Mathematics for A and AS level

Mechanics

The School Mathematics Project

CAMBRIDGE
UNIVERSITY PRESS

PUBLISHED BY THE PRESS SYNDICATE OF THE UNIVERSITY OF CAMBRIDGE
The Pitt Building, Trumpington Street, Cambridge CB2 1RP, United Kingdom

CAMBRIDGE UNIVERSITY PRESS
The Edinburgh Building, Cambridge CB2 2RU, United Kingdom
40 West 20th Street, New York, NY 10011-4211, USA
10 Stamford Road, Oakleigh, Melbourne 3166, Australia

© Cambridge University Press 1997

First published 1997

Printed in the United Kingdom at the University Press, Cambridge

Typeset in Sabon $10/12\frac{1}{2}$ pt

A catalogue record for this book is available from the British Library

Adapted from the original 16–19 Mathematics material by Chris Belsom

Main authors	Stan Dolan	Paul Roder
	Judith Galsworthy	Tom Roper
	Andy Hall	Mike Savage
	Mike Hall	Bernard Taylor
	Janet Jagger	Carole Tyler
	Ann Kitchen	Nigel Webb
	Kevin Lord	Julian Williams
	Melissa Rodd	Phil Wood
Team leaders	Ann Kitchen	Julian Williams
	Kevin Lord	
16–19 project director	Stan Dolan	

ISBN 0 521 56615 0

Acknowledgements
The publishers would like to thank the following for supplying photographs:

page vii	Ann Ronan/Image Select;
page 54	ZEFA Picture Library; Nick Judd; TM-Photo/ZEFA Picture Library;
page 65	T.C. Mettier/ZEFA Picture Library;
page 290	NASA;
page 304	NASA;
page 352	Mechanics in Action;
page 353	Mechanics in Action;
page 358	George Nelson/NASA;
page 361	Nick Judd;
page 362	Professor Harold Edgerton/Science Photo Library;
page 368	Mechanics in Action

Contents

Introduction for the student

The material in this book provides a suitable preparation for the mechanics content of most A level and AS level courses in mathematics; it is based on four units from the SMP *16–19 Mathematics* course – *Newton's laws of motion, Modelling with force and motion, Modelling with circular motion* and *Modelling with differential equations.*

The book is a self-contained resource, consisting of explanatory text and exercises. All exercises are provided with solutions at the end of the book. The textual material is written in such a way that you become involved yourself in the development of the ideas; *it is a text to be worked through, rather than read passively.* You learn mathematics by actually *doing* it, and this is constantly encouraged through the text.

Throughout the body of the text, as material is being developed, you will meet blocks of questions indicated as follows:

 .2c

> A car of mass 1 tonne, starting from rest, experiences a net forward force **F** (taking account . . .

The questions in these **development sections** are designed in such a way that ideas are opened up, explored and developed before results or observations are formalised. They are a crucial part of the learning process, making you more familiar with the ideas that you will eventually apply in more straightforward and conventional exercises. Answers, or more detailed solutions, are provided at the back of the book both for these sections and the exercises. You should check your work as you go along, correcting as necessary. Do not resort to looking at the solutions too readily when you encounter a problem – wrestling with a difficulty is a better way of resolving it than giving up too early.

At various points in the text you will also be directed towards a number of **tasksheets**. These contain essential support and enrichment material.

Chapter 4 (particularly section 4.5) requires a little familiarity with the methods of solving differential equations, especially second order differential equations with constant coefficients. The key results you will need are stated at the appropriate points in the text, but if you would like to know more of the background theory, support material can be found in the *16–19 Mathematics* text *Differential equations* (CUP, ISBN 0 521 42649 9).

Finally, a word on notation. Correct language and notation should be used consistently. You will find in this book that vector variables are generally highlighted in **bold**, although in your own work you could use any consistent method to indicate them, such as underlining.

We hope that you will find the material in this book (and the approach adopted) a challenging, enjoyable and rewarding introduction to the study of mechanics.

Sir Isaac Newton 1642–1727

1 Newton's laws of motion

.1 Modelling motion

1.1.1 Introduction

The foundations of modern mechanics were laid by Sir Isaac Newton (1642–1727) at the University of Cambridge. He published his **law of universal gravitation** in 1667 and his three **laws of motion** in the *Principia* in 1687.

A study of Newtonian mechanics will give insight into many of the natural phenomena of the world. For example, the tides, the equatorial bulge of the Earth, the time periods of the planets, the paths of comets and the variation in gravity at different latitudes were all explained by Sir Isaac Newton.

Applications of Newtonian mechanics are still extremely important today, especially in engineering, science and technology. For instance, using just A level mechanics, it is possible to:

- design road humps suitable for enforcing a 30 m.p.h. speed limit;
- estimate the best rotational speed for a tumble drier;
- choose a suitable counterweight for the design of a roadblock for a customs post or car park;
- calculate the height and speed of a geostationary communications satellite.

Your study of mechanics will help you to 'explain and predict' a range of events and phenomena in the physical world. This section will introduce you to the types of event in which we are interested, i.e. to which mechanics can contribute an important new insight.

.1A

Many simple everyday events have results you might not expect. For each of the situations below, describe what you would expect to observe. Check what happens in practice.

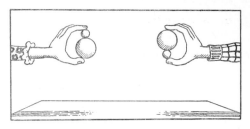

(a) What will happen if a large and a small superball are held, one on top of the other, and dropped together? Does it matter which ball is on top?

(b) A full can of cola and an empty one roll downhill. Which can takes the shorter time to roll down the slope?

(c) A friend holds a bicycle upright. What happens if you push backwards on the lower pedal?

(d) What happens when you stand on a set of bathroom scales and press down with a broom (i) on the scales, (ii) on the floor?

The situation in (b) is similar to the classic experiment conducted by Galileo Galilei (1564–1642), although he did not use cola cans! He was concerned primarily with describing the trajectory of cannon balls.

Galileo was an Italian scientist and astronomer whose work at the University of Padua preceded that of Newton and whose investigations into the motion of falling and rolling bodies included a study of the motion of spheres down inclined planes. Using planes of about 2 m in length and fixed at angles of between 1.5° and 2°, Galileo discovered a relationship between the distance travelled from rest and the time taken.

.1B

Set up and conduct a similar experiment.

What precautions should you take to make your results consistent?

How can you ensure the accuracy of your results?

What is the relationship between distance and time?

Write down your observations. You will need them later in this chapter.

1.1.2 Applied mathematical modelling

As you progress with your study of mechanics you will be able to make predictions based upon Newton's laws. You will then be able to use observations and measurements to compare your predictions with reality.

The stages in problem solving are summarised in the following diagram.

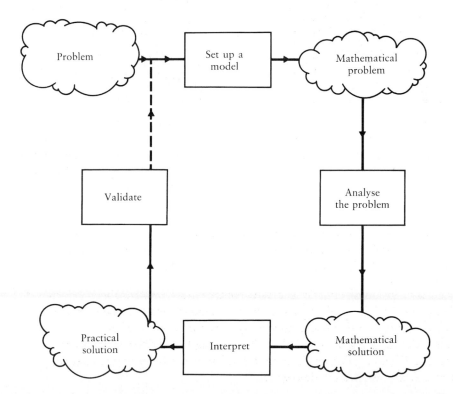

The actions you are expected to carry out during the problem-solving process are:

- identification of interesting **problems** to solve;
- formulation of the problem in mathematical terms, which involves **setting up a model**;
- **analysis of the problem** to obtain a mathematical solution;
- **interpretation** of the solution in real terms, and **validation** of it through your observations or experience.

In restaging Galileo's experiments in 1.1B, the actions you should have performed can be summarised as follows.

This stage requires the identification of a problem to be solved, such as:

- to find the distance the ball will roll down the slope in any given time;
- to find the time the ball will take to roll any given distance.

Other problems include finding the speed of the ball, or its acceleration.

Set up a model

Now you collect data on distance and time. You may choose variables to represent distance and time, d and t. The mathematical problem then is to find a relationship between d and t.

Analyse the problem

You should then analyse your data by drawing a graph and by trying to express d as a function of t, $d(t)$. A function graph plotter or a graphic calculator can be used to find a particular function such as $d = kt$ or $d = kt^2$ which best fits the data and provides a mathematical solution to the problem. Further analysis might give a formula for the speed or acceleration of the ball.

Interpret

You should now interpret your solution in ordinary English language, for example:

- the ball will roll 1 metre in 2.85 seconds;
- the ball will roll 0.38 m in 1 second;
- the ball is gaining speed;
- the average speed of the ball in the first second is ... ;

and so on.

Validate

These interpretations can now usually be validated in practice! You should check your predictions experimentally and confirm that your mathematical model is valid. If it is *not* valid, you may need to return to the first stage and reconsider your model.

This is an example of mathematical modelling. The function $d(t)$ is a mathematical model of the motion of the rolling ball, and can be used to make quantitative predictions about its real motion. Other examples of modelling will be seen throughout this chapter.

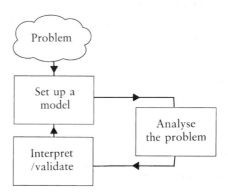

There is an alternative approach, often pursued by engineers and scientists, at the stage of setting up a model. By thinking theoretically about the factors involved in the situation and making simplifying assumptions, they can suggest a formula or equation likely to act as a suitable mathematical model. Observations can be made, the model tested and, all being well, validated.

In 1687, Sir Isaac Newton published a remarkably simple framework for a model of motion which is as relevant today as it was in the seventeenth century. As you work through this chapter you will gain an understanding of the three 'laws' of motion which formed the basis of Newton's model.

Three experiments are described on tasksheet 1. You should do *at least one* of these before discussing all the experiments with your teacher and fellow students. At this stage, there is no need to try to explain the results. You should simply attempt an analysis of your measurements to enable you to make predictions which can be tested experimentally.

You will find it helpful to use a modelling diagram for this analysis.

▶ 1.1 Tasksheet 1 – Experiments (page 347)

Each of the experiments will be followed up later in the chapter when Newtonian mechanics is introduced. You will then be able to supplement your report of the experiment with some theoretical explanation. *You should therefore save your results for later use.*

After working through section 1.1, you should:

1 have some appreciation of what is meant by a mathematical model and how you may arrive at one and test it;

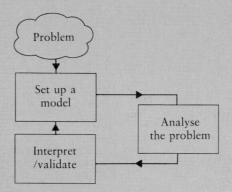

2 understand how mathematical modelling enables you to predict the motion of objects;

3 be aware that there is much you do not understand about the behaviour of things in motion!

1 Newton's laws of motion

.2 Kinematics

1.2.1 Motion

In this section you will not be trying to find out what causes something to start or stop moving. Rather, you will be investigating what the motion is like.

Traditionally this branch of mathematics is called **kinematics**, the study of movement.

To help describe a real-life example of motion, you can often set up a mathematical model of the actual motion. Various simplifying assumptions are made so that you can study the motion without having to consider all the factors which inevitably complicate matters in the real example.

You might, for example, ignore the size of an object and consider it to be a **particle** – an object whose mass is concentrated at a single point; or you might consider the motion to take place in a precise straight line, ignoring any small deviations from such a path. Whenever you set up such a model, you should be clear about the assumptions you are making.

In the remainder of this section, you will assume that you can model the motions studied by the motion of a particle.

The sorts of question you might be interested in are:

- Where is the particle at some time t?
- How far has the particle travelled?
- How fast is it moving at time t?

In the Système Internationale (SI), the basic units of length and time are metres (m) and seconds (s). The basic unit of speed is therefore metres per second (m s^{-1}).

$$\text{Average speed} = \frac{\text{Distance covered}}{\text{Time taken}}$$

Example 1

Scouts' pace consists of alternately running and walking an equal number of steps; for example, 40 running, 40 walking, 40 running, and so on. This enables large distances to be covered easily.

Problem

How long would it take a Scout to cover 2 km?
What is the average speed of the Scout?

Solution

| Set up a model |

Assumptions are made to simplify the problem; if any of these are poor assumptions you can modify them later.

- Assume the Scout's steps are all the same length, 1 metre.

- Assume the Scout runs at a steady rate of $3\,\mathrm{m\,s}^{-1}$ and walks at a steady $2\,\mathrm{m\,s}^{-1}$.

| Analyse the problem |

The distance travelled in 40 steps is 40 metres, whether the Scout walks or runs.

The time taken to run 40 steps at $3\,\mathrm{m\,s}^{-1}$ is $\frac{40}{3} = 13.3$ seconds.

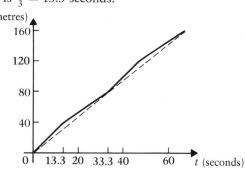

The time taken to walk 40 steps at $2\,\mathrm{m\,s}^{-1}$ is $\frac{40}{2} = 20$ seconds.

The (time, distance) graph shows the motion of the Scout.

The average speed over 80 m is $\dfrac{80}{33.3}$ or $2.4\,\mathrm{m\,s}^{-1}$.

The time taken to cover 2 km or 2000 m is approximately $\dfrac{2000}{2.4}$ or 833 seconds.

| Interpret |

Given the assumptions and their likely inaccuracy, a sensible conclusion is that a Scout will take approximately 14 minutes to travel 2 km.

Notice that the average speed is less than the mean of the two speeds. This is because the Scout spends more *time* walking than running.

1.2 Exercise 1

1 Find the average speed of a jogger who runs for 30 seconds at $5\,\mathrm{m\,s^{-1}}$ and then walks at $2\,\mathrm{m\,s^{-1}}$ for an equal period of time.

2 A jogger runs for 30 seconds at $5\,\mathrm{m\,s^{-1}}$ and then walks an equal distance at $2\,\mathrm{m\,s^{-1}}$. What is her average speed?

3 A girl runs for $60\,\mathrm{m}$ at $3\,\mathrm{m\,s^{-1}}$ and then walks twice as far at a speed of $2\,\mathrm{m\,s^{-1}}$. What is her average speed?

4 My average speed on a car journey of 210 miles (338 km) was 42 miles per hour ($18.8\,\mathrm{m\,s^{-1}}$). If my average speed for the first half of the journey's distance was 30 miles per hour ($13.4\,\mathrm{m\,s^{-1}}$), what was my average speed for the second half of the journey?

5 Repeat question 1 for a jogger who runs at $u\,\mathrm{m\,s^{-1}}$ and walks at $v\,\mathrm{m\,s^{-1}}$.

6 Repeat question 2 for a jogger who runs at $u\,\mathrm{m\,s^{-1}}$ and walks at $v\,\mathrm{m\,s^{-1}}$.

1.2.2 (Time, distance) and (time, speed) graphs

In an athletics match, the winner of the 100-metre sprint in the under-13 section took 16.8 seconds and the winner of the 100-metre sprint in the under-18 section took 13.2 seconds. This information could be represented on a graph of distance against time. Such a graph is called a (t, s) graph because the symbols s and t are often used to denote distance and time respectively.

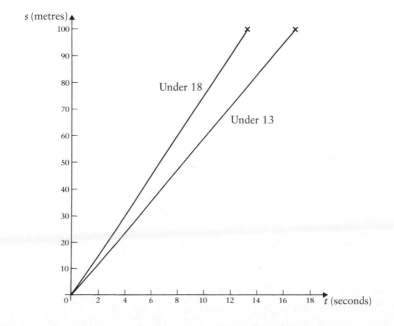

The model adopted here, and represented by the graph shown, has assumed that both runners have a constant speed over the full duration of the race. (This is hardly likely to be a realistic representation!)

The **gradient** of the line represents the speed.

> The gradient, $\dfrac{ds}{dt}$, of a (t, s) graph gives the speed of the particle at time t.

The $\left(t, \dfrac{ds}{dt}\right)$ graphs for the two sprints are shown. They are horizontal straight lines, showing that the speed for both runners is constant.

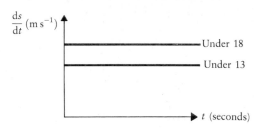

If someone alternately runs (at $3\,\mathrm{m\,s^{-1}}$) and walks (at $2\,\mathrm{m\,s^{-1}}$) between lampposts which are 180 metres apart, the $\left(t, \dfrac{ds}{dt}\right)$ graph would be as shown here.

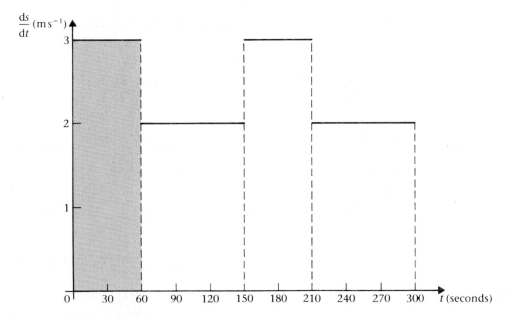

At $3\,\mathrm{m\,s^{-1}}$, it takes $60\,\mathrm{s}$ to run the $180\,\mathrm{m}$ between the lampposts. The distance travelled ($180\,\mathrm{m}$) is represented by the area underneath the $\left(t, \dfrac{ds}{dt}\right)$ graph. Check that the area of each block gives a distance of $180\,\mathrm{m}$.

The area under a $\left(t, \dfrac{ds}{dt} \right)$ graph represents the distance travelled.

1 ▶ .2A

A simplified (time, distance) graph of a college lecturer's (short) walk to work one morning is given below.

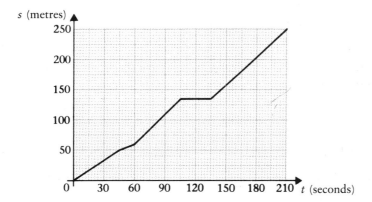

1 Explain the shape of the (t, s) graph by writing a brief account of what might have happened.

2 Draw a $\left(t, \dfrac{ds}{dt} \right)$ graph and check that the information it contains is consistent with your answer to question 1.

3 How is the total distance of the journey represented on the (t, s) graph and on the $\left(t, \dfrac{ds}{dt} \right)$ graph?

4 What was happening 2 minutes after the lecturer left home? How is this represented on each graph?

5 When did the lecturer travel most quickly? How is this represented on each graph?

The graph of distance against time for a journey made up of several sections, each taken at constant speed, is continuous and consists of jointed straight line segments.

For the situation (described on page 10) where someone alternately runs then walks between lampposts, the (t, s) graph is

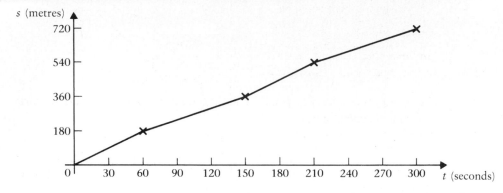

Considering the $\left(t, \dfrac{ds}{dt}\right)$ and (t, s) graphs, you can see that

> Distances covered are represented by changes in height on the (t, s) graph and by areas underneath the $\left(t, \dfrac{ds}{dt}\right)$ graph.
>
> Speed is represented by gradient on the (t, s) graph and by height on the $\left(t, \dfrac{ds}{dt}\right)$ graph.

1.2 Exercise 2

1 For part of her pre-race warm up, an athlete jogged at $2.5\,\mathrm{m\,s^{-1}}$ for 15 minutes. Represent this on a graph of speed against time. What distance did she cover? On the graph, how would you represent her coming to a standstill?

2 An athlete's training schedule consists of 20 repetitions of fast running for 1 minute followed by $1\frac{1}{2}$ minutes jog recovery. If his fast running speed is a steady $4.8\,\mathrm{m\,s^{-1}}$ and his jogging speed is $3\,\mathrm{m\,s^{-1}}$, what distance will he cover in this session?

3 Draw a graph of speed against time for the first 150 seconds of the athlete's motion in question 2. Superimpose the graph of speed against time for someone who moves with the athlete's average speed for the full 150 seconds.

4 (a) This (t, s) graph models the motion of two runners. Draw rough sketches of the corresponding $\left(t, \dfrac{ds}{dt}\right)$ graphs and compare briefly how the runners performed during the race.

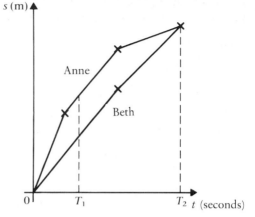

   (b) What do you notice about the runners at time T_1? Explain how this is represented in each graph.

   (c) Repeat (b) for time T_2.

5 A lorry travelling at an average speed of $11.4 \, \text{m s}^{-1}$ took $1\frac{1}{2}$ hours to reach the motorway. It then travelled at an average speed of $16.2 \, \text{m s}^{-1}$ for 2 hours before leaving the motorway and finishing the journey at an average speed of $10.5 \, \text{m s}^{-1}$ for 45 minutes. How far did the lorry travel?

6 A team of boys challenged a team of girls to see who could cover the greatest distance in 1 hour of Scouts' pace. The boys decided to run at $3 \, \text{m s}^{-1}$ for 90 seconds and to walk at $2 \, \text{m s}^{-1}$ for 135 seconds. The girls decided to run at $3 \, \text{m s}^{-1}$ for 50 seconds and to walk at $2 \, \text{m s}^{-1}$ for 75 seconds. Draw their respective graphs of speed against time for the first 6 minutes of the race. Assuming that both teams managed to keep up these paces for the full hour, which team won and by how much?

1.2.3 Speed

Section 1.2.2 considered situations where the speed was constant and the (time, speed) graph consisted of horizontal straight lines. It was clear that in such cases the gradient of the (t, s) graph gave the speed and the area under the $\left(t, \dfrac{ds}{dt}\right)$ graph gave distance. You now need to consider cases where the speed is not necessarily constant, but may change with time. You saw this in the Galileo experiment of section 1.1, where the (t, s) graph did not consist of line segments but was a smooth curve. This problem is considered below.

1 .2B

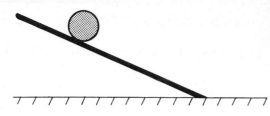

The graph shown below is drawn from data collected by students, from Galileo's experiment. Substitute your own data here if available and draw your own graph.

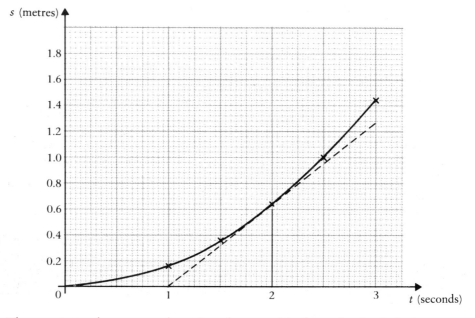

The tangent to the curve at the point where $t = 2$ is shown by the dashed line.

1 What is $\dfrac{ds}{dt}$ at $t = 2$? Describe in words what this represents and state the units in which $\dfrac{ds}{dt}$ is measured.

2 Find the gradient of the curve at half-second intervals.

3 Plot the corresponding $\left(t, \dfrac{ds}{dt}\right)$ graph. Describe in words what you note about the graph and what it implies about the motion of the ball.

The gradient of a curved (t, s) graph still represents speed, but this speed is changing. Speed (as opposed to average speed) is always understood to mean instantaneous speed, so that a speed of, say, $10\,\text{m}\,\text{s}^{-1}$ means that the object would travel 10 metres every second if it maintained the speed at that instant.

On a (t, s) graph, this imaginary motion with constant speed is represented by the tangent to the curve.

You may have obtained graphs similar to those below for the motion studied in 1.2B.

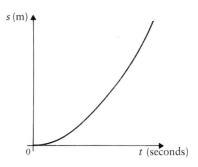 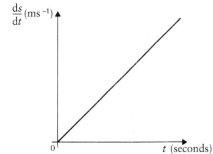

You saw earlier that if the speed is constant, then the area under the graph of speed against time gives the distance travelled. Other examples where the $\left(t, \dfrac{ds}{dt}\right)$ graph is a straight line appear to support this theory. It can be proved that this is true for any graph of speed against time.

The area under a **general** $\left(t, \dfrac{ds}{dt}\right)$ graph represents the distance travelled.

This important and remarkable result is a particular illustration of the **fundamental theorem of calculus**.

Example 2
Describe the motion represented in this $\left(t, \dfrac{ds}{dt}\right)$ graph.

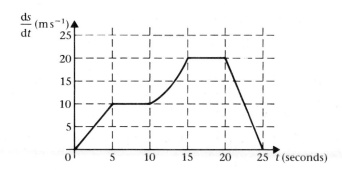

Solution

$t = 0$ to 5 There is a steady increase in speed. The distance covered each second therefore increases at a constant rate. The distance covered in the first five seconds is 25 m.

$t = 5$ to 10 Speed remains constant at $10\,\mathrm{m\,s^{-1}}$. The distance covered each second is constant. A further $50\,\mathrm{m}$ is travelled.

$t = 10$ to 15 Speed increases throughout. The distance covered each second increases.

(and so on)

1.2 Exercise 3

1 For the motion described in example 2 above, estimate the distance travelled:

(a) between $t = 10$ and $t = 15$,   (b) between $t = 20$ and $t = 25$.

2 The $\left(t, \dfrac{ds}{dt}\right)$ graph for a short jog is shown below.

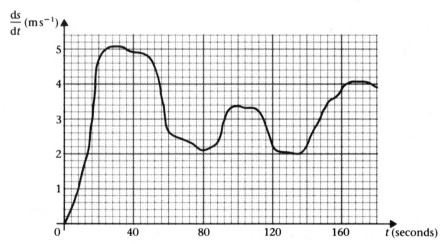

From this (time, speed) graph, estimate the distance travelled in:

(a) 40 seconds,   (b) 2 minutes.

3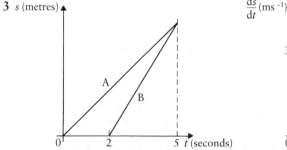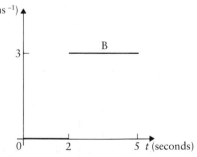

The graphs give some details of the motion of both A and B. At what distance from the start do A and B meet? What is the speed of A?

4 Tracy cycles from Aycliffe to Beford, a distance of 3 miles, in 16 minutes. She rests for 10 minutes before continuing to Ceville, a further distance of 4 miles, which takes 20 minutes.

Simon walks the same journey, does not stop to rest and takes 2 hours.

(a) If Tracy starts out 50 minutes after Simon, where will she overtake him?

(b) What is Tracy's average speed?

(c) What is Simon's average speed?

5 (a) Copy and complete the following graphs of distance against time and speed against time for the first 5 seconds of an object's motion.

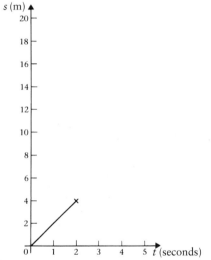
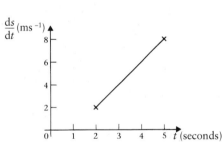

(b) What is the distance covered by the object during this motion?

6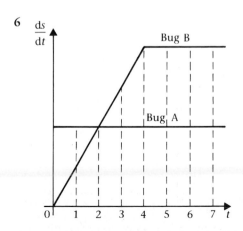

The graphs of speed against time for two gutter-bugs, starting from the same point and crawling along the same gutter, are shown.

(a) Describe the progress of bug A.

(b) Describe the progress of bug B.

(c) When is bug A moving at the same speed as bug B?

(d) When does bug B catch up with bug A?

1.2.4 Investigating speed

 .2c

The Highway Code states:

On an open road, in good conditions, a two-second gap between cars should be sufficient.

What is meant by a two-second gap?

Example 3

In many tunnels there is both a maximum and a minimum speed limit to ensure a good flow of cars through the tunnel.

Problem

The tunnel authorities want to get as many cars through the tunnel as they can in an hour. The safe gap between cars depends on their speed. Suggest sensible speed limits for the tunnel.

Solution

Suppose the cars are 4 metres long and their speed is $v\,\mathrm{m\,s^{-1}}$. There must be a two-second gap between each car. Let the number of cars entering the tunnel each minute be N. You need to maximise N.

Analyse the problem

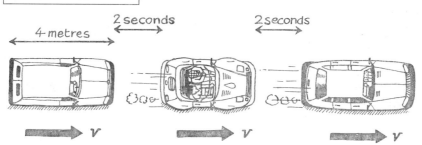

The time between the back of one car and the front of the next car passing a certain point is 2 seconds.

The time taken for one car to pass is $\dfrac{4}{v}$ seconds. So the total time between successive cars entering the tunnel is

$$2 + \frac{4}{v} \text{ seconds} = \frac{2v + 4}{v} \text{ seconds}$$

The number of cars a minute entering the tunnel is

$$N = \frac{60v}{2v + 4}$$

This is easiest to interpret from a graph.

v (m s^{-1})	N
1	10
5	21
10	25
15	26
20	27
30	28

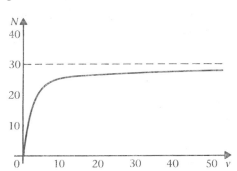

Interpret

You can see that the maximum number of cars a minute seems to be 30 when their speed is infinite. A speed of 30 m s^{-1} will enable 28 cars a minute to enter the tunnel while a speed of 20 m s^{-1} will enable 27 cars a minute to enter. It appears that a speed limit if about 20 m s^{-1} or 72 km h^{-1} will enable a reasonable number of cars to pass safely through the tunnel. However, only below 10 m s^{-1} is there a significant drop in traffic flow.

Validate

The actual speed range in the Mont Blanc tunnel is from 50 km h^{-1} to 80 km h^{-1}. In the St Bernard tunnel it is 60 km h^{-1} to 80 km h^{-1}.

Example 4

Problem

To find the passing distance needed for a car to overtake a lorry moving at a steady speed.

Solution

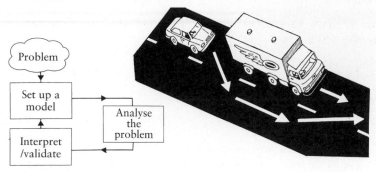

Set up a model

This is a simple model that makes a very good starting point.

Assume
- the car has length 5 metres and is moving at a constant speed of $30 \, \text{m s}^{-1}$;
- the lorry has length 15 metres and is moving at $20 \, \text{m s}^{-1}$;
- they obey the two-second rule;
- the car takes t seconds to pass.

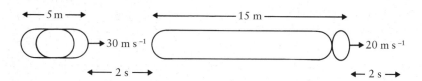

Analyse the problem

The car must travel $(5 + 60 + 15 + 40)$ metres relative to the lorry.

But the lorry will have travelled $20t$ metres so the total overtaking distance is $(120 + 20t)$ metres.

The car has speed $30 \, \text{m s}^{-1}$, so it will also have travelled $30t$ metres in t seconds.

Thus
$$30t = 20t + 120$$
$$10t = 120$$
$$t = 12 \text{ seconds}$$

Interpret/validate

The time taken to overtake safely is 12 seconds, during which time the car will have travelled 360 metres.

By choosing different values for the speed of the car you can see how the speed affects the distance needed to overtake.

 .2D

Generalise the model in example 4 for a car moving at a constant speed of $V \mathrm{m\,s}^{-1}$ passing a lorry moving at a constant speed of $U \mathrm{m\,s}^{-1}$. Suppose the car (length 5 m) takes t seconds to overtake the lorry (length 15 m).

After working through section 1.2, you should:

1 be aware that simplifying assumptions are necessary so that motion can be modelled mathematically, and be able to discuss how appropriate these assumptions are in simple cases;

2 be familiar with the concepts of distance (s metres), speed $\left(\dfrac{\mathrm{d}s}{\mathrm{d}t} \mathrm{m\,s}^{-1}\right)$ and time (t seconds);

3 know that the average speed of an object is the constant speed with which it would have covered the same total distance in the same total time, i.e.

$$\text{average speed} = \frac{\text{distance covered}}{\text{time taken}}$$

4 know that speed is the gradient of a (t, s) graph of distance against time;

5 know that the total distance travelled is the area underneath a $\left(t, \dfrac{\mathrm{d}s}{\mathrm{d}t}\right)$ graph of speed against time.

 Newton's laws of motion

.3 Vectors

1.3.1 Introduction

When both the direction and the size of a quantity are given, then you are dealing with a **vector** quantity.

Displacement is the word used to describe a distance moved in a certain direction and is an example of a vector.

A quantity which has magnitude or size but not direction is called a **scalar**.

Some scalar quantities with which you will be familiar are mass, time, speed, area and volume. Examples of vector quantities are velocity, momentum and force – all of which will be discussed in detail in later sections of this book.

> A scalar quantity has magnitude only.
>
> A vector quantity has magnitude and direction.

A displacement involves two pieces of information – the distance between two points and the direction of one point from the other. For example, a ship sails 10 km on a bearing of 037° (compass bearings are angles measured clockwise from north).

This vector can be represented by the line $\overrightarrow{AB}$ drawn to scale [1 cm : 2 km].

$\overrightarrow{AB}$ is the displacement vector representing the ship's voyage. The arrow over the letters denotes that the direction of the vector is from the first point A to the second point B.

Another way of going from A to B would be to sail 6 km due east to point C and then 8 km due north to B.

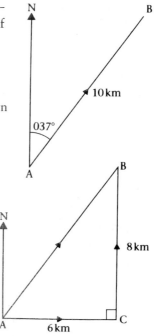

This journey has been drawn to scale [1 cm : 2 km]. You can confirm by measurement or calculation that the distance AB is 10 km, as before, and the bearing of B from A is 037°.

Thinking in terms of the rectangular coordinates of a graph, it can be said that going from A to B involves the ship moving 6 km in the x-direction and 8 km in the y-direction. The 6 and the 8 are called the x- and y-**components** of the vector.

A convention for writing down a vector in terms of its x- and y-components is to use the form $\begin{bmatrix} x \\ y \end{bmatrix}$. This is called a **column vector**.

Thus the vector $\overrightarrow{AB}$ can be expressed in two ways:

$$\overrightarrow{AB} = \begin{bmatrix} 6 \\ 8 \end{bmatrix}$$

or $\overrightarrow{AB} = 10 \, \text{km bearing } 037°$

These are two ways of saying the same thing and it is easy to convert from one to the other.

Example 1

Sketch the vector $\begin{bmatrix} 3 \\ 5 \end{bmatrix}$ and convert it to the distance and bearing form.

Solution

Start by drawing a right-angle triangle. Then,

$$AB^2 = 3^2 + 5^2 \implies AB = 5.83 \, \text{km}$$

$$\tan \alpha = \tfrac{3}{5} \implies \alpha = 31.0° \implies \text{bearing } 031°$$

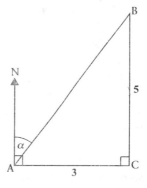

The distance from A to B is called the **magnitude** of the vector $\overrightarrow{AB}$ and is written as either $|\overrightarrow{AB}|$ or AB.

Example 2

Sketch the displacement vector, 10 km on a bearing 323°, and convert it to a column vector.

Solution

Sketch the vector. Now draw a right-angled triangle.

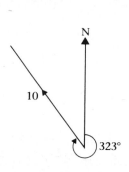
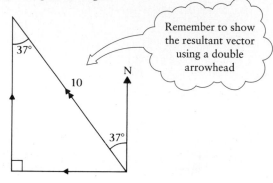

Remember to show the resultant vector using a double arrowhead

West $= 10 \sin 37° = 6.02 \approx 6$ km

North $= 10 \cos 37° = 7.99 \approx 8$ km

The column vector is $\begin{bmatrix} -6 \\ 8 \end{bmatrix}$.

Example 3

A motor boat travelling at 35 km h^{-1} on a bearing of 020° is 7.5 km west of a long reef which runs north–south. When will it cross the reef?

Solution

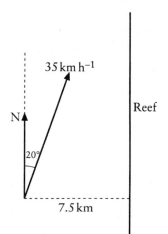

The easterly component of the boat's velocity is $35 \sin 20°$ km h^{-1}. At this easterly velocity it will cover the 7.5 km in

$$\frac{7.5}{35 \sin 20°} = 0.6265 \text{ hour}$$

$$= 38 \text{ minutes}$$

1.3 Exercise 1

1 Sketch the following vectors and convert them into column vector form. Check your answers with scale drawings.

(a) $\overrightarrow{PQ} = 7\,\text{km}$ bearing 060°   (b) $\overrightarrow{RS} = 12\,\text{km}$ bearing 200°

(c) $\overrightarrow{TU} = 5.2\,\text{km}$ bearing 310°

2 Sketch the following vectors and convert them into distance and bearing form. All units are kilometres.

(a) $\overrightarrow{AB} = \begin{bmatrix} 5 \\ 12 \end{bmatrix}$ (b) $\overrightarrow{CD} = \begin{bmatrix} 16 \\ 16 \end{bmatrix}$ (c) $\overrightarrow{EF} = \begin{bmatrix} -5.5 \\ -8.5 \end{bmatrix}$ (d) $\overrightarrow{GH} = \begin{bmatrix} 3 \\ -4 \end{bmatrix}$

3 A sailor in a catamaran starts from Seaview and sails 440 m on a bearing 064°. He then tacks (changes direction), and sails 580 m on a bearing 129°. Calculate how far east and how far south he is then from Seaview. On what bearing must he sail in order to return there? What assumption have you made when answering this question?

4 A snooker ball travels 22 cm in a direction making an angle of 33° with the x-axis. It then hits a cushion lying parallel to the x-axis, undergoing a 'perfect' rebound, so that its new direction makes −33° with the x-axis. It comes to rest after travelling a further 44 cm. Calculate how far it is then from the starting point and in what direction.

1.3.2 Vectors and maps

Ordnance Survey maps cover the whole of the UK. Each map is divided by grid lines into many squares, the distance between two adjacent lines representing one kilometre on the land. Each grid line is numbered, increasing a kilometre at a time. Places are defined by giving the numbers of the left-hand and lower boundaries of the square that they are in, just as points on a graph are located by x- and y-coordinates. For example, on the map shown on the next page, the middle of Black Head is at the intersection of the two grid lines numbered 04 and 48. It is possible to estimate a position to 0.1 of a square, or 0.1 km, and so the coordinates of Black Head can be given with greater precision as 04.0 and 48.0.

Similarly, the coordinates of Penare Point are 02.2 and 45.8.

As with graphs, the x-coordinate (or 'easting') is given first, followed by the y-coordinate (or 'northing').

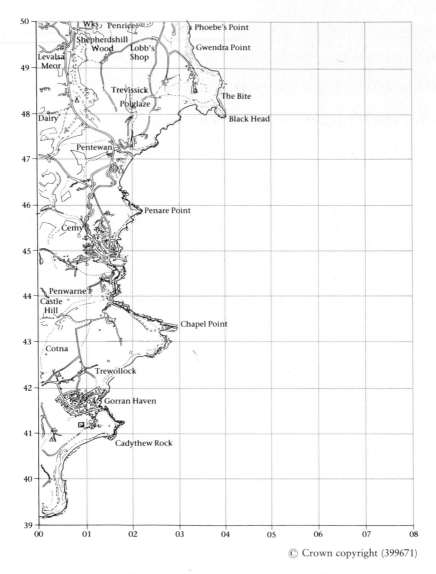

Whenever a map reference of a place is given, the six figures are written down without the decimal points. Thus,

<blockquote>Black Head is at 040480,   Penare Point is at 022458.</blockquote>

It should now be clear that a six-figure map reference contains information about distances, and moreover to an accuracy of 100 metres! Such a map reference can easily be 'dismantled' and turned back into distance coordinates – just cut it in half and insert decimal points! For example,

$$022 \quad \Big| \quad 458$$
$$\downarrow \quad \quad \downarrow$$
$$2.2 \quad \Big| \quad 45.8$$

1 .3A

Confirm your understanding of six-figure map references by:

1 writing down the references of Phoebe's Point and Cadythew Rock;

2 stating what can be found at 002480 and at 038483;

3 changing 024473 and 032505 into distance coordinates.

Starting with just the map references of two places it is easy to calculate the shortest distance between them and the direction of one from the other, using what you have learnt about vectors.

Example 4

Calculate the bearing of Black Head (040480) from Penare Point (022458) and the shortest distance between them.

Solution

Start by 'dismantling' the map references, i.e. express them as coordinates.

	x	y
Black Head (B)	4.0	48.0
Penare Point (P)	2.2	45.8
Differences	1.8	2.2

Thus B is 1.8 km east and 2.2 km north of P. Expressed as a column vector,

$$\overrightarrow{PB} = \begin{bmatrix} 1.8 \\ 2.2 \end{bmatrix}.$$

$$|\overrightarrow{PB}| = \sqrt{(1.8^2 + 2.2^2)} = 2.8 \, \text{km}$$

$$\tan \alpha = \frac{1.8}{2.2} = 0.818 \implies \alpha = 39°$$

$$\overrightarrow{PB} = 2.8 \, \text{km bearing } 039°$$

This result can be checked by making measurements on the map (remember that a side of a square represents 1 km).

1.3 Exercise 2

1 Six-figure map references for places A, B, C, D are as follows:

A 015392,   B 227461,   C 100260,   D 312329.

(a) Calculate the distance from C to B.

(b) Find the bearing of D from A.

(c) Find $\overrightarrow{BD}$ as a distance and bearing.

(d) What is the bearing of vector $\overrightarrow{DB}$?

(e) What may be said about $\overrightarrow{AB}$ and $\overrightarrow{CD}$?

2 The six-figure map reference for a town A is 214418. Town B is 12 km from A on a bearing of 120°. Calculate the map reference of B.

3 Calculate the distance and bearing of Ayton (grid reference 214300) from Botton (grid reference 318206).

1.3.3 Adding vectors

There are two ways in which a vector may be expressed:

● in terms of its components:

$$\overrightarrow{AB} = \begin{bmatrix} 3 \\ 4 \end{bmatrix}$$

● as a distance and bearing:

5 km on a bearing of 037°

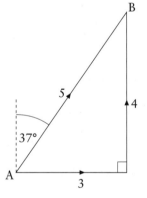

For practical purposes, such as the flight of an aeroplane or the movement of a ship, the sensible way of representing a displacement is by distance and bearing.

However, if displacements are to be combined, it is generally easier if column vectors are used.

Hence the usefulness of the form of vector depends on the purpose for which it is required.

The following questions explore how you can combine vectors by addition, where, for example, one displacement is followed by another, or you need to add two velocities together.

1 .3ʙ

1 A police helicopter is monitoring traffic flow. Trouble spots are known to be at

X (026102), Y (134154) and Z (185496).

(a) Write $\overrightarrow{XZ}$, $\overrightarrow{XY}$ and $\overrightarrow{YZ}$ as column vectors.

(b) Can you see any connection between $\overrightarrow{XZ}$, $\overrightarrow{XY}$ and $\overrightarrow{YZ}$?
$\overrightarrow{XZ}$ is called the **resultant** of $\overrightarrow{XY}$ and $\overrightarrow{YZ}$.

(c) In what direction, and how far, does the helicopter fly in going from:
(i) X to Z   (ii) X to Y   (iii) Y to Z?

2 For any vector triangle, as shown, $\overrightarrow{AC}$ is called the resultant of $\overrightarrow{AB}$ and $\overrightarrow{BC}$.

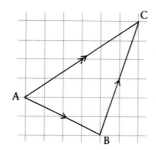

Express $\overrightarrow{AB}$, $\overrightarrow{BC}$ and $\overrightarrow{AC}$ as column vectors. What do you notice?

3 Find the resultant $\overrightarrow{AD}$ of the following vectors:

$$\overrightarrow{AB} = \begin{bmatrix} 2 \\ 2 \end{bmatrix} \qquad \overrightarrow{BC} = \begin{bmatrix} 2 \\ 0 \end{bmatrix} \qquad \overrightarrow{CD} = \begin{bmatrix} 3 \\ -4 \end{bmatrix}$$

Using squared paper, draw a vector diagram to illustrate all four vectors.

4 Find the resultant $\overrightarrow{AD}$ of the following vectors:

$$\overrightarrow{AE} = \begin{bmatrix} 3 \\ -4 \end{bmatrix} \qquad \overrightarrow{EF} = \begin{bmatrix} 2 \\ 2 \end{bmatrix} \qquad \overrightarrow{FD} = \begin{bmatrix} 2 \\ 0 \end{bmatrix}$$

Illustrate the vectors on the vector diagram used for question 3. What do you notice?

The **resultant** of a displacement from X to Y followed by a displacement from Y to Z is the displacement from X to Z.

$$\overrightarrow{XY} + \overrightarrow{YZ} = \overrightarrow{XZ}$$

Two vectors can be added by means of a scale drawing if they are drawn 'head to tail'.

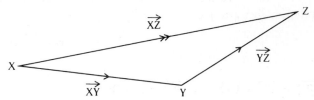

The same resultant displacement is obtained if the two displacement vectors are added in the other order.

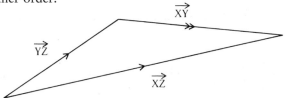

All that matters is that the 'head' of the first displacement vector you draw should be followed by the 'tail' of the next displacement vector.

To add together two vectors in column vector form, add the x-components together and add the y-components together.

$$\overrightarrow{XY} + \overrightarrow{YZ} = \overrightarrow{XZ}$$
$$\begin{bmatrix} 2 \\ 3 \end{bmatrix} + \begin{bmatrix} 4 \\ -1 \end{bmatrix} = \begin{bmatrix} 6 \\ 2 \end{bmatrix}$$

The reason they add up in this way becomes clear if the vector diagram is drawn. The vectors form the sides of the triangle XYZ.

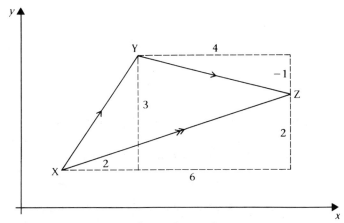

You should note that whereas $\overrightarrow{XY} + \overrightarrow{YZ} = \overrightarrow{XZ}$, it is not true that $XY + YZ = XZ$.

Example 5

Express $\overrightarrow{PQ}$ in terms of the vectors **a** and **b** shown in the diagram.

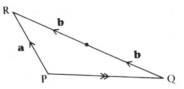

Solution

$$\overrightarrow{PQ} = \overrightarrow{PR} + \overrightarrow{RQ} \quad \Rightarrow \quad \overrightarrow{PQ} = a - 2b$$

Note that this book uses **bold** face to indicate vector quantities like **a** and **b**. You could do this in your work by underlining, writing a̲ or a̰.

1.3 Exercise 3

1 Add the vectors $\begin{bmatrix} 3 \\ -1 \end{bmatrix}$ and $\begin{bmatrix} -2 \\ 4 \end{bmatrix}$. Draw them and their resultant and show how they form a closed triangle.

2 For each of the following examples, write the vector $\overrightarrow{PQ}$ in terms of **u** and **v**.

(a)

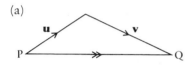

(b)

(c)

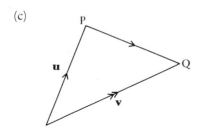

3 Four displacement vectors have a resultant of $\begin{bmatrix} 10 \\ -2 \end{bmatrix}$. If three of them are $\begin{bmatrix} -2 \\ -3 \end{bmatrix}$, $\begin{bmatrix} 5 \\ -7 \end{bmatrix}$ and $\begin{bmatrix} 16 \\ 4 \end{bmatrix}$, find the missing vector.

4 A helicopter flies from its base A (025105) to B (105155) and then to C (195400). While the helicopter is flying from B to C, a second helicopter flies parallel to it, travelling from A to D where the distances AD and BC are equal.

(a) Find the map reference for D.

(b) Express $\overrightarrow{AD}$ and $\overrightarrow{BC}$ as column vectors. What do you notice?

(c) What shape is ABCD?

1.3.4 Using vectors

You have seen that, for practical purposes, distance and bearing vectors are preferred. However, for adding vectors the column vector form is very convenient and is likely to give an accurate resultant more quickly than a scale drawing.

Example 6

One boat of a fishing fleet sails 4 km from a port in a direction 045° to investigate the prospects of good catches. The rest of the fleet travels to its usual fishing ground, 10 km from the same port in a direction 120°. In what direction does the single boat have to sail to rejoin the fleet and what distance will it cover?

Solution

Let P be the port, S the single boat and F the rest of the fleet.

First the data given is converted to column vectors.

$$\overrightarrow{PS} = \begin{bmatrix} 4\sin 45° \\ 4\cos 45° \end{bmatrix} = \begin{bmatrix} 2.83 \\ 2.83 \end{bmatrix}$$

$$\overrightarrow{PF} = \begin{bmatrix} 10\sin 120° \\ 10\cos 120° \end{bmatrix} = \begin{bmatrix} 8.66 \\ -5.0 \end{bmatrix}$$

In the triangle PSF,

$$\overrightarrow{PS} + \overrightarrow{SF} = \overrightarrow{PF}$$

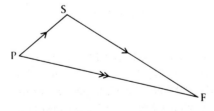

From the vector triangle $\overrightarrow{PS} + \overrightarrow{SF} = \overrightarrow{PF}$,

$$\overrightarrow{SF} = \overrightarrow{PF} - \overrightarrow{PS} = \begin{bmatrix} 8.66 \\ -5.00 \end{bmatrix} - \begin{bmatrix} 2.83 \\ 2.83 \end{bmatrix} = \begin{bmatrix} 5.83 \\ -7.83 \end{bmatrix}$$

The column vector is now converted back to a distance and bearing.

$$|\overrightarrow{SF}| = \sqrt{(5.83^2 + 7.83^2)} = 9.76$$

$$\tan \alpha = \frac{7.83}{5.83} = 1.343 \Rightarrow \alpha = 53.3°$$

Thus, to rejoin the fleet the single boat sails on a bearing of 143.3° for a distance of 9.76 km.

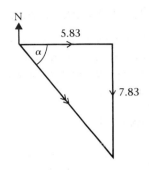

1.3 Exercise 4

1 An aircraft A develops an engine fault when it is 83 km due west of an airport P. Another airport Q is 100 km from P on a bearing 315°. Which airport is closer to the aircraft, and by how much?

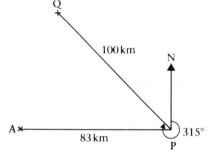

2 A ship S, having sailed 20 km from port P in a direction 127°, dropped anchor and sent an SOS for a seriously ill passenger to be lifted off. At that instant an air–sea rescue helicopter H was 5 km due east of P. In which direction and for what distance did the helicopter have to fly in order to reach the ship?

3 Storm Head Light is 4.7 km east of Black Cap Light. A fishing boat is observed at 2:15 a.m. due north of Storm Head Light. If the boat progresses on a bearing of 322° at 9.0 km h^{-1}, at what time will it be observed due north of Black Cap Light?

4 A hill walker is injured when she is 6 km north-west of Horton. The rescue helicopter is based 20 km due east of Horton. In what direction and for what distance does the helicopter have to fly in order to reach the injured walker?

5 [1 knot is a speed of 1 nautical mile per hour, a nautical mile being 1.15 land miles.]

HMS *Battledore* leaves port at 14:15 and sails at 15 knots on a bearing 119° for 24 minutes, then changes course to bearing 343°, on which the ship remains. At 14:30 HMS *Shuttlecock* leaves the same port and sails on a bearing 205° at 12 knots until 15:00 at which time its engines cease to work. How far apart are the two ships at 15:00? How long will it take HMS *Battledore* to get to HMS *Shuttlecock* at 20 knots? On what bearing must HMS *Battledore* proceed?

1.3.5 Position and displacement

At the start of this section, the word 'displacement' was defined as describing a distance moved in a certain direction. By definition, the **position vector** of a point is its **displacement from the origin**. This may be expressed in column vector form.

A point with position (x, y) has position vector $\begin{bmatrix} x \\ y \end{bmatrix}$. For example, a fishing boat and a marker buoy are spotted from a lighthouse. If the lighthouse is taken as the origin on an (x, y) grid, then the position of the boat F is given by the vector $\begin{bmatrix} -2 \\ 5 \end{bmatrix}$ and that of the buoy B is given by the vector $\begin{bmatrix} 4 \\ 3 \end{bmatrix}$.

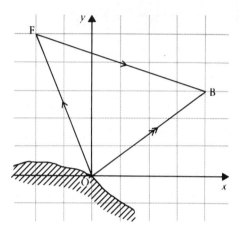

Here the movement implied by the use of the word 'displacement' is hypothetical; it can be thought of as the distance and direction of a possible journey from the origin (the lighthouse), even though no actual movement takes place.

The boat is watched (from the lighthouse) as it moves from its position at F to the position of the buoy at B. This motion is defined by the displacement vector $\begin{bmatrix} 6 \\ -2 \end{bmatrix}$.

What is actually observed is a change in the position vector, and it is this that is used to define the displacement.

Displacement = Change in position vector

$$\begin{bmatrix} -2 \\ 5 \end{bmatrix} + \begin{bmatrix} 6 \\ -2 \end{bmatrix} = \begin{bmatrix} 4 \\ 3 \end{bmatrix}$$

Original + Displacement =   New
position   position
vector   vector

.3C

Choose different examples of your own and verify that the displacement between any two positions P and Q can be defined in terms of the change in displacement *from the origin*.

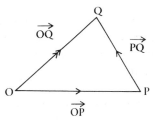

$$\overrightarrow{OP} + \overrightarrow{PQ} = \overrightarrow{OQ}$$

Example 7

A plane moves from the point with position vector $\begin{bmatrix} 3 \\ 6 \end{bmatrix}$ km to the point with position vector $\begin{bmatrix} 7 \\ -3 \end{bmatrix}$ km. Find its displacement.

Solution

Original position + Displacement = New position
vector   vector

So, $\begin{bmatrix} 3 \\ 6 \end{bmatrix} + \text{Displacement} = \begin{bmatrix} 7 \\ -3 \end{bmatrix}$

$$\text{Displacement} = \begin{bmatrix} 7 \\ -3 \end{bmatrix} - \begin{bmatrix} 3 \\ 6 \end{bmatrix} = \begin{bmatrix} 4 \\ -9 \end{bmatrix} \text{ km}$$

1.3 Exercise 5

1 Complete the following table.

	(a)	(b)	(c)	(d)
Original position vector	$\begin{bmatrix} 200 \\ 90 \end{bmatrix}$	$\begin{bmatrix} 7 \\ -7 \end{bmatrix}$	$\begin{bmatrix} -32 \\ 16 \end{bmatrix}$	
New position vector			$\begin{bmatrix} -15 \\ -4 \end{bmatrix}$	$\begin{bmatrix} -10 \\ -8 \end{bmatrix}$
Displacement	$\begin{bmatrix} 126 \\ -9 \end{bmatrix}$	$\begin{bmatrix} 66 \\ -74 \end{bmatrix}$		$\begin{bmatrix} 78 \\ 254 \end{bmatrix}$

2 A boat travels down a winding channel. Its original position vector was $\begin{bmatrix} 5.7 \\ 2.6 \end{bmatrix}$ km and its journey can be described by the successive displacement vectors $\begin{bmatrix} 0.9 \\ 0.2 \end{bmatrix}$, $\begin{bmatrix} 1.4 \\ -0.7 \end{bmatrix}$ and $\begin{bmatrix} 1.2 \\ 0.5 \end{bmatrix}$ km.

(a) Find its new position vector.

(b) What is its total displacement?

(c) How far has the boat travelled?

After working through section 1.3, you should:

1 be aware that displacement is a vector quantity and has both magnitude and direction;

2 know that the magnitude of $\overrightarrow{AB}$ is the distance from A to B and is written as $|\overrightarrow{AB}|$ or AB;

3 understand that a column vector can describe either a displacement or a position vector;

4 be able to convert column vectors to distance and bearing form and vice versa;

5 be able to convert six-figure map references to coordinates and vice versa;

6 know that vectors can be added 'head to tail' in either order,

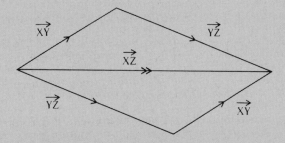

and can be added as column vectors, for example

$$\begin{bmatrix} 3 \\ 2 \end{bmatrix} + \begin{bmatrix} 5 \\ -2 \end{bmatrix} = \begin{bmatrix} 8 \\ 0 \end{bmatrix}$$

7 know that displacement is change in position vector and that

Original position vector + Displacement = Final position vector

1 Newton's laws of motion

.4 Velocity

1.4.1 Speed or velocity?

The speed of an object is simply a measure of how fast it is travelling. In everyday language, 'velocity' is often used in this way as well. However, mathematicians and scientists use the word 'velocity' in the special sense of meaning speed *and* direction.

Consider a car travelling along a winding road.

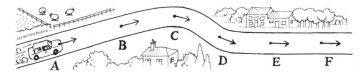

 .4A

Points A to F show the car's position at 10-second intervals. Over what parts of the journey is:

(a) the speed constant,   (b) the velocity constant?

Speed is an example of a scalar quantity; it can, for example, be read from the speedometer of a car without reference to the direction of travel.

> Velocity is a vector having the same magnitude as speed but pointing in the direction of motion.

Two cars travelling at 40 kilometres per hour ($40 \, \text{km h}^{-1}$), one going north and the other going east, have the same speed but different velocities. The velocities can be represented by arrows drawn to scale in appropriate directions, or by column vectors.

$$\begin{bmatrix} 0 \\ 40 \end{bmatrix} \quad \text{or} \quad 40 \, \text{km h}^{-1} \uparrow \qquad \begin{bmatrix} 40 \\ 0 \end{bmatrix} \quad \text{or} \quad 40 \, \text{km h}^{-1} \longrightarrow$$

Just as 'average speed' means the **equivalent constant speed**, so 'average velocity' means the **equivalent constant velocity**.

1 .4B

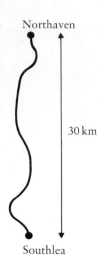

Northaven

30 km

Southlea

The village of Northaven is 30 kilometres due north of Southlea. One car travels from Southlea to Northaven at an average speed of $60 \, \text{km h}^{-1}$. A second car does the same journey with an average velocity of $60 \, \text{km h}^{-1}$ due north.

What precisely do the sentences above imply about the motion of these two cars? Do they in fact mean the same thing?

The ideas of equivalent constant speed and equivalent constant velocity are summarised as follows:

$$\text{Average speed} \quad = \frac{\text{Total distance travelled}}{\text{Time taken}}$$

$$\text{Average velocity} = \frac{\text{Change in position vector}}{\text{Time taken}}$$

Example 1
Susan walks 2 km in half an hour along a road which runs north and then runs back halfway along her route in 10 minutes.

What are her average speed and her average velocity for the whole journey?

Solution
The total time for the whole hour is 40 minutes $= \frac{2}{3}$ hour, while the total distance for the whole journey is 3 km.

Average speed $\quad = 3 \div \frac{2}{3} \, \text{km h}^{-1} = \frac{9}{2} \, \text{km h}^{-1} = 4.5 \, \text{km h}^{-1}$

Displacement $\quad = 1 \, \text{km north}$

Average velocity $= 1 \div \frac{2}{3} \, \text{km h}^{-1} \, \text{north} = 1.5 \, \text{km h}^{-1} \, \text{north}$

1.4 Exercise 1

1 A car travels 20 km at $40 \, \text{km h}^{-1}$ and then returns along the same route at $80 \, \text{km h}^{-1}$. What is the average speed for the total journey?

2 A car travels 30 km at $30 \, \text{km h}^{-1}$ and then increases its speed to $60 \, \text{km h}^{-1}$. How far does it travel on the second stage of its journey if its average speed is $45 \, \text{km h}^{-1}$?

3 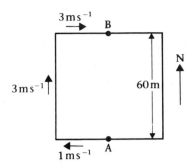 A and B are the mid-points of opposite edges of a square field. Melissa travels from A to B, around the edge of the field, with speeds as shown. What are her average speed and average velocity?

4 If an object is travelling with a constant speed, then is it necessarily travelling with constant velocity? If it travels with constant velocity, is it necessarily travelling with constant speed? Give reasons and examples.

5 State, with reasons, what can be said about the average speed of a car which travels with an average velocity of $50\,\mathrm{km\,h^{-1}}$ due east.

6

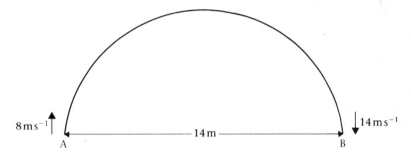

A particle moves on a semicircular path, its speed increasing uniformly with time from $8\,\mathrm{m\,s^{-1}}$ to $14\,\mathrm{m\,s^{-1}}$.

(a) What is the average speed of the particle and how many seconds does it take to complete this path?

(b) At what point on the path does the particle's speed equal $11\,\mathrm{m\,s^{-1}}$?

(c) What is its average velocity in travelling from A to B?

7 Because of engine problems, a racing car completes one lap of a race at an average speed of only $40\,\mathrm{km\,h^{-1}}$. At what speed must it complete a second lap so that its average speed for both laps is:

(a) $60\,\mathrm{km\,h^{-1}}$ (b) $80\,\mathrm{km\,h^{-1}}$?

1.4.2 Straight line motion

Even for motion in a straight line, there is a distinction between distance and displacement and between speed and velocity.

Velocity in the direction of positive displacement will be positive and in the direction of negative displacement will be negative.

Speed cannot be negative.

If the particle at P has a *velocity* of $8 \, \text{m s}^{-1}$ then it is moving from left to right. If its *velocity* is $-8 \, \text{m s}^{-1}$ then it is moving from right to left. The *speed* of the particle would be $8 \, \text{m s}^{-1}$ in both cases; the speed gives you no idea of the *direction* in which the particle is moving. If you want to know about direction of motion, you must deal with velocities.

 .4c

A ball is projected so that it rolls up an inclined track and then rolls down again. Its (time, displacement) graph is shown below.

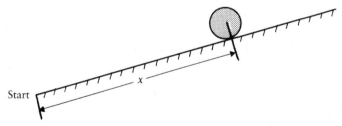

(You may wish to tackle this as a practical and substitute your own data.)

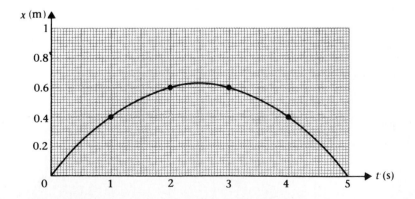

Plot a $\left(t, \dfrac{dx}{dt}\right)$ graph, either by measuring gradients or by finding the equation of the (time, displacement) graph and using calculus to find $\dfrac{dx}{dt}$.

1 What do your graphs tell you about the motion?

2 What does the area underneath the $\left(t, \dfrac{dx}{dt}\right)$ graph represent?

3 What does it mean if the area is underneath the t-axis?

4 What is the velocity of the ball after:

    (a) 1 second;   (b) 4 seconds?

5 What is the average velocity of the ball:

    (a) during the 2nd second;   (b) during the first 5 seconds?

The displacement from the origin x and velocity $\dfrac{dx}{dt}$ used in describing straight line motion are vector quantities. One direction of the line is chosen to be positive.

The area under a $\left(t, \dfrac{dx}{dt}\right)$ graph represents displacement. If the area is beneath the axis, the displacement is negative.

Example 2

(a) Describe the motion illustrated by the two graphs given below.

(b) Find T and the total distance travelled.

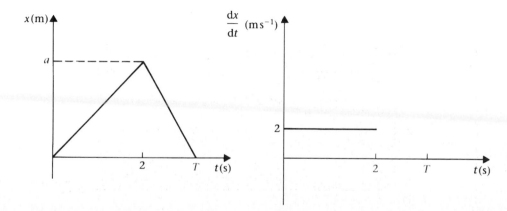

Solution

(a) The object travels away from its starting position with a constant velocity of $2\,\mathrm{m\,s}^{-1}$. When $t = 2$, it changes its velocity to $-4\,\mathrm{m\,s}^{-1}$ and returns to its starting position when $t = T$.

(b) The areas under the $\left(t, \dfrac{\mathrm{d}x}{\mathrm{d}t}\right)$ graph give the displacement during the interval of time.

The (t, x) graph shows that the position vector increases in magnitude from 0 to a in 2 seconds and becomes 0 again after T seconds.

The $\left(t, \dfrac{\mathrm{d}x}{\mathrm{d}t}\right)$ graph shows that the displacement after the first 2 seconds is 4 metres (the area under the line) so $a = 4$.

It also shows that the displacement from 2 to T seconds is $-4(T - 2)$ or $8 - 4T$, so the total displacement in T seconds is $4 + (8 - 4T) = 12 - 4T$. Hence,

$$12 - 4T = 0$$
$$T = 3$$

The total distance travelled is $4 + 4 = 8$ metres.

Example 3

A particle P moves along a straight line so that its displacement x metres from its initial position at time t seconds is

$$x = t(t - 1)$$

(a) Find: (i) the velocity of the particle when $t = 4$;
  (ii) the direction in which the particle is moving at this time.

(b) Find the velocity of the particle when it first returns to the starting position.

(c) Describe the motion of the particle.

Solution

(a) (i) $x = t^2 - t \ \Rightarrow \ $ velocity $v = \dfrac{\mathrm{d}x}{\mathrm{d}t} = 2t - 1$

When $t = 4$, the velocity is $7\,\mathrm{m\,s}^{-1}$.

  (ii) The velocity is $+7\,\mathrm{m\,s}^{-1}$, so the particle is moving from left to right along the line.

(b) The particle is at its starting position when $x = 0$.

$$0 = t(t - 1) \ \Rightarrow \ t = 0 \ \ \text{or} \ \ t = 1$$

The particle first returns to its starting position when $t = 1$. At this time it has a velocity of $1\,\mathrm{m\,s}^{-1}$.

(c) When $t = 0$, $v = -1\,\mathrm{m\,s}^{-1}$. The particle is moving left at $1\,\mathrm{m\,s}^{-1}$.
$v = 0$ when $2t - 1 = 0$,   i.e. when $t = \frac{1}{2}$ second.
When $t > \frac{1}{2}$, $v > 0$ and the particle is moving to the right.

The particle starts moving left with a speed of $1\,\mathrm{m\,s}^{-1}$; it slows down and momentarily stops when $t = \frac{1}{2}$, changing direction to move back toward its initial position. It passes through its initial position $(x = 0)$ again when $t = 1$ second, moving right at $1\,\mathrm{m\,s}^{-1}$. It continues to move away to the right, increasing its speed as it does so. It does not change direction again.

1.4 Exercise 2

1 The motion of an object is represented by the graphs shown below.

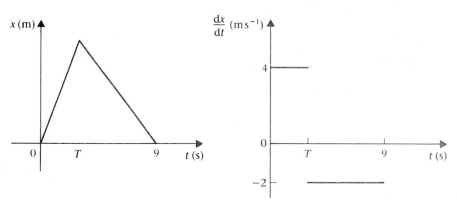

What is:

(a) the value of T;   (b) the distance covered after 9 seconds;

(c) the displacement after 9 seconds?

2 A child throws a ball up from the top of a tower. The displacement x metres from its initial position after t seconds is given by the formula $x = 6t - 5t^2$.

By using calculus or by plotting a (t, x) graph and measuring the gradient, find:

(a) the velocity of the ball after $\frac{1}{4}$ second and after 2 seconds;

(b) the average velocity of the ball for the first 3 seconds.

3 It is 10 km from A to B. Mary cycles from A to B, starting at 12 noon, at a steady speed of $15\,\mathrm{km\,h}^{-1}$ and then immediately turns and comes back to A at a speed of $7\frac{1}{2}\,\mathrm{km\,h}^{-1}$. John sets off on foot from B at noon and walks at a steady speed of $3\,\mathrm{km\,h}^{-1}$ to A.

(a) Draw (t, x) graphs of their motions on the same diagram, where t is the time in hours after 12 noon and x is the distance in kilometres from A.

(b) At what times t_1 and t_2 do Mary and John pass each other and how far are they from A at these times?

(c) At what time between t_1 and t_2 are they are the greatest distance apart?

4 Part of a (t, y) graph is shown for a ball which is dropped from a height of 10 metres onto the floor.

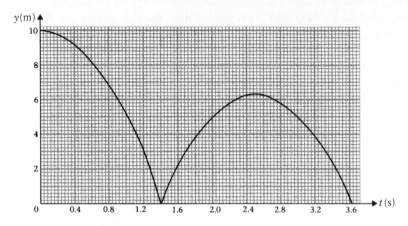

(a) Sketch the $\left(t, \dfrac{dy}{dt} \right)$ graph.

(b) Explain what happens when $t = 1.4$.

(c) Sketch a continuation of the (t, y) graph after $t = 3.6$.

(d) What is the ball's speed when $t = 1$?

1.4.3 Change in velocity

Suppose that three clockwork toy cars are each moving with a constant speed of $30\,\text{cm}\,\text{s}^{-1}$ on the surface of a floor mat. The mat is then pulled across the floor at a speed of $40\,\text{cm}\,\text{s}^{-1}$.

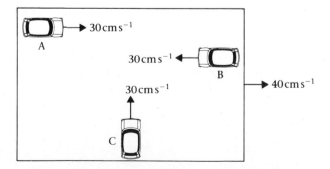

.4D

1 Find the new velocities of the cars.

2 What is the change in velocity of each car?

3 What relationship is there between the initial velocity of each car and its final velocity?

When an object moves from point P to point Q, its change in position is simply the vector $\overrightarrow{PQ}$.

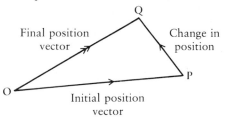

$$\begin{array}{ccc} \text{Initial position} \\ \text{vector} \end{array} + \begin{array}{c} \text{Change in position} \\ \text{vector} \end{array} = \begin{array}{c} \text{Final position} \\ \text{vector} \end{array}$$

Adding vectors 'head to tail' leads to a similar result for velocities.

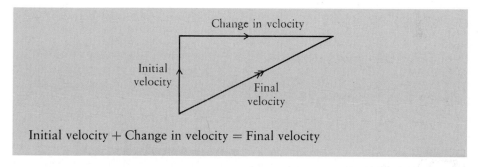

Initial velocity + Change in velocity = Final velocity

Example 4

If the initial velocity of a body is $6\,\mathrm{m\,s^{-1}}$ on a bearing of 320° and the final velocity of the body is $10\,\mathrm{m\,s^{-1}}$ due north, what is its change in velocity?

Solution

You have a choice of methods for solving this problem:

Solution by drawing (or trigonometry)
Change in velocity $= 6.6 \, \text{m s}^{-1}$ bearing $036°$

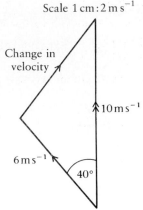

Scale $1 \, \text{cm} : 2 \, \text{m s}^{-1}$

Change in velocity

$10 \, \text{m s}^{-1}$

$6 \, \text{m s}^{-1}$

$40°$

Solution by components
Initial velocity + Change in velocity = Final velocity

Change in velocity = Final velocity − Initial velocity

$$\text{Change in velocity} = \begin{bmatrix} 0 \\ 10 \end{bmatrix} - \begin{bmatrix} 6 \sin 320° \\ 6 \cos 320° \end{bmatrix} \approx \begin{bmatrix} 3.9 \\ 5.4 \end{bmatrix}$$

1.4 Exercise 3

1 What is the change in velocity when an object's velocity changes from:

(a) $5 \, \text{m s}^{-1}$ due east to $8 \, \text{m s}^{-1}$ due west;

(b) $5 \, \text{m s}^{-1}$ due west to $8 \, \text{m s}^{-1}$ due east;

(c) $5 \, \text{m s}^{-1}$ due east to $8 \, \text{m s}^{-1}$ due north?

2 A boat is steered north-west at a speed of $4 \, \text{km h}^{-1}$. It then changes course to travel north-east at a speed of $6 \, \text{km h}^{-1}$. Find the change in velocity of the boat.

3 An aeroplane has velocity $\begin{bmatrix} 200 \\ 10 \end{bmatrix} \, \text{km h}^{-1}$. It changes its velocity by $\begin{bmatrix} -30 \\ 10 \end{bmatrix} \, \text{km h}^{-1}$. What is the final velocity of the aeroplane?

4 What is the change in velocity of a particle when its velocity changes from $\begin{bmatrix} 0 \\ -4 \end{bmatrix} \, \text{m s}^{-1}$ to $\begin{bmatrix} 6 \\ 2 \end{bmatrix} \, \text{m s}^{-1}$?

5 An aeroplane is travelling at $200 \, \text{km h}^{-1}$ on a bearing $050°$. A wind then blows so that the aeroplane ends up travelling at $200 \, \text{km h}^{-1}$ on a bearing $054°$. Find the velocity of the wind.

1.4.4 Resultant velocity

As you have seen, the idea of change of velocity is closely connected to that of the resultant velocity of an object in a moving medium, such as a floor mat or a wind.

Example 5

A boat is steered with velocity $\begin{bmatrix} 0 \\ -3 \end{bmatrix}$ km h^{-1} in a current running at $\begin{bmatrix} -5 \\ 0 \end{bmatrix}$ km h^{-1}. Find the resultant velocity of the boat:

(a) as a column vector,   (b) in speed and bearing form.

Solution
(a)

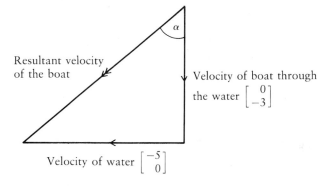

Resultant velocity of the boat

Velocity of boat through the water $\begin{bmatrix} 0 \\ -3 \end{bmatrix}$

Velocity of water $\begin{bmatrix} -5 \\ 0 \end{bmatrix}$

$$\text{Resultant velocity} = \begin{bmatrix} 0 \\ -3 \end{bmatrix} + \begin{bmatrix} -5 \\ 0 \end{bmatrix} = \begin{bmatrix} -5 \\ -3 \end{bmatrix} \text{ km h}^{-1}$$

(b) Speed $= \sqrt{(5^2 + 3^2)} \approx 5.8 \text{ km h}^{-1}$
$\tan \alpha = \frac{5}{3} \Rightarrow \alpha \approx 59°$
The bearing is $180° + 59° = 239°$.

Now consider a similar but more open-ended question.

> Problem

You want to cross a river in a boat. At what angle should you steer and how long will it take you to cross?

Set up a model

Take a simple case first.

Let the river be 100 m wide and its speed of flow be 1 m s^{-1}.

Suppose you set off from a point P at an angle α with the bank.

Assume that you can row at $2\,\mathrm{m\,s^{-1}}$ and want to land directly opposite.

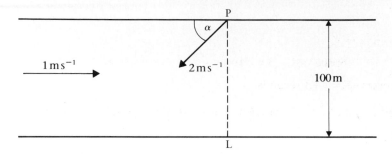

Analyse the problem

You know that your resultant velocity is

Velocity through the water + Velocity of the water

From the vector triangle, $\cos\alpha = \frac{1}{2} \Rightarrow \alpha = 60°$

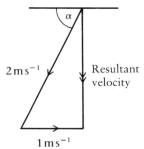

You must row at an angle of 60° to the bank.

Resultant velocity $= 1.73\,\mathrm{m\,s^{-1}}$

Time taken $= \dfrac{100}{1.73} = 57.7$ seconds

Interpret/validate

Assuming that you can row at a constant speed for almost a minute, you should reach the other side of the river at a spot opposite your departure point P. If you aim even further upstream you will land upstream.

Example 6

A canoe can travel at $4\,\mathrm{m\,s^{-1}}$ in still water. How long would it take to complete the circuit shown with a constant current of $3\,\mathrm{m\,s^{-1}}$ flowing in the direction indicated?

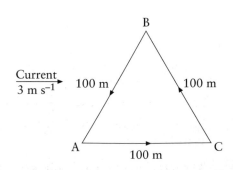

Solution

Assume the canoe travels at a constant speed of $4\,\text{m s}^{-1}$. Ignore any 'corner' effects.

From A to C

$$\text{Speed} = 4 + 3 = 7\,\text{m s}^{-1}$$

It takes $\frac{100}{7} = 14.3$ seconds

The remainder of the problem is easily tackled by scale drawing.

From C to B

The velocity vector can be found from the scale drawing below. The resultant velocity must be in the direction CB.

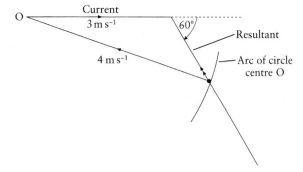

The actual velocity in the direction CB is $1.6\,\text{m s}^{-1}$ (measured).

The time taken for CB is $\dfrac{100}{1.6} = 62.5$ seconds.

From B to A

If you want to travel in direction BA then the resultant velocity must be in direction BA. By scale drawing again,

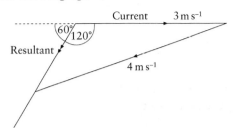

The resultant velocity is $1.6\,\text{m s}^{-1}$ (measured) on the bearing shown.

So the last leg also takes $\dfrac{100}{1.6} = 62.5$ seconds. (You may also have noticed that the two triangles drawn here are congruent, so the times for the last two legs must be the same!)

The total journey time is 139 seconds.

1.4 Exercise 4

1 A woman walks at $2\,\mathrm{m\,s}^{-1}$ across the deck of a boat. The boat is moving at $8\,\mathrm{m\,s}^{-1}$. Find the resultant speed of the woman.

2 A girl wishes to paddle her canoe across a river to the nearest point on the opposite bank of a river. If she can paddle at $1.5\,\mathrm{m\,s}^{-1}$ in still water and the river is running at $1\,\mathrm{m\,s}^{-1}$, in what direction should she point the canoe? If the river is 100 m wide, how long will it take her to cross?

Comment on any assumptions you have made.

3 A river flows with a speed of $1.5\,\mathrm{km\,h}^{-1}$. Find in what direction a swimmer, whose speed through the water is $2.5\,\mathrm{km\,h}^{-1}$, should start in order to cross at $30°$ downstream to the bank. Find his resultant speed.

4 A plane with an airspeed of $250\,\mathrm{km\,h}^{-1}$ has to fly from a town A to a town B, 100 km due east of A, in a wind blowing from $030°$ at $50\,\mathrm{km\,h}^{-1}$. Find, by drawing, the direction in which the plane must be headed and the time taken.

5 A river is 100 m wide and flows between two parallel banks at a speed of $3\,\mathrm{m\,s}^{-1}$. If you point a canoe directly across the river and paddle at $4\,\mathrm{m\,s}^{-1}$, how far downstream will you end up on the opposite bank?

How long will it take you to cross?

6 Crossing the same river in question 5, if you wish to end up directly opposite your start point, at what angle should you point and paddle the canoe?

How long will it take you to cross?

7 Again crossing the river in question 5, you point the canoe at $45°$ to the bank and into the current. Where will you end up on the other side? How long will it take you?

1.4.5 A modelling exercise

Problem

You are the pilot of a light aircraft which is capable of cruising at a steady speed in still air. You have enough fuel on board to last four hours. What is the maximum distance you can fly from your base and still return home safely?

Consider what factors are relevant, for example:

- the velocity of the plane,
- the wind velocity, and so on.

Make assumptions that will simplify the problem. For example, you could assume that the wind velocity is in a direction parallel to the velocity of the plane.

It might also help to make estimates of any relevant quantities and solve the problem for these values before you refine and generalise your model.

You should begin the modelling process by considering important factors, and assigning values where appropriate.

The key factors are:

(a) the velocity of the plane;
(b) the wind velocity;
(c) the altitude.

Assume that the velocity of the plane is constant and ignore the acceleration and retardation of starting and stopping. A speed of $150 \, \text{m s}^{-1}$ is reasonable for a light aircraft.

You may find it helpful to assume that the wind velocity is zero, in a preliminary calculation. Ignore the variation of fuel consumption with altitude. It is probably not significant for a light aircraft which will not fly very high.

Consider an initial, very simple model.

Model 1

Set up a model

Let the wind velocity be zero and the plane have velocity $150 \, \text{m s}^{-1}$.

Analyse the problem

Travelling at $150 \, \text{m s}^{-1}$ north for 2 hours gives a maximum distance from the base of $(150 \times 3600 \times 2) \, \text{m} = 1080 \, \text{km}$.

Refine the model.

Model 2

Set up a model

Now let the velocity of the wind be $30 \, \text{m s}^{-1}$ due south. Suppose that d metres is the maximum possible distance from base.

Analyse the problem

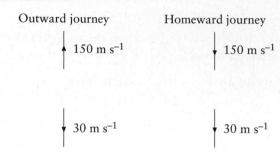

Outward journey   Homeward journey

150 m s^{-1} 150 m s^{-1}

30 m s^{-1} 30 m s^{-1}

On the outward journey the resultant speed is $120 \, \text{m s}^{-1}$ and the time taken is $d \div 120$ seconds.

On the homeward journey the resultant speed is $180 \, \text{m s}^{-1}$ and the time taken is $d \div 180$ seconds.

The total time must be 4 hours, so

$$\frac{d}{120} + \frac{d}{180} = 14\,400$$

$$\Rightarrow d = 1\,040\,000 \text{ (metres)}$$

Interpret/validate

The maximum distance that you can fly from base and return safely is $1040 \, \text{km}$.

1 ▶ **4**ᴇ

Extend the model by letting the wind speed be $v \, \text{m s}^{-1}$ due south.

After working through section 1.4, you should:

1 know that speed and distance are scalar quantities;

2 know that velocity and displacement are vector quantities which have both magnitude and direction;

3 be able to find the equivalent constant velocity from

$$\text{Average velocity} = \frac{\text{Change in position vector}}{\text{Time taken}}$$

4 know that

   Initial velocity + Change in velocity = Final velocity

and that this relationship can be represented in a vector triangle;

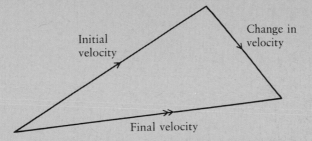

5 be able to find changes in velocity and resultant velocities using either a vector triangle or column vectors as appropriate.

1 Newton's laws of motion

1.5 Changes in motion

1.5.1 Momentum – the 'quantity of motion'

In this section you will study **changes** in motion. So far you have studied the quantities of time, distance, displacement, speed and velocity. These are not the only quantities involved when changes of motion are considered.

What makes a moving object easy or difficult to bring to rest?

First thoughts, together with everyday experience and observation, tell you that the faster something is travelling, the harder it is to stop. Conversely, the faster you wish something to go, the harder it is to achieve that speed.

You should be aware that some measure of the quantity of the object is relevant. Clearly, it is not just the volume (compare a shot-putter's shot and a beach ball) and not just the concentration of matter, or density of the object – but a combination of the two. This combination, which is called the mass of the object, is not an easy idea and is explained in this section.

Changes of motion of objects appear to be connected with the mass of the object. What precisely is meant by mass?

The **mass** of an object is the amount of matter it contains. Masses of objects of the same density can therefore be compared by simply measuring their volumes. The unit of mass, the **kilogram**, is now defined as the mass of a certain block of platinum–iridium alloy that is kept at Sèvres in France. It used to be defined as the mass of 1 litre of pure water at the temperature of its greatest density ($4\,^\circ$C). Unfortunately a mistake was made and the kilogram is actually now the mass of $1000.028\,\text{cm}^3$ of water!

The pull of the Earth on an object is proportional to its mass and so, to compare the masses of objects of different densities, we can compare the pulls the Earth exerts upon them, i.e. their weights. Greengrocers' spring balances are calibrated in kilograms as if they measured mass but they really measure weight. Six kilograms of apples would still have mass six kilograms on the Moon but such a spring balance would read only approximately 1 kg because of the much smaller gravitational pull of the Moon.

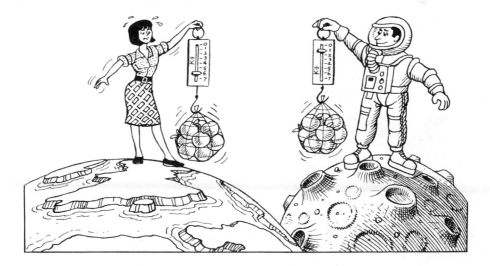

> The mass of an object is the amount of matter it contains. 1 kilogram has been defined as the mass of 1 litre of pure water.

To familiarise yourself with what Sir Isaac Newton called the 'quantities of motion' you should try the following simple experiments.

 .5A

Experiment 1

1 Place a block on the table and roll a snooker ball slowly along the table towards it.

(a) When the ball hits the block, what happens:

(i) to the ball,   (ii) to the block?

(b) Now use a table tennis ball. Try to make it travel at about the same speed. What happens now?

(c) Repeat (a) and (b) using a higher velocity for the balls.

Experiment 2

2 (a) Get a friend to drop the snooker ball from a height, allowing you to catch it in your hand. Describe what you feel as the height is increased in 50 cm steps from 50 cm to 2 metres.

(b) Repeat the experiment with the table tennis ball.

(c) What you feel is what Newton called the fundamental 'quantity of motion'. What do you think are the important factors which make up this quantity?

3 Which do you think has more 'quantity of motion', a 4 tonne lorry travelling at $1\,\mathrm{m\,s}^{-1}$ or an 800 kg car travelling at $5\,\mathrm{m\,s}^{-1}$?

The 'stoppability' of an object seems to depend upon both its mass and its speed.

The fundamental 'quantity of motion' seems to depend upon both mass and velocity. The next activity contains some experiments to investigate further the nature of this quantity in the context of collisions. It is surprising, when you consider how wild and apparently disordered collisions can be, that there should be any simple connection between the situations before and after the collision.

1 .5B

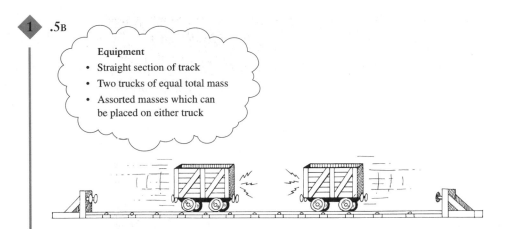

Equipment
- Straight section of track
- Two trucks of equal total mass
- Assorted masses which can be placed on either truck

Experiment 3
Set up the two trucks so that they will bounce apart. What happens if one truck is propelled towards the other stationary truck? Repeat with various masses on each truck and write down your conclusions.

Experiment 4
Set up the two trucks so that they will stick together on impact. Repeat experiment 3.

The fundamental 'quantity of motion' of an object is the product of its mass and velocity. This quantity of motion is called **momentum** (plural: momenta).

Momentum = Mass × Velocity

An object of mass $0.1\,\text{kg}$ and moving with a speed of $2\,\text{m s}^{-1}$ has momentum of $0.2\,\text{kg m s}^{-1}$. Momentum is a vector quantity and you should picture it as a vector of magnitude $0.2\,\text{kg m s}^{-1}$ in the direction of the object's velocity.

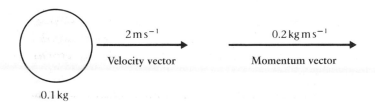

$2\,\text{m s}^{-1}$

Velocity vector

$0.2\,\text{kg m s}^{-1}$

Momentum vector

$0.1\,\text{kg}$

1.5 Exercise 1

1 Which of the following objects have the *same* momentum:

(a) a 3 kg shot rolled along the ground at $5\,\mathrm{m\,s}^{-1}$ in a northerly direction;

(b) a 6 kg shot rolled along the ground at $2.5\,\mathrm{m\,s}^{-1}$ in an easterly direction;

(c) a 3 kg shot rolled along the ground at $5\,\mathrm{m\,s}^{-1}$ in an easterly direction?

2 A woman of mass 70 kg has a velocity which can be represented by the vector $\begin{bmatrix} 3 \\ 4 \end{bmatrix}\,\mathrm{m\,s}^{-1}$, the components being in the directions east and north respectively. Find her momentum in vector form and calculate its magnitude and direction.

3 Sketch pairs of vectors to represent the momenta of the objects described below, giving reasons for the size of the vectors:

(a) a car of mass one tonne moving north at $90\,\mathrm{km\,h}^{-1}$ and a ten tonne lorry travelling east at $30\,\mathrm{km\,h}^{-1}$;

(b) a speed boat cutting across the bows of a ferry;

(c) a jeep racing a rhinoceros.

1.5.2 Conservation of momentum

In the collisions investigated in section 1.5.1, you may have observed that the total momentum after a collision was about the same as the total momentum before the collision.

Suppose a puck moving with speed $2\,\mathrm{m\,s}^{-1}$ collides with a stationary puck as shown below.

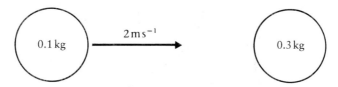

After the collision:

(a) the lighter puck might rebound, for example,

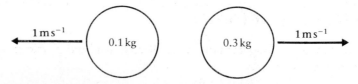

(b) or the pucks might stick together,

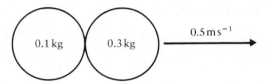

(c) or the blow might be a glancing one.

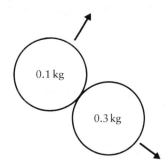

However, in each case, the momenta of the two pucks after the collision will add up vectorially (i.e. 'head-to-tail') to the original momentum of $0.2 \, \text{kg m s}^{-1}$.

Original momentum

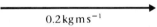

$0.2 \, \text{kg m s}^{-1}$

Final momentum
(a)

0.3

0.1

(b)

0.05   0.15

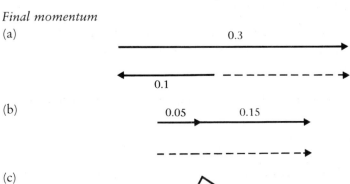

(c)

In each case, the final momenta add up to $0.2 \, \text{kg m s}^{-1}$. The total momentum has not been changed by the collision.

When total momentum is unchanged, mathematicians and physicists speak of the **conservation of momentum**.

> The law of conservation of momentum
>
> If no external forces act during a collision, the total momentum of the
> system is conserved.

The law of conservation of momentum is truly remarkable – not only is it
simple but it applies to so many different types of interaction. The law applies
equally to the motion of subatomic particles as it does to the motion of planets.
Rocket propulsion is just one practical application of this important law.

You can use conservation of momentum to help predict velocities after a
collision. This idea is illustrated in example 1.

Example 1

Louise, on a toboggan (total mass 80 kg) travelling at $4\,\mathrm{m\,s}^{-1}$, collides with
Eddie, also on a toboggan (total mass 60 kg) moving in the opposite direction at
$5\,\mathrm{m\,s}^{-1}$. The toboggans interlock and move together. What is their speed
immediately after the collision?

Solution

In the direction of motion of Louise, the momentum was

$$80 \times 4 - 60 \times 5 = 20\,\mathrm{kg\,m\,s}^{-1}$$

If $v\,\mathrm{m\,s}^{-1}$ is the new speed, then the new momentum is $(80 + 60)v\,\mathrm{kg\,m\,s}^{-1}$.
Since the momentum is conserved,

$$(80 + 60)v = 20 \quad \Rightarrow \quad v \approx 0.14$$

They move with a speed of $0.14\,\mathrm{m\,s}^{-1}$.

In the example above, the law of conservation of momentum has been assumed.

It has also been assumed that *all* of the 140 kg moves with the same velocity just
after the collision. This is *not* a reasonable assumption as the motions of Louise
and Eddie will differ initially from those of their toboggans. However, if they
remain on their toboggans and if friction has no appreciable effect, then the motion
will soon settle down into one of a uniform speed of approximately $0.14\,\mathrm{m\,s}^{-1}$.

Example 2

Two bodies, of masses 2.5 kg and 5 kg, are moving in a horizontal plane, with
respective velocities $3\,\mathrm{m\,s}^{-1}$ south and $4\,\mathrm{m\,s}^{-1}$ west, when they collide and
coalesce. Find the subsequent speed of the compound body.

Solution

The total momentum before (and after) the collision can be found by adding the vectors shown:

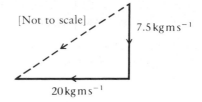

The length of the resultant can be found using Pythagoras' theorem. The momentum afterwards is 21.4 kg m s^{-1}. Since the combined mass is 7.5 kg, the subsequent speed is

$$\frac{21.4}{7.5} \approx 2.85 \text{ m s}^{-1}$$

1.5 Exercise 2

1 In each of the situations below, find the velocity of B after the collision.

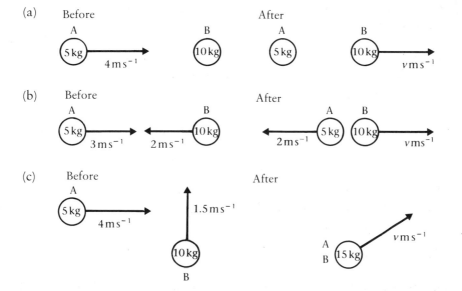

2 A car hit a parked van and after the collision the two vehicles became locked together and skidded to a stop. From the skid marks it was estimated that just after the impact the common velocity of the two vehicles was 7 m s^{-1}. If the total mass of the van and its load was 2000 kg and the mass of the car and its passengers was 1200 kg, what was the speed of the car just before impact?

3 A body A, of mass 3 kg, moving with a speed of 4 m s^{-1}, collides with a stationary body B, of mass 2 kg. After the collision A continues to move in its original direction with a speed of 2 m s^{-1}. What is the velocity of B after the collision?

4 A body P, of mass 2 kg, moving with a speed of 5 m s^{-1}, collides with a body Q which is approaching P in the same straight line, travelling in the opposite direction with a speed of 4 m s^{-1}. After the collision, both P and Q reverse their motion in the same straight line with respective speeds of 1 m s^{-1} and 2 m s^{-1}. Find the mass of Q.

5 Two bodies, of masses 3 kg and 4 kg, are each moving in a horizontal plane with a speed of 5 m s^{-1}, the first in direction 030° and the second in direction 120°. After collision, the body of mass 4 kg moves in its original direction but with a reduced speed of 3 m s^{-1}. Find, by means of a drawing, the velocity of the 3 kg mass after the collision.

1.5.3 Change in momentum

You have seen that momentum is the fundamental 'quantity of motion'. We therefore measure 'changes in motion' by calculating the **change in momentum**.

Changes in momentum can be sudden, as in the collisions of section 1.5.1. You can also observe gradual changes in momentum as when an apple falls to the ground.

One of the collisions considered in section 1.5.2 was as follows:

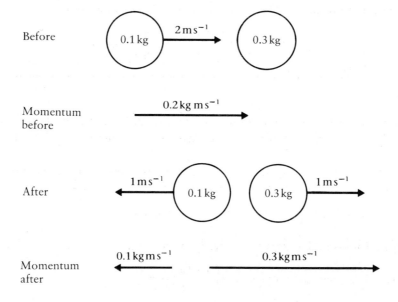

 .5c

Find the change in momentum for each puck. What do you notice? Can you explain why this should happen?

The change in momentum of an object is a measure of the action exerted upon it. (Newton called the action exerted on a body the '*vis impressa*'.) In the next section, you will consider the concept of a force and the action of one particular force, the force of gravity.

Example 3

A hockey ball of mass 0.5 kg is hit a glancing blow from a stick so that its velocity changes from $\begin{bmatrix} 6 \\ 8 \end{bmatrix}$ to $\begin{bmatrix} -9 \\ 7 \end{bmatrix}$ m s^{-1}, the axes being taken along and across the pitch. Find the ball's change in momentum in component form.

Solution

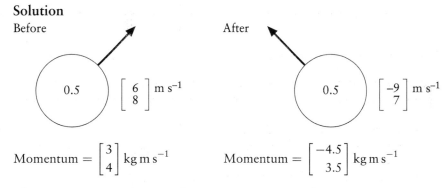

Before

After

0.5 $\begin{bmatrix} 6 \\ 8 \end{bmatrix}$ m s^{-1}

0.5 $\begin{bmatrix} -9 \\ 7 \end{bmatrix}$ m s^{-1}

Momentum $= \begin{bmatrix} 3 \\ 4 \end{bmatrix}$ kg m s^{-1}

Momentum $= \begin{bmatrix} -4.5 \\ 3.5 \end{bmatrix}$ kg m s^{-1}

Change in momentum = Final momentum − Original momentum

$$= \begin{bmatrix} -4.5 \\ 3.5 \end{bmatrix} - \begin{bmatrix} 3 \\ 4 \end{bmatrix} = \begin{bmatrix} -7.5 \\ -0.5 \end{bmatrix} \text{kg m s}^{-1}$$

1.5 Exercise 3

1 A 10 tonne truck is travelling along a straight road. Its speed increases from 65 km h^{-1} to 120 km h^{-1}. What is its change in momentum?

2 A railway truck on a straight track has a speed of 15 m s^{-1}. Its momentum decreases by 15 000 kg m s^{-1}. What is its new speed if the truck has:

(a) a mass of 2 tonnes,   (b) a mass of 10 tonnes?

3 A puck of mass 0.1 kg is travelling across an ice rink with velocity $\begin{bmatrix} 25 \\ 2 \end{bmatrix}$ m s^{-1}.

It is struck so that its new velocity is $\begin{bmatrix} -15 \\ 5 \end{bmatrix}$ m s^{-1}.

(a) What is its change in momentum?

(b) If the change in momentum had only been half this value, what would the new velocity have been?

After working through section 1.5, you should:

1   know that the 'quantity of motion' of an object is called its momentum and that it is the product of the object's mass and velocity;

2   know and understand that total momentum is conserved if there are no external forces;

3   be able to use the principle of conservation of momentum to help determine motions after collisions;

4   be able to use vector triangles to calculate changes in momentum;

5   know that a blow changes the momentum of an object in the direction of the blow.

1 Newton's laws of motion

.6 Force

1.6.1 Newton's first and second laws of motion

In section 1.5 you considered the fundamental 'quantity of motion' called momentum, and also studied changes in momentum.

To change the momentum of an object you must give it a push or a pull. The important features of a push or pull are its duration and its strength or **force**. For example, a tennis player applies a large force for a short period of time whereas a bowler in a game of cricket applies a smaller force for a longer period of time.

Without pushes or pulls the momentum of an object does not change. This important idea is called **Newton's first law of motion**.

Unless acted upon by an external force, a particle travels with constant velocity (in a straight line with constant speed).

In 1673, some 14 years before Newton's *Principia*, Huygens expressed this idea as follows:

If gravity did not exist, nor the atmosphere obstruct the motions of bodies, a body would maintain forever a motion once impressed upon it, with uniform velocity in a straight line.

It is important to note that Newton's first law states that the natural state of matter is motion with constant *velocity*. An object at rest is, of course, travelling with constant (zero) velocity!

The following two situations illustrate the application of Newton's first law.

Once a shot has left a shot-putter's hand it does not travel in a straight line with constant speed. If Newton's first law is to hold then there must be a force acting

on the shot. That force is the pull of the Earth on the shot, i.e. its weight. This
gradually changes the velocity of the shot.

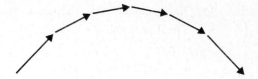

Similarly, if you push a car along a level road, when you stop pushing it quickly
comes to a halt. There must be a force acting on the car to bring it to rest. This
force is **friction**. (It might not come to rest if it is on a slope, because then the
weight of the car might overcome any frictional force.)

There are many forces, such as tension, weight, friction, and so on, which can
act on an object. The **resultant force** is the combined effect of *all* forces acting on
the object. Newton realised that if the forces acting on an object are not
balanced then the effect of the resultant force is to change the momentum of the
object according to the law known as **Newton's second law of motion**. The
questions which follow illustrate the ideas involved in the formulation of the
very important second law.

 .6A

A ball is rolled along a horizontal strip of felt. The displacement x cm of the
ball at time t seconds is recorded in the table.

Distance travelled (x cm)	0	60	80	100	120
Time taken (t seconds)	0	0.7	1.0	1.4	2.0

1 Plot the points and draw a graph showing distance travelled (vertical axis)
against time (horizontal axis).

2 As accurately as you can, draw tangents to the graph at $\frac{1}{2}$-second intervals
to show that the speed of the ball decreases at a constant rate of
approximately $40\,\text{cm s}^{-1}$ each second.

Since the mass of the ball is constant, the constant rate of change of speed
also means a constant rate of change of momentum. Newton recognised that
rate of change of momentum is a measure of the resultant force being
applied. In this case it indicates that there is a roughly constant frictional
force acting on the ball.

Newton's second law of motion states:

> **The resultant force on an object is equal to its rate of change of momentum** (its change of momentum each second).
>
> A force which causes a change in momentum of $1 \, \text{kg m s}^{-1}$ per second is said to be a force of 1 newton (1 N).

You may have already met an alternative version of Newton's second law where the resultant force is defined as the mass of the object multiplied by its 'acceleration'. This definition is consistent with the above version of the law and will be considered in section 1.6.3.

If the force acting is a constant force, then the change in momentum is simply the product of that force and the time over which it acts.

> A *constant* resultant force F acting on a body of mass m for a time t will cause a change in momentum of Ft.
>
> $$\text{Change in momentum} = \text{Resultant (constant) force} \times \text{Time}$$

Newton's first law arises as a special case of Newton's second law when the resultant force is zero.

In this case, the change of momentum is zero and therefore the momentum of the body remains constant.

$$m\mathbf{v} = \text{constant}$$

Provided the mass of the body is also constant, then the velocity ($\mathbf{v}$) is constant.

Example 1
A constant force of 15 N is applied to a body of mass 10 kg for 5 seconds. If it starts from rest, what is its final velocity?

Solution
Change in momentum = force × time taken
$$= 5 \times 15 = 75 \, \text{kg m s}^{-1}$$

Since the momentum is initially zero, the final momentum is $75 \, \text{kg m s}^{-1}$ and the final velocity is $7.5 \, \text{m s}^{-1}$ in the direction of the force.

1.6 Exercise 1

1 A constant force of 20 N is applied for 4 seconds to a body of mass 2 kg, originally at rest. What is its speed after 1, 2, 3 and 4 seconds? What does this indicate about the motion of the body?

2 What force, acting for 5 seconds, would change the velocity of a puck of mass 0.2 kg from $1.5 \, \text{m s}^{-1}$ due south to $2 \, \text{m s}^{-1}$ due north?

3 How long does it take for the speed of a car, of mass 900 kg, to be reduced from $72 \, \text{km h}^{-1}$ to $48 \, \text{km h}^{-1}$ if the net braking force is 1250 N?

4 A train of mass 35 tonnes runs with a speed of $0.3 \, \text{m s}^{-1}$ into the buffers at the end of a platform. What constant force must the buffers exert to bring the train to rest in 2 seconds?

5 A hot air balloon of mass 200 kg rises up from the ground. If the resultant force on the balloon for the first 3 seconds is 150 N vertically upwards, what is its speed at the end of that time?

1.6.2 Newton's third law of motion

Consider the collision of two snooker balls. You can model the collision by supposing that two large reaction forces (**R** and **S**) act for a very short time.

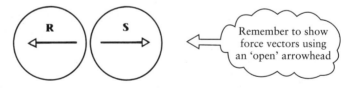

Remember to show force vectors using an 'open' arrowhead

As you found in section 1.5, the total momentum is conserved. By Newton's second law, you know that changes in momentum caused by the forces **R** and **S** are equal in magnitude and opposite in direction. For this to happen, **R** and **S** must be equal in magnitude and opposite in direction because they act for the same length of time.

This is a particular example of **Newton's third law of motion**.

When two bodies, A and B, interact, the force that A exerts on B is equal in magnitude and opposite in direction to the force that B exerts on A.

1 .6B

Two students stand on skateboards and press against each others' hands. What can you say about:

(a) the force each exerts,

(b) their subsequent motion?

If one student is twice as heavy as the other, how does this affect your answers to (a) and (b)?

Example 2

In deep space, a rocket changes its velocity by firing its engines. Explain how total momentum is conserved.

Solution

The rocket forces exhaust gases out of its motors in a given direction. These exert a force on the rocket which is equal in magnitude and opposite in direction to the force of the rocket on the gas.

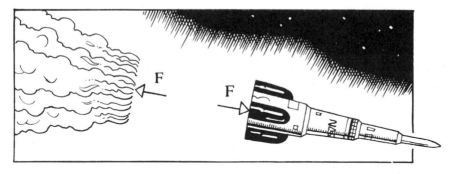

The change in momentum of the gas is therefore equal in magnitude and opposite in direction to the change in momentum of the rocket and so the total momentum of the rocket and gas is conserved.

Example 3

Draw the forces acting on a book which is on a horizontal table and pushed with a horizontal force. Consider (a) the case where the push is too small for movement, and (b) the case where the book moves at a constant speed.

Solution

(a)

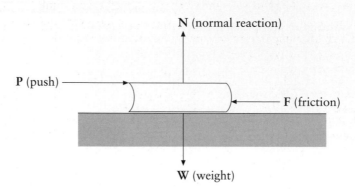

(b) The model of the forces is unchanged in the second case. There are still four forces. You need not add an extra force because the book is moving. The sizes of the push and the friction will have changed. In case (b), the push P' is bigger, so the size of the friction F' is also greater.

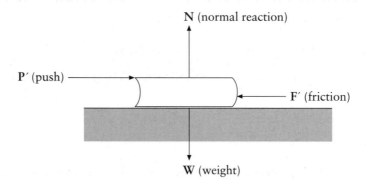

1.6 Exercise 2

1 For a falling apple of weight W, what is the 'other body' which is involved? What is the other force? What can you say about the total momentum of the apple and the Earth?

2 Draw a diagram and specify the forces of interaction involved in the motion of the Earth travelling round the Sun. Is the total momentum of the Earth and Sun constant? What does this tell you about the motion of the Sun?

3 Copy the diagrams below, describing the forces shown in the model. Show with an arrow like this ─←─ the direction in which you think the object is moving. In some of these, friction or resistance has been omitted because the force is small compared to the others. If you think forces have been neglected, make a note on your diagram.

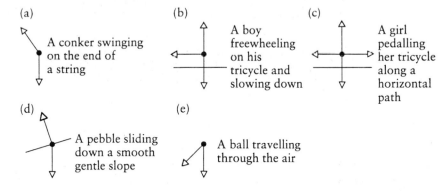

(a)   A conker swinging on the end of a string

(b)   A boy freewheeling on his tricycle and slowing down

(c)   A girl pedalling her tricycle along a horizontal path

(d)   A pebble sliding down a smooth gentle slope

(e)   A ball travelling through the air

1.6.3 Weight and change of momentum

This section considers the mechanics of objects falling freely in space and looks at the important concept of **weight**.

 .6C

1 If a golf ball is allowed to fall freely, does the pull of the Earth change as it falls? Sketch the form of (time, velocity) graph you would expect.

2 If a golf ball and cricket ball are dropped together, which will fall faster? Explain your answer.

Accurate data on falling objects can be obtained easily. Such data are studied in the following questions.

3 A 1 kg shot is dropped vertically from rest. From photographs of its motion, an accurate (time, displacement) graph has been drawn.

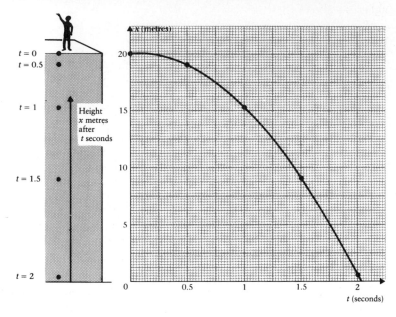

(a) From the (time, displacement) graph, estimate the velocity of the shot at half-second intervals. Hence draw the (time, velocity) graph.

(b) What is the change in momentum during:

(i) the first second, (ii) the second second?

(c) If the shot were dropped from a much greater height, what do you think the change in momentum would be during the third second, the fourth second, and so on?

(d) What do you think causes this change in momentum?

4 The track of a golf ball as it is pitched onto the green is given below. It has been marked out every quarter second for the first six seconds of its flight.

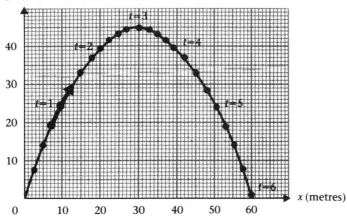

Height y (metres)

x (metres)

(a) To estimate the velocity of the ball one second after being hit, the displacement vector from $t = 0.75$ to $t = 1.25$ has been marked on the diagram. This is the displacement during a half second. A vector parallel to this but of twice the length therefore represents the average velocity during this time interval. This average velocity will be a good approximation to the velocity after one second.

Repeat this to find the velocity when $t = 2, 3, 4$ and 5 seconds.

(b) The mass of the ball is 0.1 kg. Find the five vectors representing the momenta of the ball 1, 2, 3, 4 and 5 seconds after being hit.

Draw them all with the same initial point:

(c) What do you notice about these five vectors and what does this imply about the motion of the ball?

Find the changes in momentum of the ball during the second, third, fourth and fifth seconds of its flight.

(d) What do you notice about these changes in momentum? Try to explain what you find.

The force of gravitational attraction on an object is called the **weight** of the object. For an object which remains near the Earth's surface, this force is virtually constant. It is conventional to denote the weight of a 1 kg mass by the vector **g** newtons and its magnitude by g newtons. A sufficiently accurate value of g for most purposes is either 9.8 or 10. Correspondingly, **g** is taken to be either

$$\begin{bmatrix} 0 \\ -9.8 \end{bmatrix} \quad \text{or} \quad \begin{bmatrix} 0 \\ -10 \end{bmatrix}$$

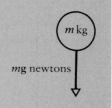

On a mass of m kg at the Earth's surface, the Earth exerts a downward force of m**g** newtons.

m**g** newtons

For an object moving freely under gravity (with negligible air resistance), the only force acting is its weight and it is easy to apply Newton's second law to its motion. For example, suppose a projectile has mass m kg and that during t seconds its velocity changes from **u** m s^{-1} to **v** m s^{-1}.

Original momentum + Time × Weight = New momentum
$$m\mathbf{u} \quad + \quad tm\mathbf{g} \quad = \quad m\mathbf{v}$$

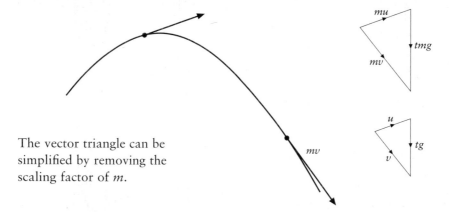

The vector triangle can be simplified by removing the scaling factor of m.

The velocity changes by **g** m s^{-1} each second. Another way of stating this is as follows.

A freely falling object has an acceleration downwards of **g** m s^{-2}.

Because of this result, $\mathbf{g}\,\mathrm{m\,s^{-2}}$ is often called the **acceleration due to gravity**.

The relationship shown in the vector triangle can therefore be written as follows.

> For an object moving freely under gravity,
>
> Initial velocity + Time × Acceleration = Final velocity
>
> $\mathbf{u}$ + $t\mathbf{g}$ = $\mathbf{v}$

A detailed study of acceleration and the corresponding form of Newton's second law,

Resultant force = Mass × Acceleration

is given in Chapter 2.

Example 4
An apple is thrown vertically upwards at $20\,\mathrm{m\,s^{-1}}$. What is its velocity after 4 seconds?

Draw a graph of velocity against time. When is its velocity zero?

Solution

$$\mathbf{v} = \mathbf{u} + t\mathbf{g} = \begin{bmatrix} 0 \\ 20 \end{bmatrix} + 4 \times \begin{bmatrix} 0 \\ -9.8 \end{bmatrix}$$

The velocity (upwards) after 4 seconds is

$$20 - 4 \times 9.8 = -19.2\,\mathrm{m\,s^{-1}}$$

From the graph you can see that the velocity is zero when $t \approx 2$.

The value from the graph can be confirmed as follows.

After t seconds, the upwards velocity is

$$20 - t \times 9.8$$

This is zero when

$$t = \frac{20}{9.8} = 2.04 \quad \text{(to 3 s.f.)}$$

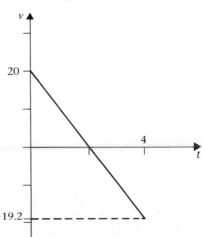

Example 5

A stone of mass 2 kg is dropped down a well. It hits the surface of the water 4 seconds later. How deep is the well?

Solution

Set up a model

Assume the stone is a particle (ignore its size).
Assume the only force acting on it is its weight so its change of velocity is a constant $9.8 \, \mathrm{m \, s^{-1}}$ each second.
Assume the stone starts from rest.

Analyse the problem

After 1 second its velocity is $9.8 \, \mathrm{m \, s^{-1}}$.

After 2 seconds its velocity is $19.6 \, \mathrm{m \, s^{-1}}$.

...

The (t, v) graph is as shown.

The shaded area under the graph gives the distance travelled as

$$x = \tfrac{1}{2} \times 4 \times 39.2 = 78.4 \text{ metres}$$

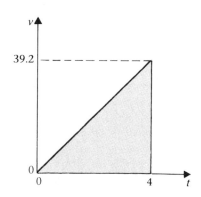

Interpret/validate

The stone travels 78.4 metres so the well is at least 78.4 metres deep.

1.6 Exercise 3

(Take $g = 9.8 \, \mathrm{m \, s^{-2}}$.)

1 A ball rolls over a high cliff.

 (a) What is its velocity after 3 seconds?

 (b) How far has it fallen?

 (c) It hits the ground after 3.5 seconds. How high is the cliff?

2 A stone is thrown vertically upwards to dislodge a conker on a tree. The maximum speed the stone can be thrown with is $14.8\,\mathrm{m\,s^{-1}}$ and it must hit the conker with a speed of at least $5\,\mathrm{m\,s^{-1}}$ to dislodge it.

(a) Draw a graph of velocity against time for the motion of the stone.

(b) Use this to calculate the height of the highest conker it can dislodge.

3 A paint tin is dislodged from a workman's platform 4 metres above the street.

(a) Draw a graph of velocity against time for the tin's motion.

(b) Use your graph to calculate the velocity with which it hits the ground.

4 A girl of mass 25 kg and her father of mass 75 kg both jump off the 5 metre board into a swimming pool. What is the momentum of:

(a) the girl,   (b) her father,

when they reach the water?

5 A pile driver of mass 2 tonnes has a momentum of $16\,000\,\mathrm{kg\,m\,s^{-1}}$ when it hits the ground. What height was it dropped from?

After working through section 1.6, you should:

1 know Newton's three laws of motion:

  ● unless acted upon by an external force, a particle travels with
    constant velocity;

  ● resultant force equals rate of change of momentum;

  ● when two bodies interact, they exert equal but opposite forces upon
    each other;

2 know that a force of magnitude 1 newton gives a mass of 1 kg a change
  in velocity of $1\,\mathrm{m\,s^{-1}}$ each second;

3 know that, on the Earth's surface, a mass of m kg has a weight of
  mg newtons, where $g \approx 9.8$;

4 be able to apply the result that, for bodies moving freely under the
  gravitational attraction of the Earth,

$$\mathbf{v} = \mathbf{u} + t\mathbf{g}$$

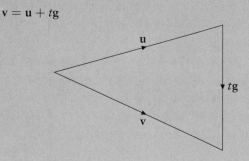

1 Newton's laws of motion

Miscellaneous exercise 1

1 A body starts from rest and moves along a straight line so that its displacement (d cm) from its start position at time t seconds is given by

$$d = t^2 + 1$$

(a) Draw a graph of displacement against time.

(b) From your graph, or otherwise, find the velocity of the body at $t = 2$.

(c) How far does the body travel:
   (i) in the first second,   (ii) in the second second?

2 A particle moves in a straight line so that its displacement d metres from its initial position is

$$d = t^2(t - 1)$$

(t is the time in seconds.)

(a) Find the velocity of the particle when $t = 2$.

(b) At what time is the velocity zero?

(c) In what direction is the particle moving when: (i) $t = 0.5$,   (ii) $t = 0.8$?

3 Calculate the components, in the x- and y-directions, of the following displacements:

(a) 3.5 cm, making an angle of 58° clockwise from the y-axis;

(b) 7.4 cm, making an angle of 237° anticlockwise from the x-axis;

(c) 11.9 cm, making an angle of 39° anticlockwise from the y-axis.

4 Nicola and Jane are on a walking holiday and set out from different youth hostels with the intention of meeting for lunch outside the *George and Dragon*. Their starting points are 5.0 km apart, with Jane due east of Nicola, at which stage the *George and Dragon* is 5.0 km north-west of Jane. Jane is good at map-reading but walks slowly: at lunchtime she has covered 3.5 km, walking in the right direction. Nicola, whose map-reading is not her strong point, has by then walked 5.5 km north-east. Calculate how far each of them is from the *George and Dragon*, and how far they are apart.

5 The position vectors **a** and **b** for two towns A and B in relation to the origin
   are as given below. Distances are in kilometres.

$$\mathbf{a} = \begin{bmatrix} 20 \\ 30 \end{bmatrix} \qquad \mathbf{b} = \begin{bmatrix} 15 \\ 20 \end{bmatrix}$$

   Calculate the distance and bearing of:

   (a) A from the origin,   (b) B from the origin,

   (c) B from A,   (d) A from B.

6 The town of Moncton, grid reference 210183, is on a bearing of 050° from
   Nawton and 16 km away. Calculate the six-figure grid reference for Nawton.

7 The towns A and B have grid references of 582108 and 413504 respectively.
   Calculate the distance between the towns, and the bearing of A from B.

8 Two larks set out in opposite directions, each flying at $10 \, \mathrm{km \, h}^{-1}$. After half
   an hour, both change course by rotating anticlockwise through 30°. Calculate
   how far they are apart after a further quarter of an hour. Would it make any
   difference if the wind was blowing?

9 The graphs below show the displacement and the velocity of a cyclist moving
   in a straight line. She pedals away from traffic lights, and then brakes gently,
   coming to rest outside a shop 12 seconds later.

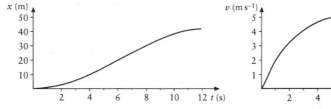 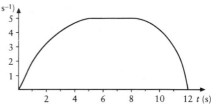

   (a) Estimate her average velocity during this period.

   (b) After approximately how many seconds does she reach the maximum
       speed? Measure the maximum speed on the first graph, and check that
       this agrees with the value given by the second graph.

10 An astronaut jumps vertically upwards from the surface of the Moon,
   and t seconds later her feet are y metres above the surface, where
   $y = 2t - 0.8t^2$.

   (a) What is her velocity when she jumps?

   (b) At what height is her velocity $1 \, \mathrm{m \, s}^{-1}$?

   (c) When do her feet make contact with the surface again?

11 A bee is travelling in a vertical line, and at time t seconds its height above the ground is y cm, where $y = 50 - 6t^2 + t^3$.

(a) Draw up a table showing the position and velocity at $t = 0, 1, 2, 3,$ 4 and 5.

(b) What is the least height of the bee above the ground?

(c) When the bee is descending, what is its maximum speed?

12 A spaceship is about to land on the planet Vulcan. The final rockets are fired and t seconds later the height of the spaceship above the surface is $(10 - 3t + 0.3t^2 - 0.01t^3)$ metres.

(a) What is the velocity when $t = 0$?

(b) Verify that the spaceship lands when $t = 10$. What is the velocity at this time?

13 A river is flowing at $2.5 \, \text{m s}^{-1}$ parallel to the banks. If you set off to swim to the other side 40 m away at $3 \, \text{m s}^{-1}$, calculate:

(a) how far you actually swim through the water;

(b) how long it takes to cross.

14 A small aeroplane, capable of an air speed of $160 \, \text{km h}^{-1}$, has to fly from Kilima to Shambani, which is 65 km away on a bearing 247°. There is a steady wind of about $40 \, \text{km h}^{-1}$ blowing from the south-east.

(a) What course should the pilot set? How long should she expect the journey to take?

(b) By evening, when she wishes to return, the wind has increased to about $50 \, \text{km h}^{-1}$ and is blowing from due east. What new course should be set and how long should the journey take?

15 A dodgem car of mass 120 kg, moving at $3 \, \text{m s}^{-1}$ with its power switched off, hits another car of mass 140 kg directly from behind. The second car was originally at rest, and moves forward after the collision at $2 \, \text{m s}^{-1}$. Find the subsequent velocity of the first car.

16 In a game of bowls, one wood of mass 0.9 kg hits a stationary jack. Its speed is reduced from $2 \, \text{m s}^{-1}$ to $1.5 \, \text{m s}^{-1}$. The whole motion takes place in the same line and the jack moves off at $3.2 \, \text{m s}^{-1}$. What is its mass?

17 Use the conservation of momentum equation $m_1\mathbf{u}_1 + m_2\mathbf{u}_2 = m_1\mathbf{v}_1 + m_2\mathbf{v}_2$ to answer the following questions.

(a) Find $\mathbf{v}_2$ when $m_1 = 3$, $m_2 = 3$, $\mathbf{u}_1 = \begin{bmatrix} 3 \\ -1 \end{bmatrix}$, $\mathbf{u}_2 = \begin{bmatrix} 1 \\ 2 \end{bmatrix}$ and $\mathbf{v}_1 = \begin{bmatrix} 3 \\ 1 \end{bmatrix}$.

(b) Find $\mathbf{v}_2$ when $m_1 = 2$, $m_2 = 3$, $\mathbf{u}_1 = \begin{bmatrix} 6 \\ -3 \end{bmatrix}$, $\mathbf{u}_2 = \begin{bmatrix} 0 \\ 0 \end{bmatrix}$ and $\mathbf{v}_1 = \begin{bmatrix} 1\frac{1}{2} \\ -3 \end{bmatrix}$.

(c) Find m_2 when $m_1 = 2$, $\mathbf{u}_1 = \begin{bmatrix} 1 \\ 2 \end{bmatrix}$, $\mathbf{u}_2 = \begin{bmatrix} 3 \\ 0 \end{bmatrix}$, $\mathbf{v}_1 = \begin{bmatrix} 3 \\ 0 \end{bmatrix}$ and $\mathbf{v}_2 = \begin{bmatrix} 2 \\ 1 \end{bmatrix}$.

18 An α-particle enters a bubble-chamber filled with liquid helium. A photograph of its track shows that, after collision with a stationary helium atom, it is deflected through $20°$ and measurements show that its speed is reduced from $2.5 \times 10^7\,\mathrm{m\,s^{-1}}$ to $2.35 \times 10^7\,\mathrm{m\,s^{-1}}$. The helium atom moves off at a right angle to the final direction of the α-particle, at $8.55 \times 10^6\,\mathrm{m\,s^{-1}}$. Show that the two particles appear to be equal in mass.

19 Two billiard balls, A and B, both of mass 0.1 kg, collide. A is moving at $2.5\,\mathrm{m\,s^{-1}}$ and B at $2\,\mathrm{m\,s^{-1}}$ at $120°$ to the direction of A's velocity. A is deflected through $80°$ by the collision and B is then moving perpendicular to it. Draw a momentum vector diagram and measure the momenta of A and B after the collision. Deduce the final velocities.

20 A dart of mass 0.12 kg travelling at $20\,\mathrm{m\,s^{-1}}$ hits a dartboard and comes to rest in 0.1 second. What is the force, assumed constant, exerted by the dartboard on the dart?

21 A bullet of mass 0.04 kg travelling horizontally at $100\,\mathrm{m\,s^{-1}}$ hits a stationary block of wood (mass 8 kg) and passes through it, emerging still travelling horizontally but now with a speed of $40\,\mathrm{m\,s^{-1}}$. If the block of wood is free to move, find its speed after the bullet has emerged.

22 A skater of mass 60 kg is gliding across the ice. The resistance is 12 N and her speed is $5\,\mathrm{m\,s^{-1}}$. Calculate the time taken for her to come to rest and the distance travelled in doing so.

23 A stone is dropped at sea and is sinking in deep water. When it is travelling at $0.2\,\mathrm{m\,s^{-1}}$ the resistance of the water is 40 N. The buoyancy of the stone does not change and is 20 N. The weight of the stone is 60 N. What is the speed of the stone when it has fallen through the sea to a depth of 1 km?

24 A ball is thrown vertically upwards with a speed of $12\,\mathrm{m\,s^{-1}}$ from a point which is 2 m above the ground. Taking $g = 9.8\,\mathrm{m\,s^{-2}}$, find the speed with which the ball hits the ground and the total distance travelled by the ball.

2 Force and motion

.1 Projectiles

2.1.1 Weight

In chapter 1, *Newton's laws of motion*, you met the idea of a force. A force is simply a measure of the strength of a push or pull. For example, you already know that an apple of mass 0.1 kg is pulled to the Earth by a force of approximately 1 newton.

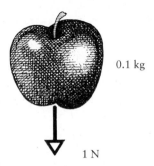

0.1 kg

1 N

This chapter examines further the connection between force and motion.

One of the remarkable features of Newton's mathematical model of mechanical motion is that you only need a knowledge of a very few different types of force to be able to model so much of the physical world. This section will reconsider the pulling force called **weight**.

Throughout history, astronomers have studied the motion of the planets. The Greeks assumed that the universe was geocentric, i.e. they assumed that the Earth was at the centre. In Alexandria, Claudius Ptolemy used this geocentric model to predict the motions of the planets, often with great accuracy. In fact the geocentric model remained dominant until 1543, when Copernicus claimed that the Sun, and not the Earth, was the centre about which the planets moved.

Later, in 1609, Johannes Kepler challenged the circular motion assumption. From observational data, Kepler realised that the paths of the planets were not perfect circles. He asserted that they move in elliptical orbits about the Sun.

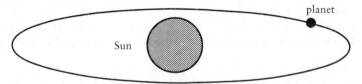

planet

Sun

It became clear that the basic assumptions of the geocentric model were false. It was replaced by a heliocentric model in which the Sun is the centre of our solar system about which the planets move in elliptical orbits.

Isaac Newton was born in 1642 and went to Cambridge to study natural science. An important problem at that time was to explain the force that kept the planets rotating about the Sun, and the Moon rotating about the Earth.

When you swing a conker round on the end of a string, the pull of the string keeps the conker rotating about your hand. Similarly, there has to be a force acting on the Moon causing it to rotate about the Earth.

Newton realised that the force which keeps the Moon spinning round the Earth is the same as that which causes objects to fall to the ground. He called it the **force due to gravity**, and in 1667 he proposed a law of gravitation.

Newton's law of gravitation

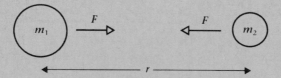

If two particles of mass m_1 kg and m_2 kg are at a distance r metres apart, they will attract each other with a force of magnitude

$$F = \frac{Gm_1m_2}{r^2} \text{ newtons}$$

where G is a universal constant, called the constant of gravitation.

The value of the universal constant can be determined by a method introduced by Henry Cavendish in 1798. He set up an experiment where two small lead spheres each of mass 0.75 kg were hung from the ends of a 2 metre wooden rod. The centre of the rod was suspended by a long fine wire. When two heavy lead spheres, each of mass 250 kg, were placed near the two small spheres the attraction between the large and small spheres caused the rod to turn.
By measuring the twist in the wire he calculated the force of attraction and hence the constant G. He placed the experiment in a draught-free room and viewed the end of the rod from the garden, using a telescope.

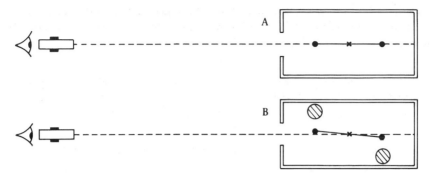

The work of Cavendish showed that $G = 0.000\,000\,000\,066\,\mathrm{N\,m^2\,kg^{-2}}$, within 1% of its modern value of $6.673 \times 10^{-11}\,\mathrm{N\,m^2\,kg^{-2}}$. This provided a direct verification of Newton's law of gravitation which had previously only been tested using astronomical data.

The consequences of Newton's law are enormous. It says that *any* two bodies will attract each other, whether they are two planetary bodies like the Moon and the Earth, or two bodies on the Earth like the book and ball shown below.

The gravitational force on an object due to the Earth is called its weight.

The force of attraction between an object on the Earth's surface and the Earth itself is given by the equation

$$F = G\frac{mE}{r^2}$$

where m is the mass of the object, E is the mass of the Earth and r is the radius of the Earth.

The radius r had been known to the ancient Greeks; it is approximately 6.4×10^6 metres. Furthermore, $\dfrac{F}{m}$ is easy to measure simply from observations of a falling object. The mass of the Earth, however, could not be calculated until Cavendish had obtained his results.

2 .1A

1 What is meant by '$\dfrac{F}{m}$ is easy to measure'? What is an approximate value for $\dfrac{F}{m}$?

2 Use Cavendish's value for G to determine the mass of the Earth.

G, the universal gravitational constant in Newton's law of gravitation, has the value

$$G = 6.673 \times 10^{-11} \, \mathrm{N\,m^2\,kg^{-2}}$$

The gravitational force per unit mass due to the Earth is g newtons per kilogram. Its effective value varies from place to place on the Earth's surface, from $9.8321 \, \mathrm{N\,kg^{-1}}$ at the poles to $9.7799 \, \mathrm{N\,kg^{-1}}$ at the equator. This is often approximated to 9.8 or $10 \, \mathrm{N\,kg^{-1}}$.

When you model the gravitational attraction of the Earth by a single 'downwards' force of mg newtons, you are making many assumptions.

 .1B

In the picture above, the Earth's gravitational attraction on the skier has been modelled by a single force, a weight **W**.

Many assumptions have been made in formulating such a simple model. List as many of these assumptions as possible, together with your own comments as to how reasonable they seem. Can you think of some situations where these assumptions would not be appropriate?

Example 1

Calculate the force of attraction between the Moon and an astronaut of mass 80 kg standing on its surface, using the following data.

Mass of Moon $= 7.34 \times 10^{22} \, \mathrm{kg}$
Approximate radius of Moon $= 1738 \, \mathrm{km}$

How does this compare with the force of attraction due to the Earth that she would experience while standing on the Earth's surface?

Solution

By Newton's law of gravitation, force $= \dfrac{80 \times 7.34 \times 10^{22} \times 6.67 \times 10^{-11}}{1\,738\,000 \times 1\,738\,000}$

$= 129.7\,\text{N}$

So the force of attraction is approximately 130 newtons.

The force of attraction she would experience on the Earth's surface is about 80g newtons. This is roughly 800 newtons; six times greater than the force on the Moon.

2.1 Exercise 1

Use $G = 6.67 \times 10^{-11}\,\text{N}\,\text{m}^2\,\text{kg}^{-2}$ and $g = 9.8\,\text{N}\,\text{kg}^{-1}$.

1 Calculate the force of attraction between a shot of mass 1 kg and a telephone directory of mass 1.5 kg if they are 1 m apart on the floor. Why do they not pull together?

2 (a) A 4 kg mass is allowed to fall from rest. What is its change in momentum after 3 seconds?

(b) During the same time interval, the Earth experiences an equal but opposite change in momentum. Assuming that the Earth has a mass of 5.98×10^{24} kg, what is the effect on the Earth's velocity?

3 A 5 kg mass is allowed to fall from rest and after t seconds the velocity is $49\,\text{m}\,\text{s}^{-1}$.

Calculate:

(a) the change in momentum;

(b) the length of time it has been falling;

(c) the distance through which it has fallen.

4 An unknown mass is allowed to fall from rest. In 4 seconds the change of momentum is $78.4\,\text{kg}\,\text{m}\,\text{s}^{-1}$. Find the mass and its velocity after the 4 seconds.

5

Assume that the Earth is a perfect sphere of mass 5.974×10^{24} kg and radius 6.378×10^6 m and that the gravitational constant is 6.673×10^{-11}. Then the weight of a stone of mass 1 kg is calculated as 9.80 newtons at sea level.

(a) Calculate its weight:

    (i) at the top of the Eiffel Tower (322 m above sea level);

    (ii) at the top of Mount Everest (8.848 km above sea level);

    (iii) at the edge of the stratosphere (928 km above sea level).

(b) Calculate its weight in a space capsule orbiting the Earth in a circular orbit whose radius is twice the radius of the Earth.

(c) Sketch a graph of weight against distance above sea level for a 1 kg mass, using the values given above.

6   A mass of 3 kg is projected vertically upwards with a speed of $49 \, \text{m s}^{-1}$. At two instants in time, the speed of the mass is measured as $9.8 \, \text{m s}^{-1}$. How long after the mass was thrown upwards were the measurements made?

7E   The forces acting on a descending parachutist of mass 70 kg are assumed to be his weight and a constant retarding force. His velocity is $24.5 \, \text{m s}^{-1}$ four seconds after starting from rest. Find the magnitude of the retarding force.

2.1.2 Motion under gravity

In chapter 1 you looked at the motion of bodies which are free to fall under the influence of gravity. How does gravity affect the motion of bodies which are launched into the air?

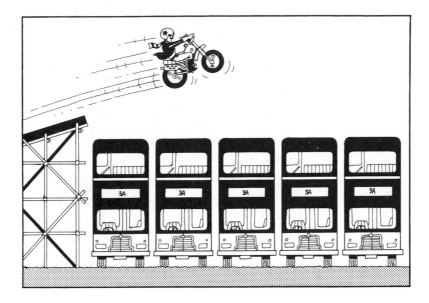

Imagine that you are asked to design a stunt like the one illustrated above. How fast should the bike go to clear 20 buses?

What can you say about its velocity on landing?

What other mathematical questions might you ask which would help you plan the stunt successfully?

In the next tasksheet you can attempt to model the motion.

▶ 2.1 Tasksheet 1 – Jumping buses (page 350)

2.1.3 Velocity

The position of the bike every fifth of a second after taking off has been marked on the graph given below.

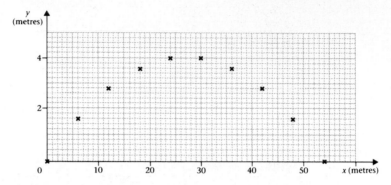

The position vectors at intervals of 0.2 second are given in the table below. (All distances are in metres.)

t	0.0	0.2	0.4	0.6	0.8	1.0	1.2	1.4	1.6	1.8
$\begin{bmatrix} x \\ y \end{bmatrix}$	$\begin{bmatrix} 0 \\ 0 \end{bmatrix}$	$\begin{bmatrix} 6 \\ 1.6 \end{bmatrix}$	$\begin{bmatrix} 12 \\ 2.8 \end{bmatrix}$	$\begin{bmatrix} 18 \\ 3.6 \end{bmatrix}$	$\begin{bmatrix} 24 \\ 4.0 \end{bmatrix}$	$\begin{bmatrix} 30 \\ 4.0 \end{bmatrix}$	$\begin{bmatrix} 36 \\ 3.6 \end{bmatrix}$	$\begin{bmatrix} 42 \\ 2.8 \end{bmatrix}$	$\begin{bmatrix} 48 \\ 1.6 \end{bmatrix}$	$\begin{bmatrix} 54 \\ 0 \end{bmatrix}$

To enable you to investigate the flight mathematically it is useful to first obtain a general expression for the position vector during the flight, t seconds after take-off.

 .1c

Complete the formula for the position at time t.

$$\begin{bmatrix} x \\ y \end{bmatrix} = \begin{bmatrix} ? \\ 9t - 5t^2 \end{bmatrix}$$

Check that your formula fits the data given above.

If a particle is travelling in a straight line with constant velocity $\mathbf{v}$, then:

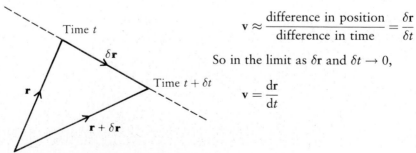

$$\mathbf{v} \approx \frac{\text{difference in position}}{\text{difference in time}} = \frac{\delta \mathbf{r}}{\delta t}$$

So in the limit as $\delta \mathbf{r}$ and $\delta t \to 0$,

$$\mathbf{v} = \frac{d\mathbf{r}}{dt}$$

Of course, the bike is *not* travelling in a straight line. However, if you magnify a small section of its flight you will find that it is locally straight.

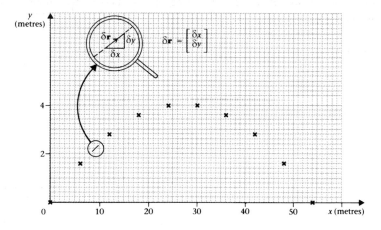

2 .1D

1 Explain why $\mathbf{v} = \begin{bmatrix} \dfrac{\mathrm{d}x}{\mathrm{d}t} \\ \dfrac{\mathrm{d}y}{\mathrm{d}t} \end{bmatrix}$.

2 Hence find $\mathbf{v}$ for $\mathbf{r} = \begin{bmatrix} 30t \\ 9t - 5t^2 \end{bmatrix}$.

3 Calculate $\mathbf{v}$ when $t = 0.7$, 0.9 and 1.1 seconds.

4 What is the speed of the bike when it lands?

5 Interpret and validate your solutions.

The position vector $\mathbf{r}$ and velocity vector $\mathbf{v}$ of a projectile (or any other particle) are connected by the equation

$$\mathbf{v} = \frac{\mathrm{d}\mathbf{r}}{\mathrm{d}t}$$

$\dfrac{\mathrm{d}\mathbf{r}}{\mathrm{d}t}$ can be found by differentiating each component of $\mathbf{r}$.

$$\frac{\mathrm{d}\mathbf{r}}{\mathrm{d}t} = \begin{bmatrix} \dfrac{\mathrm{d}x}{\mathrm{d}t} \\ \dfrac{\mathrm{d}y}{\mathrm{d}t} \end{bmatrix}$$

Example 2

The position vector of a golf ball, t seconds after being hit, is given by

$$\begin{bmatrix} x \\ y \end{bmatrix} = \begin{bmatrix} 10t \\ 30t - 5t^2 \end{bmatrix} \qquad \text{(All distances are in metres.)}$$

Find the golf ball's speed when it first strikes the ground (assumed to be horizontal).

Solution

It strikes the ground when $30t - 5t^2 = 0$

$$5t(6 - t) = 0$$
$$\Rightarrow \qquad t = 0 \text{ or } 6$$

Its velocity in m s^{-1} is given by $\mathbf{v} = \begin{bmatrix} 10 \\ 30 - 10t \end{bmatrix}$.

After 6 seconds, $\mathbf{v} = \begin{bmatrix} 10 \\ -30 \end{bmatrix}$ and its speed is $\sqrt{(10^2 + 30^2)} \approx 31.6 \, \text{m s}^{-1}$.

2.1 Exercise 2

1 For the golf ball in example 2, find:

(a) the time at which its velocity is horizontal;

(b) its maximum height;

(c) the horizontal distance it travels before it hits the ground.

2 Using the data for the motorbike given on page 90, what is the bike's speed:

(a) when it leaves the ramp;

(b) when it is at the top of its flight?

3 Cannon-ball Kate is being fired out of a cannon into a safety net in a stunt to raise money for charity. Her position vector in metres is given by

$$\mathbf{r} = \begin{bmatrix} 10t \\ 9t - 5t^2 + 2 \end{bmatrix}$$

If the landing net is 2 metres square and is placed at a height of 2 metres above the ground,

(a) should her landing net be at $\begin{bmatrix} 18 \\ 2 \end{bmatrix}$ or $\begin{bmatrix} 20 \\ 2 \end{bmatrix}$;

(b) what is her speed when she lands in the net?

4 A shot has position vector **r** metres at time t seconds given by

$$\mathbf{r} = \begin{bmatrix} 10t \\ 2 + 10t - 5t^2 \end{bmatrix}$$

Calculate:

(a) the magnitude and direction of the velocity of projection;

(b) the height above ground level at which it was released by the shot-putter;

(c) the distance of the throw;

(d) the velocity of the shot on striking the ground;

(e) when the velocity of the shot is horizontal;

(f) the maximum height it attains above the ground.

5 The centre of gravity of a long-jumper, at time t seconds, has position vector

$$\mathbf{r} = \begin{bmatrix} 0.5 + 10t \\ 0.75 + 2.8t - 5t^2 \end{bmatrix} \text{ metres}$$

where the origin is taken to be the take-off board.

(a) What is the initial or take-off velocity of the long-jumper?

(b) Where is her centre of gravity on take-off?

(c) Assume that on landing the centre of gravity is at the same height as on take-off. For how long is the jumper in the air and how long is the jump?

2.1.4 Acceleration under a constant force

The velocity of a projectile changes throughout the motion. In chapter 1 you obtained the following result for the flight of a golf ball:

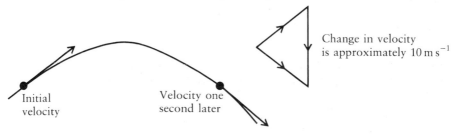

Change in velocity is approximately $10\,\mathrm{m\,s^{-1}}$

Initial velocity

Velocity one second later

The change in velocity each second is always constant at $10\,\mathrm{m\,s^{-1}}$ downwards.

so $\dfrac{d\mathbf{v}}{dt} = \begin{bmatrix} 0 \\ -10 \end{bmatrix}$

Initial velocity **v**

Change in velocity $\delta\mathbf{v}$

Final velocity $\mathbf{v} + \delta\mathbf{v}$

The vector $\dfrac{d\mathbf{v}}{dt}$ is called the **acceleration** of the projectile.

For the motion of the motorbike described earlier, you found the position vector **r**, where

$$\mathbf{r} = \begin{bmatrix} 30t \\ 9t - 5t^2 \end{bmatrix}$$

Hence

$$\mathbf{v} = \frac{d\mathbf{r}}{dt} = \begin{bmatrix} 30 \\ 9 - 10t \end{bmatrix}$$

and

$$\mathbf{a} = \frac{d\mathbf{v}}{dt} = \frac{d^2\mathbf{r}}{dt^2} = \begin{bmatrix} 0 \\ -10 \end{bmatrix}$$

You should note that the acceleration is a vector in the same direction (vertically downwards) as the only force acting on the projectile − its weight. This can be obtained directly from Newton's second law:

$$\text{force} \times \text{time} = \text{change in momentum}$$

 .1E

1 From the equation

$$\text{force} \times \text{time} = \text{change in momentum}$$

explain how to obtain the alternative form of Newton's second law,

$$\text{force} = \text{mass} \times \text{acceleration}$$

2 Hence explain the connection between the acceleration of a projectile and **g**, the gravitational force (or weight) per unit mass.

For any motion,

$$\text{force} = \text{mass} \times \text{acceleration}$$

where acceleration is the rate of change of velocity.

For a projectile, the acceleration due to gravity is approximately
$\begin{bmatrix} 0 \\ -10 \end{bmatrix} \text{m s}^{-2}$.

It is important to note that $\mathbf{F} = m\mathbf{a}$ is a vector equation, so acceleration is a vector quantity and the acceleration vector and the force vector must act in the same direction. Any object will therefore accelerate in the direction of the resultant force acting upon it. This is true even if the force is not constant.

Example 3

A 3 kg stone slides across the surface of a frozen lake in such a way that its position vector **r** metres at time t seconds is given by

$$\mathbf{r} = \begin{bmatrix} t^2 - 20t + 80 \\ -2t^2 + 40t \end{bmatrix} \qquad 0 \le t \le 10$$

Find the force acting on the stone. Show that this force is constant and acts in the opposite direction to the velocity of the stone.

Solution

By differentiating,

$$\mathbf{v} = \begin{bmatrix} 2t - 20 \\ -4t + 40 \end{bmatrix} \qquad \mathbf{a} = \begin{bmatrix} 2 \\ -4 \end{bmatrix}$$

From Newton's second law, $\mathbf{F} = m\mathbf{a} = 3\begin{bmatrix} 2 \\ -4 \end{bmatrix} = 6\begin{bmatrix} 1 \\ -2 \end{bmatrix}$; therefore the force is $\begin{bmatrix} 6 \\ -12 \end{bmatrix} = 6\begin{bmatrix} 1 \\ -2 \end{bmatrix}$ newtons.

The force is constant and parallel to the vector $\begin{bmatrix} 1 \\ -2 \end{bmatrix}$.

For $0 \le t \le 10$, $\mathbf{v} = (20 - 2t)\begin{bmatrix} -1 \\ 2 \end{bmatrix}$ is in the direction of the vector $\begin{bmatrix} -1 \\ 2 \end{bmatrix}$.

Hence **F** acts in the opposite direction to the motion of the stone and is presumably due to friction or air resistance.

2.1 Exercise 3

1 A ball is thrown so that it has position vector $\mathbf{r} = \begin{bmatrix} 5t \\ 6t - 5t^2 + 1 \end{bmatrix}$ metres.
Calculate the velocity and acceleration of the ball.

2 An ice hockey puck is hit so that it has position vector $\mathbf{r} = \begin{bmatrix} 9t - t^2 \\ 9t - t^2 + 1 \end{bmatrix}$ metres for $0 \le t \le 4.5$ seconds.

If the puck has mass 100 grams, find the force acting on the puck.

3 A skater's position on the ice is given by the position vector
$$\mathbf{r} = \begin{bmatrix} 5t - t^2 \\ 3 + 5t - t^2 \end{bmatrix} \text{ metres for } 0 \le t \le 2.5 \text{ seconds.}$$

Calculate the velocity and acceleration of the skater.

If the skater weighs 70 kg, calculate the force acting on him.

4 A child pulls a toy car along by means of a string, exerting a constant force on the string. If the position vector of the car, **r** metres at time t seconds, is given by $\mathbf{r} = \begin{bmatrix} 3t^2 \\ 4t^2 \end{bmatrix}$ and its mass is 500 grams, calculate the magnitude and direction of the pull exerted by the child.

5 In each of the following cases a particle is moving in such a way that its position vector is **r** metres at time t seconds. In each case:

- sketch the course on which the particle moves between $t = 0$ and $t = 4$;
- find its acceleration;
- find its acceleration at $t = 2$ and sketch its vector representation on your curve.

(a) $\mathbf{r} = \begin{bmatrix} t \\ t^2 \end{bmatrix}$ (b) $\mathbf{r} = \begin{bmatrix} 4t \\ 4t^{-1} \end{bmatrix}$

(c) $\mathbf{r} = \begin{bmatrix} \cos t \\ \sin t \end{bmatrix}$ (d) $\mathbf{r} = \begin{bmatrix} t \\ 3t \end{bmatrix}$

2.1.5 Projectile motion

The motion of bodies which are thrown, dropped or launched into the air under the influence of gravity is called **projectile motion**. You can study this motion using vector equations for position, velocity or acceleration.

For any projectile motion, the only force acting is taken to be weight, $\mathbf{W} = m\mathbf{g}$, acting downwards.

Taking axes horizontally and vertically upwards, $\mathbf{W} = \begin{bmatrix} 0 \\ -mg \end{bmatrix}$

Hence Newton's second law, $\mathbf{F} = m\mathbf{a}$, gives $\mathbf{a} = \begin{bmatrix} 0 \\ -g \end{bmatrix}$

In order to find out more about the velocity and position vector of a projectile, you will need to set up a model and analyse it. You can do this analysis in the problem which follows.

Problem

To find the highest point, the landing point and the flight time for an elastic band fired at a speed of $4.4\,\mathrm{m\,s}^{-1}$ at an angle of $30°$.

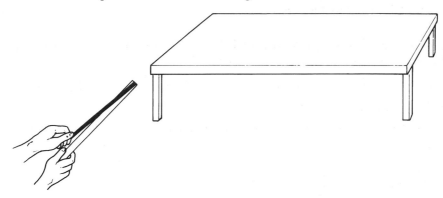

Set up a model

Assume the elastic band is a particle, projected from point A with a speed of $4.4\,\mathrm{m\,s}^{-1}$ at $30°$ to the horizontal table AB. The elastic band then flies for t seconds and lands R metres along the table at B.

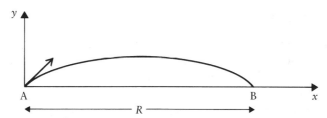

Choose x- and y-axes as shown, so that A has coordinates $(0,0)$ and B has coordinates $(R,0)$. Assume that the elastic band of mass m has constant weight mg, and take $g = 10\,\mathrm{m\,s}^{-2}$. What other assumptions are made in this model?

Analyse the problem

The problem is to calculate R and t.

The acceleration is $\mathbf{a} = \begin{bmatrix} 0 \\ -g \end{bmatrix} = \begin{bmatrix} 0 \\ -10 \end{bmatrix}\,\mathrm{m\,s}^{-2}$

You need to find the velocity $\mathbf{v}$ after any time t. Remember that if you can differentiate $\mathbf{v}$ to obtain $\mathbf{a}$, you can integrate $\mathbf{a}$ to obtain $\mathbf{v}$.

$$\frac{d\mathbf{v}}{dt} = \begin{bmatrix} 0 \\ -10 \end{bmatrix}$$

Integrating, $\mathbf{v} = \begin{bmatrix} C_1 \\ -10t + C_2 \end{bmatrix}$ where C_1 and C_2 are constants.

The initial velocity is $4.4\,\text{m s}^{-1}$ at an angle of $30°$ and so

$$\mathbf{v} = \begin{bmatrix} 4.4\cos 30° \\ 4.4\sin 30° \end{bmatrix} = \begin{bmatrix} 3.81 \\ 2.2 \end{bmatrix} \quad \text{when } t = 0$$

Therefore $\begin{bmatrix} C_1 \\ C_2 \end{bmatrix} = \begin{bmatrix} 3.81 \\ 2.2 \end{bmatrix}$ and $\mathbf{v} = \begin{bmatrix} 3.81 \\ 2.2 - 10t \end{bmatrix}$

The horizontal component of velocity is a constant $3.81\,\text{m s}^{-1}$, but the vertical component is decreasing at $10\,\text{m s}^{-2}$.

The band is at its highest point when $\mathbf{v} = \begin{bmatrix} 3.81 \\ 0 \end{bmatrix}\,\text{m s}^{-1}$, i.e. when

$0 = 2.2 - 10t \Rightarrow t = 0.22$ seconds.

 .1F

1 Integrate $\mathbf{v}$ to find the position vector $\mathbf{r}$ of the elastic band at time t. Check that you get the answers shown on the graph below.

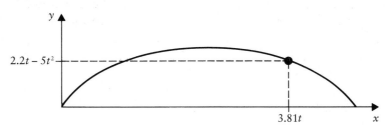

At the band's highest point $t = 0.22$ seconds, $y = 2.2t - 5t^2$ and so $y = 0.24$ metres.

Now consider the time, t, taken to land at B, where the y-coordinate is zero.

$$2.2t - 5t^2 = 0$$

2 (a) Solve the equation $2.2t - 5t^2 = 0$ to find t.

  (b) Use this value to find the range.

3 What are your conclusions?

4 You could validate your results experimentally. What difficulties and errors might arise?

$\mathbf{a} = \dfrac{d\mathbf{v}}{dt}$, so integrating acceleration gives velocity.

$\mathbf{v} = \dfrac{d\mathbf{r}}{dt}$, so integrating velocity gives displacement.

The initial conditions of motion give the constants of integration.

Example 4

A girl puts a shot with velocity $\begin{bmatrix} 4 \\ 3.5 \end{bmatrix}$ m s^{-1}. If she releases it 1.5 metres above the ground, show that it hits the ground after 1 second. Find its speed of impact.

Solution

Assume that the shot is a particle of mass m kg and that air resistance can be neglected. Let the point of release be O and the point where it hits the ground be A.

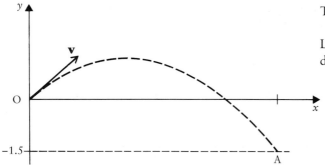

Take axes as shown.

Let $g = 10$ m s^{-2} downwards.

The force acting is $\begin{bmatrix} 0 \\ -mg \end{bmatrix}$ so the acceleration is $\dfrac{d\mathbf{v}}{dt} = \begin{bmatrix} 0 \\ -10 \end{bmatrix}$

By integration, $\mathbf{v} = \begin{bmatrix} 0 + c_1 \\ -10t + c_2 \end{bmatrix}$

When $t = 0$, $\mathbf{v} = \begin{bmatrix} 4 \\ 3.5 \end{bmatrix}$ $\Rightarrow$ $\mathbf{v} = \begin{bmatrix} 4 \\ 3.5 - 10t \end{bmatrix}$

Thus $\dfrac{d\mathbf{r}}{dt} = \begin{bmatrix} 4 \\ 3.5 - 10t \end{bmatrix}$ $\Rightarrow$ $\mathbf{r} = \begin{bmatrix} 4t + d_1 \\ 3.5t - 5t^2 + d_2 \end{bmatrix}$

When $t = 0$, $\mathbf{r} = \begin{bmatrix} 0 \\ 0 \end{bmatrix}$ $\Rightarrow$ $\mathbf{r} = \begin{bmatrix} 4t \\ 3.5t - 5t^2 \end{bmatrix}$

When $t = 1$, $\mathbf{r} = \begin{bmatrix} 4 \\ -1.5 \end{bmatrix}$

The shot hits the ground 4 metres away after 1 second.

When $t = 1$, $\mathbf{v} = \begin{bmatrix} 4 \\ -6.5 \end{bmatrix}$

The speed of impact is $\sqrt{(16 + 42.25)} = 7.6\,\mathrm{m\,s^{-1}}$.

2.1 Exercise 4

In this exercise, ignore the effect of air resistance and take g to be $10\,\mathrm{m\,s^{-2}}$.

1   Ann throws a ball to Julian with initial velocity $\begin{bmatrix} 7 \\ 5 \end{bmatrix}\,\mathrm{m\,s^{-1}}$ and Julian catches it at the same height. For how long is the ball in the air? How far apart are Ann and Julian?

2   A high-jumper takes off with initial velocity $\begin{bmatrix} 3 \\ 5 \end{bmatrix}\,\mathrm{m\,s^{-1}}$.

At take-off her centre of gravity is approximately 1 metre above the ground. Write down the velocity and position vector of her centre of gravity at time t seconds after take-off.

What is the maximum height of her centre of gravity?

3   A discus is projected at an angle of $40°$ with a speed of $21\,\mathrm{m\,s^{-1}}$ and from a height above the ground of 2 metres.

Calculate its velocity and position vector at time t. What is the length of the throw?

4E

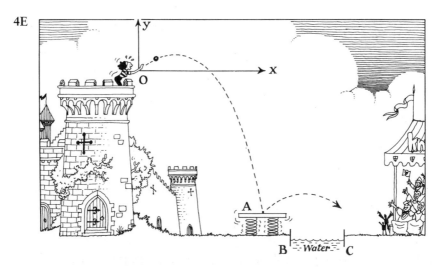

The picture shows a contestant in a TV game show standing on top of a tower. She hurls a cannon-ball of mass 8 kg from point O. Her objective is to make the cannon-ball bounce on a smooth horizontal platform at A, and then rebound across the water hazard BC. Taking axes through O as shown and with units of metres, A is the point $(8, -10)$ and C is $(11, -12)$.

(a) If the initial velocity is $\begin{bmatrix} 4 \\ 5 \end{bmatrix}$ m s^{-1} show that the cannon-ball will land at A when two seconds have elapsed, with velocity $\begin{bmatrix} 4 \\ -15 \end{bmatrix}$ m s^{-1}.

(b) Assuming that momentum is conserved in the collision between the cannon-ball and the sprung platform (which can be modelled as a heavy, smooth rigid block of mass 48 kg, and which acquires a velocity $\begin{bmatrix} 0 \\ -3 \end{bmatrix}$ m s^{-1} immediately after impact), show that the initial velocity of the cannon-ball as it bounces off the block is $\begin{bmatrix} 4 \\ 3 \end{bmatrix}$ m s^{-1}.

(c) Does the cannon-ball clear the water hazard?

5E   A missile leaves a plane at a height of 3000 m and moves so that t seconds later its displacement **r** in metres is given by

$$\mathbf{r} = \begin{bmatrix} 3t \\ 4t \\ -5t^2 \end{bmatrix}$$

with respect to axes in the directions south, east and vertically upwards respectively.

(a) Find its velocity after t seconds.

(b) Show that initially the missile is travelling horizontally, and calculate its bearing.

(c) Show that its speed after 2 seconds is $5\sqrt{17}$ m s^{-1}.

(d) Calculate the missile's distance from its starting point after 2 seconds.

(e) Find when it hits the ground.

(f) Calculate its acceleration and hence state, with a brief reason, whether it is powered or not.

2.1.6 The general case

For a more general case of projectile motion, you could take axes to be horizontal (x) and vertical (y) such that, at $t = 0$, the projectile has position vector $\begin{bmatrix} a \\ b \end{bmatrix}$ and initial velocity $\begin{bmatrix} u_x \\ u_y \end{bmatrix}$.

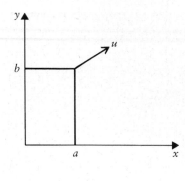

Assume that the only force acting is gravity.

So $\mathbf{a} = \dfrac{d\mathbf{v}}{dt} = \begin{bmatrix} 0 \\ -g \end{bmatrix}$ and, integrating this,

$\mathbf{v} = \begin{bmatrix} u_x \\ -gt + u_y \end{bmatrix}$ since $\mathbf{v} = \begin{bmatrix} u_x \\ u_y \end{bmatrix}$ when $t = 0$

Since $\mathbf{v} = \dfrac{d\mathbf{r}}{dt}$, direct integration gives

$\mathbf{r} = \begin{bmatrix} u_x t + a \\ -\frac{1}{2}gt^2 + u_y t + b \end{bmatrix}$

since $\mathbf{r} = \begin{bmatrix} a \\ b \end{bmatrix}$ when $t = 0$

Often, projectile motion assumes projection from the origin with velocity of magnitude u at an angle ϕ to the horizontal.

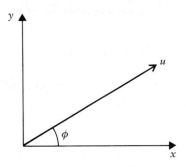

So $u_x = u \cos \phi$
$u_y = u \sin \phi$

and a and b are zero.

This gives $\mathbf{v} = \begin{bmatrix} u \cos \phi \\ -gt + u \sin \phi \end{bmatrix}$ and $\mathbf{r} = \begin{bmatrix} ut \cos \phi \\ -\frac{1}{2}gt^2 + ut \sin \phi \end{bmatrix}$

 .1G

1 (a) When $t = \dfrac{2u \sin \phi}{g}$, calculate $\mathbf{r}$.

(b) Interpret your result. How can it be validated?

2 (a) At the highest point on the path of a projectile, the vertical component of the velocity is zero. Use this fact to find an expression, in terms of u, g and ϕ, for the time taken to reach the highest point.

(b) Use this result to show that the height reached is $\dfrac{u^2 \sin^2 \phi}{2g}$.

(c) Interpret this result as u and ϕ vary. Validate it practically in a suitable experiment.

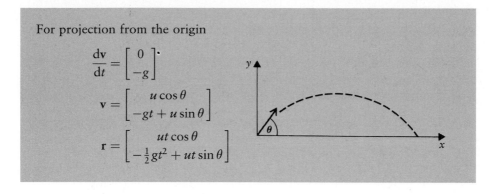

For projection from the origin

$$\frac{d\mathbf{v}}{dt} = \begin{bmatrix} 0 \\ -g \end{bmatrix};$$

$$\mathbf{v} = \begin{bmatrix} u\cos\theta \\ -gt + u\sin\theta \end{bmatrix}$$

$$\mathbf{r} = \begin{bmatrix} ut\cos\theta \\ -\frac{1}{2}gt^2 + ut\sin\theta \end{bmatrix}$$

2.1 Exercise 5

Take g as $10\,\mathrm{m\,s}^{-2}$ unless stated otherwise and ignore air resistance.

1 At a given instant, a group of objects is projected horizontally from the edge of a table. Each object has a different initial speed.

What can you say about the motion of each object as time increases?

2 A golf ball is hit so that it leaves the ground with initial velocity of magnitude $25\,\mathrm{m\,s}^{-1}$, at an angle α, where $\tan\alpha = \frac{4}{3}$, as shown in the diagram.

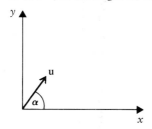

(a) How high does the ball go?

(b) How far does it travel before its first bounce if the ground is horizontal?

3 Two children throw stones into the sea. Jill throws her stone at an angle of $60°$ to the horizontal and speed $20\,\mathrm{m\,s}^{-1}$, while Jack throws his stone at a $40°$ angle and can only manage an initial speed of $15\,\mathrm{m\,s}^{-1}$. Both stones are thrown simultaneously and both are released at a height $1.4\,\mathrm{m}$ above sea level.

(a) How high does Jill throw her stone?

(b) Which stone lands in the water first?

(c) Whose stone lands further away?

4 A small relief plane is flying horizontally at $30\,\mathrm{m\,s}^{-1}$. Its height is $210\,\mathrm{m}$.
A package, released from the plane, just clears some trees which are $30\,\mathrm{m}$ high.

(a) At what horizontal distance from the trees is the package released?

(b) How far beyond the trees does the package land?

5 Ahmed throws a ball to Susan who is 80 m away and who catches it at the same height as it was thrown. The ball is in the air for 5 seconds. Taking the acceleration g as $9.8\,\mathrm{m\,s^{-2}}$, find the initial velocity of the ball.

6 At what angle should a projectile be launched if it is to achieve the maximum possible horizontal range?

Find out the greatest recorded distance a cricket ball has ever been thrown. Estimate the initial speed of the ball.

7 A rugby player takes a penalty kick. He places the ball at a point O on the ground, 12 metres away from the goal line and directly in front of the goal, and he kicks it at a right angle to the goal line at an angle /of $40°$ to the horizontal. The ball passes over the crossbar at point P, 4 metres above the ground. Estimate the initial speed of the ball.

After working through section 2.1, you should:

1 know that Newton's law of gravitation states that

$$F = \frac{Gm_1m_2}{r^2}$$ where G is a universal constant called the constant of gravitation;

2 know that the acceleration of a body is its rate of change of velocity

$$\mathbf{a} = \frac{d\mathbf{v}}{dt} = \frac{d^2\mathbf{r}}{dt^2}$$

(acceleration is a vector and has both magnitude and direction);

3 know that Newton's second law of motion can be stated as

$$\mathbf{F} = m\mathbf{a}$$

(the force and acceleration must act in the same direction);

4 know that in projectile motion, the only force is assumed to be weight, acting vertically downwards;

5 know how to model projectile motion in a variety of problems and situations.

2 Force and motion

2 .2 Forces

2.2.1 Contact forces

In chapter 1 you saw that:

- Unless acted upon by an external force, a particle travels with constant velocity.

- The resultant force on an object is equal to its rate of change of momentum (its change in momentum each second).

- When two bodies interact, they exert equal but opposite forces upon each other.

One type of pushing force with which you will be very familiar is that of a contact force between surfaces.

If a box rests on a table then the box pushes against the table and the table pushes against the box. **R** is the total contact force on the box from the table. In this case, Newton's third law of motion says that there is an equal but opposite force acting on the table.

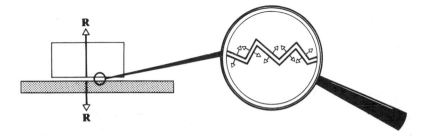

You can model the situation with a large number of 'contact forces'. Note that the sum of all the contact forces on the box gives the total contact force. This is conventionally modelled as a single force.

The most useful force diagram to draw is usually one showing *all* the forces acting on one object. For a box on a table you might draw:

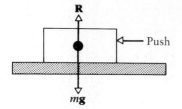

There is no acceleration vertically, and so by Newton's first law

$$\mathbf{R} = -m\mathbf{g}$$

in vector form or, considering only magnitudes,

$$R = mg$$

Even when the box is on a slope, if it does not move then the contact force is vertically upwards to maintain the equilibrium and again $\mathbf{R} = -m\mathbf{g}$. Note that $\mathbf{R}$ is not perpendicular to the surface.

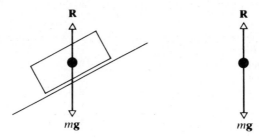

Objects are modelled as particles. This is done by drawing a dot in the object and showing *all* the forces acting on the dot, as shown above.

It is sometimes convenient to consider the contact force as a combination of two forces, a **normal contact force** perpendicular to the surface and a force called **friction** which acts parallel to the surfaces in such a direction as to oppose any tendency to slide.

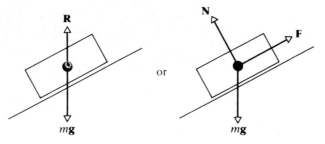

or

$\mathbf{N}$ and $\mathbf{F}$ are called components of the contact force $\mathbf{R}$. This idea is studied further in a later section. It is important to note that you can use either $\mathbf{R}$ or its components but *not both* on the same diagram.

If a box is pushed across a rough horizontal surface, friction opposes the motion and the force diagram is:

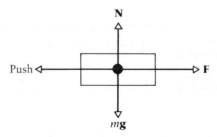

If the box does not move then there is no change in momentum. The resultant force on the box is therefore zero. The normal contact force is balanced by the weight and the push is balanced by the friction force.

The normal contact force and the frictional force may be represented by a single contact force, **R**. The force diagram for this is:

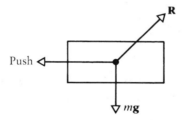

In the illustration, a loaded sledge is being pulled up a slight incline.

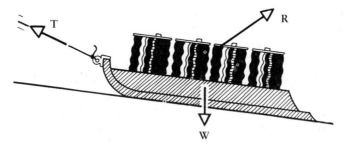

The forces acting on the sledge can be modelled by the force diagram shown.

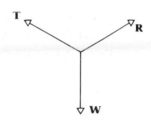

There are three forces – the pull of the rope on the sledge, the weight of the sledge and the contact force between the slope and the sledge. This last force (**R**) is split into a normal contact force **N** and a frictional force **F** in the figure below.

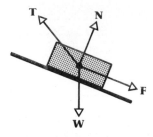

The contact force, **R**, of one object on another may be replaced by a normal contact force, **N**, perpendicular to the surface, and a friction force, **F**, parallel to the surface which acts to oppose motion. This friction force may, of course, be zero.

2.2 Exercise 1

1 The six diagrams provide models of the forces acting on various objects. For each, give a possible description of the forces.

(a)

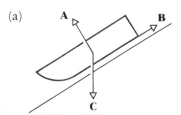

A sledge sliding
down a slope

(b)

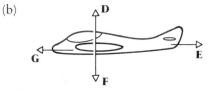

An aeroplane in flight

(c)

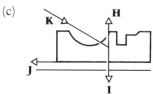

A toy being pushed across
a floor by a child leaning over it

(d)

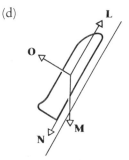

An injured climber being
pulled up an ice face

(e)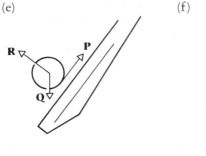

(f)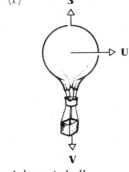

A ball being
struck with a bat

A hot-air balloon ascending and
being blown by a side wind

2 Draw a force diagram for the injured climber of question 1(d) if she is being winched *down* the cliff face.

3 Draw a force diagram for a toy being pulled across the floor by a string:

(a) if the contact force between the floor and the toy is shown as a single force;

(b) if the contact force is divided into its two components.

4 For each of the following situations draw a diagram to model the forces you think are appropriate. Consider the object in bold type.

(a) a **girl** sliding on a toboggan

(b) the **toboggan** in part (a)

(c) a **car** being given a push start by a man

(d) the **man** in part (c)

(e) a **ship** at anchor

(f) a **ski-jumper** when she is in the air

(g) a **parachutist** in mid-air falling straight down

2.2.2 Adding forces

 .2A

The picture shows two girls using ropes to hold a heavy object just above the ground.

Describe what happens to the pull from the ropes if the girls are standing:

(a) close together,

(b) one metre apart,

(c) four metres apart.

Try this practically using a heavy school-bag and some string. Can you lift the bag high enough so that the strings are horizontal? Explain your answer.

You know that forces are vectors. This implies that they can be added in just the same way as displacement and velocity.

You saw in section 1.6 that the combined effect of a number of forces is known as the *resultant* force. The resultant of two forces can be found by adding the forces as vectors. This can be done by drawing either a triangle of forces or a parallelogram of forces.

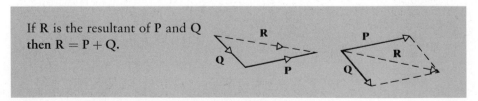

If **R** is the resultant of **P** and **Q** then **R** = **P** + **Q**.

Example 1

Find the resultant of the two forces 5 newtons and 7 newtons which contain an angle of 70°.

Solution

Draw a parallelogram ABCD with AD = 5 units and AB = 7 units and angle BAD = 70°.

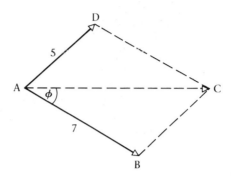

Measure AC and angle ϕ.

AC = 9.9 units and angle $\phi = 28°$.

Hence the resultant is a force of 9.9 newtons at an angle of 28° to the 7 newton force.

[The cosine and sine rules could be used instead of drawing.]

For three forces **X**, **Y**, **Z** with resultant force **R**,

$$\mathbf{R} = \mathbf{X} + \mathbf{Y} + \mathbf{Z} = (\mathbf{X} + \mathbf{Y}) + \mathbf{Z} = \mathbf{X} + (\mathbf{Y} + \mathbf{Z}) = (\mathbf{X} + \mathbf{Z}) + \mathbf{Y}$$

This can be found by drawing the resultant of any pair of the vectors, then adding the resultant to the third vector. Alternatively the vectors can be drawn nose to tail to form a polygon. The resultant is the vector that joins the start of the vector chain to the finish.

For example:

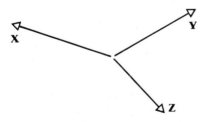
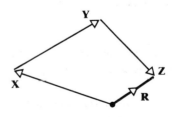

If a body is either at rest or moving with constant velocity, its acceleration is zero. The vector sum of the forces acting on the body is zero and hence the forces form a closed polygon.

Example 2

The three forces shown acting on a particle are in equilibrium. Find the magnitude and direction of **P**.

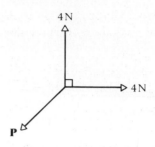

Solution

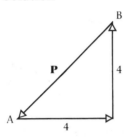

The forces are in equilibrium so their resultant is zero. Their vectors form a closed polygon.

P is therefore represented in magnitude and direction by $\overrightarrow{BA}$.

So **P** has magnitude $4\sqrt{2}$ newtons and acts in a direction of 135° with each 4 N force.

The experiments in tasksheet 1 will enable you to investigate these ideas practically. Your class could split into groups, with each group reporting back to the whole class and giving a clear description of their experiment and the conclusions they have reached.

▶ 2.2 **Tasksheet 1 – Investigating forces (page 352)**

2.2 **Exercise 2**

1 Find the resultants of the pairs of forces shown in the diagrams.

(a)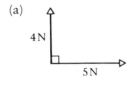

(b)

2 Gillian and Paul give Zia's car a push start. Gillian pushes straight ahead with a force of 420 N. Paul pushes with a force of 500 N at an angle of 25° to the line of the car. Use a scale drawing to find both the magnitude and the direction of the resultant of these two pushes.

3 Two tugs are towing a large ship into harbour, pulling on the bows of the ship with horizontal cables. The far tug is pulling with a force of 52 000 N at an angle of 23° to the forward motion of the ship and the near tug pulls with a

force of 68 000 N at an angle of 18° to the motion. Use a scale drawing to find the resultant pull on the ship.

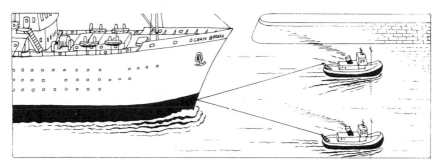

4 The frictional force between an object and the ground is 80 N. If the normal contact force is 200 N then calculate the magnitude and direction of the total contact force.

5 Two forces of magnitude 3 N and 4 N have a resultant of magnitude 6 N. Find, by scale drawing, the angle between the two forces.

6 The following groups of forces are in equilibrium. Find the magnitude and direction of the forces labelled by letters.

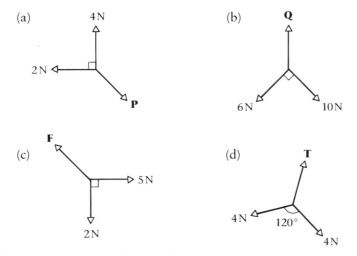

7 A shopping bag of mass 15 kg is carried by two people. If they walk so that their arms make an angle of 50° with the horizontal, what force must each of them exert on the bag? Estimate the likely minimum angle at which they can hold the bag.

2.2.3 Resolving forces

You know that total contact force **R** may be considered as the sum of a frictional force **F** and a normal contact force **N**.

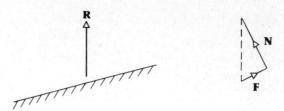

Splitting a force into components at right angles to each other is easy to do using simple trigonometry.

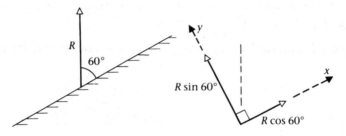

The use of components can be helpful in solving problems because the components in a particular direction can be added very easily.

Example 3

Calculate the answer to question 3 of exercise 2.2 by splitting the forces in this way.

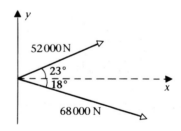

Solution

$$\mathbf{R} = \begin{bmatrix} 52\,000\cos 23° \\ 52\,000\sin 23° \end{bmatrix} + \begin{bmatrix} 68\,000\cos 18° \\ -68\,000\sin 18° \end{bmatrix} = \begin{bmatrix} 112\,538 \\ -695 \end{bmatrix}$$

$$R^2 = 112\,538^2 + 695^2 \qquad R = 112\,540$$

$$\tan \phi = \frac{-695}{112\,538} \quad \Rightarrow \quad \phi = -0.4° \quad \text{(to 1 d.p.)}$$

The resultant pull is 113 000 N (to 3 s.f.) at an angle of 0.4° (to the nearest 0.1°) to the line of motion of the ship.

In general, any force **F** can be resolved into two perpendicular components $F \cos \phi$ and $F \sin \phi$ acting in the directions shown.

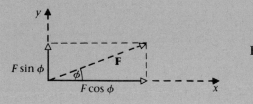

$$\mathbf{F} = \begin{bmatrix} F \cos \phi \\ F \sin \phi \end{bmatrix}$$

2.2 Exercise 3

1 The force **F** is of magnitude 50 newtons at 30° to the horizontal. In each of the following cases resolve **F** into its components:

(a) horizontally and vertically,

(b) up the slope and perpendicular to the slope,

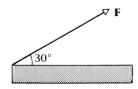

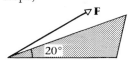

(c) down the slope and perpendicular to the slope.

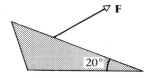

2 Resolve the following forces into perpendicular components in the directions indicated.

(a)

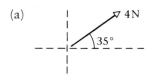

(b)

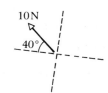

(c)

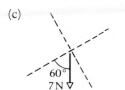

(d)

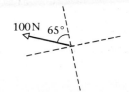

3 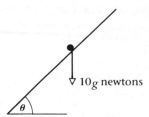 A mass of 10 kg is resting on a rough inclined plane as shown.

(a) Draw a force diagram and, by considering components parallel to the plane, calculate the magnitude of the force of friction, F, if $\theta = 20°$.

(b) If N is the magnitude of the normal contact force, show that

$$\frac{F}{N} = \tan \theta$$

4 By resolving one or both forces into components, calculate the resultant of the forces 11 N and 9 N shown in the diagram.

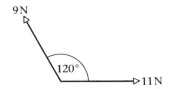

5 By resolving each force into components, find the resultant of the following sets of forces.

(a)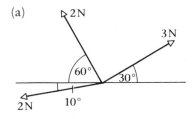

(b)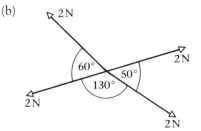

6 Three children each think that a parcel has stopped at them in a game of 'pass the parcel'. They pull on parts of the parcel with forces of 20 N, 40 N and 35 N at angles of 120°, 150° and 90° with each other as shown in the diagram.

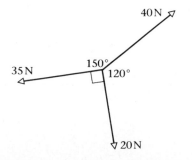

If the parcel does not break, in which direction will it move?

7 The diagram shows a boy held (at rest) by two ropes. The mass of the boy is 60 kg. Find the tension in each of the ropes:

(a) by taking components horizontally and vertically;

(b) by taking components parallel and perpendicular to one of the ropes.

8 Two masses of *m* grams each are suspended over two friction-free pulleys. A mass of 60 grams is hung between them as shown. If the strings both make an angle of 45° to the vertical, find *m*.

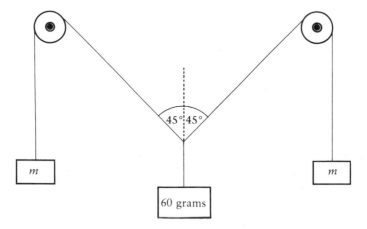

9 A mass of 20 kg is supported by two strings inclined to the vertical at 30° and 60°. Calculate the tension in each string.

2.2.4 Force and acceleration

The following diagram was obtained earlier, when modelling a sledge (of mass 750 kg) being pulled up the slope.

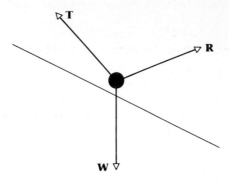

The values for some of the angles and forces have been included on the diagram below. The total contact force is split into a normal contact force and a friction force of 250 N.

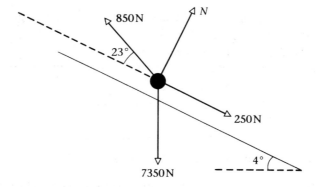

The weight of the sledge is $750 \times 9.8 = 7350$ N.

Finding the normal contact force **N** is easy enough if you choose sensible directions in which to resolve the forces. In this case, a sensible choice would be parallel and perpendicular to the plane. This is because there is no acceleration perpendicular to the plane.

The set of forces is equivalent to:

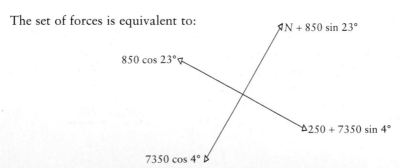

Newton's second law gives

$$\begin{bmatrix} 850\cos 23° - 250 - 7350\sin 4° \\ N + 850\sin 23° - 7350\cos 4° \end{bmatrix} = m\begin{bmatrix} a \\ 0 \end{bmatrix}$$

This gives $N = 6999.97$ or 7000 newtons.

The resultant force $= 850\cos 23° - 250 - 7350\sin 4°$
$= 19.719$ or 20 newtons up the plane

The acceleration $a = \dfrac{19.719}{750} = 0.026 \text{ m s}^{-2}$ up the plane

The choice of directions in which to resolve the forces can be critical for finding straightforward solutions to problems.

Example 4

A book of mass 3 kg is placed on a smooth slope of angle 25°. It starts to slide down the slope. What is the contact force on the book?
What is its acceleration?   (Take $g = 10 \text{ N kg}^{-1}$.)

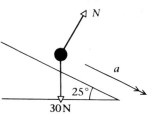

Solution

The slope is smooth so the contact force is normal to the slope. The acceleration is $a \text{ m s}^{-2}$ down the slope. Taking axes along and perpendicular to the slope,

by Newton's second law $\begin{bmatrix} 30\sin 25° \\ N - 30\cos 25° \end{bmatrix} = 3\begin{bmatrix} a \\ 0 \end{bmatrix}$

$$30\sin 25° = 3a \quad \Rightarrow \quad a = 4.23$$

and $\quad N - 30\cos 25° = 0 \quad \Rightarrow \quad N = 27.2$

The contact force is 27.2 newtons at right angles to the slope (to 3 s.f.).
The book accelerates down the slope at 4.23 m s^{-2} (to 3 s.f.).

▶ 2.2 **Tasksheet 2 – Modelling with force (page 354)**

2.2 Exercise 4

(Take $g = 10 \text{ N kg}^{-1}$.)

1 A block is sliding down a slope. The forces acting on it are shown in the diagram (in newtons).
Find the normal contact force N newtons.
What is the acceleration of the block?

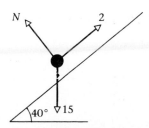

2 A trolley of mass 200 kg is being pulled up a smooth slope of 20° by a rope parallel to the slope. If the tension in the rope is 800 newtons, find the acceleration of the trolley.

3 A girl of mass 65 kg is abseiling down a rope fixed to the top of a cliff. If the tension in the rope is 540 newtons, what is the resultant force on the girl? Find her acceleration. What happens if the rope breaks?

4 A ball of mass 1 kg is falling through the air with an acceleration of $6\,\mathrm{m\,s^{-2}}$. Calculate the air resistance.

5 A woman weighing 60 kg is standing in a lift. What is the magnitude of the contact force between her and the lift if the lift is moving:

(a) upwards with constant speed,

(b) upwards with acceleration $1.5\,\mathrm{m\,s^{-2}}$,

(c) downwards with acceleration $1.5\,\mathrm{m\,s^{-2}}$?

2.2.5 Models of static friction

 .2B

A man is trying to push a heavy crate across the floor. It is too hard to move so more and more people come to help. It finally moves when there are 5 people pushing.

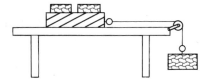

Consider the friction force between the crate and the floor. Is it constant the whole time? What might it depend on? Set up an experiment, as shown, to find out how static friction, F newtons, depends on the normal contact force, N newtons.

Data from friction experiments often give a variety of linear and non-linear models for **limiting friction**. The limiting friction may vary dramatically from point to point on a surface of contact. The models below were fitted to experimental data collected by some students.

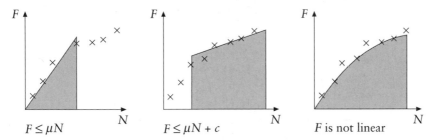

$F \le \mu N$ $F \le \mu N + c$ F is not linear

The models are valid for different ranges of N. The first model applies to the data for small N. The second applies for large N. The third is an attempt to fit a curve that would be valid for most N. The inequality is used because friction can take any value up to the limiting value depending on the force being applied to the body.

For static friction, the model usually used is $F \le \mu N$.

Static friction

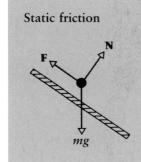

Friction acts in a direction along the surface of contact to prevent motion.

$$F \le \mu_S N$$

where μ_S is the coefficient of static friction, which depends upon the nature of both surfaces.

Typical values and ranges of values of μ_S are indicated in the table.

Surfaces in contact	μ_S
Wood against wood	0.2–0.5
Wood against metal	0.2–0.6
Metal against metal	0.15–0.3
Plastic against rubber	0.7
Sandpaper against sandpaper	2.0
Metal on snow	0.02

Example 5

A box is placed on a rough plane which is gradually tilted. The box is on the point of sliding when the plane makes an angle of α to the horizontal. Find the coefficient of static friction between the box and the plane.

Solution

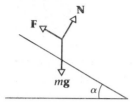

Let the friction force be **F** newtons and the normal contact force be **N** newtons, as shown. The forces are in equilibrium. Using Newton's second law,

$$\mathbf{F} + \mathbf{N} + m\mathbf{g} = 0$$

$$\begin{bmatrix} F \\ 0 \end{bmatrix} + \begin{bmatrix} 0 \\ N \end{bmatrix} + \begin{bmatrix} -mg\sin\alpha \\ -mg\cos\alpha \end{bmatrix} = \begin{bmatrix} 0 \\ 0 \end{bmatrix}$$

$$\Rightarrow \quad F = mg\sin\alpha \quad \text{and} \quad N = mg\cos\alpha$$

But $F = \mu N$ as the box is about to slide

so $mg\sin\alpha = \mu mg\cos\alpha$

$$\Rightarrow \quad \mu = \tan\alpha$$

2.2 Exercise 5

Take $F \leq \mu_S N$ for your model of static friction and $g = 10\,\mathrm{m\,s^{-2}}$.

1 A crate of weight 100 newtons rests on a rough plane inclined at 30° to the horizontal. It is just about to slip.

(a) What is the force due to friction on the crate?

(b) Find the coefficient of static friction between the crate and the plane.

2 A rubber of mass m kilograms is placed on a table. The coefficient of static friction between the two surfaces is 0.7. What is the greatest angle at which the table can be tilted before the rubber starts to slide?

3 A climber of mass 65 kg is practising traversing a slab of rock. The coefficient of friction between her feet and the rock is 1.2.

(a) What is the greatest angle of slope she can walk on?

(b) What is the force due to friction at that point?

4 A sledge of mass 150 kg is being held on a snowy slope by a rope parallel to the slope. If the slope makes an angle of 35° to the horizontal and the coefficient of static friction is 0.02, what is the least force required:

(a) to hold it stationary;

(b) to start it moving up the slope?

5 A climber of mass 100 kg is being held stationary on a rough slope of angle 80°
   to the horizontal by his partner at the top of the slope.

   If the coefficient of static friction between the climber and the slope is 0.9,
   what are the limits on the tension in the rope?

2.2.6 Models of sliding friction

When you solve problems you generally need to make assumptions about the
forces which act. In particular, you need to have reasonable 'models' for friction,
tension and air resistance in various situations. A 'reasonable model' for a force
involves making assumptions about the force which experience tells you have
worked well in similar situations. Scientists and engineers have collected a
number of 'standard models' of this kind which are now in common use,
though it is *impossible to guarantee* that they will work in any new situation and
they are usually only *approximately* true. In section 2.2.5 you looked at some
models for static friction. Here you will consider friction when objects are
sliding.

 .2c

 Problem

What model of friction would be
appropriate for a curling stone
travelling along the ice?

The data below were collected for a curling stone from the moment it left the
curler's hand until it came to rest.

Displacement x (metres)	0	5	10	15	20	25	30	35	40
Time t (seconds)	0	2.5	5.5	8.5	11.9	16.2	21.7	31.1	–

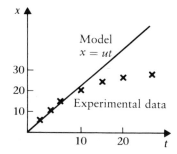

Set up a model

Assume that the stone is a particle of mass m kg and that air resistance can be ignored. Let the friction force be F and the velocity be $v\,\mathrm{m\,s}^{-1}$.

The key assumption concerns the friction F. First, try the model $F = 0$.

Model 1: Sliding friction is zero

Analyse the problem

Apply Newton's second law:

$$\begin{bmatrix} -F \\ N - mg \end{bmatrix} = m \begin{bmatrix} \dfrac{dv}{dt} \\ 0 \end{bmatrix}$$

$F = 0$ and so $\dfrac{dv}{dt} = 0$

Therefore v is a constant, u, say.
Then $x = ut$

Interpret/validate

The stone continues to slide at speed u for ever.
In fact this result is a reasonable model for the first 20 metres of the motion.

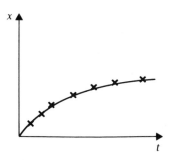

1 Find a value for u which best fits the first 20 metres of the motion.

You can see that the model does not fit the data well for values of t greater than 10 seconds.

It is clear that the graph of (t, x) should be a curve.

2 What conclusion should you reach about the model $F = 0$

(a) for the first few seconds of the motion;

(b) for the motion when $t > 10$ seconds?

You can now refine the model for the second part of the motion.

Set up a model

The only assumption you need to change is $F = 0$.
Now let F be constant throughout the motion.

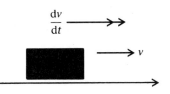 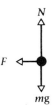

Model 2: Sliding friction is constant during the motion

Analyse the problem

Applying Newton's second law,

$$\begin{bmatrix} -F \\ N - mg \end{bmatrix} = m \begin{bmatrix} \dfrac{dv}{dt} \\ 0 \end{bmatrix}$$

Therefore, $\quad -F = m\dfrac{dv}{dt} \quad$ and $\quad N - mg = 0$

so $\qquad \dfrac{dv}{dt} = \dfrac{-F}{m}$

Integrating gives $v = u - \dfrac{Ft}{m} \quad$ and $\quad x = ut - \dfrac{Ft^2}{2m}$

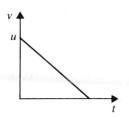 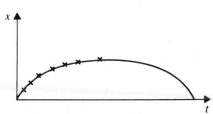

Interpret/validate

The stone comes to rest after $t = \dfrac{um}{F}$ seconds.

The faster it is projected, the longer it takes to stop. It is clear that after this point the model becomes invalid.

You must now match the equation

$$x = ut - \frac{F}{2m}t^2$$

against the data collected previously.

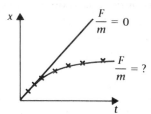

3 (a) What value of $\dfrac{F}{m}$ will give a reasonable fit for this set of data?

   (b) What can you conclude about the model $F = $ constant for a stone sliding until it comes to rest?

Sliding friction

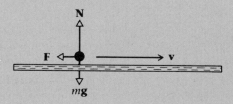

The friction force always acts in the direction opposed to the velocity of the body relative to the surface of contact.

(a) $F = 0$ if the object is moving on a smooth surface (e.g. a puck on ice for a short period of time).

(b) $F = \mu_D N$ where μ_D is the coefficient of sliding friction ('D' stands for dynamic) and N is the normal contact force.

μ_D is normally less than μ_S for any two bodies in contact.

Example 6

A box of mass $20\,\text{kg}$ is being pushed across a rough floor at constant velocity by a horizontal force of 20 newtons. Using the model for sliding friction $F = \mu N$, what is the coefficient of sliding friction μ?

What force must be used if the mass of the box is doubled?

Solution

Let the friction be F and the normal contact force be N. The box does not accelerate vertically or horizontally, so by Newton's second law,

$$N = 200\,\text{N} \quad \text{and} \quad F = 20\,\text{N}$$

Then $F = \mu N \Rightarrow \mu = 0.1$.

If the mass of the box is doubled, N is doubled and $F = 0.1 \times 400 = 40$. The push must be 40 newtons horizontally.

2.2 Exercise 6

1   A block of mass 6 kg will move at constant velocity when pushed along a table by a horizontal force of 24 N. Find the coefficient of friction between the block and the table.

2   A puck of mass 0.1 kg is sliding in a straight line on an ice rink. The coefficient of sliding friction between the puck and the ice is 0.02. Find the resistive force due to friction and then find the speed of the puck after 20 seconds if its initial speed is $10\,\text{m}\,\text{s}^{-1}$.

3   A particle of mass 1 kg is projected at $5\,\text{m}\,\text{s}^{-1}$ along a rough horizontal surface. The coefficient of sliding friction is 0.3. Assuming that $F = \mu N$, how far does the particle move before coming to rest?

4   A gymnast of mass 80 kg is sliding down a vertical climbing rope with constant speed. The coefficient of friction between his hands and the rope is 0.3. Calculate the total normal contact between his hands and the rope. State any assumptions you make.

5E A particle rests on a rough plane inclined at an angle ϕ to the horizontal.

When an additional force P is applied as shown, the particle slides down the slope at constant speed.

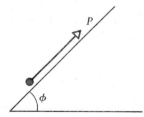

Show that $P = mg(\sin\phi - \mu\cos\phi)$ where m is the mass of the particle and μ is the coefficient of friction.

If the additional force is trebled to $3P$, and the particle now moves up the plane with constant speed, show that $\tan\phi = 2\mu$.

After working through section 2.2, you should:

1 be able to find the resultant of several forces on a particle;

2 be able to use this resultant to find the acceleration of the particle;

3 know that if a particle is in equilibrium then the resultant force acting on it is zero; a particle that is in equilibrium will either remain at rest or travel with constant velocity;

4 be able to resolve a force, $\mathbf{F}$, into two components, $F \sin \phi$ and $F \cos \phi$;

5 be able to model situations involving friction, tension and resistance.

2 Force and motion

.3 Acceleration and circular motion

2.3.1 The motion of the Moon

This section will consider acceleration which is not constant. Acceleration is a vector and can therefore change its magnitude or its direction or both.

The direction of the acceleration of a body is always in the direction of the resultant force acting. This may not be in the direction of motion, as can be seen clearly by considering the motion of the Moon.

The Moon experiences many forces due to its attraction by the other bodies in the solar system. Discussion will be limited initially to the force of attraction between the Moon and the Earth. This force, as with all gravitational attraction, acts along the line of centres of the two bodies. The magnitude of the force is approximately 2.0×10^{20} N.

As the force acts towards the Earth, the acceleration of the Moon is also towards the Earth. The direction of travel of the Moon is perpendicular to its acceleration. As the Moon does not disappear into deep space or crash into the Earth and always appears to be approximately the same size when seen from Earth it is reasonable to assume that it is travelling in a circle about the Earth.

As the Moon travels around the Earth the direction of the line of centres changes. Thus the directions of both the velocity and the acceleration change. As the Moon's orbit around the Earth is nearly circular and the forces of attraction can be taken as constant, both velocity and acceleration change in direction but not in magnitude.

2.3 Exercise 1

Use $G = 6.67 \times 10^{-11}$ N m^2 kg^{-2}.

1 (a) Calculate the magnitude of the force due to the Earth acting on the Moon, using the following data:
- mass of Moon $= 7.34 \times 10^{22}$ kg
- mass of Earth $= 5.98 \times 10^{24}$ kg
- average radius of the Moon's orbit $= 3.8 \times 10^8$ metres

(b) Use Newton's second law to deduce the magnitude and direction of the Moon's acceleration.

2 (a) Calculate the force of attraction of the Sun on the Earth using Newton's law of gravitation and hence deduce the magnitude and direction of the acceleration of the Earth due to the pull of the Sun.

The mass of the Sun is 2.0×10^{30} kg, that of the Earth is 5.98×10^{24} kg and the average distance between their centres is 1.50×10^{8} km.

(b) The maximum distance between the centres of the Sun and the Earth is 1.52×10^{8} km and the minimum distance is 1.47×10^{8} km. Find the range of the force of attraction between the Sun and the Earth.

3 The first orbiting laboratory, Skylab, was set in orbit at an altitude of 434 km on 14 May 1973. Crews were ferried to and from the laboratory by means of Apollo-type spacecraft. With the Apollo command and service module (CSM) attached, Skylab had an overall length of 36 m and a mass of 82 000 kg.

Calculate the force of attraction of the Earth on Skylab.

2.3.2 Angular speed and velocity

The motion of the Moon can be modelled by that of a penny stuck onto a rotating turntable.

 .3A

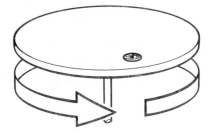

A penny is placed on the turntable so that its centre is 0.06 metre from the centre of the turntable. The turntable rotates through an angle of 2 radians every second.

1 The angular speed is 2 radians per second. What is this in revolutions per minute (r.p.m.)?

2 What is the speed of the penny in metres per second?

3 What can you say about the velocity of the penny?

4 Where could you place a second penny so that:

(a) its speed is half that of the first penny;

(b) its speed is twice that of the first penny;

(c) its velocity is twice that of the first penny?

The motion of the penny can be plotted on a grid.

5 How long does it take the penny to reach $(0, 0.06)$?

6 Find the coordinates of the penny after:

(a) 0.25 second,

(b) 0.5 second,

(c) 1 second,

(d) 2 seconds.

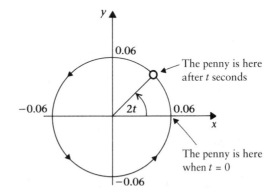

7 What are the coordinates of the penny after t seconds?

If the penny is 0.1 m from the centre of rotation and it rotates at $2\,\text{rad}\,\text{s}^{-1}$, then the position of the penny at any time t is defined by the vector $\mathbf{r}$, measured in metres, where

$$\mathbf{r} = \begin{bmatrix} 0.1\cos 2t \\ 0.1\sin 2t \end{bmatrix}$$

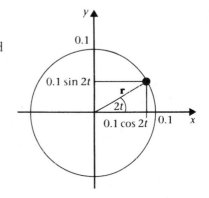

Being able to express precisely the position of the penny, for any value of t during the time it rotates, enables you to investigate its motion mathematically.

The velocity of the penny $\mathbf{v} = \dfrac{\mathrm{d}\mathbf{r}}{\mathrm{d}t}$ where $\mathbf{v}$ is measured in $\text{m}\,\text{s}^{-1}$.

So if $\mathbf{r} = \begin{bmatrix} 0.1\cos 2t \\ 0.1\sin 2t \end{bmatrix}$, then differentiating $\mathbf{r}$ gives $\mathbf{v} = \begin{bmatrix} -0.2\sin 2t \\ 0.2\cos 2t \end{bmatrix}$.

.3ʙ

1 Calculate the position vector **r** and the velocity vector **v** for time t where $t = 0.5, 1, 1.5, 2, 2.5$ and 3 seconds.

2 On a sheet of graph paper, draw a circle (reduced scale) to represent the penny on the turntable and mark the position and velocity vectors calculated above.

What can you say about the magnitude and direction of the velocity vector?

What can you say about the acceleration, $\dfrac{d\mathbf{v}}{dt}$, of the penny?

If a particle is rotating with a constant angular speed of ω rad s^{-1} at a distance r from the centre, then in 1 second the particle travels a distance $r\omega$. The speed of the particle is given by

$$v = r\omega$$

(ω is the Greek letter omega.)

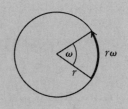

Example 1

A wheel of radius 5 cm is rotating at 6 r.p.m. What is its angular speed in rad s^{-1} and what is the speed of the edge of the wheel?

Solution

6 r.p.m. $= 6 \times 2\pi$ or 37.7 radians per minute

i.e. $\dfrac{37.7}{60} = 0.628$ rad s^{-1} (to 3 s.f.)

The radius of the wheel is 5 cm, so in one second the edge of the wheel has moved a distance 5×0.628 cm. The speed is 3.14 cm s^{-1} (to 3 s.f.).

2.3 Exercise 2

1 A helicopter's rotor blade is 4 metres long and is rotating at 50 r.p.m. Find the speed of the blade tip.

2 An outboard motor is started by pulling a cord wound around a grooved wheel of radius 10 cm. If the cord is pulled at 1 m s^{-1} what is the angular speed of the wheel in rad s^{-1}?

3   The drum of a washing machine can rotate at between 500 and 1000 r.p.m. What are these in rad s^{-1}? If the diameter of the drum is 1.2 metres what is the range of speeds of points on the drum?

4   The Earth has radius 6.37×10^6 metres. It spins about its axis approximately once every 24 hours. What is the approximate speed of an object due to this rotation:

   (a) on the Earth's equator,   (b) at the north pole?

5   (a) The hand of a dial is rotating with angular speed 3 rad s^{-1}. What is the time for one revolution?

   (b) If its angular speed is ω rad s^{-1} and the time for one revolution is T seconds, find an equation linking T and ω.

6E   The cotton from a cotton reel of radius 2 cm is pulled out with a constant speed of 3 m s^{-1}. What is the angular speed of the reel in rad s^{-1}? If the radius of an empty reel is 1 cm and the reel takes 50 minutes to empty, sketch a rough graph of angular speed against time. Give reasons for your sketch.

2.3.3 Uniform circular motion

You have seen that the Moon travels around the Earth in an approximately circular orbit due to a force acting towards the Earth. When any particle moves uniformly in a circle, it is straightforward to show that its acceleration is always directed towards the centre.

Consider a particle P moving about O in a circle radius r with uniform speed (starting from the x-axis).

Moving uniformly means that the angle ϕ changes at a constant rate.

Thus $\phi = \omega t$ where ω is the angular speed, measured in rad s^{-1}.

The displacement $\mathbf{r} = \begin{bmatrix} r\cos \omega t \\ r\sin \omega t \end{bmatrix}$

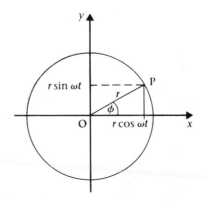

.3c

1 Find the velocity by differentiation and show that its magnitude is constant. What is its direction?

2 Show that the acceleration can be written as

$$\mathbf{a} = r\omega^2 \begin{bmatrix} -\cos \omega t \\ -\sin \omega t \end{bmatrix} \quad \text{or} \quad \mathbf{a} = -\omega^2 \mathbf{r}$$

What is its direction?

Show that its magnitude is $a = r\omega^2 = \dfrac{v^2}{r}$.

Example 2

An astronaut is orbiting the Earth at a steady speed in a space capsule. The capsule is, on average, 12 800 km from the Earth's centre.

Problem

What is the time taken to complete an orbit?

What if the orbit radius were larger?

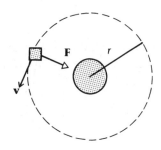

Set up a model

Assume the space capsule is a particle and its weight, **F**, is the only force acting. Let its mass be m kg. Assume the mass of the Earth is 5.98×10^{24} kg and $G = 6.67 \times 10^{-11}$ N m^2 kg^{-2}. Assume the orbit is a circle of radius 12 800 km.

Analyse the problem

Working in SI units and using Newton's law of gravitation, $F = \dfrac{GMm}{r^2}$

$$F = \frac{6.67 \times 10^{-11} \times 5.98 \times 10^{24} \times m}{(1.28 \times 10^7)^2}$$

$$= 2.43m \text{ newtons}$$

Using Newton's second law radially, $F = ma$ so $a = 2.43 \text{ m s}^{-2}$

But $a = r\omega^2$ so $2.43 = 1.28 \times 10^7 \omega^2$

$\Rightarrow \omega = 4.36 \times 10^{-4}$ rad s^{-1}

But $\omega = \dfrac{2\pi}{T}$ where T is the time for one orbit,

$\Rightarrow T = 14\,400$ seconds   (to 3 s.f.)

Interpret/validate

The space capsule orbits the Earth once every four hours.

If the orbit radius is r then $F = \dfrac{GMm}{r^2}$ and $F = mr\omega^2$.

Therefore, $\dfrac{GM}{r^2} = r\omega^2 \Rightarrow \omega^2 = \dfrac{GM}{r^3}$

So ω^2 is proportional to $\dfrac{1}{r^3}$.

Since $T = \dfrac{2\pi}{\omega}$, T^2 varies as $\dfrac{1}{\omega^2}$.

T^2 is therefore proportional to r^3.

So for a satellite, the greater the orbit radius, the greater the time taken for an orbit. Equally, the greater the radius, the smaller the angular speed.

> If a particle rotates with constant angular speed ω rad s^{-1} at a distance r metres from the centre of rotation then the speed of the particle is given by $r\omega$ m s^{-1} and the acceleration is $r\omega^2$ m s^{-2} towards the centre of the circle.
>
> $$v = r\omega \quad \text{and} \quad a = r\omega^2 = \dfrac{v^2}{r}$$

▶ 2.3 **Tasksheet 1 – Satellites (page 357)**

2.3 Exercise 3

1   (a)   Calculate the angular speed of the Moon about the Earth. (One revolution takes 27.32 days.)

　　(b)   Use the result $a = r\omega^2$ to calculate the acceleration of the Moon. (The radius of the Moon's orbit $= 3.8 \times 10^8$ metres.)

　　(c)   Compare your answer with the acceleration you calculated in 2.3 exercise 1, question 1.

2   A racing car is travelling at a constant speed of $120\,\mathrm{km\,h^{-1}}$ around a bend consisting of part of a circle. The magnitude of its acceleration is $30\,\mathrm{m\,s^{-2}}$. What is the radius of the bend?

3   A roundabout in a children's playground is rotating at 10 revolutions a minute. The radius of the roundabout is 2 metres. A child of mass $30\,\mathrm{kg}$ sits on the seat. What are her speed and acceleration if she sits:

(a) 1 metre from the centre;   (b) 2 metres from the centre?

Describe how the force acting on the child alters as she changes her position on the roundabout.

4   A coin of mass 4 grams is placed on a turntable and rotates with constant angular speed $0.5\,\mathrm{rad\,s^{-1}}$. Write down its acceleration in metres per second^2 when it is placed $15\,\mathrm{cm}$ from the axis of rotation. Calculate the magnitude of the resultant force on the coin. What can you deduce about the coefficient of friction between the turntable and the coin?

5   The coefficient of static friction between a block of wood and a turntable surface has been found to be 0.3. The block is placed $20\,\mathrm{cm}$ from the axis of rotation and the speed of the turntable is gradually increased. How fast is it rotating when the block slides off?

6E A group of ten skaters have linked arms to form the rotating diameter of a circle.

(a) If they make one complete revolution every 6 seconds, describe the probable speeds of the various members of the group.

(b) What is the acceleration of the outside pair?

(c) Estimate the force needed to produce such an acceleration.

2.3.4 Acceleration

The diagram below shows the figure-of-eight track for a model car. A car is travelling around it at a constant speed of $2\,\mathrm{m\,s^{-1}}$.

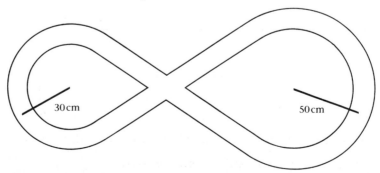

In considering the *velocity* and the *acceleration* of the car as it moves around the track, you can make the following observations.

- The velocity is constant on all the straight sections, as both speed and direction are constant. However, on the bends, the velocity at any point is perpendicular to the radius of the bend and so its direction is changing there. The magnitude of the velocity remains constant.

- The acceleration is zero on the straight sections. On the bends the acceleration is radially inwards.
  Where $r = 30$ cm $= 0.3$ m, the acceleration is about 13 m s^{-2}.
  Where $r = 50$ cm $= 0.5$ m, the acceleration is about 8 m s^{-2}.

- The maximum acceleration is therefore 13 m s^{-2} and the minimum is zero.

The velocity and acceleration can be shown conveniently on a diagram of the path of the model car by representing them by arrows, in the appropriate directions, of length proportional to the magnitudes involved. For instance, using a scale of 1 cm : 1 m s^{-1} and 1 cm : 10 m s^{-2}, you can draw a diagram to show velocities and accelerations in three positions, P, Q and R below.

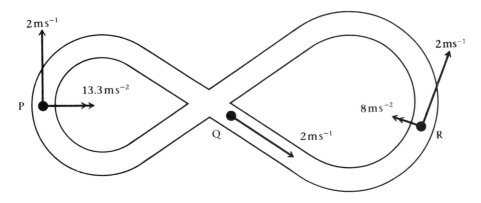

Many people think of acceleration as rate of change of speed, a scalar quantity. In mechanics the correct use of the term is as rate of change of velocity. Remember that it is a vector and has both magnitude and direction. The direction is always in the direction of the resultant force.

2.3 Exercise 4

1 An ice-skater moves with constant speed 20 m s^{-1} around a circle of radius 6 m.

    (a) Calculate his acceleration and show on a diagram the directions of his velocity and acceleration at two separate points on the circle.

    (b) The speed is constant, but is the velocity constant? Justify your answer.

    (c) Explain why the acceleration is not constant.

2 The drum of a small centrifuge spins at a constant 100 r.p.m. about a vertical axis. If the inside of the drum is 27 cm across, show that the acceleration of an object of mass 200 grams pressed against the wall of the drum is approximately $15 \, \mathrm{m \, s^{-2}}$. What are the magnitude and direction of the resultant force required to produce this acceleration?

3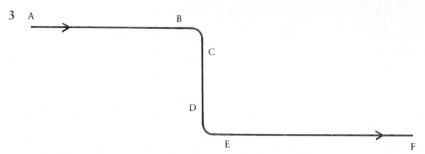

The diagram illustrates the shape of part of the layout for a model railway. The bends at BC and DE are circular, the other sections being straight. The train increases speed between A and B, travels with constant speed from B to E and then slows down from E to F.

(a) Mark on a diagram the direction of the acceleration between A and B, B and C, C and D, D and E, and E and F.

(b) How does the acceleration differ from the rate of change of speed at these various points?

4 At the points A, B, C and D, draw vectors representing the acceleration of a car moving around the track at a constant speed of $20 \, \mathrm{m \, s^{-1}}$.

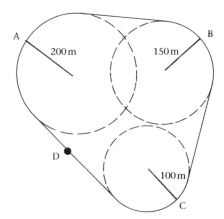

5E   A particle moves around a circle of radius 10 metres such that its angular speed is not constant, but in fact at time t seconds, its position vector, **r** metres, is given by

$$\mathbf{r} = \begin{bmatrix} 10\cos t^2 \\ 10\sin t^2 \end{bmatrix} = 10\begin{bmatrix} \cos t^2 \\ \sin t^2 \end{bmatrix}$$

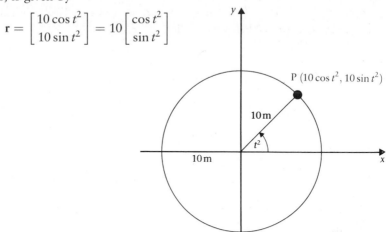

(a) Calculate its velocity vector $\mathbf{v}\,\mathrm{m\,s}^{-1}$.
     Interpret the result.

(b) Calculate its acceleration vector, $\mathbf{a}\,\mathrm{m\,s}^{-2}$, and show that

$$\mathbf{a} = 20\begin{bmatrix} -\sin t^2 \\ \cos t^2 \end{bmatrix} - 40t^2\begin{bmatrix} \cos t^2 \\ \sin t^2 \end{bmatrix}$$

Interpret the two parts of this vector as components of acceleration in the radial and tangential directions (i.e. towards the centre and along the tangent).

(c) When a particle moves in a circle, is the acceleration necessarily towards the centre?

After working through section 2.3, you should:

1 be familiar with examples of motion which can be appropriately measured as the motion of a particle rotating with constant angular speed ω at a distance r from an axis of rotation;

2 know that, for a particle rotating with constant angular speed:

 • the velocity of the particle will have magnitude $r\omega$ and the direction of the velocity, although constantly changing, will always be tangential to the circle;
 • the vector acceleration of the particle will have magnitude $r\omega^2$ $\left(= \dfrac{v^2}{r} \right)$ and the direction (again constantly changing) will always be towards the axis of rotation;
 • the time for one revolution is $T = \dfrac{2\pi}{\omega}$;

3 be able to apply Newton's laws of motion to various situations involving uniform circular motion;

4 know that the acceleration of a particle is in the direction of the resultant force and not necessarily in the direction of motion;

5 know that if a particle is travelling at constant speed it may still have a vector acceleration.

2 Force and motion

.4 Rigid bodies

2.4.1 Rotating objects – moments

Up to now, you have modelled various objects, in motion and at rest, by considering them to be **particles**. There are situations when this model must be extended.

If you watch from the side as one person throws a tennis racket through the air to another person, does it behave like a projectile?

If it did, you would expect to see a parabolic path. Here, however, the rotation of the racket itself makes it difficult to see exactly what happens.

If you tried this in practice it would be helpful to have a marker, for example a red dot, on the racket and to watch it move through the motion. However, where would you place the red dot?

If you placed it on the lower part of the handle then its path would look something like this.

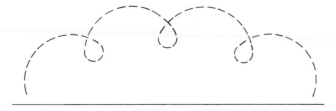

Alternatively, you could place the marker at the 'balance point' for the racket – the point about which the weight of the racket is equally distributed. In this case, the path of the dot *would* appear to be a simple parabola.

One of the important properties of a particle is that it does not have shape or size. This means that you can think of all the forces as acting at a single point. However, it also means that you cannot take into account any rotational motion which might be caused by the forces.

A **rigid body** is an extended body which has a fixed size and shape. Where forces act on a body to try to rotate it, you may have to take into account the size and shape of the body in question and model it as a rigid body.

The particle model used previously is not always suitable for rigid bodies. If a body is modelled as a particle, the forces acting on it are concurrent, whereas for an extended body you will find that the points of application of the forces are as important as their magnitudes. This section considers a different model; one which can be applied to rigid bodies in both static and dynamic situations. This model is referred to as the **rigid body model**.

Consider a heavy rod on a smooth table with two forces of magnitude P acting as shown in the plane of the table.

The sum of the forces is zero, but the rod will start to turn and so is not in equilibrium. The two forces have a turning effect on the rod.

If the effect of a force being applied to an object is to cause it to rotate about a pivot, then this effect is called the **moment of the force about the pivot**. A **pivot** is a line or axis through a particular point.

The moment of a force about an axis, O, is the product of the magnitude of the force applied and the perpendicular distance between the line of action of the force and the axis, O.

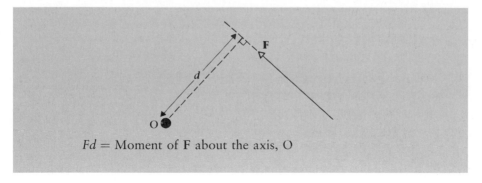

Fd = Moment of F about the axis, O

The sense of a moment is either clockwise or anticlockwise.
By convention anticlockwise is taken as positive.

The units of a moment are newton metres (N m).

Example 1

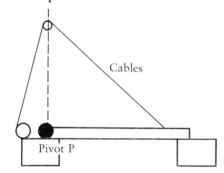

A drawbridge of mass 500 kg and length 5 m is to be winched into the upright position by two cables. The cables make an angle of 35° with the bridge and are attached to the bridge 4 m from the pivot, P. What is the moment of the weight of the drawbridge about the hinge? If the tension in each cable is 2724 newtons, what is the moment of these forces about the pivot?

Solution
Assume that the bridge is uniform and that the cables are light. There are four forces acting on the bridge when it is on the point of being raised; its weight, the tensions in the two cables, and a reaction, **R**, at the hinge. Assume that $g = 10 \, \text{N kg}^{-1}$.

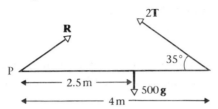

Moment of the weight about the pivot, P = $500g \times 2.5$ N m clockwise
$= 12\,500$ N m clockwise

Moment of each cable about the pivot, P = $2724 \times 4 \sin 35°$ N m anticlockwise
$= 6250$ N m anticlockwise

Note that, since **R** acts through the pivot P, it has no turning effect about P.

2.4 Exercise 1

1   Bob and Sally are pushing open an enormous gate hinged at A with forces as shown in the diagram.

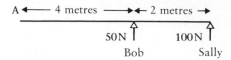

Calculate the total turning effect of the forces on the gate about the pivot at A.

2   A light rod OA is pivoted at O as shown. If $P = 6$ newtons, $Q = 7$ newtons and $R = 5$ newtons, find the moments of **P**, **Q** and **R** about the pivot at O.

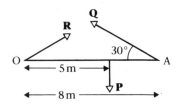

3   A uniform rod OA is pivoted at O and held at an angle ϕ to the vertical (as shown) by a horizontal force P newtons.

If $OA = 2a$ metres, find the moment of the weight **W** and the force **P** about the axis through O. (The force at O has been omitted from the diagram.)

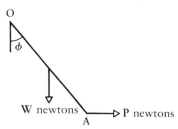

4   Find the moment of each force shown in the diagram about:

(a) the pivot point O,

(b) the point A.

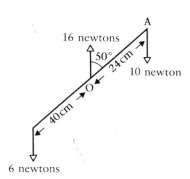

5   A plank of length l is lying horizontally on the ground and is pivoted at one end. Bronwen lifts up the other end with a force **T** newtons at an angle ϕ as shown.

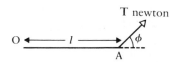

Find the moment of **T** about the pivot O. At what angle should she apply the force in order to maximise the turning effect?

6   Carole lifts a wheelbarrow full of brick rubble (combined mass 90 kg). Estimate the lifting force.

7E Josie and her son Winston are on a swing see-saw. Josie has mass 60 kg and Winston 20 kg. Does the gravitational force acting on Winston or that acting on his mother provide the greater moment about the pivot when the see-saw is in the position shown?

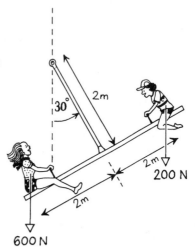

8E

Josie (in the example above) makes a simple see-saw by placing a 3 m plank of wood on a pivot which is positioned closer to her than to her son.

(a) How close to Josie should the pivot be placed if the see-saw is to balance?

(b) The plank of wood is quite heavy. Does this make a difference to your answer?

2.4.2 Equilibrium

A *particle* is in equilibrium when the vector sum of the forces acting on it is zero. This is not necessarily true for a *rigid body*.

This section is concerned with the conditions which must be satisfied by the forces acting on a rigid body *in equilibrium*.

.4A

1 A light rod is
suspended at its
mid-point from a
spring balance.
100-gram and
200-gram weights
are attached as
shown and the
rod hangs
horizontally in
equilibrium.

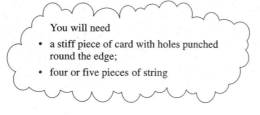

100 grams

200 grams

(a) Draw a force diagram for the rod. What would you expect the reading,
    R, of the spring balance to be?

(b) Apart from the value of R, what else can be deduced from the fact that
    the rod is in equilibrium?

(c) Can you state what general conditions must be satisfied by the forces
    acting on a rigid body in equilibrium?

The following simple experiment will illustrate a number of important ideas
concerned with the equilibrium of a rigid body.

You will need
• a stiff piece of card with holes punched
  round the edge;
• four or five pieces of string

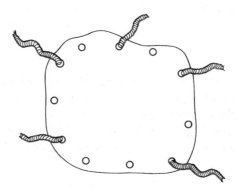

Thread each length of string through a different hole and tie a knot on the underside of the card so that the string swivels freely.

- Take two strings and pull.
- Now pull on three strings.
- What about four strings?
- Describe the lines of action of the forces when the body is in equilibrium.
- Make notes about what you see.

2 If a rigid body is in equilibrium under the action of three forces is it possible for:

(a) the three forces to be parallel;

(b) the lines of action of the forces to lie through a point;

(c) the forces to be non-planar;

(d) neither (a) nor (b) to hold?

3 What happens if there are four forces acting on the body?

> A body is in equilibrium when the vector sum of the forces acting on the body is zero *and* the sum of their moments about any axis is zero. If only three forces act on the body then they either pass through a point or are parallel.

For a body which is in equilibrium you can write down equations representing these results.

Example 2
A ladder of length 2 m and weight 200 N rests against a smooth vertical wall with its foot on horizontal rough ground, making an angle of 60° with the ground. Find the magnitude of the normal contact force which the wall exerts on the top of the ladder. Find also the magnitude and direction of the contact force exerted by the ground on the foot of the ladder.

Solution

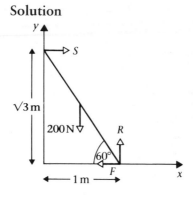

Since the wall is 'smooth', only a normal contact force S acts at the top of the ladder; friction acts only at the foot of the ladder.

The ladder is in equilibrium so the sum of the forces is zero.

$$\begin{bmatrix} S \\ 0 \end{bmatrix} + \begin{bmatrix} -F \\ 0 \end{bmatrix} + \begin{bmatrix} 0 \\ R \end{bmatrix} + \begin{bmatrix} 0 \\ -200 \end{bmatrix} = 0$$

So $S = F$
and $R = 200$

The sum of the moments of the forces on the ladder about any axis is zero, so taking moments about an axis through the foot of the ladder,

$$200 \times \tfrac{1}{2} - S \times \sqrt{3} = 0, \qquad \text{so } S = 57.7$$

The contact force exerted by the wall on the ladder is 57.7 newtons (to 3 s.f.).

The contact force exerted by the ground on the ladder is
$\sqrt{(200^2 + 57.7^2)} = 208$ newtons
at an angle ϕ where $\tan \phi = \dfrac{200}{57.7} \Rightarrow \phi = 74°$

The force is 208 newtons (to 3 s.f.) at an angle of 74° to the horizontal (to the nearest degree).

Example 3

A uniform ladder of length 4 metres and weight 200 newtons rests against a smooth vertical wall with its foot on rough horizontal ground, making an angle of 60° with the ground. If the coefficient of static friction between the foot of the ladder and the ground is $\tfrac{1}{2}$, is it possible for a man of weight 700 newtons to climb to the top of the ladder without it slipping?

Solution

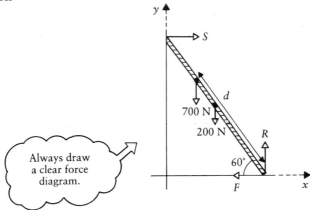

The ladder is in equilibrium, so the sum of the forces is zero.

$$\begin{bmatrix} S \\ 0 \end{bmatrix} + \begin{bmatrix} -F \\ 0 \end{bmatrix} + \begin{bmatrix} 0 \\ R \end{bmatrix} + \begin{bmatrix} 0 \\ -700 \end{bmatrix} + \begin{bmatrix} 0 \\ -200 \end{bmatrix} = 0$$

$$\Rightarrow S = F \quad \text{and} \quad R = 900$$

Taking moments about the foot of the ladder,

$$S \times 4 \sin 60° - 700d \cos 60° - 200 \times 2 \cos 60° = 0$$

$$S = \frac{350d + 200}{3.464} = F$$

For static equilibrium $F \leq \mu R$, so

$$\frac{350d + 200}{3.464} \leq \frac{1}{2} \times 900$$

$$350d \leq 1559 - 200$$

$$d \leq 3.88 \quad \text{(to s.f.)}$$

It is not possible for the man to climb to the top of the ladder. Limiting friction will be reached when he is 3.88 metres along the ladder. After this, the ladder will slip at the ground. However, in reality he is unlikely to want to stand on the very top rung. It depends what is meant by the top of the ladder.

2.4 Exercise 2

1 A uniform ruler, supported at the centre, has two masses dangling from it at distances of 10 cm and 7 cm from the centre as shown.

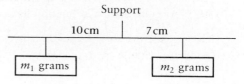

If the rod is horizontal, find an equation linking m_1 and m_2.

Hence find m_2 if $m_1 = 49$.

2

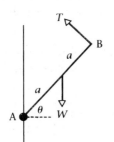

AB is a uniform rod of length $2a$ units hinged to a wall at A and held in equilibrium by a string at B pulling at right angles to the rod.

By taking moments about A, show that

$$T = \tfrac{1}{2} W \cos \theta$$

3 If the angle between the string and BA in question 2 is only $60°$, show that the tension required is greater than before.

4 A force $\begin{bmatrix} 3 \\ 4 \end{bmatrix}$ newtons acts at the point $(5, 2)$.

Find the moment of the force about the origin by finding:

(a) the sum of the moments of the components about 0,

(b) the moment of the resultant force about 0.

(Hint: graph paper may help.)

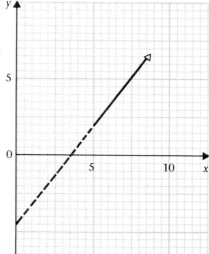

5   Two removal men are carrying a loaded rectangular box at a steady rate up a flight of stairs, inclined at 45° to the horizontal. The loaded box is of weight 750 newtons, its length is 2 m and its square ends have edges of length 0.8 m.

Calculate the part of the weight supported by each of the hands of each man if they are holding the underneath of each square end. What assumptions are you making?

What do the results suggest about the position for the stronger man of the two?

6   (a) A car weighing 6800 N has its axles 3 m apart. If its centre of gravity is 1.2 m in front of the rear axle, what force will be exerted by the road on each wheel? What assumptions are you making?

   (b) If luggage of weight 600 N is placed on the roof rack so that its weight acts through the centre of gravity of the car, what force will then be exerted on each wheel by the road?

   (c) If the luggage is placed centrally in the boot so that its weight acts at a distance of 0.6 m beyond the rear axle, what force will then be exerted on each wheel by the road?

7   A man's forearm is 0.3 m from the elbow joint to the palm, its weight is 27 N and its centre of gravity is 0.13 m from the joint. The biceps muscle, which raises the forearm, is 0.02 m from the joint. Assume that the forearm is horizontal and the biceps muscle is vertical.

Find the tension in the biceps:

   (a) when the hand is empty,

   (b) when a weight of 45 N is held in the palm.

8E A uniform ladder of weight W N and length 4 m rests against a smooth vertical wall with its foot on rough horizontal ground. If the coefficient of friction at the ground is $\frac{1}{2}$, what is the minimum angle of inclination of the ladder to the ground?

9E A walking stick of weight 5 N and length 1 m rests against the rail of a hatstand as shown.

The stick makes an angle of 60° with the horizontal and the rail is 0.75 m above the base of the stand. If contact with the rail is rough and that with the base is smooth, find the coefficient of friction necessary to maintain equilibrium.

2.4.3 Centre of gravity

'Josie is 2 m from the pivot.'

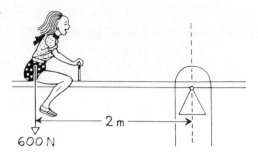

A statement like this really means that Josie's **centre of gravity** is 2 m from the pivot. The gravitational pull on the woman acts on all parts of her, but, from the point of view of taking moments about a pivot, the effect of the gravitational pull is that of a single force acting at a point which is called the centre of gravity.

The position of the centre of gravity of the human body is important. Many of the movements you make throughout the day are purely to make small adjustments to the position of your centre of gravity in order to maintain balance.

You can alter the position of your centre of gravity by changing your shape, but the centre of gravity of a rigid body is a fixed point, no matter what the orientation of the body or how it is moving.

The following example illustrates how you can calculate the location of the centre of gravity of a compound object.

Example 4

An object consists of a 400-gram mass on one end of a rod and a 100-gram mass on the other. The rod itself is a uniform cylinder of mass 100 g and length 40 cm. The location of the centres of gravity of the individual masses and of the rod are shown on the diagram below, but where is the centre of gravity when the three of them together form 'a single object'?

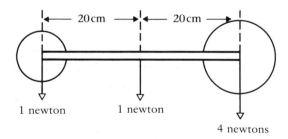

Solution

Suppose the object is pivoted about the left-hand end of the rod.

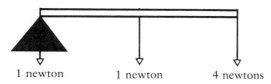

1 newton   1 newton   4 newtons

The moment of the 100-gram mass will be zero because its line of action passes through the pivot.

The moment of the 400-gram mass will be $4 \times 0.4 = 1.6 \, \text{N m}$ clockwise. The moment of the rod itself will be $1 \times 0.2 = 0.2 \, \text{N m}$ clockwise. Thus the total moment about the pivot is $1.8 \, \text{N m}$ clockwise.

The total gravitational force acting on the object is 6 newtons, so if the centre of gravity is a distance d metres from the pivot, it follows that the moment of the object as a whole about the pivot is $6 \times d$. This must be the same as the sum of the moments of the three parts of the object about the pivot, so

$$6 \times d = 1.8 \implies d = 0.3$$

The weighted rod will behave as though a single force of 6 newtons was acting at a point 30 cm along its length measured from the centre of the 100-gram mass. It is this point, the centre of gravity, which will obey Newton's laws of motion and follow a parabolic path if the rod is thrown.

2 .4B

For the weighted rod of example 4, take the pivot at any point you choose and check that you obtain the same position for the centre of gravity.

▶ 2.4 **Taksheet 1 – Modelling the Fosbury flop (page 359)**

The centre of gravity of a compound body is the point at which the total weight of the body can be said to act. If the body is symmetrical, it lies on the line, or lines, of symmetry of the body.

The moment of the weight of the whole body about *any* pivot, O, is equal to the sum of the moments of the weights of the component parts of the body about O.

2.4 Exercise 3

1 Find the centre of gravity of the following objects.

(a)

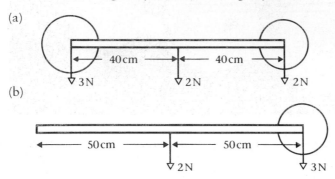

(b)

2 The diagram shows a person standing upright with both arms stretched out sideways parallel with the ground.

Axes are drawn with the person facing in the direction of the x-axis, and with the origin vertically below the person's centre of gravity.

The arms are moved as indicated below. All movements are from the original starting position.

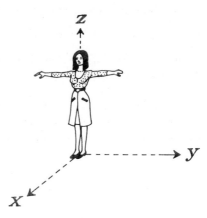

(a) Both arms are rotated through 90° to a vertically upward position.

(b) The right arm is lowered to a vertically downward position.

(c) The left arm is held horizontally outwards towards the front.

(d) The left arm is lowered to a vertically downward position and the right arm is held horizontally outwards towards the front.

For each of the movements, describe whether the displacement of the centre of gravity from its *original* position is positive, negative or zero in the direction of the x-, and y- and z-axes.

2.4.4 Centre of mass

A space platform orbiting the Earth consists of three spherical modules attached to a rigid connecting walkway as shown in the diagram. (The walkway is of negligible mass compared with the mass of the modules.) The gravitational force per unit mass is g newtons.

Small booster rockets, used to manoeuvre the platform, are located near the platform's centre of gravity.

In the absence of further information you can assume that:

(a) the masses of the three modules are m_1, m_2 and m_3;

(b) the distances of the centres of gravity of the modules are x_1, x_2 and x_3 from the end of the walkway.

You can find the centre of gravity of the space platform by taking moments about the imaginary pivot O shown in the diagram.

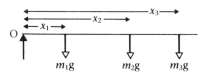

Total moment $= m_1gx_1 + m_2gx_2 + m_3gx_3$ clockwise.

If the centre of gravity is located a distance $\bar{x}$ from O then

$$(m_1g + m_2g + m_3g)\bar{x} = m_1gx_1 + m_2gx_2 + m_3gx_3$$

$$\bar{x} = \frac{m_1x_1 + m_2x_2 + m_3x_3}{m_1 + m_2 + m_3} = \frac{\sum mx}{\sum m}$$

Note that $\bar{x}$ is independent of g, and so the gravitational attraction makes no difference to the position of the centre of gravity.

The position where $\bar{x} = \dfrac{\sum mx}{\sum m}$ is also referred to as the **centre of mass** of the object.

The assumption made in solving the problem is that g is constant in magnitude and direction. This is reasonable when the object is near a much larger body such as the Earth or the Moon.

However, if the space platform was in deep space near an asteroid of comparable size then the gravitational force per unit mass would not be constant for the whole of the platform and the orientation of the body would affect the position of the centre of gravity.

Note that the position of the centre of mass of a body is always the same but that of the centre of gravity can vary in exceptional circumstances.

In the questions which follow, you will discover how to find the centre of mass of a two-dimensional shape (sometimes referred to as a **lamina**).

 .4c

A group of students was about to test a model bridge to destruction by gradually increasing the weight placed on the centre span. Before the test they were asked to predict the maximum weight the bridge could carry.

The breaking strain data from repeated tests are shown in the histogram below.

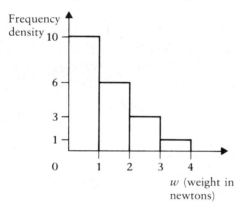

$$\bar{w} = \frac{\sum fx}{\sum f}$$

$$= \frac{\begin{aligned}10 \times 0.5 + 6 \times 1.5 +\\ 3 \times 2.5 + 1 \times 3.5\end{aligned}}{10 + 6 + 3 + 1}$$

$$= \frac{25}{20}$$

$$= 1.25$$

1 Draw a histogram on stiff card, using a scale of 2 cm per unit for the x-axis and 1 cm per unit for the y-axis, and cut it out.

   The centre of gravity of the resulting lamina is situated at $(\bar{x}, \bar{y})$.

   Locate the centre of gravity of the lamina by balancing it on the edge of a table or suspending it from a pin.

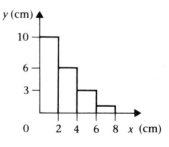

2 By modelling each rectangle as a point mass at its centre, the location of the centre of gravity can be calculated taking moments about the pivot shown in the diagram.

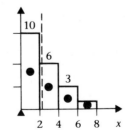

$$\bar{x} = \frac{10 \times 1 + 6 \times 3 + 3 \times 5 + 1 \times 7}{10 + 6 + 3 + 1} = \frac{50}{20} = 2.5$$

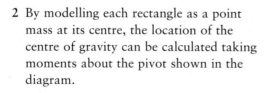

Turn the lamina around so that the y-axis is horizontal and use the same technique to find $\bar{y}$.

3 In what sense is the point $(\bar{x}, \bar{y})$ the mean of the lamina?

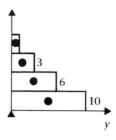

In 2.4c you saw how to calculate the position of the centre of mass of a two-dimensional shape and you saw why it is sensible to refer to the centre of mass as the mean or average position of the mass.

If a body can be modelled as a number of rigidly connected point masses $m_1, m_2, m_3, m_4 \ldots$ located at points $(x_1, y_1), (x_2, y_2) \ldots$ then the centre of mass will be located at $(\bar{x}, \bar{y})$ where

$$\bar{x} = \frac{\sum mx}{\sum m} \qquad \bar{y} = \frac{\sum my}{\sum m}$$

Under normal circumstances the position of the centre of gravity is independent of the gravitational force per unit mass and hence is the same as the position of the centre of mass, and can be calculated in the same way. These two terms are used interchangeably.

Example 5

A space platform consists of four modules, of masses 1, 2, 3 and 4 tonnes, at the corners A, B, C and D respectively of a light square framework of side a metres. Locate the position of the centre of mass.

Solution

The platform is modelled as four point masses located at $(0,0)$, $(a,0)$, (a, a), $(0, a)$.

The centre of mass lies at $(\bar{x}, \bar{y})$ where

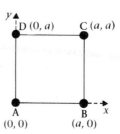

$$\bar{x} = \frac{\sum mx}{\sum m} = \frac{1 \times 0 + 2 \times a + 3 \times a + 4 \times 0}{1 + 2 + 3 + 4} = 0.5a$$

$$\bar{y} = \frac{\sum my}{\sum m} = \frac{1 \times 0 + 2 \times 0 + 3 \times a + 4 \times a}{1 + 2 + 3 + 4} = 0.7a$$

The centre of mass is at $(0.5a, 0.7a)$.

The centres of gravity of many objects are easy to find using symmetry. For example, it is reasonable to assume that the centre of gravity of the Earth is at its geometric centre and the centre of gravity of a rectangular lamina is at its point of symmetry. In other cases, a combination of symmetry and the mean position idea can be used.

2.4 Exercise 4

1 A balancing toy is made by soldering two spheres of the same uniform density to an L-shaped wire as shown. A small metal pin of negligible mass is to be soldered to the longer arm so that its point is at the centre of gravity of the object.

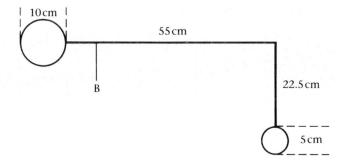

If the mass of the wire can be ignored and the spheres have mass 20 grams and 80 grams find the length and position of the balance pin, B.

2 Find the centre of gravity of each of the following laminae.

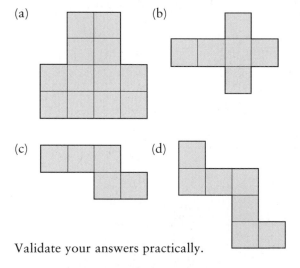

Validate your answers practically.

3 Obtaining suitable data from an encyclopaedia or other source, find the centre of mass of the Earth and Moon together.

▶ 2.4 Tasksheet 2E – Which slides first? (page 361)

2.4.5E Solid shapes

The definition of the centre of mass can be extended for more than two particles. For a collection of particles in space of masses $m_1, m_2, \ldots, m_n$ with position vectors $\mathbf{r}_1, \mathbf{r}_2, \ldots, \mathbf{r}_n$, respectively,

$$(m_1 + m_2 + \ldots + m_n)\bar{\mathbf{r}} = m_1\mathbf{r}_1 + m_2\mathbf{r}_2 + \ldots + m_n\mathbf{r}_n$$

Thus, $M\bar{\mathbf{r}} = \displaystyle\sum_{i=1}^{n} m_i\mathbf{r}_i$

where M is the total mass of the particles.

$$M\bar{\mathbf{r}} = \sum_{i=1}^{n} m_i\mathbf{r}_i$$

Example 6
Find the centre of mass of a uniform solid cone.

Solution
Since the cone is symmetrical, the centre of mass will lie on its axis, so let this be the x-axis in the chosen coordinate system. The cone is then divided up into suitable pieces whose centres of mass lie on the x-axis. This suggests the use of thin slices whose planes are at right angles to the x-axis.

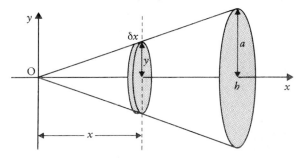

Each slice is so thin that it can be regarded as a circular disc.

$$\text{Volume of disc} = \pi y^2 \, \delta x$$

$$\text{Mass of disc} \quad = \rho \pi y^2 \, \delta x,$$

where $\rho = $ mass per unit volume

Let the centre of mass be a distance $\bar{x}$ from O.

Then, using $M\bar{r} = \sum\limits_{i=1}^{n} m_i r_i$,

$$\sum_{x=1}^{n} \rho\pi y^2 \, \delta x \, \bar{x} = \sum_{x=1}^{n} \rho\pi y^2 x \, \delta x$$

Taking limits as $\delta x \to 0$ and recognising ρ and π as constants,

$$\int_0^b y^2 \, dx \, \bar{x} = \int_0^b xy^2 \, dx$$

But $y = \dfrac{a}{b}x \implies y^2 = \dfrac{a^2}{b^2}x^2$ where a and b are constant, and so,

$$\int_0^b \frac{a^2}{b^2}x^2 \, dx \, \bar{x} = \int_0^b \frac{a^2}{b^2}x^3 \, dx$$

$$\left[\frac{x^3}{3}\right]_0^b \bar{x} = \left[\frac{x^4}{4}\right]_0^b$$

$$\bar{x} = \tfrac{3}{4}b$$

Example 7
A uniform solid cone and hemisphere, made of the same material, are joined at their circular faces. Find the centre of mass of the combined solid if the height of the cone is h metres and the circular faces are each of radius r metres.

Solution
The position of the centre of the hemisphere is $\tfrac{3}{8}r$ metres from the plane face. This is found by using calculus in a similar method to that used for the cone.

The mass of the cone is $\tfrac{1}{3}\pi r^2 h\rho$ where ρ is the mass per unit volume. Its centre of mass is $\tfrac{3}{4}h$ from the vertex.

The mass of the hemisphere is $\tfrac{2}{3}\pi r^3 \rho$ and the centre of mass is $\tfrac{3}{8}r$ from the plane face.

The x-coordinate of the centre of mass of the composite body is $\bar{x}$.

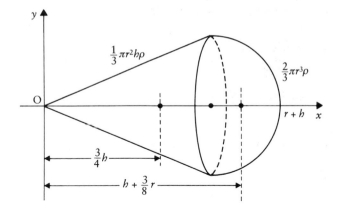

$$(\tfrac{1}{3}\pi r^2 h\rho + \tfrac{2}{3}\pi r^3 \rho)\bar{x} = \tfrac{1}{3}\pi r^2 h\rho(\tfrac{3}{4}h) + \tfrac{2}{3}\pi r^3 \rho(h + \tfrac{3}{8}r)$$

$$(h + 2r)\bar{x} = \tfrac{3}{4}h^2 + \tfrac{1}{4}r(8h + 3r)$$

The distance in metres of the centre of mass of the solid from the vertex of the cone is

$$\frac{3h^2 + 8rh + 3r^2}{4(h + 2r)}$$

It lies on the axis of symmetry.

2.4 Exercise 5E

1 Show that the centre of mass of a uniform solid hemisphere of radius r is $\tfrac{3}{8}r$ along the axis of symmetry from the plane circular face.

2 Find the positions of the centres of mass of the following composite bodies formed by combinations of a uniform solid cone, height h, base radius r; a uniform solid circular cylinder, height h, base radius r; and a uniform solid hemisphere of radius r. The bodies are all made of the same material.

(a) The cone and cylinder joined at their circular faces.

(b) The cylinder and the hemisphere joined at their circular faces.

3 A 'wobbly man' is made by joining two uniform solid shapes, a cone and hemisphere, by their circular faces. Find the condition on the height of the cone in terms of the radius of their joint circular faces if the wobbly man is always to return to an upright position when placed with any point of the hemisphere on a horizontal surface.

4 At the start of the evening a full can of cola stands on the table. Later it stands empty on the table. The centre of mass is in the same place in each case. Where has it been in between times, when the can was partially full? How low down the can did it go?

After working through section 2.4, you should:

1 know that the moment of a force about a pivot is the product of the magnitude of the force and the distance between the pivot and the line of action of the force (units are usually in newton metres, i.e. N m);

2 be able to find the total moment of several forces about a pivot by summing the individual moments (it is conventional for anticlockwise moments to be taken as positive and clockwise moments as negative);

3 know that, for an object to be in equilibrium,
  - the sum of the forces acting upon it must be zero;
  - the sum of moments of these forces about any pivot must be zero;
  - if three forces act on the object then they either pass through a point or are parallel;

4 be able to use the equilibrium conditions listed above to solve statics questions;

5 know that the centre of gravity of a body is the point at which the total gravitational force on the body appears to act;

6 be able to find the position of the centre of gravity of an object by using moments and understand that the centre of mass and centre of gravity of an object are normally coincident where
$$(\bar{x}, \bar{y}) = \left(\frac{\sum mx}{\sum m}, \frac{\sum my}{\sum m} \right);$$

7 appreciate that (as a first approximation) it is convenient to model an object as a point mass, at the centre of gravity, with all forces acting at this point;

8 appreciate that the particle model is not always appropriate;

9 know that the centre of gravity of a projectile follows a parabolic path;

10E know how to use calculus to calculate the positions of the centres of mass of various basic uniform rigid bodies;

11E be able to calculate the positions of the centres of mass of combinations of such rigid bodies.

2 Force and motion

Miscellaneous exercise 2

Take $g = 9.8\,\mathrm{m\,s^{-2}}$ unless otherwise stated. Other physical constants can be found in Appendix 1 on page 493.

1   A meteorite is 1200 km above the Earth's surface. If its mass is 2000 kg, what is its weight? Calculate the mass of a body which has this weight at the surface of the Earth.

2   In an experiment similar to the original carried out by Cavendish in 1798, two spheres of mass 1 g placed with their centres at a distance 1 cm apart were found to attract each other with a force of 6.66×10^{-13} N. Deduce Cavendish's value of G in units of newtons, kilograms and metres.

3   The Moon's mass is approximately $\frac{1}{80}$ that of the Earth, and its radius is about $\frac{3}{11}$ that of the Earth. If a man of 60 kg were to stand on the surface of the Moon, estimate what his weight would be relative to the Moon.

4   The path of a projectile is given by the equation

$$\mathbf{r} = \begin{bmatrix} t \\ 2t - t^2 \end{bmatrix}$$

   (a) What is the magnitude and direction of the velocity when $t = \frac{1}{2}$? What is the magnitude and direction of the acceleration at this time?

   (b) At what time is the velocity parallel to the x-axis?

   (c) At what time is the velocity perpendicular to that at $t = \frac{1}{2}$?

   (d) Is the acceleration constant?

5   A body moving with constant acceleration changes its velocity from $\begin{bmatrix} 3 \\ -2 \end{bmatrix}\mathrm{m\,s^{-1}}$ to $\begin{bmatrix} 8 \\ 18 \end{bmatrix}\mathrm{m\,s^{-1}}$ in 5 seconds.

   (a) Find the acceleration.

   (b) Show that the displacement during the 5 seconds is parallel to $\begin{bmatrix} 11 \\ 16 \end{bmatrix}$.

6 The velocity of a bee is given by $\begin{bmatrix} t-1 \\ t^2 \\ 1-t \end{bmatrix}$ m s^{-1}. Find the acceleration and

position vectors at time t, given that the displacement when $t = 0$ is $\begin{bmatrix} 0 \\ 9 \\ \frac{1}{2} \end{bmatrix}$ m.

What is the magnitude of the acceleration when the bee is travelling in the y-direction?

7 A tennis ball is volleyed down the centre of the court. The position of the ball is given by

$$\begin{bmatrix} 7t \\ t - \frac{1}{2}t^2 \\ 4t - 5t^2 + 2 \end{bmatrix}$$

where distances are in metres and time in seconds. The x-, y- and z-axes are taken to be down the centre line, across the court and vertically upwards respectively. Given that the ball is struck when $t = 0$ and strikes the opponent's racket 7 m away in the x-direction, find:

(a) the velocity at time t;

(b) the velocity, speed and position of the ball when it strikes the racket.

8 The speed of a car in m s^{-1} after t seconds is modelled by $v = 2t - \frac{1}{30}t^2$. Find:

(a) the initial acceleration;

(b) the acceleration after 20 seconds;

(c) the time at which the acceleration becomes zero;

(d) the maximum speed of the car.

9 A tennis ball is hit horizontally from the top of a cliff. Its initial velocity is 20 m s^{-1} and the acceleration g is 9.8 m s^{-2} downwards. The ball first bounces 50 m from the base of the cliff. For how long was the ball falling, and how high is the cliff?

10 A dart is thrown horizontally at 18 m s^{-1} at the centre of a dartboard 6 m away. The acceleration is $\begin{bmatrix} 0 \\ -9.8 \end{bmatrix}$ m s^{-2}. Where and with what speed will the dart land?

11 A ball is thrown from the ground with a speed of $25\,\mathrm{m\,s^{-1}}$ at $20°$ to the horizontal. Assuming that the ground is flat and horizontal, find the time the ball is in the air, the range and the greatest height attained. Take the acceleration to be

$$\mathbf{g} = \begin{bmatrix} 0 \\ -10 \end{bmatrix} \mathrm{m\,s^{-2}}$$

12 A cuckoo pushes a small bird out of its nest with an initial velocity of $\begin{bmatrix} 2 \\ 0 \end{bmatrix} \mathrm{m\,s^{-1}}$, taking components horizontally and vertically. The nest is $7\,\mathrm{m}$ above the horizontal ground and the bird moves with acceleration $\begin{bmatrix} 0.1t \\ 10t - 10 \end{bmatrix} \mathrm{m\,s^{-2}}$. After how many seconds is the bird next moving in a horizontal direction? What is its speed at this instant, and how high above the ground is it?

13 Find, as a column vector, the resultant of forces **P**, **Q**, **R** and **S** where

$$\mathbf{P} = \begin{bmatrix} -5 \\ 7 \end{bmatrix} \mathrm{N}, \quad \mathbf{Q} = \begin{bmatrix} 2 \\ 3 \end{bmatrix} \mathrm{N}, \quad \mathbf{R} = \begin{bmatrix} 4 \\ 4 \end{bmatrix} \mathrm{N} \quad \text{and} \quad \mathbf{S} = \begin{bmatrix} 1 \\ -8 \end{bmatrix} \mathrm{N}$$

Demonstrate, with sketches on squared paper, the truth of your result, drawing three different vector polygons:

(a) linking the forces in the order **P**, **Q**, **R**, **S**;

(b) linking the forces in the order **Q**, **P**, **R**, **S**;

(c) linking the forces in another order of your choice.

14 Find the resultant of these forces:

$36\,\mathrm{N}$ making $342°$ with the x-axis;

$54\,\mathrm{N}$ making $97°$ with the x-axis;

$45\,\mathrm{N}$ making $216°$ with the x-axis.

15 Find the resultant of forces $80\,\mathrm{N}$ making $60°$ with the x-axis, $40\,\mathrm{N}$ making $180°$ with the x-axis, and $80\,\mathrm{N}$ making $300°$ with the x-axis.

16 (a) A car of mass $700\,\mathrm{kg}$ is parked on a $10°$ slope. Find the minimum possible value of the coefficient of friction between the tyres and the ground.

(b) What is the steepest slope on which the car can be parked if the coefficient of friction is 0.4?

(c) With what acceleration will the car slide down the $10°$ slope if $\mu = 0.1$?

17 A block of mass 10 kg is pulled along a horizontal surface by a horizontal force of 100 N. The coefficient of dynamic friction between the block and the surface is 0.4.

   (a) What is the magnitude of the limiting friction between the block and the surface?

   (b) Work out the acceleration of the block.

   (c) If a second block, also of mass 10 kg, is placed on top of the first one, what will the new acceleration be?

18 The driver of a car travelling at 80 km h^{-1} puts on his brakes hard and goes into a skid. Find μ if the car travels 30 m before stopping. (Assume that it skids all the time.)

19 A book, mass 1 kg, is at rest on a desk lid. The book will slide down if the desk lid is at an angle greater than 30°. Find μ, the coefficient of static friction, and find what force parallel to the lid would be needed to move the book (a) up and (b) down the lid when it is inclined at 25° to the horizontal.

20 A rocket orbits the Earth at twice the radius of the Earth. At what speed is it travelling? (Assume the Earth is a sphere of radius $R = 6400$ km.)

21 An astronaut finds herself in orbit around the Earth at an unknown height. Her rocket and remaining fuel have a total mass of 60 000 kg, and she completes one orbit every six hours. Find the mutual force of attraction between the Earth and the rocket.

22 Find the distance above the Equator at which a satellite is in stationary orbit, that is, appears to remain stationary relative to an observer on the Earth's surface.

23 A girl of mass 40 kg is sitting on a horizontal roundabout 3 m from the central axle. The roundabout rotates at 2 rad s^{-1}. Find the radial force on the girl to keep her position at this point on the roundabout.

24 A conker of mass 10 grams is attached to one end of a string of length 50 cm. The other end is held fixed, while the conker makes horizontal revolutions below, with the string at 30° to the vertical. Find the tension in the string and the angular velocity of the conker.

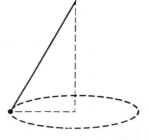

25 A windmill with four sails is rotating in a steady breeze at a rate of 3 revolutions every 20 seconds. Find the linear speed and acceleration of a point on the tip of a sail which is 5 m from the axle of the mill.

26 A uniform ladder of length 2 metres and weight 200 newtons rests against a smooth vertical wall at one end and rough, horizontal ground at the other. The angle of inclination to the horizontal is 60°. If a man of weight 1000 newtons has to be able to climb to the top of the ladder, what is the minimum value of the coefficient of friction?

27 A uniform ladder leans against a smooth wall with its foot on rough horizontal ground. It is about to slip when its angle to the horizontal is 32°. What is the coefficient of friction between the ladder and the ground?

28 Equal masses are placed at the three points $(4, 8)$, $(5, -2)$ and $(6, 4)$. Find the coordinates of their centre of mass.

29 Find the centre of mass of the triangle ABC where $\mathbf{a} = \begin{bmatrix} 4 \\ 3 \end{bmatrix}$, $\mathbf{b} = \begin{bmatrix} 5 \\ -2 \end{bmatrix}$ and $\mathbf{c} = \begin{bmatrix} -6 \\ 5 \end{bmatrix}$.

30 A square of side p is removed from a corner of a uniform square lamina of side $2p$. Where is the centre of gravity of the remaining piece?

31 A mass of 2 kg is placed at the point $(4, 1)$. Find the masses which should be placed at $(-1, 3)$ and $(-2, -1)$ in order that the centre of mass of the three masses should be at the origin.

32 A cube of side 1 m is removed from a corner of a uniform solid cube of side 2 m. How far has the centre of mass been displaced?

3 Towards circular motion

.1 Circular motion

3.1.1 Modelling horizontal circular motion

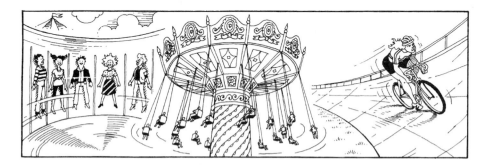

The sketches above illustrate the types of situation which an understanding of circular motion will help explain.

For example, how can you design a chair-o-plane (pictured in the centre above) which is safe, or a cycle racing track with the correct angle of banking to ensure that the cycles actually stay on the track? In these situations, circular motion can be fun, but is it safe? To answer this question it is necessary to analyse the forces involved.

A designer of a chair-o-plane at a fun-fair would have asked questions such as:

- Will a child swing out at a greater angle than a much heavier adult?
- Will the people on the inside swing out at the same angle as those on the outside?
- Will empty chairs be a problem?
- What will happen as the speed increases?

Although the chair-o-plane is slightly more complicated, analysing the motion of a simple conical pendulum is a sensible first step.

If you tie a small mass or bob to the end of a piece of
string and set the bob moving in a horizontal circle, then
you have a conical pendulum.

Two forces act on the bob, weight, **W**, and tension, **T**.

The string experiences two forces, the pull of the bob on one end and the pull of
the hand on the other. The string is said to be in tension.

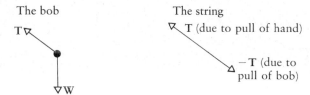

The bob   The string

T ↖   ↖ **T** (due to pull of hand)

                                   △ −**T** (due to
                                     pull of bob)

↓**W**

Weight is a constant force; tension is not. Although the magnitude of
tension may be assumed to be constant in this type of motion, the *direction*
is not.

If the angular speed of the bob is increased, then the radius of the circular
motion also increases. In reality, as the angular speed increases, you can feel the
tension increasing. Similarly, as you decrease the angular speed and the tension
decreases, then the radius of the circle decreases. You could also keep the
angular speed the same but change the length of the string.

Your hand feels an 'outward' and 'downward' force due to the tension in the
string pulling your hand. This is equal and opposite to the 'inward' and 'upward'
force you apply to the string to pull the bob around in a circle. This is an
example of Newton's third law of motion.

The bob of a conical pendulum performs horizontal circular motion with
constant angular speed. In Chapter 2, *Force and motion*, a mathematical analysis
of circular motion yielded a number of useful results.

If a particle is rotating with a constant angular speed of ω rad s^{-1} at a distance r metres from the centre, then the velocity of the particle will have magnitude $r\omega$ m s^{-1} and its direction, although constantly changing, will always be tangential to the circle.

$$v = r\omega$$

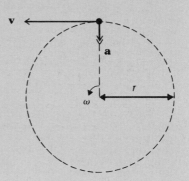

The vector acceleration of the particle will have magnitude $r\omega^2$ and its direction (again, constantly changing) will always be towards the axis of rotation.

$$a = r\omega^2 \implies a = \frac{v^2}{r}$$

Acceleration directed towards the centre of a circular motion is called **centripetal acceleration**.

Some real situations such as the chair-o-plane, the rotor and the cyclist shown in the picture at the start of the chapter lend themselves to further investigation as extended pieces of work. The chair-o-plane will be considered in 3.1A and the other two situations can be found in exercise 1.

Example 1

A child of mass 40 kg is sitting on a roundabout 3 metres from the central axle. The roundabout rotates at 2 rad s^{-1}. Find the horizontal force acting on the child.

Solution

Newton's second law of motion states

$$\text{horizontal force} = \text{mass} \times \text{acceleration}$$

The acceleration of the child is

$$a = r\omega^2$$

$$= 3 \times 2^2 = 12 \, \text{m s}^{-2} \text{ towards the central axle}$$

$$\implies \text{horizontal force} = 40 \times 12 = 480 \text{ newtons towards the} \\ \text{central axle}$$

The first question a design engineer working on a chair-o-plane must ask is, 'Will a child swing out at a greater angle than a much heavier adult?' Some insight into the problem can be gained by simplifying the situation and asking a similar question about the conical pendulum.

.1A

Problem

Does a heavy bob swing out at the same angle as a light bob if they are both rotating at the same angular speed?

Set up a model

Assume that the bob may be modelled by a particle of mass m, distance r from the axis of rotation. The angular speed of the bob is a constant ω radians per second and the bob swings out at an angle θ radians to the vertical when the length of the string is l. You can also assume that air resistance is negligible so that there are just two forces acting on the bob, weight, $\mathbf{W}$, and the tension in the string, $\mathbf{T}$.

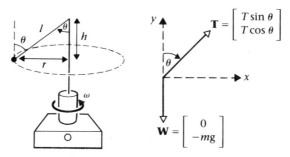

Analyse the problem

Resolving forces horizontally and vertically and adding the forces to obtain the resultant, Newton's second law gives

$$\begin{bmatrix} T \sin \theta \\ T \cos \theta \end{bmatrix} + \begin{bmatrix} 0 \\ -mg \end{bmatrix} = m \begin{bmatrix} r\omega^2 \\ 0 \end{bmatrix}$$

$\Rightarrow T \sin \theta = mr\omega^2$ and $T \cos \theta = mg$

But $r = l \sin \theta$ $\Rightarrow$ $T \sin \theta = ml\omega^2 \sin \theta$

$\Rightarrow$ $T = ml\omega^2$ or $\sin \theta = 0$ (i.e. $\theta = 0$)

1 Show that for $\theta > 0$, $\cos \theta = \dfrac{g}{l\omega^2}$

Interpret

The cosine of the angle (and hence the angle itself) depends on the gravitational force per unit mass, g, the angular speed, ω, and the length, l, of the string.

2 Explain why the analysis suggests that the heavier bob will swing out at the same angle as the lighter bob.

Validate

This may be validated by tying two bobs (one heavy and one light) to the spindle of the conical pendulum using strings of the same length. A visual check will show that they both swing out at the same angle.

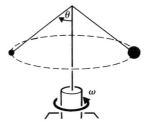

3 Use the analysis to solve, interpret and (where possible) validate the following problems.

   (a) What happens to the angle θ as the angular speed ω increases?

   (b) How big can the angle become?

   (c) What happens if you keep the angular speed the same but increase the length of the string?

   (d) Explain why h is the same for two bobs of different masses, tied to the spindle with different lengths of string.

Sometimes, a mathematical analysis of a problem suggests 'solutions' to new problems. For example, it is interesting to note that for the conical pendulum,

$$\cos\theta \le 1 \quad \Rightarrow \quad \frac{g}{l\omega^2} \le 1 \quad \Rightarrow \quad \omega \ge \sqrt{\left(\frac{g}{l}\right)}$$

4 What happens if $\omega < \sqrt{\left(\frac{g}{l}\right)}$?

   What does this tell you about the motion of a conical pendulum?

5 What is the main difference between a chair-o-plane and a conical pendulum?

Example 2

A penny is placed on a turntable 0.12 m from the axis of rotation. A second penny is placed on the turntable so that its speed is half that of the first penny. The first penny starts to slide when the angular speed reaches $4\,\mathrm{rad\,s^{-1}}$.

(a) How far from the axis of rotation is the second penny?

(b) At what angular speed would the second penny start to slide?

Solution

(a) The penny is modelled as a particle of mass m rotating with angular speed ω, distance r from the axis of rotation.

The speed of the first penny is $v = \omega r$.

The speed of the second penny is $\dfrac{v}{2}$ or $\omega\left(\dfrac{r}{2}\right)$, so it must be placed a distance 0.06 m from the axis of rotation.

(b) There are just two forces acting on the first penny, gravity and a contact force. The contact force has two components, the normal contact force, N, and friction, F.

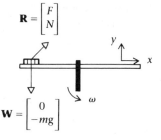

The penny has acceleration $\begin{bmatrix} r\omega^2 \\ 0 \end{bmatrix}$.

By Newton's second law, $\quad \begin{bmatrix} 0 \\ -mg \end{bmatrix} + \begin{bmatrix} F \\ N \end{bmatrix} = m\begin{bmatrix} r\omega^2 \\ 0 \end{bmatrix}$

Therefore $F = mr\omega^2$.

As the angular speed increases, friction will increase in magnitude until it reaches a limit (**limiting friction**), at which point the penny will start to slide.

The first penny starts to slide when $\omega = 4\,\mathrm{rad\,s^{-1}}$
so limiting friction is $\quad (0.12 \times 4^2)m = 1.92m$ newtons

Assume that limiting friction will be the same for the second penny.

$$1.92m = 0.06\,m\omega^2$$

$$\Rightarrow \quad \omega = 5.66\,\mathrm{rad\,s^{-1}}$$

The second penny will start to slide when the angular speed reaches $5.66\,\mathrm{rad\,s^{-1}}$.

3.1 Exercise 1

Take $g = 9.8 \, \text{N kg}^{-1}$ where necessary.

1 A racing car is travelling at a constant speed of $120 \, \text{km h}^{-1}$ around a circular bend. The centripetal acceleration is $30 \, \text{m s}^{-2}$. What is the radius of the bend?

2 A conical pendulum has length 80 cm and a bob of mass 0.5 kg, which is rotating in a horizontal circle of radius 30 cm. Find the angle between the string and the vertical, the tension in the string and the linear speed of the bob.

3 A thin string of length 1 metre has a breaking strain of 60 newtons. A mass of 4 kg is attached to one end and made to rotate as a conical pendulum. Draw diagrams and form an equation to describe the motion. Hence find the largest angular speed that can be attained and the angle the string makes with the vertical in this case.

4 A fairground machine consists of a large hollow cylinder of internal radius 5 metres. This can be made to rotate about its axis and a floor can be raised or lowered. When stationary, a door opens to allow a man of mass 75 kg to enter and then closes flush with the wall. The cylinder rotates faster and faster until the friction between the man's back and the wall is equal to his weight. Then the floor drops away.

Draw a force diagram showing **W** (weight), **F** (friction) and **N** (normal reaction) acting on the man. Given that the magnitude of **F** is two-fifths that of **N**, write down a vector equation and hence find the angular speed of the cylinder.

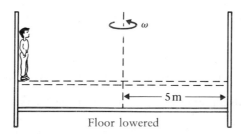

Floor lowered

5 Given below is a force diagram modelling a cyclist rounding a bend of radius 10 metres. The road is banked at an angle of 30°. The total mass of the cyclist and the bicycle is 100 kg. The speed of the cyclist is such that there is no frictional force acting sideways on the cycle tyres up or down the slope. Find the speed of the cyclist.

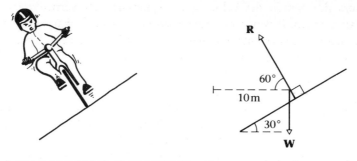

3.1.2 Investigating vertical circular motion

Fairground rides must be designed to be safe. An engineer will formulate a mathematical model of a ride, analyse the model and then validate that the ride is safe by simulating it under laboratory conditions.

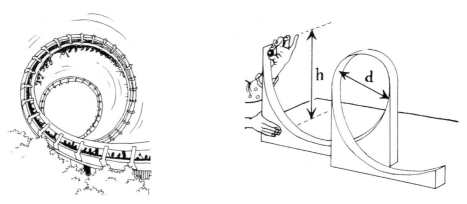

There seem to be three different possibilities for the motion of the marble illustrated above on the right.

 (i) The marble completes a loop safely.

 (ii) The marble falls off before it reaches the top of the loop and becomes a projectile until it lands on the track on the other side (if you are lucky).

 (iii) The marble goes part way up the loop before it rolls back down again.

This can be validated by setting up the apparatus and releasing the marble from different heights. Even when the marble completes a full vertical circle, its speed varies. It goes more slowly at the top of the loop than it does at the bottom.

The horizontal circular motion which you have analysed so far has always assumed constant angular speed. You will not necessarily be able to assume constant speed (or angular speed) in situations involving vertical circular motion.

However, it would be wrong to assume that constant speed is *never* found in vertical circular motion. Several fairground rides *do* have vertical circular motion *and* constant speed. It would be equally wrong to assume that constant speed is always a feature of horizontal circular motion. When you negotiate a bend in a car you do not necessarily do so at a constant speed!

Chapters 1 and 2 dealt with many of the concepts needed to analyse motion. The further concepts of **work** and **energy**, which you will need to analyse examples of vertical circular motion, form the central theme of this chapter. The aim is to show you some of the mathematical techniques associated with these concepts so that you can use them with confidence when formulating a mathematical model to describe situations such as those shown above.

After working through section 3.1, you should:

1 know that the acceleration directed towards the centre of circular motion is called centripetal acceleration;

2 know how to set up, analyse and interpret a mathematical model for horizontal circular motion where more than one force is acting on a body travelling with constant angular speed;

3 appreciate that many instances of circular motion, especially those involving vertical motion, do not involve constant angular speed.

3 Towards circular motion

.2 Work and kinetic energy

3.2.1 Areas under graphs

Measurements taken during a simulation of a car crash produced the graph shown below.

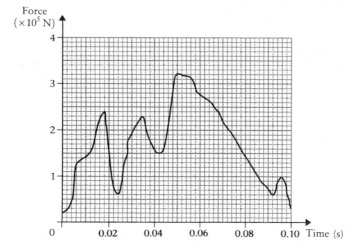

If the mass of the car was 1200 kg, can you estimate the original speed of the car if it came to rest after 0.1 second?

The variable force experienced by the car can be approximated by a series of forces, constant over short time-intervals.

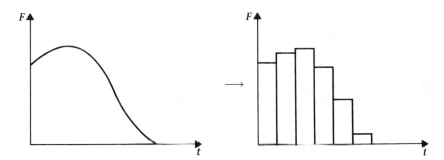

The area under the step graph measures a succession of 'changes in momentum'. To find the change in momentum of the car it is therefore necessary to find the area under the (time, force) graph. This can be estimated by counting squares or using trapezia.

The area under the graph is approximately 17 000 N s.

So $17\,000 \approx 1200v$, where v is the original speed.

$$v \approx 14\,\mathrm{m\,s}^{-1}$$

 .2A

Consider a car accelerating in a straight line along a horizontal stretch of road. The forces acting on the car in motion are

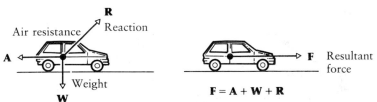

$$\mathbf{F} = \mathbf{A} + \mathbf{W} + \mathbf{R}$$

The car has mass 800 kg and accelerates from 0 to 30 m s^{-1} in 20 seconds. The velocity of the car is modelled by the functions:

$$v = \frac{-5t^2 + 20t}{4} \qquad 0 < t \le 2$$

$$v = \frac{-7t^2 + 70t - 67}{9} \qquad 2 < t \le 5$$

$$v = \frac{-8t^2 + 160t - 300}{25} \qquad 5 < t \le 10$$

$$v = \frac{-t^2 + 40t - 100}{10} \qquad 10 < t \le 20$$

1 At the times $t = 1, 3$ and 7 seconds,

    (a) evaluate the momentum of the car;

    (b) find the acceleration of the car;

    (c) find the resultant force acting on the car.

2 (a) Sketch the (time, momentum) graph for $0 < t < 10$.

    (b) Sketch the (time, force) graph for $0 < t < 10$.

3 Evaluate the area under the (time, force) graph. What does this area represent?

You found that the area under the (time, force) graph represented the change in momentum.

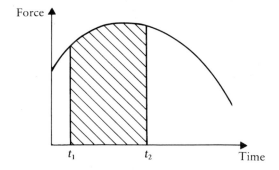

The direction of the force was constant, although the magnitude varied. Newton's second law of motion states

$$\mathbf{F} = \frac{d}{dt}(m\mathbf{v})$$

From the fundamental theorem of calculus it follows that

$$\int_{t_1}^{t_2} \mathbf{F}\,dt = m\mathbf{v}_2 - m\mathbf{v}_1$$

where $\mathbf{v}_1$ and $\mathbf{v}_2$ are the velocities at t_1 and t_2 respectively. It therefore follows that the area under any (time, force) graph represents change in momentum. (We will be considering one-dimensional motion only, so momentum and force only vary in magnitude.) The change in momentum due to a force is known as the **impulse** of the force and is measured in newton seconds (N s) or, equivalently, in $\mathrm{kg\,m\,s^{-1}}$.

The area under a (time, force) graph represents change in momentum.

Example 1

The force acting on a golf ball of mass 45 g when it is struck may be modelled approximately by the function

$$F = 10^{11}t(t - 0.004)^2 \qquad 0 < t < 0.004$$

Find the velocity with which it leaves the club.

Solution

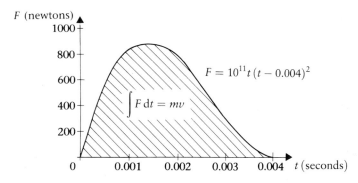

The area under the graph gives the change in momentum, or impulse. Since the initial velocity (and hence momentum) is zero, the momentum of the ball when it leaves the club face is represented by the area

$$mv = 10^{11} \int_0^{0.004} t(t - 0.004)^2 \, dt$$

$$0.045v = 2.13$$

$$\Rightarrow \quad v = 47 \, \text{m s}^{-1}$$

The integral can be evaluated numerically, or algebraically by multiplying out the bracket

The ball leaves the club face with an initial velocity of 47 m s^{-1} in the direction of the force.

3.2 Exercise 1

1 A ball of mass 90 grams strikes a wall at right angles when moving at $8\,\mathrm{m\,s^{-1}}$. It rebounds along the same line with a speed of $6\,\mathrm{m\,s^{-1}}$. A very simple force–time model assumes that the force between the wall and the ball increases uniformly with time up to a maximum and then decreases at the same rate. Use this model to estimate the maximum force (in newtons) on the ball if the total contact time is 0.002 second.

2 A car of mass 1 tonne started from rest and accelerated for 60 seconds. During this time the propulsive force was measured at 10-second intervals.

Force (N)	1050	650	480	260	170	130	80
Time (s)	0	10	20	30	40	50	60

Use this information to estimate the final speed of the car.

3 A ball of mass $0.5\,\mathrm{kg}$ is moving with velocity $\begin{bmatrix} 8 \\ 4 \end{bmatrix}\,\mathrm{m\,s^{-1}}$ when it receives a blow that changes its velocity to $\begin{bmatrix} 4 \\ 6 \end{bmatrix}\,\mathrm{m\,s^{-1}}$. What was the impulse due to the blow?

4

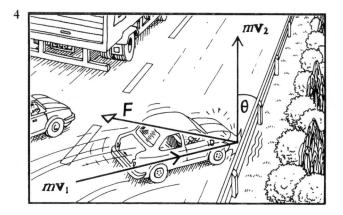

When a car runs off the road into a certain type of wire crash-barrier, the force exerted by the barrier on the car is given approximately by the function $F = 42\,000\sin(2\pi t)$, where F is measured in newtons and t in seconds. This force acts perpendicular to the barrier.

A car of mass 1200 kg hits such a barrier at an angle of 30° while travelling at 20 m s^{-1}. The impact lasts 0.5 second.

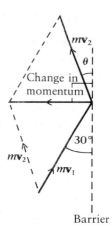

(a) Evaluate the impulse of the force, i.e.

$$\int_0^{0.5} 42\,000 \sin(2\pi t) \, dt.$$

(b) Explain why the change in momentum is perpendicular to the barrier.

(c) Calculate the initial momentum of the car.

(d) Find the momentum of the car after impact by scale drawing or otherwise.

(e) What is the velocity of the car after impact?

3.2.2 Speed and distance

When investigating a car crash, police and insurance claim investigators need to know at what speed the crashed vehicle was travelling before the brakes were applied. The length of time taken for skidding cannot be measured but the distance of the skid is often easy to measure.

You are familiar with the momentum equation for motion under a constant force,

$$\mathbf{F}t = m\mathbf{v} - m\mathbf{u}$$

If the force is in the direction of motion, this becomes a relationship between *speed* and *time*,

$$Ft = mv - mu$$

This section investigates the relationship between *speed* and *distance*.

 .2B

1 A series of skid tests is carried out in which a car skids to rest with its wheels locked by the brakes. The table below shows the lengths of skid marks, x metres, for various speeds, u km h^{-1}.

u	0	40	60	80	100
x	0	9	20	36	56

What would you expect the length of the skid marks to be for an initial speed of 120 km h^{-1}? Find x in terms of u.

2 An object of mass m is accelerated in a straight line by a constant force F, from speed u to speed v. Its (t, v) graph is as shown.

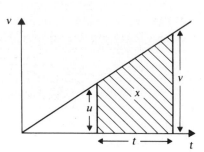

Find the distance covered, x, in terms of u, v and t.

Use the equation $Ft = mv - mu$ to obtain the expression

$$Fx = \tfrac{1}{2}mv^2 - \tfrac{1}{2}mu^2$$

for the product, force × distance.

The concept of 'force × distance' is as useful as that for 'force × time' which you have used previously. The expenditure of energy involved in pushing something along for some distance has come to be known as 'doing work'. To be more precise, Fx is known by engineers, physicists and mathematicians as the **work done** by the force.

The energy of motion acquired by the object as a result of being pushed (and having 'work' done on it) is represented by $\tfrac{1}{2}mv^2$. This form of energy is called **kinetic energy**, from the Greek word for motion, κινεσις (kinesis). Other forms of energy will be introduced later in this chapter.

For a constant force accelerating an object in a straight line,

$$Fx = \tfrac{1}{2}mv^2 - \tfrac{1}{2}mu^2$$

Work done = Change in kinetic energy

The units of energy are known as **joules** (abbreviated to J). These are named after James Prescott Joule (1818–89), an English physicist who established that the various forms of energy known at that time – mechanical, electrical and heat – are basically equivalent. Each can be transformed into any of the others.

1 N m (from force × distance) is the same as 1 joule.
Also, $1 \, \text{kg} \, \text{m}^2 \, \text{s}^{-2}$ (from $\tfrac{1}{2}$ mass × speed^2) is the same as 1 joule.

Example 2

(a) A sports car of mass $1000\,kg$ is travelling at $50\,m\,s^{-1}$. What is the work done by the frictional forces which bring it to rest?

(b) If it is brought to rest in 50 metres, what is the total retarding force (assumed to be constant)?

Solution

(a) Work done = change in kinetic energy

$$= \tfrac{1}{2}mv^2 - \tfrac{1}{2}mu^2 = \tfrac{1}{2} \times 1000 \times 0^2 - \tfrac{1}{2} \times 1000 \times 50^2$$
$$= -1\,250\,000 \text{ joules}$$

(b) Let the total retarding force be F newtons.

$$\text{Work done} = F \times 50 = -1\,250\,000$$
$$\Rightarrow \qquad F = -25\,000 \text{ newtons}$$

Note that the force is negative because it acts in the opposite direction to the direction of the motion. A general extension of the work and energy equation to cases where the force and motion are not in the same direction requires a vectorial treatment. This will be considered later.

Example 3

A car hits a telegraph pole head-on. There are skid marks of length 27 metres, and it is established from analysis of the impact damage that the car must have been travelling at $55\,km\,h^{-1}$ on impact. A skid test shows that, in similar circumstances, from the speed of $70\,km\,h^{-1}$, the car would have been expected to stop in 25 metres. At what speed was the car travelling when the brakes were applied?

Solution

Speeds in $km\,h^{-1}$ must be converted to speeds in $m\,s^{-1}$. In this case,

$$70\,km\,h^{-1} \approx 19.5\,m\,s^{-1} \quad \text{and} \quad 55\,km\,h^{-1} \approx 15.3\,m\,s^{-1}$$

For the skid test, let F be the resultant force on the car.

$$F \times 25 = \tfrac{1}{2}m \times 0^2 - \tfrac{1}{2}m \times 19.5^2 \quad \Rightarrow \quad \frac{F}{m} = -7.6$$

For the pre-collision skid,

$$F \times 27 = \tfrac{1}{2}m \times 15.3^2 - \tfrac{1}{2}mu^2$$

$$\Rightarrow \frac{F}{m} \times 27 = \tfrac{1}{2} \times 15.3^2 - \tfrac{1}{2}u^2$$

$$\Rightarrow -7.6 \times 27 = \tfrac{1}{2} \times 15.3^2 - \tfrac{1}{2}u^2$$

$$\Rightarrow u = 25.4$$

When the brakes were applied, the car was travelling at about $25.4\,m\,s^{-1}$ or $91\,km\,h^{-1}$.

3.2 Exercise 2

1 A car of mass 1500 kg is travelling at 150 km h^{-1}. Considering this motion only, and neglecting any energy associated with rotation of moving parts of the car, how much kinetic energy does the car possess? Give your answer in joules.

If the car's brakes are applied, locking the wheels and causing the car to skid to a halt in 100 metres, what is the average retarding force due to friction between the tyres and the road?

2 A bullet of mass 15 grams passes horizontally through a piece of wood 2 cm thick. If its speed is reduced from 500 m s^{-1} to 300 m s^{-1}, find the average resistive force exerted by the wood.

3 A car of mass 1 tonne accelerates with a constant acceleration from 0 to 108 km h^{-1} in 15 seconds. Find the net forward force on the car. If the engine is then switched off and the car is allowed to come to rest under the action of a resistive force of 500 newtons, find the total distance travelled by the car.

4 A car of mass 800 kg is capable of producing a net force of 3100 newtons in first gear, 2000 newtons in second gear, 1500 newtons in third gear and 1100 newtons in top gear. Find the speed attained if the car is driven from rest for 10 metres in first, 20 metres in second, 30 metres in third and 40 metres in top gear.

5 A van of mass 2250 kg hit a low obstruction which caused it to turn on its side and slide 32 metres before hitting a barrier. Impact tests suggest that it hit the barrier at 50 km h^{-1}. Tests involving towing the remains of the van, on its side, on the same road surface in similar conditions, suggest that the friction forces retarding the sliding van amount to about 2×10^4 newtons.
At approximately what speed did the van start to slide on its side?

6 Find the kinetic energy of the Earth due to its motion around the Sun. (You may assume the mass of the Earth to be 6.04×10^{24} kg, the mean radius of its orbit to be 1.5×10^8 km and the length of the year to be 365 days.)

3.2.3 Work done by a variable force

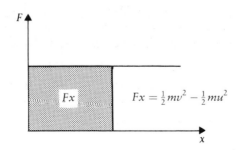

For a constant force **F**, acting in the direction of the displacement x, the area under the (displacement, force) graph is the work done and equals the change in kinetic energy. Considering a (displacement, force) graph will help you to see how to calculate the work done by a variable force.

3 .2c

A car of mass 1 tonne, starting from rest, experiences a net forward force **F** (taking account of resistances to motion). During the first 50 metres of motion, the force is as given in the table below.

Distance travelled (metres), x	5	15	25	35	45
Net forward force (newtons), F	3800	3675	3500	3275	3000

1 Estimate the speed of the car after it has travelled 10, 20, 30, 40 and 50 metres.

2 How would you expect the result
$$Fx = \tfrac{1}{2}mv^2 - \tfrac{1}{2}mu^2$$
to generalise for a variable force?

You saw earlier that the area under a (time, force) graph represents the **change in momentum**.

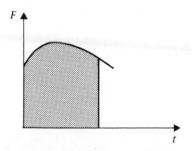

$$\int F \, dt = m\mathbf{v} - m\mathbf{u}$$

For a constant force, this simplifies to

$$\mathbf{F}t = m\mathbf{v} - m\mathbf{u}$$

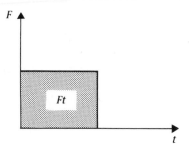

Similarly, for a force *in the direction of displacement*, the area under a (displacement, force) graph represents **work done** and equals the **change in kinetic energy** (which is a scalar quantity).

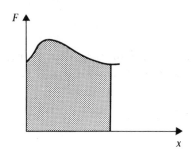

$$\int F\,\mathrm{d}x = \tfrac{1}{2}mv^2 - \tfrac{1}{2}mu^2$$

For a constant force, this simplifies to

$$Fx = \tfrac{1}{2}mv^2 - \tfrac{1}{2}mu^2$$

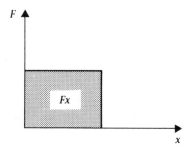

The change in momentum and the change in kinetic energy equations can both be shown to be integrals of Newton's second law of motion, $\mathbf{F} = m\mathbf{a}$. It is often considerably easier to apply these equations than to use Newton's second law.

The work–energy equation for straight-line motion may be derived using calculus as follows.

For straight-line motion, Newton's second law can be written as

$$F = m\frac{\mathrm{d}v}{\mathrm{d}t}$$

$$= m\frac{\mathrm{d}v}{\mathrm{d}x}\frac{\mathrm{d}x}{\mathrm{d}t}$$

$$= mv\frac{\mathrm{d}v}{\mathrm{d}x}, \quad \text{since } \frac{\mathrm{d}x}{\mathrm{d}t} = v$$

$$\Rightarrow \int F\,\mathrm{d}x = \int mv\frac{\mathrm{d}v}{\mathrm{d}x}\,\mathrm{d}x$$

$$= \int mv\,\mathrm{d}v$$

$$= \left[\tfrac{1}{2}mv^2\right]_u^v$$

$$= \tfrac{1}{2}mv^2 - \tfrac{1}{2}mu^2$$

Example 4

A car of mass 1 tonne, starting from rest, experiences a resultant force F newtons. During the first 50 metres of motion, the force is related to the distance travelled, x, by the relationship $F = 4025 - x^2$.

Calculate the speed of the car after it has travelled 50 metres.

Solution

$$\text{Total work done} = \int_0^{50} (4025 - x^2)\,\mathrm{d}x$$

$$= \left[4025x - \tfrac{1}{3}x^3\right]_0^{50} \approx 159\,600\,\mathrm{J}$$

Total work done = change in kinetic energy

$$159\,600 = \tfrac{1}{2} \times 1000 \times v^2 - 0 \quad \Rightarrow \quad 319.2 = v^2$$

The speed is approximately $17.9\,\mathrm{m\,s^{-1}}$.

3.2 Exercise 3

1 An object of mass 10 kg is accelerated from rest by a machine with the following force–distance relationship.

Distance (metres)	0	1	2	3	4	5	6	7	8
Force (newtons)	400	300	240	210	190	160	130	80	0

Estimate the speed of the object at intervals of one metre during the thrust.

2 The effective force forward, F newtons, on a van of mass 1.4 tonnes accelerating from rest, is given by the equation $F = 4000 - 22.5x - 0.25x^2$, where x metres is the distance travelled from rest.

Find, by integration, the speed achieved by the van when it has gone 50 metres.

3 A car of mass 1 tonne starts from rest on a level road. The net forward force initially is 3300 newtons but this falls linearly with the distance travelled so that after 200 metres its value is zero. Find the force in terms of x. Hence find the speed of the car every 50 metres and sketch a graph to show the relationship between the speed and the distance travelled.

4 A stone is dropped down a well and takes 3 seconds to reach the bottom. Find the speed with which the stone hits the bottom. Use the work–energy equation to find the depth of the well. [Take $g = 10 \, \text{m s}^{-2}$.]

3.2.4 Collisions

In earlier work you saw that momentum is conserved. However, knowledge of this fact alone will not enable you to predict the outcome of collisions, as illustrated in the following three cases.

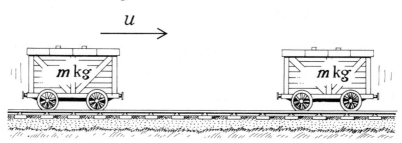

	Before collision	After collision
Collision (i)	$\boxed{m} \mapsto u \quad \boxed{m}$	$\boxed{m} \qquad \boxed{m} \mapsto u$
Collision (ii)	$\boxed{m} \mapsto u \quad \boxed{m}$	$\boxed{m} \mapsto \dfrac{u}{2} \quad \boxed{m} \mapsto \dfrac{u}{2}$
Collision (iii)	$\boxed{m} \mapsto u \quad \boxed{m}$	$\boxed{m} \mapsto \dfrac{u}{4} \quad \boxed{m} \mapsto \dfrac{3u}{4}$

3 .2D

1 Check that momentum is conserved in all three collisions.

2 The three collisions involve the trucks:

    (a) coupling together,   (b) using spring buffers,

    (c) using cork buffers.

    Which is which?

3 Is kinetic energy conserved in any or all of these collisions?

Although momentum is always conserved, you have seen that the same is not necessarily true for kinetic energy.

> Kinetic energy is always lost when two bodies collide. However, it is useful to consider an idealised collision in which there is no loss of kinetic energy, called a **perfectly elastic collision.**

If two objects collide along a straight line and if you can assume that both kinetic energy and momentum are conserved, then it is not too difficult to obtain an interesting and very useful result.

Consider the following collision where both kinetic energy and momentum are conserved.

Speed of approach $= u_1 - u_2$ Speed of separation $= v_2 - v_1$

$\boxed{m_1} \rightarrow u_1$ $\boxed{m_2} \rightarrow u_2$ $\boxed{m_1} \rightarrow v_1$ $\boxed{m_2} \rightarrow v_2$

Kinetic energy: $\frac{1}{2}m_1u_1{}^2 + \frac{1}{2}m_2u_2{}^2 = \frac{1}{2}m_1v_1{}^2 + \frac{1}{2}m_2v_2{}^2$

Momentum: $m_1u_1 + m_2u_2 = m_1v_1 + m_2v_2$

$\Rightarrow \quad m_1(u_1{}^2 - v_1{}^2) = m_2(v_2{}^2 - u_2{}^2)$ and $m_1(u_1 - v_1) = m_2(v_2 - u_2)$

$\Rightarrow \quad \dfrac{m_1(u_1{}^2 - v_1{}^2)}{m_1(u_1 - v_1)} = \dfrac{m_2(v_2{}^2 - u_2{}^2)}{m_2(v_2 - u_2)}$

$\Rightarrow \quad \dfrac{(u_1 - v_1)(u_1 + v_1)}{(u_1 - v_1)} = \dfrac{(v_2 - u_2)(v_2 + u_2)}{(v_2 - u_2)}$

$\Rightarrow \quad u_1 + v_1 = v_2 + u_2$

$\Rightarrow \quad u_1 - u_2 = v_2 - v_1$

This result shows that the speed of separation is the *same* as the speed of approach. Although the analysis above only considers the particular case when the velocities before and after collision are all in the same direction, you can see by imagining negative values for some of the velocities that it is true for all perfectly elastic collisions.

In a perfectly elastic collision, the speed with which the colliding objects separate is the *same* as the speed with which they initially approached each other.

> For a perfectly elastic collision,
>
> $$\text{Speed of separation} = \text{Speed of approach}$$

This fact, together with the principle of conservation of momentum, can be used to predict the outcome of perfectly elastic collisions.

Example 5

Predict the outcome of this collision between trucks with spring buffers.

$$\boxed{3m} \longmapsto u \qquad \boxed{m}$$

Solution

Assume the collision is perfectly elastic so the speed of separation must also be u.

$$\boxed{3m} \longmapsto v \qquad \boxed{m} \longmapsto v + u$$

For conservation of momentum,

$$3mv + m(v + u) = 3mu$$

$$\Rightarrow \quad 3v + v + u = 3u$$

$$\Rightarrow \quad 4v = 2u$$

$$\Rightarrow \quad v = \frac{u}{2}$$

giving speeds of $\dfrac{u}{2}$ and $\dfrac{3u}{2}$, as shown.

$$\boxed{3m} \longmapsto \frac{u}{2} \qquad \boxed{m} \longmapsto \frac{3u}{2}$$

3.2 Exercise 4

1 Consider the following three perfectly elastic collisions between trucks which each have spring buffers.

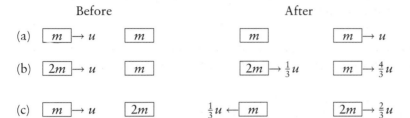

         Before   After

(a) $m \to u$ m m $m \to u$

(b) $2m \to u$ m $2m \to \frac{1}{3}u$ $m \to \frac{4}{3}u$

(c) $m \to u$ $2m$ $\frac{1}{3}u \leftarrow m$ $2m \to \frac{2}{3}u$

For each of the collisions above, show that:

 (i) momentum is conserved;   (ii) kinetic energy is conserved;

(iii) speed of separation = speed of approach.

2 (a) Two trucks, each of mass m, approach each other from opposite directions, each travelling with speed v. Assuming the collision to be perfectly elastic, what will be the speed of each truck after the collision?

  (b) If the experiment is repeated with one of the trucks now having speed u, what will be the velocity of each truck after the collision?

  (c) Compare the total kinetic energy of the two trucks before and after each collision.

▶ 3.2 **Tasksheet 1E – Sporting collisions (page 362)**

After working through section 3.2, you should know that:

1 for one-dimensional motion, the area under a (time, force) graph represents the change in momentum or impulse,

$$\int F \, dt = m\mathbf{v} - m\mathbf{u}$$

2 for one-dimensional motion, the area under a (displacement, force) graph represents work done and equals the change in kinetic energy, and

$$\int F \, dx = \tfrac{1}{2}mv^2 - \tfrac{1}{2}mu^2$$

3 momentum is conserved in all collisions, but kinetic energy is conserved only in a perfectly elastic collision;

4 in a perfectly elastic collision, the speed of separation is equal to the speed of approach.

3 Towards circular motion

.3 Using scalar products

3.3.1 Work done in two dimensions

This section extends the ideas of 'work done' into two dimensions.

Example 1
A lifebelt is thrown horizontally from a ship and lands in the water near a swimmer.

The only force acting is gravity and so $\dfrac{\mathrm{d}\mathbf{v}}{\mathrm{d}t} = \begin{bmatrix} 0 \\ -g \end{bmatrix}$.

The initial velocity is $\begin{bmatrix} u \\ 0 \end{bmatrix}$,

so $\mathbf{v} = \begin{bmatrix} u \\ 0 \end{bmatrix} + \begin{bmatrix} 0 \\ -gt \end{bmatrix} = \begin{bmatrix} u \\ -gt \end{bmatrix}$, by integration.

Similarly, $\mathbf{r} = \begin{bmatrix} 0 \\ 0 \end{bmatrix} + \begin{bmatrix} ut \\ -\frac{1}{2}gt^2 \end{bmatrix}$, taking $\mathbf{r} = \begin{bmatrix} 0 \\ 0 \end{bmatrix}$ when $t = 0$.

3 .3A

The deck of the ship is 20 metres above sea level and the lifebelt has mass 3 kg. Assume $g = 10\,\mathrm{N\,kg^{-1}}$.

Suppose the lifebelt is projected horizontally with speed:

(a) $10\,\mathrm{m\,s^{-1}}$ (b) $20\,\mathrm{m\,s^{-1}}$ (c) $30\,\mathrm{m\,s^{-1}}$ (d) $u\,\mathrm{m\,s^{-1}}$

For each speed of projection calculate:

(i) the displacement vector, **r**, of the swimmer from the deck;

(ii) the change in the kinetic energy of the lifebelt from the point of projection to when it lands in the water.

What does this suggest about work done on the belt during this time?

Calculate the work done by gravity if the lifebelt is *dropped* from the deck into the sea.

You have seen that, in one dimension, the work done by the resultant force acting on a body is equal to the change in kinetic energy of the body.
For projectile motion, if you ignore air resistance, gravity is the only force acting. The work done by gravity is independent of the horizontal displacement of the body and is equal to the change in kinetic energy. When several forces act on a body, each force may do work. However, the change in kinetic energy is caused by the work done by the resultant force. In the situation above, only one force is assumed to be acting, so the work done by gravity is equal to the change in kinetic energy.

In addition, in one-dimensional situations, the work done by a constant force was defined as force × distance.

A ← $\xrightarrow{\textbf{F}}$ - - - - - - - → B   Work done $= F \times d$
　　 d

In the example of the lifebelt, even though the direction of the motion was not the same as the direction of the force acting, work was done by gravity to change the kinetic energy of the belt. You saw that

work done = magnitude of weight × vertical distance travelled

In general, the work done by a constant force is defined as the product of the magnitude of the force and the distance moved in the direction of the force.

The work done is $F \times d = Fr\cos\theta$

Example 1

A child of mass 30 kg is sliding down a slide of length 4 metres inclined at 40° to the vertical. What work does the gravitational force do?

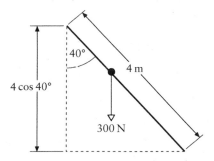

Solution

Work done $= Fr \cos \theta$

$$= 300 \times 4 \cos 40°$$

$$\approx 900 \, \text{joules}$$

3.3 Exercise 1

Take $g = 10 \, \text{m} \, \text{s}^{-2}$.

1 A ski-jumper of mass 75 kg is practising on a dry ski slope. He travels 35 metres down a slope inclined at 55° to the vertical. What is the work done by gravity?

2 A trolley of mass 15 kg is pulled up a ramp, inclined at 25° to the horizontal, by means of a rope parallel to the slope. If the tension in the rope is 100 newtons, find the work done by this force when the trolley is raised 5 metres vertically.

3 A sledge of mass 10 kg slides 25 metres down a slope. If the work done by gravity is 500 joules, what is the angle of elevation of the slope?

4 A girl of mass 50 kg walks 100 metres up a slope of 30° to the horizontal. What is the work done against gravity?

3.3.2 The scalar product

The work done by a constant force **F** displaced through a vector **r** is written as **F** · **r** (read as **F** 'dot' r) and is called the **scalar product** of vectors **F** and **r**. (It is called a product because it involves multiplication and it is called a scalar because the result is *not* a vector.)

Example 2

Calculate the scalar product $\mathbf{F} \cdot \mathbf{r}$ in the following instances.

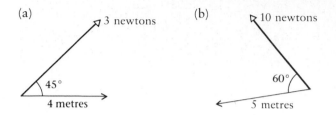

(a)   3 newtons   (b)   10 newtons

45°   4 metres

60°   5 metres

Solution

(a) $\mathbf{F} \cdot \mathbf{r} = 3 \times 4 \times \cos 45° = 8.5$ joules

(b) $\mathbf{F} \cdot \mathbf{r} = 10 \times 5 \times \cos 60° = 25$ joules

Example 3

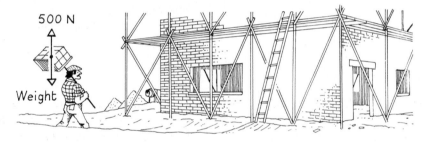

500 N

Weight

A labourer has to move bricks from the ground floor to the first floor of a building. Using a hod to carry the bricks, he walks up a 4 metre slope of angle 15° and then climbs a 5 metre ladder inclined at 70° attached to the scaffolding. The force he exerts on the bricks is modelled as a constant vertical force of magnitude 500 newtons.

What is the work done by the 500 newton force acting on the bricks?

5 m

70°

4 m

15°

Solution

Total work done $= 500 \times 4 \cos 75° + 500 \times 5 \cos 20°$

$\qquad\qquad\qquad = 518 + 2349 = 2867$ joules

The work done can also be found by the following method.

The bricks are raised to a total height of

$$4 \sin 15° + 5 \sin 70° = 5.734 \text{ metres}$$

The work done is therefore $500 \times 5.734 = 2867$ joules.

The work done by a constant force **F** when displaced through a vector **r** is

$$\mathbf{F} \cdot \mathbf{r} = Fr \cos \theta$$

where θ is the angle between the directions of **F** and **r**.

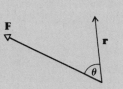

In example 3, the work done by the 500 N force acting on the bricks as they are displaced up the first incline is:

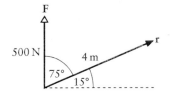

Work done $= 500 \times 4 \cos 75°$

$$= \mathbf{F} \cdot \mathbf{r}$$

Properties of the scalar product are investigated in the following questions.

 .3B

1 A man pulls a 20 kg block along a smooth horizontal surface. He exerts a tension of 200 newtons in the chain. Find the work done by the tension in moving the block 4 metres along the surface when the chain makes an angle with the surface of:

(a) 0°   (b) 30°   (c) 60°

2 Judith calculates the scalar product of the two vectors shown as

$$5 \times 7 \times \cos 60°$$

Her friend Carole says the angle between the vectors is 300° and therefore calculates the scalar product as

$$5 \times 7 \times \cos 300°$$

Who is right?

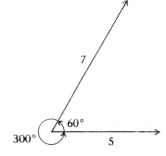

3 A 3.5 kg mass is pulled up a slope inclined at 30° to the horizontal.

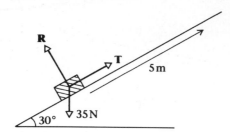

(a) What is the work done by the normal contact force when the mass moves 5 metres up the slope?

(b) What is the work done by the weight in moving 5 metres up the slope?

4 A box is pulled 2 metres across the floor with a force of 30 newtons.

(a) What is the work done by the force?

The box is then pushed back to its original position by a force of 30 newtons.

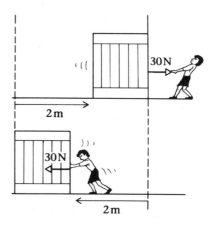

(b) What is the work done by this force?

(c) What can you say about the size and direction of these forces and displacements?

(d) Explain why $(-\mathbf{p}) \cdot (-\mathbf{q}) = \mathbf{p} \cdot \mathbf{q}$ for any vectors $\mathbf{p}$ and $\mathbf{q}$.

5 (a) A vertical force of 7 newtons lifts a box 7 metres vertically. What is the work done by this force?

(b) What is $\mathbf{p} \cdot \mathbf{p}$ if $\mathbf{p}$ is any vector?

6 It is estimated that a vertical force of 500 newtons is needed to lift bricks 5 metres up a ramp inclined at 25° to the horizontal.

(a) What would be the work done by the force?

(b) How much more work would be done if the bricks had to be moved three times as far up the ramp?

(c) What would happen to your calculation of work done in part (a) if the force needed to lift the bricks was found to be twice as much as originally estimated?

(d) How much more work would be done if the force were doubled *and* the distance was three times as far?

(e) Show that $(k\mathbf{p}) \cdot (l\mathbf{q}) = kl(\mathbf{p} \cdot \mathbf{q})$ for any vectors $\mathbf{p}$ and $\mathbf{q}$ and scalars l and k.

7 A suitcase of mass 10 kg slides
   4 metres down a smooth ramp
   inclined at 25° to the
   horizontal and then 6 metres
   down another smooth ramp
   inclined at 10° to the
   horizontal.

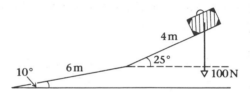

   What is the total work done by the weight of the suitcase?

8 The two ramps in question 7 are replaced by a single ramp (with the same
   starting and finishing points) and an identical suitcase slides down it.

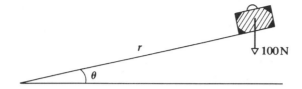

   (a) Find r and θ.

   (b) Find the work done by the weight of the suitcase.

   (c) The identity $\mathbf{p} \cdot (\mathbf{q} + \mathbf{r}) = \mathbf{p} \cdot \mathbf{q} + \mathbf{p} \cdot \mathbf{r}$ is valid for any three vectors $\mathbf{p}$,
        $\mathbf{q}$ and $\mathbf{r}$. Explain how your answers to the questions above support this
        statement.

9 A builder can lift bricks with a vertical force of 500 newtons, either up a
   ramp 5 metres long inclined at 30° to the horizontal, or up another ramp
   4 metres long inclined at 48.6° to the horizontal. What would be the
   difference in the work done by the force?

Some of the results investigated in 3.3B above are listed here.

Suppose that a force $\mathbf{F}$ is displaced through a vector $\mathbf{r}$.

- When $\theta = 0°$ the work done is Fr.

  If the force and displacement are
  in the same direction then the
  work done is simply force
  multiplied by distance.

- When $\theta = 90°$ the work done is zero.

  If the direction of the force and
  displacement are at right angles
  to each other, then the distance
  moved in the direction of the
  force is zero and no work is
  done.

- $(k\mathbf{F}) \cdot \mathbf{r} = kFr \cos\theta$
  $$= Fkr \cos\theta$$
  $$= \mathbf{F} \cdot k\mathbf{r}$$
  $$= k(\mathbf{F} \cdot \mathbf{r})$$

If the magnitude of either the force or the displacement is increased by a factor of k, then the work done is also increased by a factor of k.

- $\mathbf{F} \cdot (\mathbf{r} + \mathbf{s}) = \mathbf{F} \cdot \mathbf{r} + \mathbf{F} \cdot \mathbf{s}$

  Work done from A to C $= \mathbf{F} \cdot (\mathbf{r} + \mathbf{s})$
  Work done from A to B $= \mathbf{F} \cdot \mathbf{r}$
  Work done from B to C $= \mathbf{F} \cdot \mathbf{s}$

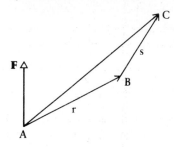

- $\mathbf{F} \cdot \mathbf{r} = F \times r \cos\theta$
  $$= r \times F \cos\theta$$
  $$= \mathbf{r} \cdot \mathbf{F}$$

Work done is also the component of the force in the direction moved multiplied by the distance moved.

Example 4

A trolley of mass 2 kg is pulled along the floor by a string held at an angle of 30° to the horizontal.

If the tension in the string is 40 newtons, find the work done by this force in pulling the trolley 3 metres across the floor.

Solution

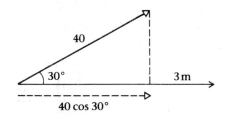

Work done $= \mathbf{r} \cdot \mathbf{F}$
$$= rF \cos\theta$$
$$= 3 \times 40 \cos 30°$$
$$= 103.9 \text{ J}$$

3.3 **Exercise 2**

1 A force of 5 newtons acts on a particle at A, which is displaced 4 metres along AB.

(a) Calculate the work done by the force.

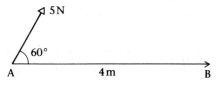

(b) If the direction of the force is reversed but the displacement remains the same, i.e. $\overrightarrow{AB}$, calculate the work done by this new force.

2 Calculate the scalar product of the following pairs of vectors.

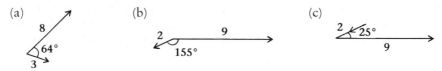

(a)
8
64°
3

(b)
2
9
155°

(c)
2 25°
9

3 A roller is pulled 7 metres across a cricket pitch. The handle is pulled with a force of 100 newtons at an angle of 70° to the vertical.

(a) What is the work done by this force?

(b) What is the work done if the handle is pushed with the same force?

4 A horse pulls a barge of mass 30 tonnes along a canal by means of a rope which makes an angle of 20° with the direction of the barge.

If the tension in the rope is 200 newtons, find the work done by this force in pulling the barge 1 km.

3.3.3 Using column vectors

Vectors are often used in *component* form, where the components of the vector are expressed in a column vector. For example, suppose a force $\mathbf{F} = \begin{bmatrix} 3 \\ 3 \end{bmatrix}$ newtons moves its point of application through a displacement $\mathbf{r} = \begin{bmatrix} 0 \\ 4 \end{bmatrix}$ metres. What is the work done by the force $\mathbf{F}$?

A diagram will help you see what is going on.

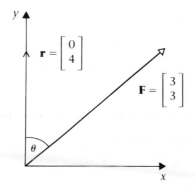

You could tackle the problem by working out the magnitude and direction of each of the two vectors as shown earlier, i.e.

$$F = \sqrt{(9+9)}, \quad r = 4, \quad \theta = 45°, \quad \sqrt{18} \times 4 \times \cos 45° = 12\,\text{N m}$$

Can the problem be tackled in component form?

You know that a force $\mathbf{F} = \begin{bmatrix} a \\ b \end{bmatrix}$ can be replaced

by component forces $\mathbf{a} = \begin{bmatrix} a \\ 0 \end{bmatrix}$ and $\mathbf{b} = \begin{bmatrix} 0 \\ b \end{bmatrix}$

as shown. Similarly, a displacement $\mathbf{r} = \begin{bmatrix} c \\ d \end{bmatrix}$

can be written as $\mathbf{r} = \mathbf{c} + \mathbf{d}$ where $\mathbf{c} = \begin{bmatrix} c \\ 0 \end{bmatrix}$

and $\mathbf{d} = \begin{bmatrix} 0 \\ d \end{bmatrix}$.

So $\mathbf{F} \cdot \mathbf{r} = (\mathbf{a} + \mathbf{b}) \cdot (\mathbf{c} + \mathbf{d})$

$= \mathbf{a} \cdot \mathbf{c} + \mathbf{a} \cdot \mathbf{d} + \mathbf{b} \cdot \mathbf{c} + \mathbf{b} \cdot \mathbf{d}$

$= ac \cos 0° + ad \cos 90° + bc \cos 90° + bd \cos 0°$

$= ac + bd$

Applying this method to the example above,

work done $= 3 \times 0 + 3 \times 4 = 12$ joules

Since the magnitudes and angles do not need to be calculated to find the work done, the actual arithmetic is simpler and there is less likelihood of error.

When a force $\mathbf{F} = \begin{bmatrix} a \\ b \end{bmatrix}$ moves its point of application a distance $\mathbf{r} = \begin{bmatrix} x \\ y \end{bmatrix}$ then the work done by the force is

$$\mathbf{F} \cdot \mathbf{r} = \begin{bmatrix} a \\ b \end{bmatrix} \cdot \begin{bmatrix} x \\ y \end{bmatrix} = ax + by$$

That is, the value of the work done is obtained by first multiplying the corresponding elements together and then summing the results.

Example 5

A particle is acted upon by two forces $\begin{bmatrix} 3 \\ 4 \end{bmatrix}$ and $\begin{bmatrix} 5 \\ -12 \end{bmatrix}$ newtons. If it is displaced through $\begin{bmatrix} 16 \\ -16 \end{bmatrix}$ metres, find the work done by each of the forces.

Solution

Work done by the $\begin{bmatrix} 3 \\ 4 \end{bmatrix}$ force is

$$\begin{bmatrix} 3 \\ 4 \end{bmatrix} \cdot \begin{bmatrix} 16 \\ -16 \end{bmatrix} = 48 + -64 = -16 \text{ joules}$$

Work done by the $\begin{bmatrix} 5 \\ -12 \end{bmatrix}$ force is

$$\begin{bmatrix} 5 \\ -12 \end{bmatrix} \cdot \begin{bmatrix} 16 \\ -16 \end{bmatrix} = 80 + 192 = 272 \text{ joules}$$

3.3 Exercise 3

1 Find the work done when a force **F** newtons acts on a particle which subsequently moves through a displacement **r** metres where:

(a) $\mathbf{F} = \begin{bmatrix} 2 \\ 4 \end{bmatrix}$, $\mathbf{r} = \begin{bmatrix} 12 \\ -4 \end{bmatrix}$ (b) $\mathbf{F} = \begin{bmatrix} 1 \\ -2 \end{bmatrix}$, $\mathbf{r} = \begin{bmatrix} -3 \\ 4 \end{bmatrix}$

2 A force of $\begin{bmatrix} 3 \\ -5 \end{bmatrix}$ newtons acts on a particle moving parallel to the vector $\begin{bmatrix} 5 \\ 12 \end{bmatrix}$. If the work done by the force is 90 joules, what is the distance travelled?

3 Forces of $\begin{bmatrix} 3 \\ -3 \end{bmatrix}$ and $\begin{bmatrix} 9 \\ 15 \end{bmatrix}$ newtons act on a particle. If its displacement is parallel to the resultant of the two forces and the total work done by both forces is 120 joules, find the displacement.

4 A particle of mass 5 kg is moved 12 metres down a slope inclined at an angle θ to the horizontal where $\tan \theta = 0.75$. Find the work done by:

(a) the gravitational force, assuming $g = 10 \, \text{m s}^{-2}$;

(b) the normal contact force.

5 The work done by a force **F** displaced through vector **r** is $Fr \cos \theta$.

(a) 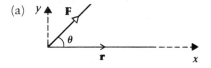 (b)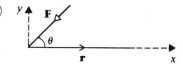

Does the definition $\mathbf{F} \cdot \mathbf{r} = Fr \cos \theta$ hold for both of these diagrams?

3.3.4 Work done by several forces

A stationary engine pulls a load at a constant speed up a slope with gradient 1 in 4. The load is pulled along a channel which has been smoothed by the constant passage of material, so that the frictional force opposing the motion of the load is negligible. The load is pulled from A to B.

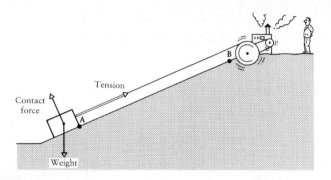

The forces acting on the load are shown below in column vector form. The forces are measured in newtons and the displacement in metres.

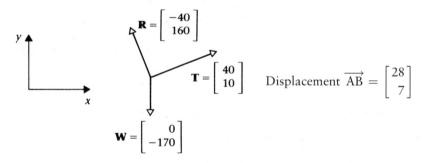

How can you calculate the total work done on the load?

The work done by the separate forces is

$$\text{work done by force } \mathbf{R} = \begin{bmatrix} -40 \\ 160 \end{bmatrix} \cdot \begin{bmatrix} 28 \\ 7 \end{bmatrix}$$

$$= -1120 + 1120 = 0 \text{ joules}$$

$$\text{work done by force } \mathbf{T} = \begin{bmatrix} 40 \\ 10 \end{bmatrix} \cdot \begin{bmatrix} 28 \\ 7 \end{bmatrix}$$

$$= 1120 + 70 = 1190 \text{ joules}$$

$$\text{work done by force } \mathbf{W} = \begin{bmatrix} 0 \\ -170 \end{bmatrix} \cdot \begin{bmatrix} 28 \\ 7 \end{bmatrix}$$

$$= -1190 \text{ joules}$$

So the total work done on the load is

$$\text{total work done} = 0 + 1190 + (-1190)$$

$$= 0 \text{ joules}$$

But if the separate forces are replaced by a single *resultant* force, you can see why no work is done.

$$\text{Resultant force} = \begin{bmatrix} -40 \\ 160 \end{bmatrix} + \begin{bmatrix} 40 \\ 10 \end{bmatrix} + \begin{bmatrix} 0 \\ -170 \end{bmatrix}$$

$$= \begin{bmatrix} 0 \\ 0 \end{bmatrix} \text{newtons}$$

The work done by the resultant force is $\begin{bmatrix} 0 \\ 0 \end{bmatrix} \cdot \begin{bmatrix} 28 \\ 7 \end{bmatrix} = 0$ joules.

In this example it appears that the work done by the resultant force is equal to the sum of the work done by the individual forces. This is explored further in the following questions.

 .3c

1 Three forces of $\begin{bmatrix} 2 \\ 3 \end{bmatrix}$, $\begin{bmatrix} 4 \\ -1 \end{bmatrix}$ and $\begin{bmatrix} -3 \\ -2 \end{bmatrix}$ newtons act on a particle which is displaced $\begin{bmatrix} 5 \\ 7 \end{bmatrix}$ metres.

   (a) Calculate the work done by each of these forces.

   (b) What is the resultant of the three forces?

   (c) Calculate the work done by the resultant force.

   (d) What is the connection between your answers to (a) and (c)?

2 Repeat question 1 for any three (or more) forces and a displacement of your own choice.

3 Four forces of $\begin{bmatrix} 3 \\ 2 \end{bmatrix}$, $\begin{bmatrix} 4 \\ -8 \end{bmatrix}$, $\begin{bmatrix} 2 \\ -6 \end{bmatrix}$ and $\begin{bmatrix} 3 \\ 6 \end{bmatrix}$ newtons act on an object which is displaced $\begin{bmatrix} 6 \\ -3 \end{bmatrix}$ metres.

   (a) Find the work done by each force.

   (b) Find the work done by the resultant of the four forces.

   (c) One of the forces does no work. What can you say about its direction?

4 Two forces of $\begin{bmatrix} 22 \\ -4 \end{bmatrix}$ and $\begin{bmatrix} -6 \\ -8 \end{bmatrix}$ newtons act on an object.

Calculate the work done if the object moves 30 cm in the direction $\begin{bmatrix} 4 \\ -3 \end{bmatrix}$.

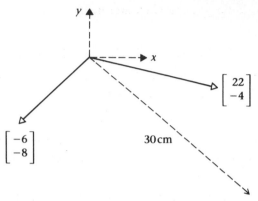

Several of the forces acting on an object may do work on the object, but it is the *total* work done by all the forces on the object which accounts for its final change in kinetic energy.

> The energy equation
>
> $$\text{Work done} = \text{Change in kinetic energy}$$
>
> refers to the work done on an object by the *resultant* force.

This result follows directly from the **distributive law**.

Consider two forces **S** and **T** acting on an object. If the displacement of the object is **r**, then

$$\mathbf{S} \cdot \mathbf{r} + \mathbf{T} \cdot \mathbf{r} = (\mathbf{S} + \mathbf{T}) \cdot \mathbf{r}$$

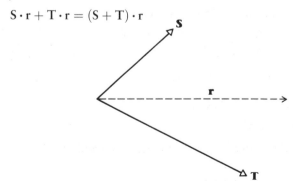

The sum of the work done by each of the two forces equals the work done by the resultant of the two forces.

It is often necessary to calculate the change in kinetic energy of an object when solving certain types of problem.

When calculating the change in kinetic energy you can either:

(a) calculate the work done by the resultant force;

or

(b) calculate the sum of the work done by the individual forces.

In complicated examples the second method is often preferred, especially if you can identify one of the forces as 'doing no work'.

Example 6

A swimmer of weight 700 newtons slides into a swimming pool down a 5 metre long straight chute inclined at 30° to the horizontal. (Assume a constant friction force of 100 newtons.)

(a) Draw a diagram showing the forces acting on the swimmer.

(b) With what speed does the swimmer enter the water?

Solution

(a)

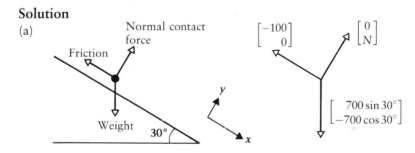

(b) The displacement is $\begin{bmatrix} 5 \\ 0 \end{bmatrix}$.

To calculate the speed of the swimmer you must calculate the total work done and hence the change in kinetic energy (KE).

$$\text{Work done} = \begin{bmatrix} 700\sin 30° \\ -700\cos 30° \end{bmatrix} \cdot \begin{bmatrix} 5 \\ 0 \end{bmatrix} + \begin{bmatrix} -100 \\ 0 \end{bmatrix} \cdot \begin{bmatrix} 5 \\ 0 \end{bmatrix} + \begin{bmatrix} 0 \\ N \end{bmatrix} \cdot \begin{bmatrix} 5 \\ 0 \end{bmatrix}$$

$$= 1750 - 500 + 0 \text{ joules}$$

Total work done $= 1250$ joules

So change in KE $= 1250$

But change in KE $= \frac{1}{2}mv^2 - \frac{1}{2}mu^2$ where $u = 0$ and $m = 70$

so $v^2 = \dfrac{2 \times 1250}{70}$

$v = 6.0 \,\text{m s}^{-1}$

3.3 Exercise 4

When answering the following questions state clearly what simplifying assumptions you make. Take $g = 10\,\text{m s}^{-2}$.

1 A ski slope consists of three parts, as shown in the diagram. A skier, mass 80 kg, starts from rest at A.

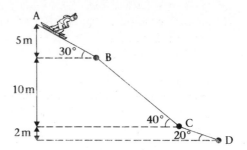

(a) What work is done at each stage?

(b) What work is done altogether?

(c) What is the skier's speed at D?

2 A man cycles 50 metres up a slope. The diagram shows a simplified model of the forces acting on the cyclist.

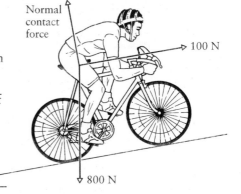

(a) Suggest what causes the 100 newton force up the slope.

(b) Calculate the work done by each of the forces shown in the diagram.

(c) What can you say about the speed with which the man cycles?

3 A girl of weight 450 newtons pulls her small brother, of weight 300 newtons, on a sledge of weight 40 newtons. She pulls him 80 metres along flat ground in a straight line, at a steady speed of $1.2\,\text{m s}^{-1}$, using a rope at $55°$ to the horizontal. Assume the retarding force (friction) is a constant 50 newtons.

(a) Draw a diagram showing the forces acting on the boy.

(b) What is the work done by each of the forces?

4 A toboggan of mass 5 kg slides from rest down a slope inclined at an angle of $\sin^{-1}\left(\tfrac{1}{6}\right)$ to the horizontal. After travelling 80 metres it has reached a speed of $10\,\text{m s}^{-1}$. Find the resistance (assumed to be constant).

5 A particle of mass 10 grams is initially moving with velocity $\begin{bmatrix} 4 \\ 16 \end{bmatrix}\,\text{m s}^{-1}$.

Later, its velocity is $\begin{bmatrix} 8 \\ -20 \end{bmatrix}\,\text{m s}^{-1}$.

Calculate the work that has been done on the particle.

6   A boy lets go of his sports-bag at the top of a grassy slope inclined at 30° to the horizontal. The bag weighs 10 newtons and is released from rest. If it travels 5 metres down the slope against friction and reaches a speed of $4\,\mathrm{m\,s^{-1}}$, show that the force of friction has magnitude 3.4 newtons.

7E A block of mass 6.5 kg is projected with a velocity of $4\,\mathrm{m\,s^{-1}}$ up a line of greatest slope of a rough plane. Calculate the initial kinetic energy of the block.

The coefficient of friction between the block and the plane is $\frac{2}{3}$ and the plane makes an angle θ with the horizontal, where $\sin\theta = \frac{5}{13}$. The block travels a distance of d metres up the plane before coming to rest instantaneously. Express in terms of d:

(a) the work done by gravity;

(b) the work done against friction by the block in coming to rest.

Hence calculate the value of d.

8E A body of mass m is projected up a rough inclined plane with speed $u\,\mathrm{m\,s^{-1}}$ from a point P. It moves up to Q, a distance d from P, and then slides back down to P. Show that:

(a) the total work done by friction is $2\mu mgd\cos\theta$ (where μ is the coefficient of friction and θ is the inclination of the plane to the horizontal);

(b) $u = \sqrt{(2gd(\sin\theta + \mu\cos\theta))}$;

(c) the speed of the body when it returns to P is $\sqrt{(2gd(\sin\theta - \mu\cos\theta))}$.

3.3.5 Variable forces

Not all forces acting on an object do work. If a force acting on an object does no work then its direction must be at right angles to the direction of motion. Not all forces acting on an object will be constant forces. For example, consider the forces acting on a pendulum bob as shown.

The forces acting on the bob of the pendulum are:

(i) the tension in the string, **T**;

(ii) the weight of the bob, **W**.

The weight remains constant, but the tension varies in both magnitude and direction.

The tension force does no work as it is always perpendicular to the direction of motion.

The work done by the weight $= \mathbf{W} \cdot \mathbf{r}$

$$= \begin{bmatrix} 0 \\ -mg \end{bmatrix} \cdot \overrightarrow{AB}$$

$$\overrightarrow{AB} = \begin{bmatrix} -AN \\ -NB \end{bmatrix}$$

$$\begin{bmatrix} 0 \\ -mg \end{bmatrix} \cdot \begin{bmatrix} -AN \\ -NB \end{bmatrix} = mg(NB)$$

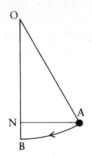

So the work done by the weight $= W \times$ vertical distance between A and B

Example 7

A circus performer (mass 70 kg) swings on a rope of length 8 metres. He starts from rest, holding the rope at A, 1 metre below the point of suspension. The rope is taut throughout. What is his maximum speed?

Solution

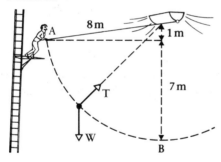

The tension in the rope is a variable force. However, the tension is always perpendicular to the direction of the velocity. Tension therefore does no work.

If air resistance is ignored, the only other force acting on the man is gravity and so it is this force which does the work which changes his kinetic energy.

Assume $g = 10 \, \text{N} \, \text{kg}^{-1} \Rightarrow \mathbf{W} = \begin{bmatrix} 0 \\ -700 \end{bmatrix}$

then $\mathbf{W} \cdot \mathbf{r} = \dfrac{mv^2}{2} - \dfrac{mu^2}{2}$

$\Rightarrow \begin{bmatrix} 0 \\ -700 \end{bmatrix} \cdot \begin{bmatrix} x \\ -7 \end{bmatrix} = \dfrac{70v^2}{2}$ as $u = 0$

$\Rightarrow \qquad 4900 = 35v^2$

$\Rightarrow \qquad v = 11.8 \, \text{m} \, \text{s}^{-1}$

.3D

1 How can you be sure the maximum speed is reached at point B?

2 Would taking the more accurate value $g = 9.81\,\mathrm{N\,kg^{-1}}$ make a big difference to your answer?

3 The man's partner (of smaller mass) performs the same manoeuvre. Will her maximum speed be less than the man's?

A constant force does no work if the direction of its line of action is perpendicular to the displacement of its point of application.

An example is the normal contact force on a straight slide.

A force with variable direction does no work if the object on which it acts has a variable velocity which changes direction in such a way that the direction of the line of application of the force is always perpendicular to the velocity of the object.

An example is the normal contact force on a curved slide.

3.3 Exercise 5

1 A girl (mass 40 kg) swings on the end of a 5 metre rope in a gymnasium. If she initially jumped at $3 \, \mathrm{m \, s^{-1}}$ off a horse 2 metres high on a level 4 metres below the point of suspension of the rope, which was taut, find:

(a) her maximum speed;

(b) her maximum height above the ground.

(c) Did you need to know her mass?

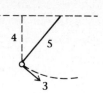

2 A Scout sets up an aerial runway starting from 10 metres up a tree.

(a) If the lowest point is 2 metres off the ground, at what speed will someone using the runway pass that point? (State clearly what assumptions you make.)

(b) If the end of the aerial runway is 4 metres off the ground, with what speed will someone reach this point?

(c) Do you think such a runway would be safe?

3 A force of $\begin{bmatrix} 2 \\ 5 \end{bmatrix}$ newtons moves a bead of mass 0.1 kg along a smooth wire from A $(6, 7)$ to B $(9, 8)$.

(a) Calculate the work done by the force.

(b) If the bead starts from rest, what is its speed at B?

4 The resultant force on a ball of mass 0.2 kg is $\begin{bmatrix} 6 \\ 5 \end{bmatrix}$ newtons. It causes the ball to move from A, $\begin{bmatrix} 6 \\ 7 \end{bmatrix}$ to B, $\begin{bmatrix} 10 \\ 12 \end{bmatrix}$.

(a) Calculate the work done by the force.

(b) What can you say about the velocity of the ball at A?

After working through section 3.3, you should know that:

1 the work done by a constant force **F** is the scalar product **F** · **r** where **r** is the displacement;

$$\text{if } \mathbf{F} = \begin{bmatrix} p \\ q \end{bmatrix} \quad \text{and} \quad \mathbf{r} = \begin{bmatrix} x \\ y \end{bmatrix}$$

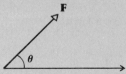

$$\mathbf{F} \cdot \mathbf{r} = Fr\cos\theta = px + qy$$

2 the work done by a force may be calculated as either:
 (i) the magnitude of the force multiplied by the distance moved in the direction of the force,

 or

 (ii) the magnitude of the displacement multiplied by the component of the force acting in the direction of the displacement;

3 the sum of the work done by several forces equals the work done by the resultant force;

4 Change in KE = Total work done by all the forces

3 Towards circular motion

.4 Potential energy

3.4.1 Gravitational potential energy

Push a pencil across the table in a straight line, keeping its speed constant.

Look at the forces involved in this apparently simple action.

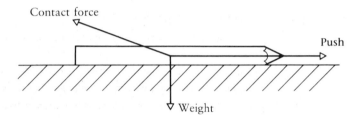

Although only three forces are involved it is sometimes useful to split the contact force into two components, one normal to the table and one parallel to the table.

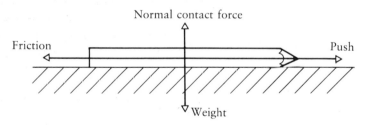

The pencil was stationary before you started to push and it is stationary when you stop pushing, so there is no change in kinetic energy. Does this mean that no work has been done?

As both the normal contact force and the weight are perpendicular to the motion of the pencil, neither do any work and so you should focus on the work done by friction and the work done by the push.

In a simple model of motion you could imagine the pencil going through three distinct stages:

- a (short) period of constant acceleration during which the force provided by the push is greater than that of friction;

- a period of constant velocity during which time the force provided by the push is equal and opposite to that of friction;

- a (short) period of constant deceleration during which time the force of friction is greater than that provided by the push.

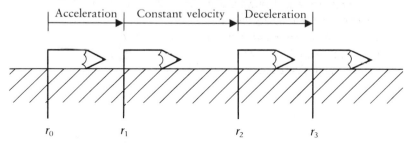

If you take the direction of motion as being positive for the purpose of defining the vectors of force and displacement, then the (displacement, force) graphs will look like this.

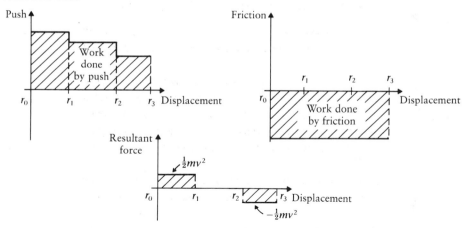

While the force provided by the push does positive work on the pencil, the friction force does negative work because its direction opposes the motion of the pencil. Both forces do work, but the net work done on the pencil is zero and hence there is no change in kinetic energy.

3 .4A

Lift a pencil vertically through a height h.

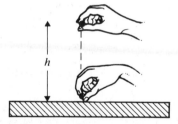

1 What is the total work done?

2 What forces act on the pencil?

3 What is the work done by each force?

You may think that this situation is similar to that of pushing the pencil across the table, but there is one very important difference. When you release the pencil after pushing it across the table, it remains stationary because the friction force vanishes when you stop pushing. When you release the pencil above the table it does not remain stationary. It falls down because gravity is still acting on it. The pencil held at rest above the table has zero kinetic energy, but it can acquire kinetic energy because gravity has the potential to do positive work on it as it falls to the table. For this reason, the pencil is said to have **gravitational potential energy** (PE) *before* it falls.

- The gravitational potential energy (PE) of a body is always measured relative to an arbitrary fixed reference position where its value is taken to be zero. It is defined as the work that would be done by gravity if the body were to move from its present position to the fixed reference position.

- A particle of mass m kg, at height h metres above the floor, has gravitational potential energy mgh N m (or joules) relative to the floor.

$$h \quad \text{PE} = mgh$$

$$mg$$

- If you raise a mass m kg a distance h metres in a vertical direction, you increase the gravitational potential energy by mgh N m, where g is the gravitational force per unit mass.

Example 1
Calculate the gravitational potential energy, relative to the ground, of a 2 kg mass at a height of 3 metres above the ground.

Solution
$$\text{PE} = mgh = 2 \times 10 \times 3$$

$$= 60 \, \text{joules}$$

Note that the mass has this potential energy whether or not it is allowed to fall.

Example 2
A child of mass 20 kg is sitting at the top of a slide of length 4 metres which is inclined at 25° to the horizontal. Find her gravitational potential energy relative to B. (Take $g = 9.8 \, \text{N} \, \text{kg}^{-1}$.)

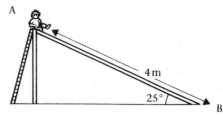

Solution

The child's height above B is $4 \sin 25°$ metres.

So her $PE = 20g \times (4 \sin 25°)$

$\qquad\qquad = 331 \text{ joules}$

3.4 Exercise 1

Take $g = 10 \, \text{N kg}^{-1}$.

1 Calculate the gravitational potential energy, relative to the ground, of a particle of mass 5 kg if it is 2 metres above the ground.

2 Calculate the gravitational potential energy, relative to the ground, of a child of mass 30 kg sitting at the top of a slide of length 5 metres and inclined at 36° to the horizontal.

3 A circus performer of mass 70 kg swings on a rope of length 8 metres.

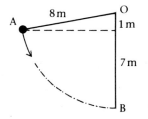

Calculate the change in his potential energy as he moves from A to B.

4 (a) Calculate the work done by gravity (to the nearest joule) when a 50 kg hod of bricks is carried up a ramp which has length l and is inclined at an angle θ to the horizontal if:

(i) $l = 34.4$ metres, $\theta = 5°$ (ii) $l = 8.0$ metres, $\theta = 22°$

(b) Explain why the increase in the gravitational potential energy of the bricks is approximately the same for each of the ramps.

5 A bricklayer carries a hod of bricks (50 kg) up a ladder. Calculate the length of the ladder if it is inclined at 70° to the horizontal and the increase in the gravitational PE of the bricks is 4300 J.

3.4.2 Conserving energy

You may have been told that 'energy cannot be created or destroyed'. This suggests that energy is conserved. Yet, when two bodies collide, unless the collision is perfectly elastic, there will be a loss of kinetic energy.

Look at the following situation.

A child (40 kg) slides down a water chute. The chute is very slippery and there is no friction to oppose motion.

The child initially travels at $3\,\mathrm{m\,s^{-1}}$, having been given a push at the start.

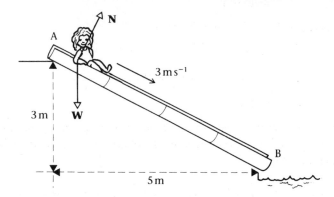

There are two forces on the child, **N** and **W**.

N is the contact force from the chute and it acts at 90° to the direction of motion. Since the distance moved in the direction of **N** is zero, the work done by **N** on the child is zero.

W is the weight of the child, i.e. the gravitational attraction of the Earth on the child.

$$W = 40\,\mathrm{kg} \times 10\,\mathrm{N\,kg^{-1}} = 400\,\mathrm{newtons}$$

W acts vertically and the distance moved in this direction is 3 metres.

The work done by **W** on the child $= 400\,\mathrm{newtons} \times 3\,\mathrm{metres}$
$$= 1200\,\mathrm{N\,m} \ (\mathrm{or}\ \mathrm{J})$$

You can calculate the speed with which the child enters the water.

Work done = change of KE
$$1200 = \tfrac{1}{2}mv^2 - \tfrac{1}{2}mu^2$$
$$= 20v^2 - 20 \times 3^2$$
$\Rightarrow \qquad 60 = v^2 - 9$
$\Rightarrow \qquad v^2 = 69$
$\Rightarrow \qquad v = 8.3\,\mathrm{m\,s^{-1}} = \text{final speed of child}$

So the child will enter the water at a speed of $8.3\,\mathrm{m\,s^{-1}}$.

If you consider the total energy at both points A and B,

energy at A = PE at A + KE at A

$$= mgh + \tfrac{1}{2}mu^2$$

$$= 4 \times 10 \times 3 + \tfrac{1}{2} \times 40 \times 3^2$$

$$= 1380 \text{ J}$$

energy at B = PE at B + PE at A

$$= mgh + \tfrac{1}{2}mv^2$$

$$= 40 \times 10 \times 0 + \tfrac{1}{2} \times 40 \times 8.3^2$$

$$= 1380 \text{ J}$$

Energy is conserved because the only force doing work is gravity. Conservation of energy was assumed when the speed of the child was calculated earlier. However, this model ignores friction.

If a constant frictional force of 100 newtons acts in a direction parallel to the chute then the work done against friction is

$$100\sqrt{(3^2 + 5^2)} = 100\sqrt{34} = 583 \text{ J}$$

This amount of energy is dissipated from the system as heat and so the child starts with 1380 J at the top but has only $1380 - 583 = 797$ J of mechanical energy at the bottom. Since this is in the form of KE, the child's speed at B is now

$$\sqrt{\left(\frac{2 \times 797}{40} \right)} = 6.3 \text{ m s}^{-1}$$

These ideas are explored further in the questions which follow.

 .4B

A snooker ball of mass 50 grams is thrown vertically upwards with a speed of 10 m s^{-1}. Assume that there is no air resistance and that $g = 10 \text{ N kg}^{-1}$.

1 Make a table of the ball's kinetic and potential energies as it rises.

Height above point of projection (metres)	KE (joules)	PE relative to point of projection (joules)
0		
1		
2		
3 etc.		

2 How high does it rise?

3 State the sum of the potential and kinetic energies at each height. Is energy conserved?

4 Describe (in words) how kinetic energy and potential energy vary as the ball rises.

5 If, instead of a snooker ball, a tennis ball of the same mass is used, what difference will this make?

Assume that the resistance to motion is a constant 0.125 newton due to air resistance and draw up a similar table including a column for the sum of the kinetic and potential energies.

6 Is energy conserved in this case?
What has happened to the energy?

You have seen that in the absence of friction or air resistance, potential energy changes into kinetic energy (or vice versa) in such a way that the total energy is constant.

On the other hand, if friction or air resistance is present, some of the energy appears to be lost.

If gravity is the only force doing work, then it is always true that the total energy is constant.

> If the only force doing work is gravity, then at any two positions A and B,
>
> $$(KE + PE) \text{ at } A = (KE + PE) \text{ at } B$$

Example 3
A marble rolls down a chute and becomes a projectile.

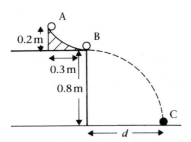

(a) Calculate its speed as it leaves the chute.

(b) The marble lands at distance d metres from the table. Calculate d.

Solution

Assume that the marble is a particle of mass m kg and that there is no friction.

(a) The normal contact force is always perpendicular to the velocity and so does no work. The only force doing work is gravity, so

$$(KE + PE) \text{ at } B = (KE + PE) \text{ at } A$$

Choose values for the potential energy relative to the level of B.

$$\tfrac{1}{2}mv^2 + 0 = 0 + mg(0.2)$$

$$\Rightarrow \qquad v = 2$$

Therefore the speed of the marble at B is $2\,\mathrm{m\,s^{-1}}$.

(The change in potential energy is of course independent of the reference point chosen, in this case, B. The problem could equally be solved by taking C as the arbitrary reference point.)

(b) Assume that the motion is horizontal at B.

The initial velocity is $\mathbf{u} = \begin{bmatrix} 2 \\ 0 \end{bmatrix}$. The acceleration is $\mathbf{a} = \begin{bmatrix} 0 \\ -g \end{bmatrix}$.

Since $\mathbf{u} = \begin{bmatrix} 2 \\ 0 \end{bmatrix}$, $\qquad \mathbf{v} = \begin{bmatrix} 2 \\ -gt \end{bmatrix}$

Since $\mathbf{r_B} = \begin{bmatrix} 0 \\ 0 \end{bmatrix}$, $\qquad \mathbf{r} = \begin{bmatrix} 2t \\ -\tfrac{1}{2}gt^2 \end{bmatrix}$

Taking $g = 10\,\mathrm{m\,s^{-2}}$, $\qquad \mathbf{r} = \begin{bmatrix} 2t \\ -5t^2 \end{bmatrix}$. At C, $\mathbf{r} = \begin{bmatrix} d \\ -0.8 \end{bmatrix}$.

$\Rightarrow \quad d = 2t \quad$ and $\quad -0.8 = -5t^2$
$\Rightarrow \quad t = 0.4 \quad$ and $\quad d = 0.8$

3.4 Exercise 2

1 A squash ball of mass 20 grams is hit vertically upwards with speed $15\,\mathrm{m\,s^{-1}}$.

(a) What is its potential energy relative to its initial position when it has travelled 3 metres?

(b) What is its speed at that point?

(c) What is its potential energy at the highest point of its path?

2 A bob of mass 100 grams, on a string of length 1 metre, is released from rest when the string makes an angle of 80° with the vertical as shown. What is its speed at the lowest point of its path?

3 Two ball bearings (one twice as heavy as the other) can swing freely on the ends of light strings as shown in the diagram. The lighter ball bearing swings down and collides with the heavier one, which has a piece of Blu-Tack on it so that the two stick together on impact.

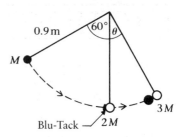

(a) What is the speed of the lighter ball bearing just before impact?

(b) What is the speed of the combined mass immediately after impact?

(c) Predict the angle of swing of the combined mass.

3.4.3 Elastic potential energy

If you stretch a bow, the (positive) work done by the pull you apply (in the direction of displacement) will be equal and opposite to the (negative) work done by the tension in the bow. However, the tension, like gravity, does not disappear once motion stops; it has the *potential* to do positive work. Such energy is called **elastic potential energy** (abbreviated to EPE) and this is the energy which is transferred to the arrow as kinetic energy when the bow is released.

▶ 3.4 **Tasksheet 1 – Tension (page 364)**

> The tension in a stretched spring is proportional to the extension of the spring.
>
> $$T = kx$$
>
> where k is called the **spring constant.**

If a spring with spring constant k is stretched (or compressed) a distance x beyond its natural length, it can be shown that the elastic potential energy of the spring is

$$\frac{kx^2}{2}$$

as follows.

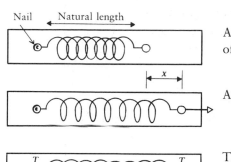

A spring is anchored by a nail to a strip of wood.

A force extends the spring a distance x.

This end is also anchored with a nail, and the force is removed. The tension in the spring is $T = kx$.

In this situation there is a store of potential energy. The tension in the spring has the potential to do some work if, for example, one end is connected to an object which is free to move when the nail is removed.

If this were to happen, then the tension would decrease linearly from kx to zero as the displacement of the object increases from zero to x.

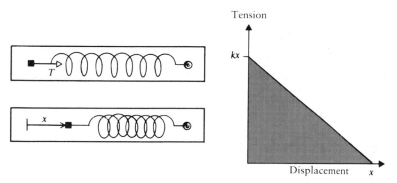

Work done by tension = Area under the graph

$$= \frac{kx^2}{2}$$

The tension in the spring has the potential to do $\dfrac{kx^2}{2}$ joules of work.

Example 4

A spring of length $10\,\text{cm}$ is stretched to a length of $12\,\text{cm}$ by a pull of 10 newtons.

(a) What is its spring constant?

(b) What work must be done to stretch it a further $2\,\text{cm}$?

Solution

(a) $T = kx$

So $10 = k \times 0.02$

$$\Rightarrow k = \frac{10}{0.02} = 500 \,\text{N}\,\text{m}^{-1}$$

(b) Work done to stretch the spring to 12 cm $= 500 \times \dfrac{(0.02)^2}{2} = 0.1 \,\text{J}$

Work done to stretch the spring to 14 cm $= 500 \times \dfrac{(0.04)^2}{2} = 0.4 \,\text{J}$

Work done to stretch the spring from 12 cm to 14 cm $= 0.3 \,\text{J}$

3.4 Exercise 3

1 A spring has a spring constant of $100 \,\text{N}\,\text{m}^{-1}$.

   (a) What is the work done if it is stretched by 5 cm?

   (b) What is the work done if the spring is stretched by 15 cm?

2 The work done to stretch an elastic band by 10 cm from its natural length is 0.2 joules. What is its spring constant?

3 A spring is compressed by a distance of 5 cm. Its spring constant is $500 \,\text{N}\,\text{m}^{-1}$.

   (a) What work has been done?

   (b) What work must be done to compress it by a further 5 cm?

3.4.4 Conserving mechanical energy

Three quantities with the name 'energy' have so far been introduced: kinetic energy, gravitational potential energy and elastic potential energy. Energy, however, appears in many different forms. Heat and electrical energy are both forms of energy. Some substances possess energy which can be released when they undergo a chemical change; for example, when coal is burnt it releases energy in the form of heat and light. A person has a similar store of 'chemical energy' which can be released in the form of mechanical energy when movement is required.

Energy is continually changing from one form to another. When you push a pencil across the table the chemical energy you release is changed into heat energy. (The temperatures of both the table and the pencil increase due to the action of friction.) When you lift a pencil up, the chemical energy released is changed into gravitational potential energy. This can be changed into kinetic energy if the pencil is allowed to fall. Gravitational potential energy and kinetic energy are both forms of **mechanical energy**. A spring has mechanical energy when extended or compressed.

Many problems are very much easier to solve if you can assume that mechanical energy is conserved. While this may be a reasonable assumption in many situations, you need to check carefully that energy is not added to the system from outside and that there are no dissipative forces (such as friction) which would change the energy from mechanical energy to a different form of energy such as heat or light.

> If there are no dissipative forces, such as friction, and no energy is added from outside, then the total mechanical energy of a system is conserved.

Example 5
A marble travels down a chute from A to B.

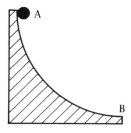

What assumptions are made if it is assumed that the decrease in PE is equal to the increase in KE?

Solution
You would assume that:

(i) the chute is smooth, so there is no friction;
(ii) there is no air resistance.

There would, in practice, be some doubt about the validity of these assumptions. Although air resistance *is* likely to be negligible, the assumption of a smooth chute is unlikely to be valid and so any analysis based on this assumption must be interpreted accordingly.

The presence of friction will mean that not all of the decrease in potential energy will be converted into an increase in kinetic energy. Some of it will be 'lost' to other forms of energy. If the marble slides, mechanical energy will be lost to heat energy; if the marble rolls it will gain 'rotational' kinetic energy as well as 'translational' kinetic energy. Either way, the speed of the marble at the bottom of the chute will be less than expected.

(An object may be stationary in the sense that its centre of mass is stationary. It may, however, still have kinetic energy if it is rotating about an axis through its centre of mass. This form of kinetic energy is looked at in section 3.6.)

Example 6

A 200 gram mass is attached to the end of a spring (natural length 0.3 metre) and hangs at rest (in equilibrium). The mass is then pulled down a distance 0.15 metre (to position A) and released. The mass oscillates as shown. Assume the spring obeys Hooke's law, with spring constant $8\,\mathrm{N\,m}^{-1}$.

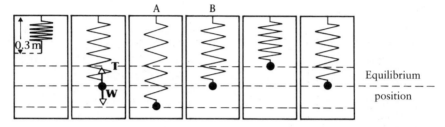

What is the resultant force acting on the mass when it is in position B and what is its velocity at that time?

Solution

Position B is the equilibrium position so the resultant force is zero (i.e. the tension in the spring is equal and opposite to the gravitational pull).

 3 .4c

Explain why the spring is extended 0.25 m beyond its natural length when the mass is in position B.

Being in equilibrium does not mean the mass is not moving. The direction of its motion is obvious. The problem is how to calculate the magnitude of the velocity.

As no energy from outside is put into the system once it is in motion and as energy loss due to air resistance is negligible, it is reasonable to assume that the total mechanical energy of the system is constant.

(In fact, mechanical energy is gradually lost, mostly as heat. In the short term, however, this is a reasonably good model.)

Position A

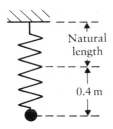

KE $\quad \dfrac{mv^2}{2} = 0$

PE $\quad mgh = 0 \quad$ (relative to position A)

EPE $\quad \dfrac{kx^2}{2} = \dfrac{8 \times 0.4^2}{2}$

$\qquad = 0.64$ joules

Position B

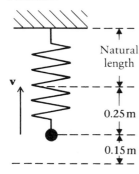

KE $\quad \dfrac{mv^2}{2} = \dfrac{0.2v^2}{2}$

$\qquad = 0.1v^2$ joules

PE $\quad mgh = 0.2 \times 10 \times 0.15$

$\qquad = 0.3$ joules

EPE $\quad \dfrac{kx^2}{2} = \dfrac{8 \times 0.25^2}{2}$

$\qquad = 0.25$ joules

Total mechanical energy at A = total mechanical energy at B

$$0.64 = 0.1v^2 + 0.3 + 0.25$$

$\Rightarrow \qquad\qquad 0.9 - v^2$

The velocity of the mass is $0.95\,\mathrm{m\,s^{-1}}$.

3.4 Exercise 4

1 A light spring, of natural length 0.2 m, is extended to a length of 0.3 m when a mass of 100 g is hung on it. It is then pulled down a further 0.1 m and released.

(a) Find the velocity of the mass when the spring next has length 0.3 m.

(b) Where is its elastic potential energy greatest?

2 A mass of 2 kg is hung from a spring with spring constant $500\,\mathrm{N\,m^{-1}}$.

(a) Find the extension when the mass hangs in equilibrium.

(b) The mass is pulled down until the extension is 0.1 m and then released. Find the speed of the mass when the spring reaches its unstretched length.

3

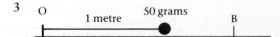

The diagram shows a mass of 50 grams lying on a smooth table. It is fixed to point O by an elastic string of length 1 metre. It is held at point B by a force of 4 newtons and then released. OB is 1.5 metres.

At what speed is the mass travelling when it passes O?

4 A stunt actor attaches one end of a nylon rope to himself and the other end to an anchor point on the edge of the roof of a high-rise building. He then steps off the roof and falls vertically. The actor has mass 76 kg and the roof is 200 metres above an air bag on the ground. The rope has unstretched length 100 metres and its tension, T newtons, when stretched by a further x metres, is given by the formula

$$T = 30x$$

(a) Given that the actor reaches the air bag, calculate the loss of PE of the actor and the gain in EPE of the rope.

(b) Hence estimate the speed with which the actor hits the air bag.

5 A child's toy rocket (mass 20 grams) is fired by releasing a compressed spring. The natural length of the spring is 5 cm, the compressed length is 1 cm and the spring constant is $1000\,\mathrm{N\,m^{-1}}$.

Estimate the height the rocket will reach when fired vertically up in the air.

After working through section 3.4, you should know that:

1 the gravitational potential energy (PE) of a body is always measured relative to an arbitrary fixed reference position (it is defined as the work that would be done by gravity if the body were to move from its present position to the fixed reference position);

2 a particle of mass m kg, at a height h metres above the floor, has gravitational potential energy mgh joules relative to the floor;

3 if gravity is the only force doing work then, at any two positions A and B,

$$(KE + PE) \text{ at } A = (KE + PE) \text{ at } B$$

4 if a spring, with spring constant k, is stretched or compressed a distance x metres beyond its natural length, then its elastic potential energy (EPE) is $\dfrac{kx^2}{2}$ joules;

5 kinetic energy, gravitational potential energy and elastic potential energy are all forms of mechanical energy;

6 if there are no dissipative forces, such as friction, and no energy is added from outside, then the total mechanical energy of a system is conserved.

3 Towards circular motion

.5 Modelling circular motion

3.5.1 Changing speed, changing energy

In section 3.1 you looked at some examples of bodies in horizontal circular motion – the chair-o-plane, conical pendulum, rotor, cyclist on a circular track – and in each case the speed was assumed to be constant. By contrast, when bodies move in a vertical circle their speed may change continually.

For example,

A conker on a string

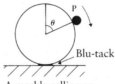

A marble rolling on
the surface of a cylinder

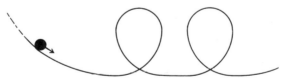

A marble rolling on a loop-the-loop track

 .5A

1 In which of the situations above is it reasonable to assume conservation of mechanical energy?

2 Describe what happens to the kinetic and potential energies of the marble as it moves along the track.

3 How would using a toy car rather than a marble affect what happens?

Set up the apparatus to validate your conjectures.

When tackling the more complicated problems in circular motion, an important principle to use is the conservation of mechanical energy. This is illustrated in the following example.

Example 1

A marble is released from rest at A and loops the loop.

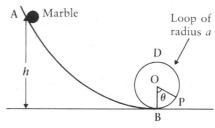

Calculate its speed on reaching:

(a) the lowest point B of the loop;

(b) the highest point D;

(c) the general point P, where angle BOP $= \theta$.

What have you assumed?

Solution

Some assumptions are:

- the rotational energy of the marble is ignored:
- the marble can be modelled as a particle of mass m kg;
- energy is conserved (i.e. resistance is ignored);
- the initial speed is zero;
- the height of h is sufficient for the marble to reach D;
- the gravitational force per unit mass is $10 \, \text{N} \, \text{kg}^{-1}$.

(a) At B:
$$10mh = \tfrac{1}{2}mv^2 - \tfrac{1}{2}mu^2$$
$$v^2 = 20h$$
$$v = \sqrt{(20h)}$$

(b) At D:
$$10mh = \tfrac{1}{2}mv^2 + 10m \times 2a$$
$$v^2 = 20h - 40a$$
$$v = \sqrt{(20(h - 2a))}$$

(c) At P:
$$10mh = \tfrac{1}{2}mv^2 + 10m(a - a\cos\theta)$$
$$v^2 = 20h - 20a(1 - \cos\theta)$$
$$v = \sqrt{(20(h - a + a\cos\theta))}$$

For a gravitational force per unit mass of $g \, \text{N} \, \text{kg}^{-1}$, the velocity at the general point P is given by

$$v = \sqrt{(2g(h - a + a\cos\theta))}$$

3.5.2 Acceleration

When solving real problems in circular motion the energy equation is usually insufficient. You must, in addition, consider the forces acting (which may introduce extra energy into the system) and apply Newton's second law, $\mathbf{F} = m\mathbf{a}$.

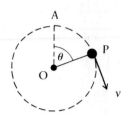

A conker of mass m on the end of a string moves in a vertical circle of radius r.

At time t, its speed is v and angle AOP $= \theta$.

The questions in 3.5B below will show you how to analyse the motion of the conker and enable you to deduce some useful general results about acceleration and circular motion.

 .5B

1 (a) What forces are acting on the conker?

  (b) Does the resultant force act towards the centre of circular motion?

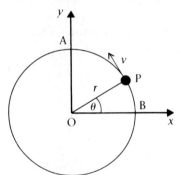

A particle moves in a vertical circle of radius r. (It could represent a conker on a string or a marble rolling on the outside of a cylinder.) At time t, its speed is v and angle POB $= \theta$. Its angular speed is the rate of change of θ, $\dfrac{d\theta}{dt}$.

A useful notation is to write $\dot{\theta}$ for $\dfrac{d\theta}{dt}$ and $\ddot{\theta}$ for $\dfrac{d^2\theta}{dt^2}$.

2 Show that $\begin{bmatrix} \cos\theta \\ \sin\theta \end{bmatrix}$ is a unit vector in the direction $\overrightarrow{OP}$.

3 With respect to the (x, y) axes shown in the diagram, the displacement $\overrightarrow{OP}$ is given by

$$\mathbf{r} = r \begin{bmatrix} \cos\theta \\ \sin\theta \end{bmatrix}$$

Find the velocity $\mathbf{v}$ and show that its magnitude is $r\dot{\theta}$.

4 (a) Show that the acceleration is given by

$$\mathbf{a} = -r\dot{\theta}^2 \begin{bmatrix} \cos\theta \\ \sin\theta \end{bmatrix} + r\ddot{\theta} \begin{bmatrix} -\sin\theta \\ \cos\theta \end{bmatrix}$$

  (b) Show that $\begin{bmatrix} -\sin\theta \\ \cos\theta \end{bmatrix}$ is a unit vector in a direction perpendicular to $\overrightarrow{OP}$.
  (Hint: use the scalar product.)

  (c) Show that the component of acceleration in the direction $\overrightarrow{PO}$ has magnitude $\dfrac{v^2}{r}$.

When the motion of an object follows a circular path, its acceleration has two components, radial and tangential.

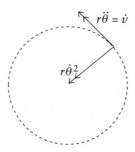

$$r\ddot{\theta} = \dot{v}$$

$$r\dot{\theta}^2$$

The radial component has magnitude $r\dot{\theta}^2 = r\omega^2 = \dfrac{v^2}{r}$.

The tangential component has magnitude $r\ddot{\theta} = r\dot{\omega} = \dot{v}$.

The tangential component will be new to you, but the radial component should be familiar from your work with horizontal circular motion at a constant angular speed.

Example 2

A 2 kg mass is connected to a point A by a light string. The string is 1.2 metres long and has a breaking strain of 50 newtons.

B O — — — — A   The mass is released from the point B, where AB is
   θ horizontal and of length 1.2 metres. The string breaks
                     when the mass reaches point C.

C

Find the angle θ.

Solution

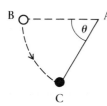

These are just two forces acting on the mass if air resistance is taken as being negligible.

By Newton's second law,

    tangentially: $mg\cos\theta = mr\dot{\omega}$ ①

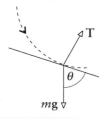

    radially: $T - mg\sin\theta = \dfrac{mv^2}{r}$ ②

By conservation of mechanical energy,

$$mgr\sin\theta = \tfrac{1}{2}mv^2 \qquad\qquad ③$$

Combining equations ② and ③,

$$T - mg \sin\theta = 2mg \sin\theta$$

$$\Rightarrow \qquad T = 3mg \sin\theta$$

Assuming $T = 50\,\mathrm{N}$, $m = 2\,\mathrm{kg}$ and $g = 10\,\mathrm{N\,kg^{-1}}$

$$\Rightarrow \qquad 50 = 60 \sin\theta$$

$$\Rightarrow \qquad \theta = 56.4°$$

Notice that equation ①, for the tangential component of force, was not needed to obtain a solution. Notice also that the solution is independent of the length of the string. When solving problems on vertical circular motion, you will find that it is often sufficient to use:

- the energy equation;
- Newton's second law in the radially inward direction.

Example 3

A girl of mass 30 kg is sitting on a swing. The ropes of the swing are 2 metres long and they make an angle of 60° with the vertical when she reaches the top point of her swing. Find:

(a) the greatest tension in the ropes,

(b) the greatest speed of the girl.

Solution

Assume the girl is a particle on the end of a light string of length 2 metres. Let $g = 10\,\mathrm{N\,kg^{-1}}$ and let the tension in the string be T newtons.

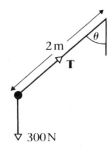

Using Newton's second law radially,

$$T - 300 \cos\theta = 30a$$

But $a = \dfrac{v^2}{r} = \dfrac{v^2}{2}$

$$\Rightarrow \qquad T - 300 \cos\theta = 15v^2 \qquad ①$$

By conservation of energy,

$$\tfrac{1}{2}mv^2 = mg(2\cos\theta - 2\cos 60°)$$

$$v^2 = 20(2\cos\theta - 1)$$

Substitute in ①

$$T = 300(2\cos\theta - 1) + 300\cos\theta$$

$$= 900\cos\theta - 300$$

So T is greatest when $\theta = 0°$

$$T_{\text{max}} = 600\,\text{N}$$

The greatest speed of the girl is when her PE is least, i.e. at the bottom of the swing.

$$v^2 = 20(2\cos\theta - 1)$$

$$= 20$$

$$v = 2\sqrt{5}\,\text{m s}^{-1}$$

3.5 Exercise 1

1 A girl is skateboarding on a rink which is the shape of a bowl whose cross-section is given below.

She has mass $40\,\text{kg}$ and her maximum speed is $5\,\text{m s}^{-1}$.

(a) How high up the slope can she go?

(b) What is the reaction between the skateboarder and the skateboard at this point?

2 A small boy of mass $40\,\text{kg}$ holds on to the end of a rope in the gym and jumps off a bar. The length of the rope is 5 metres and the height of the bar is 4 metres below the point of suspension of the rope. Find:

(a) the speed of the boy at the bottom of his swing;

(b) the tension in the rope at the bottom of his swing;

(c) the tension in the rope when he reaches the highest point at the other end of his swing.

3 A girl swings a conker around in a vertical circle. The conker has mass 10 grams and its velocity is $3\,\mathrm{m\,s}^{-1}$ downwards when the string is horizontal. The string is 50 cm long and the conker hits another when it makes an angle of 120° with the upward vertical. Find:

(a) the conker's velocity at this point;

(b) the tension in the string at this point.

3.5.3 Losing contact

When a marble is released from rest at some position, A, on the approach track to a loop-the-loop, it will do one of three things: oscillate to and fro about B, loop the loop or lose contact with the track at some position between C and D.

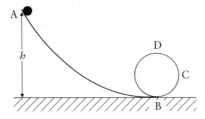

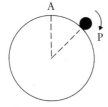

In the case of the marble rolling around the perimeter of a cylinder, a position P is reached at which the marble loses contact.

If the marble is assumed to be a particle of mass m and the effects of air resistance and friction are ignored, then the forces acting are the normal contact force **N** and the weight mg. If the normal contact force equals zero, then the marble will lose contact with the surface.

Once the marble loses contact with the track/cylinder it becomes a projectile and it is of interest to know where contact is lost and where the marble lands. These problems are tackled below, in the context of downhill skiing.

.5c

Starting from rest on the horizontal, a skier travelling down a convex slope picks up speed as she moves downhill and may take off into the air at some position.

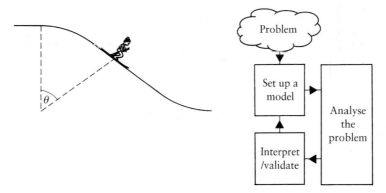

Her motion might be modelled by a marble rolling around the outside of a cylinder, for example, a cake tin, fixed to a table with Blu-Tack.

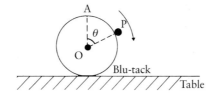

Problem

To find θ at the take-off position.

Set up a model

Set up a simple model in which the effect of friction is ignored.

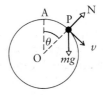

Assume that the skier (marble) is a particle of mass m, sliding on a smooth cylindrical surface of radius r.

1 What other assumptions should you make?

Analyse the problem

If friction can be ignored, you can apply the energy equation

total energy at A = total energy at P
(PE + KE)   (PE + KE)

$$mg2r + 0 = mgr(1 + \cos\theta) + \tfrac{1}{2}mv^2$$

$$\Rightarrow \quad v^2 = 2gr(1 - \cos\theta) \qquad ①$$

By Newton's second law, $F = ma$ in the direction PO gives

$$mg\cos\theta - N = \frac{mv^2}{r}$$

When the particle loses contact with the surface, $N = 0$ and so

$$v^2 = gr\cos\theta \qquad ②$$

2 Use equations ① and ② to show that $\theta = \cos^{-1}(\tfrac{2}{3})$.

Interpret

3 Explain why the marble leaves the surface at a distance $\dfrac{r}{3}$ below A.

Validate

Validation can be achieved by coating the cylinder with talcum powder (to show up the marble's track) and measuring the length, s, of the arc from A to the take-off position; $\dfrac{s}{r}$ gives θ (in radians).

4E Determine where the marble should land on the table.

After working through section 3.5, you should know that:

1 when a body moves in a vertical circle, its speed is not necessarily constant;

2 when the motion of an object follows a circular path, its acceleration has two components, radial and tangential; the radial component has magnitude $r\omega^2$ towards the centre of the circle; and the tangential component has magnitude $r\dot{\omega}$;

3 if gravity is the only force doing work on a particle travelling in a vertical circle, then the velocity at any point can be found by using the principle of conservation of mechanical energy.

3 Towards circular motion

.6E Rotation and energy

3.6.1 Rotational energy

A man walks up to a stationary revolving door and pushes it. It starts to revolve and he walks through.

- Does the man do work when he pushes the door?
- Does it matter where he pushes?
- Does the door have any energy as it rotates?

Experience and theory suggest that he will need to do work in order to start the door rotating. You know that he needs to apply a force to the push bar and the point of application of his force, i.e. the bar, will move as he pushes.

The distance his hands move will be $r\theta$ metres, where r metres is the distance of his hands from the pivot and θ radians is the angle through which the door has turned.

If he applies a force of magnitude F newtons, then, since
work done = force × distance,

$$\text{Work done} = Fr\theta \text{ joules}$$

What about the energy of the rotating door?

Consider a heavy rod of length $2a$ metres spinning about its centre of mass with an angular speed of $\omega\,\text{rad}\,\text{s}^{-1}$.

Suppose the rod is modelled as a particle at the rod's centre of mass. The particle does not move so it does not have any kinetic energy.

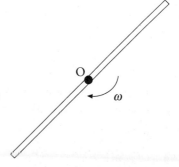

However, if the rod is modelled as a set of small particles, then each of those particles (except the particle at the centre) is moving.

Consider a particle P of mass m kilograms a distance r metres from the centre.

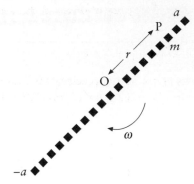

It is moving with speed $v = r\omega \text{ m s}^{-1}$ at right angles to the rod.

Its kinetic energy is $\frac{1}{2}mv^2 = \frac{1}{2}m(r\omega)^2$ joules.

Every particle is moving with the same angular speed ω, so the total KE is

$$\sum_{r=-a}^{a} \tfrac{1}{2}mr^2\omega^2 = \tfrac{1}{2}\left(\sum mr^2\right)\omega^2 \text{ joules}$$

So, even though the centre of mass of the rod is not moving, the rod has kinetic energy due to its rotation. This is called **rotational kinetic energy** and is measured in $\text{kg m}^2 \text{ s}^{-2}$ or joules (the same units as those used for linear kinetic energy).

You have seen that the kinetic energy of the rod is $\frac{1}{2}\left(\sum mr^2\right)\omega^2$ joules.

The quantity $\sum mr^2$ is called the **moment of inertia** of the rod and is usually represented by I.

> The rotational kinetic energy of any body spinning about a fixed axis with angular speed $\omega \text{ rad s}^{-1}$ is given by
> $$\text{KE} = \tfrac{1}{2}\left(\sum mr^2\right)\omega^2 = \tfrac{1}{2}I\omega^2 \text{ joules}$$

The similarity between the formulas $\frac{1}{2}I\omega^2$ and $\frac{1}{2}mv^2$ for kinetic energy of rotational and linear motion is striking. Moreover, the energy principle

> Sum of work done by forces = change in kinetic energy

applies to rotational as well as to linear motion.

Example 1

A turntable is rotating at an angular speed of 45 r.p.m. Its moment of inertia about the axis of rotation is $0.2 \, \text{kg} \, \text{m}^2$.

(a) What is its rotational kinetic energy?

(b) If the turntable has radius 16 cm and is accelerated from rest by a force of 1 newton acting on the rim, how many revolutions does it take to reach 45 r.p.m?

Solution

(a) Angular speed $= 45 \times 2\pi \div 60 \, \text{rad} \, s^{-1}$

$$= 1.5\pi \, \text{rad} \, s^{-1}$$

Rotational KE $= \frac{1}{2} I \omega^2$

$$= 0.1 \times (1.5\pi)^2 = 0.225\pi^2 \, \text{joules}$$

(b) Assuming there are no energy losses as the turntable turns through θ radians,

work done from rest $= Fr\theta = 0.16\theta$

work done $=$ KE gained

so $\qquad\qquad 0.16\theta = 0.225\pi^2 \Rightarrow \theta \approx 13.88$

The number of revolutions is 2.2 (to 2 s.f.).

3.6 Exercise 1

1 A turntable is rotating at 78 r.p.m. Its moment of inertia about the axis of rotation is $0.1 \, \text{kg} \, \text{m}^2$. What is its rotational kinetic energy?

2 The moment of inertia of a bicycle wheel about its axis is $0.05 \, \text{kg} \, \text{m}^2$. Assuming the axis is smooth, what work must be done to make it spin at $40 \, \text{rad} \, s^{-1}$ from rest?

3 A rotating disc loses 1000 joules of rotational kinetic energy when its angular speed drops from $10 \, \text{rad} \, s^{-1}$ to $5 \, \text{rad} \, s^{-1}$. What is its moment of inertia about the axis of rotation?

4 A light rod of length 2 metres has a particle of mass 10 grams at each end. The rod is spinning about an axis through its centre, perpendicular to the plane of the rod, at an angular speed of $4 \, \text{rad} \, s^{-1}$. Find the rotational kinetic energy of the system.

5 A large cotton reel of radius 5 cm is free to rotate on a smooth vertical spindle. The cotton is pulled with a constant force of 2 newtons. The moment of inertia of the reel is 0.0003 kg m^2 and the reel starts from rest. After one revolution, find:

(a) the kinetic energy of the reel,   (b) the angular speed of the reel.

6E A light rod of length d metres has n particles, each of mass $\dfrac{m}{n}$ kilograms, distributed equally along its length (with one at each end). The rod is spinning about an axis through one end, perpendicular to the rod, at an angular speed of ω rad s^{-1}. Find the kinetic energy of the rod if:

(a) $n = 3$ (b) $n = 5$ (c) $n = 101$

3.6.2 Moment of inertia

You have now seen that a body rotating around a fixed axis has a rotational inertia called its moment of inertia. This quantity, I, depends upon the distribution of the mass of the body about the axis.

$$I = \sum mr^2$$

The calculation of the moment of inertia of a rigid body about a fixed axis can be done in one of two ways:

• by simple summation, for a body made up from a finite number of particles;
• by integration, for a solid body whose mass is distributed over the body.

The methods are illustrated in the following examples.

Example 2

Two rods of negligible mass and each of length $2a$ metres are fixed together at their common mid-point O to form a cross as shown. Particles A, B, C and D of mass m, $2m$, $3m$ and $4m$ kilograms respectively are fixed to the ends of the rods.

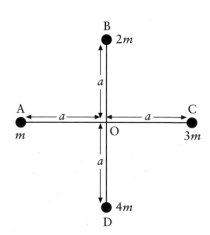

Find the moment of inertia of the body:

(a) about an axis perpendicular to the plane ABCD through O;

(b) about an axis along AB;

(c) about an axis along AC.

Solution

(a) A is a distance a from the pivot at O, so the moment of inertia of the particle at A is ma^2. Similarly, the moments of inertia of particles B, C and D are $2ma^2$, $3ma^2$ and $4ma^2$.

Thus, the moment of inertia of the whole body about an axis perpendicular to the plane ABCD through O is

$$ma^2 + 2ma^2 + 3ma^2 + 4ma^2 = 10ma^2 \text{ kg m}^2$$

(b) A lies on AB, so the moment of inertia of A about AB is zero. Similarly, the moment of inertia of B about AB is zero. C is a distance $a\sqrt{2}$ from AB so the moment of inertia of C about AB is

$$3m(a\sqrt{2})^2 = 6ma^2$$

D is a distance $a\sqrt{2}$ from AB so the moment of inertia of D about AB is

$$4m(a\sqrt{2})^2 = 8ma^2$$

The total moment of inertia about AB is $14ma^2$ kg m^2.

(c) A lies on AC, so the moment of inertia of A about AC is zero. Similarly, the moment of inertia of C about AC is zero. B is a distance a from AC, so the moment of inertia of B about AC is $2ma^2$. D is a distance a from AC, so the moment of inertia of D about AC is $4ma^2$. The total moment of inertia of the system about AC is $6ma^2$ kg m^2.

Example 3

Find the moment of inertia of a uniform rod of length $2a$ metres and mass per unit length ρ kilograms:

(a) about an axis through its centre of gravity perpendicular to the rod;

(b) about an axis through one end of the rod perpendicular to the rod;

(c) about an axis parallel to the rod a distance h metres away.

Solution

The mass M of the rod is $2\rho a$ kilograms.

(a) The mass of an element of length δx is $\rho\,\delta x$.

If the element is a distance x from the axis, then the moment of inertia about the axis is $\rho\,\delta x\,x^2$. For the whole rod you need to sum these quantities.

$$\text{Moment of inertia} = \int_{-a}^{a} \rho x^2 \, dx$$

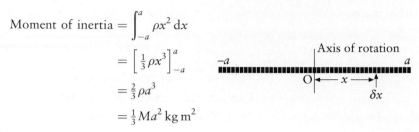

$$= \left[\tfrac{1}{3} \rho x^3 \right]_{-a}^{a}$$

$$= \tfrac{2}{3} \rho a^3$$

$$= \tfrac{1}{3} M a^2 \text{ kg m}^2$$

(b) Let the moment of inertia of the rod about an axis through one end be I.

$$I = \int_{0}^{2a} \rho x^2 \, dx$$

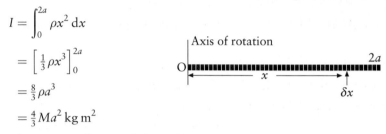

$$= \left[\tfrac{1}{3} \rho x^3 \right]_{0}^{2a}$$

$$= \tfrac{8}{3} \rho a^3$$

$$= \tfrac{4}{3} M a^2 \text{ kg m}^2$$

(c) Every element is a distance h from the axis.

The moment of inertia of each element about the axis is $\rho \, \delta x \, h^2$.

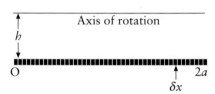

$$\text{Moment of inertia of whole rod} = \int_{0}^{2a} h^2 \rho \, dx = M h^2 \text{ kg m}^2$$

You can see that there is no unique value for the moment of inertia of a body. It depends upon the position of the body relative to the axis of rotation.

> The moment of inertia of a rigid body about an axis is $\sum m r^2$ where m is the mass of a typical element of the body and r is the perpendicular distance of the element from the axis.
>
> The moment of inertia of a composite body about an axis is equal to the sum of the moments of inertia of the components about the axis.

The table opposite gives the moments of inertia of several simple bodies about various axes. Unless specifically asked to derive these results, you may quote them without proof.

Uniform body of mass M	Axis	Moment of inertia
Rod of length $2a$	Through centre, perpendicular to rod	$\frac{1}{3}Ma^2$
	Through end, perpendicular to rod	$\frac{4}{3}Ma^2$
Ring of radius r	Through centre, perpendicular to plane of ring	Mr^2
	Along diameter	$\frac{1}{2}Mr^2$
Disc of radius r	Through centre, perpendicular to disc	$\frac{1}{2}Mr^2$
	Along diameter	$\frac{1}{4}Mr^2$
Solid sphere of radius r	Through centre	$\frac{2}{5}Mr^2$
Hollow sphere of radius r	Through centre	$\frac{2}{3}Mr^2$
Square lamina of side $2a$	Along one side	$\frac{4}{3}Ma^2$
	Through centre, perpendicular to plane	$\frac{2}{3}Ma^2$
	Through centre, in the plane of the lamina	$\frac{1}{3}Ma^2$

3.6 Exercise 2

1 Find the moment of inertia of a system of three particles, each of mass 1 kg and fixed at the vertices of a light equilateral triangle of side 1 metre, about an axis:

   (a) through one vertex parallel to the opposite side;

   (b) through one vertex perpendicular to the plane of the triangle;

   (c) along one side of the triangle.

2 Find the moment of inertia of a thin hollow cylinder of mass M kilograms, and radius r metres, about the axis of the cylinder.

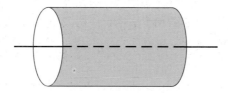

3 Find the moment of inertia of a uniform rod of length 10 cm and mass 10 grams about an axis perpendicular to the rod and 3 cm along the rod from its centre:

   (a) from first principles,

   (b) by considering the rod as two rods joined end to end.

4 Find the moment of inertia of a solid uniform sphere of mass 5 kg and radius 20 cm about an axis through the centre of the sphere.

5 A body is made from two uniform rods, each of length $2l$ metres and mass M kilograms, fixed together to form an L-shape. Find its moment of inertia about an axis perpendicular to the plane of the shape through the point at which they join.

3.6.3 Conservation of mechanical energy

In section 3.4.4 you learnt that if no external work is done on a particle, other than by gravity, then the total mechanical energy of the particle remains constant.

This principle applies equally to rotating rigid bodies. The sum of (gravitational) potential and kinetic energy remains constant as long as no work is done other than by gravity. In this case, if the body is rotating around a fixed axis or pivot then there must be no resistance to rotation due to friction at the pivot. The body is then said to be **rotating freely** about the pivot.

There is nearly always a force acting on the body due to the pivot but if the body rotates freely and the pivot is stationary this force will do no work.

The potential energy of a particle of mass M kilograms at a height of h metres above the ground is Mgh joules relative to the ground. What is the potential energy of a rigid body of equal mass?

 .6A

1 Find the gravitational potential energy of a rod of length $2d$ metres relative to a line through its mid-point A.

Model the rod by a set of n particles, each of mass $\dfrac{M}{n}$, equally spaced along the rod.

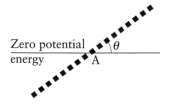

2 Does its gravitational potential energy depend on the angle of slope, θ, of the rod to the horizontal?

The potential energy of a rigid body is easy to calculate using the following result.

> The gravitational potential energy of a rigid body is equal to that of a particle of the same mass situated at the centre of gravity of the body.

You will now be able to use the principle of conservation of mechanical energy for a rotating body.

Example 4

A gymnast balances on her hands on a high bar. She then rotates freely about the bar until she is hanging vertically below it.

(a) Assuming that she is modelled as a uniform rod, if the distance between her centre of gravity and her hands is 1 metre and her mass is 60 kg, estimate her moment of inertia about the bar and hence estimate her angular speed when she reaches her lowest point.

(b) What would your answer be if you had modelled the gymnast as a light rod with a particle of mass 60 kg one metre from the pivot?

Solution

Set up a model

(a) Assume that the gymnast can be modelled as a uniform heavy rod of length 2 metres and mass 60 kg rotating freely about an axis 1 metre from her centre of gravity. Assume that she has an angular speed of ω when she reaches the bottom of her swing.

Analyse the problem

Her moment of inertia about the bar is
$\frac{4}{3} \times 60 \times 1^2 = 80 \, \text{kg m}^2$.

Initial KE $= 0$ Initial PE $= 0$

Final KE $= \frac{1}{2} I \omega^2 = 40 \omega^2$

Final PE $= mgh = -60 \times 10 \times 2 = -1200$ joules

But mechanical energy is conserved, so

$$0 = 40 \omega^2 - 1200$$

$$\omega^2 = \frac{1200}{40}$$

$$\omega = 5.48 \, \text{rad s}^{-1}$$

Level of zero potential energy

Centre of gravity

2 m

ω

Centre of gravity

(b) Assume the gymnast can be modelled as a particle of mass 60 kg at the end of a light rod of length 1 metre.

Initial PE = 0   Initial KE = 0

Final PE = mgh = −1200 joules

Final KE = $\frac{1}{2}mv^2 = \frac{1}{2}mr^2\omega^2 = 30\omega^2$

But energy is conserved, so $30\omega^2 = 1200$

$$\omega = 6.32\,\text{rad}\,\text{s}^{-1}$$

Interpret

The particle model has given a higher estimate of angular speed than the rigid body model because it has ignored the motion of the athlete's body relative to her centre of mass. The true answer should be between the two estimates, because the limbs contain less mass than the head and torso.

3.6 Exercise 3

1 A girl balances a pencil vertically on its point on a table. The pencil then topples. Find its angular speed as it hits the table, assuming that it may be modelled as a uniform rod of length 15 cm, and that it topples without sliding.

2 A barrier at a car park is in the form of a uniform pole of mass 20 kg and length 5 metres, freely pivoted about a point 1 metre from its end. When it is vertical, it is displaced slightly by a gust of wind. Estimate its angular speed as it reaches the horizontal.

3 A uniform body of mass 2 kg is pivoted a distance 20 cm from its centre of gravity. It swings under gravity at exactly the same angular speed as a particle of equal mass on the end of a light string of length 30 cm. What is the moment of inertia of the body?

4 A tree of height 50 metres and mass 2 tonnes is to be cut down.

(a) Assuming it can be modelled as a uniform rod freely rotating about a pivot at the base, find its angular speed as it hits the ground.

(b) What is the speed of the top of the tree as it hits the ground?

(c) Discuss why your answer is likely to be either an underestimate or an overestimate.

Validate your answer by making cardboard models of a pine tree and an oak tree, with the same mass. Stand them side by side on a table and release them together. Which hits the table first?

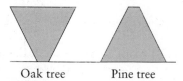

Oak tree   Pine tree

5 A boy is swinging on the end of a heavy rope. His speed when at the bottom of his swing is $6\,\mathrm{m\,s}^{-1}$. The rope has mass $20\,\mathrm{kg}$ and length 10 metres and the boy can be modelled as a heavy particle of mass $25\,\mathrm{kg}$ hanging at the end of the rope. Find the greatest angle the rope makes with the vertical.

3.6.4 Parallel axis theorem

In section 3.6.2 you saw that the moment of inertia of a rod is different for different axes of rotation. If the moment of inertia about an axis through the centre of mass is known, then its moment of inertia about any parallel axis can be calculated.

The parallel axis theorem states:

If the moment of inertia of a body of mass M kilograms about a fixed axis through its centre of mass is I_G then its moment of inertia about a parallel axis a distance d metres from this fixed axis is given by

$$I_D = I_G + Md^2$$

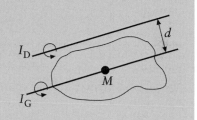

The fact that the theorem is always true can be proved as follows.

Consider a body of mass M which has a moment of inertia I_G about an axis GG_1 through its centre of mass G.

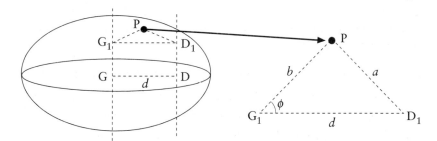

If m is the mass of a typical particle and b is its distance from GG_1, then $I_G = \sum mb^2$.

Let a parallel axis DD_1 be a distance d from the axis GG_1.

The moment of inertia of the body about DD_1 is $\sum ma^2$, where $a^2 = b^2 + d^2 - 2bd\cos\phi$.

So the moment of inertia about DD_1 is $\sum mb^2 + d^2 \sum m - 2d \sum mb \cos \phi$

$$\Rightarrow \quad I_D = I_G + d^2 M - 2d \sum mb \cos \phi$$

Taking G as the origin and the direction $\overrightarrow{GD}$ for the x-axis,

$$\sum mb \cos \phi = \sum mx = M\bar{x}$$

$$= 0 \qquad (\text{since } \bar{x} = 0)$$

Therefore $\quad I_D = I_G + Md^2$

Example 5

Use the parallel axis theorem to find the moment of inertia of a uniform rod of length $4d$ metres and mass M kg about an axis perpendicular to the rod passing through a point on the rod a distance d metres from the mid-point.

Solution

The moment of inertia of the rod about an axis through its centre of gravity is $\frac{1}{3}M(2d)^2 = \frac{4}{3}Md^2$.

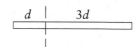

By the parallel axis theorem, the moment of inertia about the new axis is $\frac{4}{3}Md^2 + Md^2 = \frac{7}{3}Md^2$.

3.6 Exercise 4

1 (a) Find the moment of inertia of a hollow sphere of mass 10 kg and radius 15 cm about an axis 1 metre from its centre.

   (b) Find the moment of inertia of a solid sphere of the same mass and radius about an axis 1 metre from its centre.

2 Find the moment of inertia of a disc of mass 1 kg and radius 50 cm about an axis perpendicular to the disc through a point on the circumference of the disc.

3 A drum majorette's baton is made from two solid spheres, each of radius 5 cm and mass 100 grams, joined by a uniform rod of mass 100 grams and length 1 metre. Find the moment of inertia of the baton about an axis perpendicular to the rod:

   (a) through the mid-point of the rod,

   (b) through the centre of one of the spheres.

4 The pendulum of a grandfather clock is made from a rod of length 1 metre and mass 0.1 kg with a disc of radius 3 cm and mass 0.2 kg fixed to the rod a distance 80 cm from the axis of rotation through the end of the rod.

(a) Find the moment of inertia about its axis of rotation.

(b) How will the moment of inertia of the system change if you move the disc nearer the axis of rotation?

5 The moment of inertia of a solid cylinder of mass 12 kg about an axis 50 cm from its centre of gravity is 5.5 kg m². Find its moment of inertia about a parallel axis a distance 20 cm from its centre of gravity.

3.6.5 Perpendicular axes theorem

Another useful theorem relating to moments of inertia is the perpendicular axes theorem. This holds only for thin laminae, *not* for three-dimensional bodies.

The perpendicular axes theorem states:

If the moments of inertia of a plane lamina about two perpendicular axes in the plane of the body are I_A and I_B respectively, then the moment of inertia of the body about an axis through the same point perpendicular to the lamina is $I_A + I_B$.

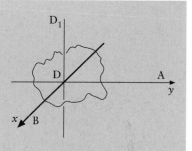

 .6A

Test this theorem using some of the moments of inertia given in the table in 3.6.2 (on page 247), for example those for (a) the ring and (b) the square lamina.

You should be aware that this test does not constitute a proof. It only tells you that the theorem may be true.

Consider a body of mass M kilograms which has a moment of inertia I_A about an axis DA in the plane of the lamina through a point. Let the moment of inertia of the body about a perpendicular axis DB, also in the plane, be I_B. Let its moment of inertia about an axis DD_1 through D, perpendicular to the lamina, be I. You need to prove that $I = I_A + I_B$.

Let m kilograms be the mass of a typical particle, x metres its distance from the first axis, y metres its distance from the second axis and r metres its distance from the axis perpendicular to the lamina.

Then $I_A = \sum mx^2$ and $I_B = \sum my^2$

The moment of inertia of each particle about the axis perpendicular to the lamina is mr^2 where $r^2 = x^2 + y^2$.

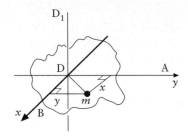

So $I = \sum mr^2 = \sum m(x^2 + y^2)$

$\qquad = \sum mx^2 + \sum my^2$

$\Rightarrow \quad I = I_A + I_B$

Example 6

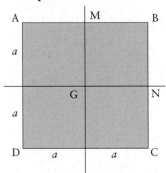

The moment of inertia of a uniform square lamina ABCD of side $2a$ metres and mass M kg about an axis parallel to one side through its centre of gravity, G, is $\frac{1}{3}Ma^2$.

Find the moment of inertia, I, of the lamina about an axis through G perpendicular to the plane ABCD, and hence find the moment of inertia of the lamina about AC.

Solution

The moment of inertia of the lamina about GM is $\frac{1}{3}Ma^2$.

By symmetry, the moment of inertia of the lamina about GN is also $\frac{1}{3}Ma^2$.

Therefore $I = \frac{1}{3}Ma^2 + \frac{1}{3}Ma^2 = \frac{2}{3}Ma^2$

As the lamina is square, AC is perpendicular to BD and, by symmetry, the moment of inertia of the lamina is the same about each.

Hence $I = I_{AC} + I_{BD} = 2I_{AC}$ so $I_{AC} = \frac{1}{3}Ma^2$

3.6 **Exercise 5**

1 A rectangular lamina ABCD of mass M kg has sides AB $= a$ metres and BC $= b$ metres. Its moment of inertia about AD is $\frac{1}{3}Ma^2$. Find its moment of inertia about an axis perpendicular to ABCD through A.

2 A lamina of mass 3 kg is in the shape of a quadrant of a circle of radius 40 cm. Find its moment of inertia about one of its straight edges.

3 A circular turntable has mass M kg, internal radius 1 metre and external radius 2 metres. Find its moment of inertia about an axis along a diameter. (The moment of inertia of a disc about a perpendicular axis through its centre is $\frac{1}{2}Ma^2$.)

4 A table tennis player balances the end of the handle of his bat on his finger. It starts to topple. Assume that the bat can be modelled as a circular disc of mass 30 grams and radius 8 cm on a rod of mass 30 grams and length 10 cm. Find its angular speed when it is horizontal if it rotates:

(a) about an axis perpendicular to the face of the bat,

(b) about an axis parallel to the face of the bat.

After working through section 3.6, you should:

1 know that the rotational kinetic energy of any body rotating about a fixed axis with angular speed ω rad s^{-1} is given by the formula $\text{KE} = \frac{1}{2}I\omega^2$, where I is the moment of inertia of the body about the axis;

2 be able to find the moment of inertia, about a given axis, of a body composed of a finite number of particles;

3 be able to apply the table of moments of inertia on page 247;

4 know that the moment of inertia of a composite body about an axis is equal to the sum of the moments of inertia of its component parts about that axis;

5 know that the gravitational potential energy of a rigid body relative to a given position is equal to the potential energy of a particle of equal mass situated at the centre of gravity of the rigid body;

6 understand and be able to apply the parallel and perpendicular axes theorems;

7 know that if a body is rotating freely about a fixed axis then its mechanical energy is conserved.

3 Towards circular motion

Miscellaneous exercise 3

Take $g = 9.8\,\mathrm{ms}^{-2}$.

1 A big wheel at a fair rotates in a vertical plane at a rate of $1\,\mathrm{rad\,s}^{-1}$. A man of mass $75\,\mathrm{kg}$ sits in a chair which is $5\,\mathrm{m}$ from the axle of the wheel. Find the horizontal and vertical reaction forces acting on the man at the top, bottom, half-way up and half-way down.

2 A stone is attached to a string and is made to move in horizontal circles at an angular speed of $4\,\mathrm{rad\,s}^{-1}$. The stone has a mass of $1.2\,\mathrm{kg}$ and the string has length $1.4\,\mathrm{m}$. Find:

  (a) the tension in the string,

  (b) the angle the string makes with the vertical.

3 Find the angle of banking of a bend of radius $30\,\mathrm{m}$ if a cyclist travelling at $12\,\mathrm{m\,s}^{-1}$ experiences no sideways frictional force up or down the slope.

4 (a) If a track curves in a horizontal circle of radius $300\,\mathrm{m}$, at what angle should it be banked so that there may be no tendency to side-slip at a speed of $40\,\mathrm{m\,s}^{-1}$?

  (b) If in fact it is banked at $20°$, what sideways frictional force will be necessary for a car of mass $1400\,\mathrm{kg}$ moving at $40\,\mathrm{m\,s}^{-1}$?

5 A car C is rounding a corner, which is a circular arc with centre O and radius $300\,\mathrm{m}$, at a steady $25\,\mathrm{m\,s}^{-1}$. Find:

  (a) the angular velocity of OC;

  (b) the acceleration of the car.

6 An engine exerts a constant force of $8 \times 10^4\,\mathrm{N}$ on a train of total mass 300 tonnes, moving against a resistance of $3 \times 10^4\,\mathrm{N}$ on a straight level track. Find the increase in speed in the first 25 seconds.

7 An electron of mass $10^{-30}\,\mathrm{kg}$ is moving at a speed of $4 \times 10^5\,\mathrm{m\,s}^{-1}$ when it enters an electrical field. 4×10^{-9} seconds later it is moving in a direction perpendicular to its initial direction with a speed of $6 \times 10^5\,\mathrm{m\,s}^{-1}$. Find:

  (a) the impulse,

  (b) the work done on the electron during the interval.

8 A destroyer slows down from $30\,\text{km}\,\text{h}^{-1}$ to $20\,\text{km}\,\text{h}^{-1}$. If the mass of the destroyer is 5000 tonnes and it travels 200 m while slowing down, calculate:

(a) the loss in kinetic energy,

(b) the retarding force.

9 A car which has a mass of 1 tonne experiences a constant resistance to motion of 150 N. When it has travelled a distance x m, the force exerted by the engine is given by the following table.

Distance (m)	0	10	20	30	40	50
Force (N)	4000	3900	3750	3550	3300	3000

Draw a graph showing the acceleration of the car plotted against x and find the speed of the car when it has travelled 50 m, assuming that it starts from rest.

10 A truck of mass 3 tonnes moving at $3\,\text{m}\,\text{s}^{-1}$ catches up and collides with one of mass 2 tonnes moving at $2\,\text{m}\,\text{s}^{-1}$. The trucks remain coupled together after the collision. With what speed will they be moving immediately after collision and how much kinetic energy is lost?

11 (a) A rugby player of mass 70 kg moving at $6\,\text{m}\,\text{s}^{-1}$ tackles another player of mass 80 kg moving at $4\,\text{m}\,\text{s}^{-1}$ in the same direction. Calculate their combined speed after collision and the loss of kinetic energy due to the impact. If they slither to a halt after travelling 2 m, calculate the frictional resistance of the ground, assumed constant throughout.

(b) If the players were moving in opposite directions at impact, calculate the loss in kinetic energy and, assuming the same frictional resistance as in (a), calculate how far they will slide before stopping.

12E (a) A pile-driver of mass 100 kg is dropped through 2 m on to a pile of mass 1 tonne. The driver does not bounce. If the pile is driven 10 cm into the earth, what resistance does the earth offer if it is assumed constant?

(b) Find the height from which a pile-driver of mass 200 kg must be dropped on to a pile of mass 1 tonne if the combined pile and driver drive the pile 15 cm into the earth. Assume the same resistance as in (a).

13 A railway truck of mass 5 tonnes runs freely from rest down an incline of 1 in 100, 100 metres in length. Find the work done by the forces on the truck and calculate the final velocity.

14 A particle of mass 200 grams moves through a displacement of r m under the action of a force $\mathbf{F}$ N. If its initial speed is u m s^{-1} and its final speed is v m s^{-1}, find:

(a) the value of v if $\mathbf{F} = \begin{bmatrix} -5 \\ 10 \\ 4 \end{bmatrix}$, $\mathbf{r} = \begin{bmatrix} 16 \\ -4 \\ -4 \end{bmatrix}$, $\mathbf{u} = \begin{bmatrix} 10 \\ 20 \\ 30 \end{bmatrix}$;

(b) the value of u if $\mathbf{F} = \begin{bmatrix} 4 \\ -8 \\ 10 \end{bmatrix}$, $\mathbf{r} = \begin{bmatrix} -50 \\ 20 \\ -8 \end{bmatrix}$, $\mathbf{v} = \begin{bmatrix} -3 \\ 2 \\ 5 \end{bmatrix}$.

15 A particle of mass 5 kg is acted on by a force of $\begin{bmatrix} 12 \\ -5 \\ 5 \end{bmatrix}$ N while it is displaced through $\begin{bmatrix} 5 \\ 4 \\ 2 \end{bmatrix}$ m. If its final speed is 6 m s^{-1}, calculate its initial speed.

16 A body of mass 6 kg moving with velocity $\begin{bmatrix} 3 \\ 6 \\ 11 \end{bmatrix}$ m s^{-1} collides with and sticks to a body of mass 10 kg moving with velocity $\begin{bmatrix} 3 \\ -2 \\ 3 \end{bmatrix}$ m s^{-1}. Find the change in kinetic energy due to the impact.

17 (a) A ball, mass 0.2 kg, with velocity $\begin{bmatrix} 5 \\ 0 \\ -1 \end{bmatrix}$ m s^{-1} is in contact with a bat for 0.01 second, as a result of which its new velocity is $\begin{bmatrix} 3.5 \\ 2 \\ 0 \end{bmatrix}$ m s^{-1}.

Calculate the average force exerted by the bat on the ball.

(b) An impulse of $\begin{bmatrix} 3 \\ -9 \\ 6 \end{bmatrix}$ N s causes the final momentum of a 3 kg body to be $\begin{bmatrix} 6 \\ 3 \\ 9 \end{bmatrix}$ N s. Calculate the initial velocity of the body.

18   In (a), (b) and (c), find the work done by the force **F** newtons in displacement **r** metres.

(a) $\mathbf{F} = \begin{bmatrix} 1 \\ 2 \\ 3 \end{bmatrix}$, $\mathbf{r} = \begin{bmatrix} 3 \\ -4 \\ 1 \end{bmatrix}$;

(b) $\mathbf{F} = \begin{bmatrix} -3 \\ 2 \\ 5 \end{bmatrix}$, $\mathbf{r} = \begin{bmatrix} 1 \\ -2 \\ 4 \end{bmatrix}$;

(c) $\mathbf{F} = \begin{bmatrix} 3 \\ 5 \\ 2 \end{bmatrix}$, $\mathbf{r} = \begin{bmatrix} 5 \\ -4 \\ 1 \end{bmatrix}$;

(d) A particle of mass 5 kg is moved 12 m down a slope making an angle $\tan^{-1}\frac{3}{4}$ with the horizontal. Find the work done by each of the forces shown.

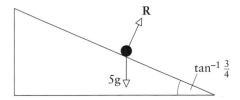

19   A child sitting on a mat slides down a helter-skelter. If the friction is negligible and the helter-skelter is 10 m high, what will be the child's speed at the bottom?

20   A space capsule of mass 10 tonnes is moving towards the Earth's surface at 50 m s^{-1}. It is required to reduce its speed to 5 m s^{-1} before splashdown by applying a constant retarding force P newtons provided by a series of parachutes. If the force is to act for a total distance of 1 km find:

(a) the kinetic energy of the capsule just before splashdown,

(b) the magnitude of **P**.

21   A light spring of natural length 20 cm, which requires a force of 1.5 N to stretch it 1 cm, is attached to a fixed point at one end and hangs freely. A 1 kg mass is hung from the lower end and it is released from rest with the spring unstretched. How long is the spring when the mass comes instantaneously to rest?

22 A child whirls a conker of mass m in a vertical circle by means of a string of length l. The speed of the conker is u at the lowest point A of the circle.

(a) Find the speed of the conker when its height above A is h.

(b) Find the tension in the string at the top of the vertical circle.

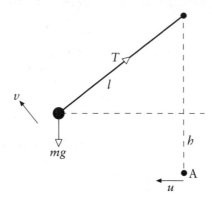

23 A woman of mass $60\,\text{kg}$ swings on a rope of length $8\,\text{m}$. She starts with the rope taut from a platform A which is $1\,\text{m}$ below the point of suspension of the rope.

(a) What must be the minimum breaking strain of the rope if she is to reach the lowest point B without the rope snapping?

(b) If the rope has a breaking strain of $1500\,\text{N}$, at what depth below A will the woman be when the rope snaps?

24 A marble is placed on the top of a smooth up-turned hemispherical bowl and gently pushed off. If the radius of the outside of the bowl is $20\,\text{cm}$ and the marble is of mass 2 grams, find the speed after descending through a vertical distance of $4\,\text{cm}$, $8\,\text{cm}$, $12\,\text{cm}$, $16\,\text{cm}$ and $20\,\text{cm}$. If R is the normal reaction between the bowl and the marble, find R for each of the speeds found above. Comment on your results.

If the question was about a bead threaded on a smooth semicircular wire standing in a vertical plane, what modifications would you make to your answers?

25 An olympic athlete of mass $70\,\text{kg}$ is swinging in vertical circles on the high horizontal bar. Assuming that his motion can be described as the same as a mass of $70\,\text{kg}$ concentrated at a distance of $120\,\text{cm}$ from the bar, find the tension or thrust in his arms at the top and bottom of the circle given that the angular velocity of the athlete at the top is

(a) $0.5\,\text{rad s}^{-1}$,

(b) $1\,\text{rad s}^{-1}$.

(c) What must be the angular velocity at the top if the athlete's arms are to remain in tension throughout the motion? What would be the tension in his arms at the lowest point of swing in this case?

26E A uniform rod of length 20 cm and mass 300 grams is rotating about a point 5 cm from one end. Its speed of rotation is 20 rad s^{-1}. Find the kinetic energy of the rod.

27E A swingboat can be modelled as two uniform rods, AB and CD, each 12 m long as shown. AB has mass 200 kg and CD has mass 600 kg.

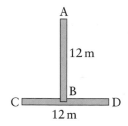

(a) Find the moment of inertia of the boat about an axis through A, perpendicular to AB and CD.

(b) Assuming that the boat can rotate freely about A, find the maximum height B can reach if it has an angular speed of 0.5 rad s^{-1} in the position shown.

(c) A different model is set up assuming that the boat is a particle of mass 800 kg at B suspended by a light rod from A. Find the maximum height B could reach using this model.

4 Modelling with differential equations

.1 Modelling resisted motion

4.1.1 Resistance to motion

In your earlier work in mechanics, you generally assumed resistance forces due to the medium (air or water) in which a body moves to be negligible. This led to equations of motion that were relatively straightforward to solve. However, in some cases the resistance force of the medium, or **drag**, cannot be ignored.

Air resistance restricts the speed of movement through air. In parachuting, this air resistance is used to reduce speed sufficiently to enable a person to land safely.

Air resistance also plays an important role in many sports. Its effect on a badminton shuttlecock is especially easy to observe. A sky-diver can alter his or her speed significantly either by curling up or by falling in a spread-eagled position.

Drag can be minimised by keeping speeds low. In cases where this is impractical it can be reduced by aerodynamically shaping (streamlining) objects and smoothing their surfaces.

In this chapter you will be looking at the effects of introducing resistance and other variable forces into the model, at how this changes the equation of motion, and at the new methods needed to solve the resulting equation of motion.

 .1A

1 If you drop a ball of paper and a sheet of paper at the same time, which falls faster? Account for your observations.

2 Imagine holding your hand out of the window of a moving car. Describe what it would feel like.

3 What is the force resisting motion in each of questions 1 and 2?

4 What two factors seem to affect the magnitude of this force?

In order to analyse the motion of some objects, you need to develop a suitable model for air resistance. However, to do this you need a better understanding of the factors which affect the magnitude of the force.

▶ 4.1 Tasksheet 1 – Sky-diving (page 365)

Sophisticated experiments have been performed on smooth spheres positioned in a wind tunnel. The air is blown past them, and the resistance is measured.

It has been found that the force due to air resistance, R, can be modelled by an expression of the type

$$A\,f(v)$$

where A is the cross-sectional surface area of the object perpendicular to the direction of motion and $f(v)$ is an increasing function of the speed v of the object through the air.

In many situations, the area for a particular object can be considered as constant, so that resistance can be modelled simply as a function of speed.

Although there is no simple formula relating the force, R, to speed, experiments suggest that two models are reasonable.

$R = Kv$ is a suitable model for the air resistance at 'low' speeds

$R = kv^2$ is a suitable model for the air resistance at 'high' speeds

where K and k are constants which depend on the size and shape of the object.

4.1 Exercise 1

1 The examples in the picture show (i) a sky-diver free-falling,   (ii) a person using a parachute and   (iii) a rhinoceros using an identical parachute.

   If the resistance force in each example is of the form $R = kv^2$, for which situation would k be   (a) smallest,   (b) largest?

   (i)   (ii)   (iii)

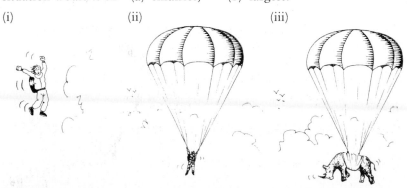

2 The resistance force on a wooden block when in orientation A is $R = 16v$ newtons. What would be the resistance force on the block falling in orientation B?

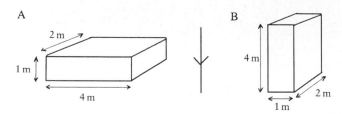

3 Two identical cones are dropped from a high tower, one base first and one point first. The cross-sectional areas of the cones are equal. Comment on the size of the resistance force on each cone.

4.1.2 Modelling a sky-diver's descent

Imagine a sky-diver making a jump from 3700 metres. At first, she accelerates at approximately 10 m s^{-2} since the air resistance is small. At this rate, after 5 seconds she would be travelling at 50 m s^{-1} and would continue to accelerate. However, this does not happen because the air resistance quickly becomes significant. The resistance force or drag gradually increases as her speed increases. At some point, the resistance force balances her weight of 600 newtons and she stops accelerating. From then on she will travel with constant speed, her **terminal speed**.

At terminal speed, the weight is balanced by the air resistance force, i.e.

$$mg = R$$

Hence there is no resultant force and so the acceleration is zero.

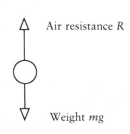

For a body falling from rest through air, the resistance increases with speed until it balances the weight. The body then falls with constant terminal speed because there is no acceleration.

 .1B

1 Model the sky-diver with a force diagram.

2 Assume that her terminal speed is $50\,\mathrm{m\,s^{-1}}$ and that air resistance is modelled by the force $R = Kv$. Hence deduce the value of K.

3 Show how Newton's second law of motion can be used to obtain the differential equation of motion

$$\frac{dv}{dt} = 10 - 0.2v$$

The graph shows the direction field (where the gradient is plotted at various points) for solutions to the equation

$$\frac{dv}{dt} = 10 - 0.2v$$

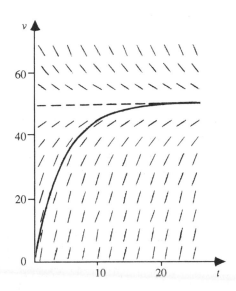

By starting a numerical solution at $(0,0)$, you can obtain a solution for $v(t)$ which is relevant to the sky-diver jumping with zero initial speed. You can check that it takes about 20 seconds for her to 'more or less' reach terminal speed.

By starting from other points, you can obtain solutions relevant to other situations. For example, a sky-diver who ejects from the aeroplane at $10 \, \text{m s}^{-1}$ downwards would reach terminal speed more quickly.

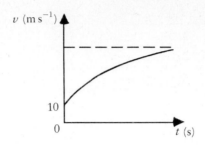

In the following questions, a different resistive model is used. The model above assumes that air resistance is proportional to velocity, but suppose now that resistance is proportional to the square of the velocity.

 .1c

A sky-diver jumps from a plane at a height of 3700 metres. In order to make a safe landing, the parachute must be opened before a height of 610 metres is reached.

Problem

To estimate the length of time the sky-diver is in free-fall.

Set up a model

Let the air resistance be modelled by the force $R = kv^2$ newtons.

1 List the other assumptions about mass, motion and terminal speed for the sky-diver which were made in section 4.1.2. Hence obtain the equation of motion

$$\frac{dv}{dt} = 10 - 0.004v^2$$

Analyse the problem

A numerical method can be used to calculate the velocity, acceleration and height of the sky-diver after successive small increments of time.

From the equation of motion above, the acceleration $a = 10 - 0.004v^2$. The speed is found by considering a small change in time of δt.

Then the acceleration is $a = \dfrac{dv}{dt}$

$\Rightarrow \delta v \approx a\,\delta t$

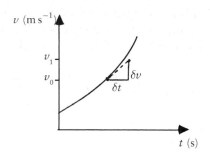

From the graph the new speed is approximately

$$v_1 = v_0 + \delta v = v_0 + a\,\delta t$$

Similarly, the change in height is approximately $\delta h = v_0\,\delta t$.

Since the sky-diver is falling, the new height $h_1 = h_0 - \delta h \Rightarrow h_1 = h_0 - v_0\,\delta t$.

The table shows the first few calculations of the numerical solution for a step size δt of 0.1 second.

Time $t_{n+1} = t_n + 0.1$	Velocity $v_{n+1} = v_n + 0.1a_n$	Acceleration $a_{n+1} = 10 - 0.004v_n^2$	Height $h_{n+1} = h_n - 0.1v_n$
0	0	10	3700
0.1	1.00	10.000	3700.0
0.2	2.00	9.996	3699.9
0.3	3.00	9.984	3699.7
0.4	4.00	9.964	3699.4
...	...	...	...

Many steps are required for a complete solution. To save time, it is possible to write a short program for a computer or a calculator to perform these calculations. (See the programs in Appendix 2, pages 495–6.)

2 Use a program to check the calculations in the table above and complete the calculations for the first second of the motion.
(Save your program as you will use it again later.)

3 By adapting your program, calculate the velocity and height at regular intervals (for example, every 1 or 5 seconds) and use the results to plot the graphs of speed v and height h against time for the descent to 610 metres.

4 How long does it take the sky-diver to approximately reach her terminal speed?

5 How long can she spend in free-fall?

The article in tasksheet 1 states:

'Her speed increases for about eight seconds, reaching a "terminal speed" of approximately 120 m.p.h. (190 km h^{-1}). This is the highest speed she will achieve in this position. Her altimeter tells her the height, second by second, as she plunges earthward, and she knows that to make a safe landing, she must open her parachute before she reaches 2000 ft. (610 m). So the free-fall will last less than one minute – a brief, floating interlude during which the parachutist carries out the acrobatics which are the real purpose of sky-diving.'

6 Use the information above to validate your solution. Try to account for any discrepancies.

7E Investigate the accuracy of your solution by changing the step size.

Example 1

A beach ball is thrown vertically upwards with a speed of $8\,\mathrm{m\,s}^{-1}$. It has a mass of 100 grams. The resistance force due to the air, R newtons, is modelled by $R = 0.25v$, where $v\,\mathrm{m\,s}^{-1}$ is the speed of the ball.

Using a numerical method, find the maximum height the ball reaches above the point of projection.

Solution

Set up a model

Assume that the only forces acting on the ball are its weight and air resistance. Let h metres be the height of the centre of mass of the ball above the point of projection. Initially, $h = 0$. Assume $g = 10\,\mathrm{m\,s}^{-2}$.

Analyse the problem

Using Newton's second law upwards,

$$0.1\frac{\mathrm{d}v}{\mathrm{d}t} = -0.1g - 0.25v \quad \Rightarrow \quad \frac{\mathrm{d}v}{\mathrm{d}t} = -10 - 2.5v$$

Using the Euler step-by-step program (see Appendix 2, pages 495–6) with a step size of 0.01 second, the expression for the acceleration is $a = -10 - 2.5v$.

The table opposite shows results for the first four steps, and is then continued until $v \le 0$ (i.e. until the maximum height has been reached).

Time $t_{n+1} = t_n + 0.01$	Speed $v_{n+1} = v_n + 0.01a_n$	Acceleration $a_{n+1} = -10 - 2.5v_n$	Height $b_{n+1} = b_n - 0.01v_n$
0.00	8.0	−30.0	0.00
0.01	7.7	−30.0	0.08
0.02	7.4	−29.3	0.16
0.03	7.1	−28.5	0.23
0.04	6.8	−27.8	0.30
...	...	...	...
		continue until $v \le 0$	
0.41	0.1	−10.6	1.43
0.42	0.0	−10.3	1.43
0.43	−0.1	−10.1	1.43

Interpret/validate

When $v \approx 0$, the ball has reached 1.43 metres. To obtain a more accurate answer for the maximum height, i.e. when the speed is exactly zero, a smaller step size should be used, for example, 0.005 or 0.001. Decreasing the step size will give a more accurate solution providing the step size is not so small that rounding errors are compounded.

Numerical methods can be used to solve any differential equation. The step size should be as small as is practical. A very small step size may lead to computational errors.

4.1 Exercise 2

In the following questions take $g = 10 \, \text{m s}^{-2}$.

1 A mouse of mass 45 grams falls from the top of a building 12 metres high. Air resistance is modelled by the force $R = 0.3v$ newtons, where $v \, \text{m s}^{-1}$ is the speed of the mouse.

(a) Show that the differential equation for the fall is

$$\frac{dv}{dt} = 10 - \frac{20v}{3}$$

(b) Use the step-by-step method to calculate the time taken for the mouse to fall 12 metres. (A suggested step size is 0.01 second.)

(c) Find the speed of the mouse on impact.

(d) Repeat the calculations with step sizes of 0.005 and 0.001. Compare the results for the time of fall.

2 A water-skier is pulled from rest by a speed-boat exerting a constant horizontal force of 180 newtons. The mass of the skier and her skis is 60 kg. Her maximum speed is $9\,\mathrm{m\,s}^{-1}$. The total resistance force due to the water and air is modelled by $R = Kv$ newtons, where $v\,\mathrm{m\,s}^{-1}$ is her speed.

(a) Draw a force diagram for the water-skier when moving at $9\,\mathrm{m\,s}^{-1}$.

(b) Calculate the value of the constant K.

(c) Write down the equation of motion for the skier.

3 The motion of a downhill skier, of mass 65 kg, is modelled by the equation of motion

$$65g \sin 20° - 0.5v^2 = 65\frac{dv}{dt}$$

(a) State three main assumptions that have been made to obtain the equation of motion.

(b) Calculate the terminal speed of the skier.

4 The skier in question 3 crouches into a more tucked position, so the resistance force is now modelled as $R = 0.2v^2$.

(a) Calculate her new terminal speed.

(b) Use a numerical method to find her time to complete a straight course 2.5 km long.

4.1.3 Terminal speed

For most of the free-fall, the sky-diver of section 4.1.2 is travelling at terminal speed. You will now examine this part of the motion in greater detail.

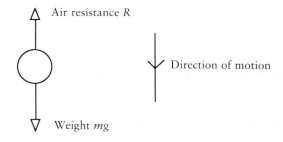

Using Newton's second law downwards,

$$mg - R = m\frac{dv}{dt}$$

When the resultant force acting on a moving object is zero, it will continue to move with constant velocity. It is then said to be in **dynamic equilibrium.**

So at terminal speed there is no resultant force, i.e. $mg = R$, and the acceleration is zero.

 .1D

Two models for the resistance force have been suggested,

$$R = Kv \quad \text{and} \quad R = kv^2$$

1 Given a terminal speed of w metres per second, show that these models lead respectively to the following expressions for w.

$$w = \frac{mg}{K} \quad \text{and} \quad w = \sqrt{\left(\frac{mg}{k}\right)}$$

The graphs for both resistance models show how the terminal speed, w, of an object varies as its mass increases (with no change in the size or shape of the object).

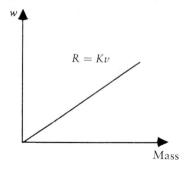 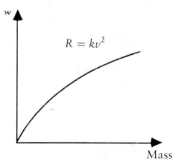

2 Interpret the expressions $w = \dfrac{mg}{K}$ and $w = \sqrt{\left(\dfrac{mg}{k}\right)}$.

3 Explain how a sky-diver is able to change terminal speed during the free-fall.

4 Why is the sky-diver's terminal speed much slower once the parachute is opened?

5 Would the sky-diver have the same terminal speed on the Moon?

6 Explain why, when two or more sky-divers link up in free-fall, their terminal speed does not increase significantly.

It is possible to use a simple experiment to investigate how terminal speed varies with mass. The data can be used to validate one of the models for the resistance force. If terminal speed is proportional to mass, then the $R = Kv$ model is appropriate. However, if terminal speed is proportional to the square root of mass, then $R = kv^2$ is a better model.

▶ 4.1 **Taksheet 2 – Resistance experiments (page 367)**

> In experiments where the speeds are low, $R = Kv$ is an appropriate model for the air resistance force. However, when the speeds are higher, $R = kv^2$ is a more suitable model.
>
> In addition, it can be found from experiment that the resistance force is proportional to the cross-sectional area of the object.

4.1 Exercise 3

1 In a wind tunnel experiment, a small disc is placed in the air flow. A spring balance is used to measure the resistance force, R newtons, for different wind speeds. The data collected are recorded below.

Wind speed (m s^{-1})	7.46	10.06	15.09	19.22	21.21	24.53
Resistance force (N)	0.27	0.49	1.11	1.78	2.18	3.03

Find a suitable function to model the resistance force in terms of the wind speed.

2 In an experiment, spheres of different masses, but equal diameter, were dropped in a long column of oil. The time taken to travel a distance of one metre was found, after each sphere had reached terminal speed.

Mass (grams)	8.25	2.66	2.31	1.225
Terminal speed (m s^{-1})	0.704	0.235	0.188	0.040

(a) Plot the data on suitable axes.

(b) What type of model for the resistance force seems more appropriate, $R = Kv$ or $R = kv^2$?

(c) Calculate the value of K or k.

3 An A4 sheet of card falling vertically through the air is found to have a terminal speed of $w\,\mathrm{m\,s}^{-1}$. At such slow speeds, $R = Kv$ is found to be a good model of the air resistance, where K is proportional to the surface area of the card.

$w\,\mathrm{m\,s}^{-1}$

Predict the terminal speeds, in terms of w, for the following objects.

(a) Two pieces of A4 card stuck face to face

(b) An A3 (double sized) sheet of the card

(c) Half of an A4 sheet of card

(d) An A4 sheet folded in half

4 For the models of air resistance, $R = Kv$ or $R = kv^2$, the velocity v is actually the **relative velocity** of the object through the medium.

The equation of motion of a car of mass m kilograms moving at speed $v\,\mathrm{m\,s}^{-1}$ in still air is modelled by

$$T - Kv = m\frac{\mathrm{d}v}{\mathrm{d}t}$$

where T and K are constants.

(a) Deduce the equation of motion for the same car moving against a headwind of $10\,\mathrm{m\,s}^{-1}$.

(b) What effect does the headwind have on the car's maximum speed?

(c) Explain the slipstream effect which allows a racing car to make use of the slipstream behind another vehicle.

4.1.4 Another force – upthrust

Consider the motion of an airship rising slowly after its mooring ropes are released. What forces are acting on it and how should they be modelled?

It is clear that there is a resultant force acting on the airship.

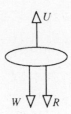

The force due to air resistance, R, and the weight, W, of the airship both act downwards and there is a force, U, acting upwards called the **upthrust**.

The equation of motion of the airship would be

$$U - W - R = m\frac{dv}{dt}$$

where m kilograms is the mass of the fully inflated airship.

Until now the effects of upthrust have been ignored in the setting up of a model. However, any body totally or partially immersed in a fluid, such as air, water, oil, and so on, experiences an upwards force due to the pressure of the surrounding fluid.

The effect of upthrust can be demonstrated by lowering an object on a newton meter or spring balance into water. The decrease in the reading on the meter is the magnitude of the upthrust force of the water on the object.

The model for upthrust is based on Archimedes' principle,

Upthrust = Weight of fluid displaced

Alternatively,

$$U = \rho V g$$

where $\rho \, \text{kg m}^{-3}$ is the density of displaced fluid,
$V \, \text{m}^3$ is the volume of the body, and
$g \, \text{N kg}^{-1}$ is the acceleration due to gravity.

 .1E

1 Describe how the upthrust on the airship might vary as it rises to the stratosphere (about 18 km above the Earth's surface).

2 Why is the upthrust due to air negligible for a cannon-ball, but significant for a child's helium balloon?

4.1 Exercise 4

In the following questions take $g = 10\,\text{N}\,\text{kg}^{-1}$.

1 Two metal spheres of equal radius 10 cm, one of lead (density $11\,000\,\text{kg}\,\text{m}^{-3}$) and the other of iron (density $8000\,\text{kg}\,\text{m}^{-3}$) are dropped into a tank of water. The resistance force on each sphere due to the water is modelled as $R = 16v$ newtons where $v\,\text{m}\,\text{s}^{-1}$ is the speed of the sphere.

(a) Derive an equation of motion for each sphere if upthrust is not ignored.

(b) Calculate their terminal speeds.

2 Estimate the upthrust force on yourself:

(a) in air of density $1.29\,\text{kg}\,\text{m}^{-3}$;

(b) floating in water;

(c) fully immersed in water.

3 A balloon has a volume of $2200\,\text{m}^3$ and is filled with hot air of density $0.98\,\text{kg}\,\text{m}^{-3}$. The deflated balloon, equipment and passengers together have a mass of 0.6 tonnes.

(a) Calculate the upthrust force on the inflated balloon given that the surrounding air has density $1.29\,\text{kg}\,\text{m}^{-3}$.

(b) Find the initial acceleration of the balloon.

(c) What effect will air resistance have on the balloon's ascent?

(d) Describe the effect of the upthrust as the balloon rises through the atmosphere.

After working through section 4.1, you should:

1 be able to model the motion in one dimension of bodies subject to weight, upthrust and a variable resistance force (for example, air resistance);

2 understand what is meant by the terms terminal speed and dynamic equilibrium;

3 know that accepted models for resistance are

Kv for low speed,
kv^2 for high speed;

4 be able to solve, by numerical methods, differential equations of the form

$$\frac{dv}{dt} = f(v)$$

5 be able to interpret graphical and numerical solutions to problems in the context of resisted motion.

4 Modelling with differential equations

.2 Analytical methods

4.2.1 Motion at low speeds

In this section, you will discover how to solve the differential equation for resisted motion at low speeds using the method of separation of variables. This will give an algebraic solution which is more powerful than numerical solutions such as those obtained in section 4.1. (The method of integration by separation of variables is an example of an **analytical method**.)

Consider the motion of a weighted bob tied on the end of a thin cord and being used to test the depth of water in a river.

Problem

To find a general solution for the motion of the bob as it sinks to the bottom.

Set up a model

The following assumptions are made.

- The bob is a particle of mass m kilograms.
- The cord is light and does not restrict the motion of the bob in any way.
- The force due to upthrust on the bob is negligible.
- The bob enters the water with zero speed.
- The model used for the resistance force at low speed is $R = Kv$ newtons, where K is a constant and the speed of the bob is $v\,\mathrm{m\,s}^{-1}$.

Hence the only forces acting on the bob are its weight and water resistance.

Analyse the problem

Using Newton's second law,

$$mg \quad R = m\frac{dv}{dt}$$

Substituting $R = Kv$,

$$mg - Kv = m\frac{dv}{dt} \quad \Rightarrow \quad \frac{dv}{dt} = g - \frac{Kv}{m}$$

Separating variables,

$$\int \frac{dv}{(g - Kv/m)} = \int dt$$

$$-\frac{m}{K}\ln \left| g - \frac{Kv}{m} \right| = t + \text{constant}$$

The *initial conditions* are $t = 0$ and $v = 0$,

so $\text{constant} = -\dfrac{m}{K}\ln |g|$

and $t = -\dfrac{m}{K}\ln \left| g - \dfrac{Kv}{m} \right| + \dfrac{m}{K}\ln |g|$

Rearranging for v,

$$\frac{-Kt}{m} = \ln \left| \frac{g - Kv/m}{g} \right| \quad \Rightarrow \quad e^{-Kt/m} = 1 - \frac{Kv}{mg}$$

(the modulus signs can be dropped since $v < \dfrac{mg}{K}$, the terminal velocity).

Therefore the speed of the falling bob at time t is

$$v = \frac{mg}{K}\left(1 - e^{-Kt/m}\right)$$

Interpret/validate

This is a general solution which applies to any object falling under gravity, where the resistance force is modelled by $R = Kv$. Using this expression with appropriate values for the constants, graphs can easily be sketched to compare the motion of bodies of different mass, size and shape. The graphs show speed against time for identically shaped bobs of different masses, where $K = 5$.

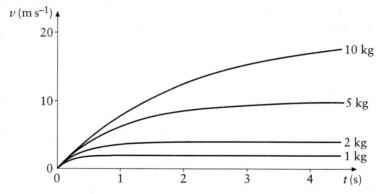

All the graphs above show that the speed of the bob increases as the bob falls and that the acceleration decreases as the bob approaches a terminal speed. The heavier the bob, the greater its terminal speed, and the longer it takes for this speed to be reached. (For example, the 10 kg bob is not yet close to terminal speed after 2 seconds.) Initially the bobs have the same acceleration.

You can obtain an expression for the distance fallen, x, by integrating the expression for v.

$$\frac{dx}{dt} = \frac{mg}{K}\left(1 - e^{-Kt/m}\right)$$

$$x = \frac{mg}{K}\int\left(1 - e^{-Kt/m}\right)dt \quad \Rightarrow \quad x = \frac{mg}{K}\left(t + \frac{m}{K}e^{-Kt/m} + c\right)$$

The initial conditions were $x = 0$, $t = 0$, so $c = -\dfrac{m}{K}$. So,

$$x = \frac{mg}{K}\left(t + \frac{m}{K}e^{-Kt/m} - \frac{m}{K}\right) \quad \Rightarrow \quad x = \frac{mg}{K}\left(t + \frac{m}{K}\left(e^{-Kt/m} - 1\right)\right)$$

Graphs of distance against time for identically shaped bobs of masses 1, 2, 5 and 10 kg, with $K = 5$, are as follows.

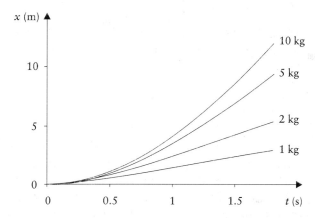

The following investigation applies the ideas developed here to model the motion of a falling feather.

 .2A

Feathers of all kinds fall slowly because their motion is greatly dependent on air resistance. For such a feather of mass m kilograms, assume that the air resistance force is modelled by $R = Kv$ newtons and assume a terminal speed of $w\,\mathrm{m\,s^{-1}}$.

1 Express K in terms of m and w.

2 Show that the equation of motion for the feather travelling at speed $v\,\mathrm{m\,s^{-1}}$ can be written as

$$\frac{dv}{dt} = g\left(1 - \frac{v}{w}\right)$$

3 Interpret this expression for the acceleration when:

(a) $v < w$ (b) $v = w$ (c) $v > w$

4 Integrate the expression and show that, for a feather falling from rest, the solution for v is

$$v = w(1 - e^{-gt/w})$$

5 Does the feather actually reach terminal speed? Comment on your answer.

6 Taking $w = 1$ and $g = 10$, use a graphical method or otherwise to find the time taken for the feather to reach the following percentages of terminal speed.

(a) 50%   (b) 90%   (c) 99%

7 Interpret these results and comment on their validity for a falling feather.

Instead of finding an expression for speed in terms of time, there are situations in which the speed at different heights is required and so a function $v(x)$ is more appropriate.

8 (a) Show that an alternative form for the acceleration $\dfrac{dv}{dt}$ is $v \dfrac{dv}{dx}$.

  (b) Using this form for acceleration, rewrite the equation of motion for the feather.

9 Show that $\dfrac{v}{v - w} = 1 + \dfrac{w}{v - w}$ and hence show that the equation of motion has a solution

$$x = \frac{-w}{g}\left(v + w \ln \left|\frac{v - w}{w}\right|\right)$$

10 Sketch the graph of distance fallen against speed. (Assume $w = 1$.)

11 Find the distance the feather has to fall to reach the following percentages of terminal speed.

(a) 50%   (b) 90%   (c) 99%

Solutions obtained numerically can now be checked with this general solution. For instance, graphs from the general solution can be superimposed on the numerical solutions.

The advantage of a general solution is that it enables much more interpretation, for example, of the effects of changing parameters such as mass. It is easier to sketch graphs for different values of the parameters K and m, instead of solving the equation numerically each time. Even for a particular case, it may be quicker, more accurate and more reliable to substitute particular values into your general solutions.

Acceleration can be written in various forms.

$$\frac{dv}{dt} = v\frac{dv}{dx} = \frac{d^2x}{dt^2}$$

The choice depends on the final solution required.

- For solutions in v and t, use $\frac{dv}{dt}$.

- For solutions in v and x, use $v\frac{dv}{dx}$.

- For solutions in x and t, use $\frac{dv}{dt}$ and then $v = \frac{dx}{dt}$, or $\frac{d^2x}{dt^2}$ directly.

Example 1

A fisherman casts a line with a spinner attached to the end. The spinner sinks slowly in the water before being reeled in, imitating the movement of a small fish.

The fisherman chooses a spinner of mass 30 grams, which sinks with terminal speed $1.5\,\mathrm{m\,s^{-1}}$.

(a) Find a suitable model for the force due to the water resistance.

(b) Calculate the depth to which the spinner sinks in 3 seconds.

(c) Estimate the time taken for the spinner to fall to a depth of 15 metres.

Solution

Assume that the spinner is small in comparison with its weight. The upthrust force is then negligible. Assume the spinner sinks vertically downwards, entering the water at time $t = 0$ with speed $v = 0$. For low speeds, the appropriate model for resistance is $R = Kv$ newtons.
Let x metres be the depth to which the spinner sinks in time t seconds.
Take $g = 10\,\mathrm{m\,s^{-2}}$.

Thus the only forces acting on the spinner are its weight and water resistance.

(a) Using Newton's second law,

$$0.3 - Kv = 0.03\frac{dv}{dt}$$

At terminal speed, $K \times 1.5 = 0.3 \quad \Rightarrow \quad K = 0.2$

Hence a suitable model for the force due to the water resistance is
$R = 0.2v$.

(b) Substituting $K = 0.2$ in the equation of motion,

$$\frac{dv}{dt} = \frac{10}{3}(3 - 2v)$$

Separating variables and integrating (with the initial conditions $v = 0$ when $t = 0$ 'written in' as limits of integration),

$$\int_0^v \frac{1}{3 - 2v}\, dv = \int_0^t \frac{10}{3}\, dt \quad \Rightarrow \quad -\tfrac{1}{2}\ln|3 - 2v| + \tfrac{1}{2}\ln 3 = \frac{10t}{3}$$

Rearranging this,

$$\ln\left|\frac{3 - 2v}{3}\right| = -\frac{20}{3}t \quad \Rightarrow \quad v = 1.5(1 - e^{-20t/3})$$

Integrating again for depth x at time t,

$$\int_0^x dx = \int_0^t 1.5(1 - e^{-20t/3})\, dt = \left[1.5(t + \tfrac{3}{20}e^{-20t/3})\right]_0^t$$

$$\Rightarrow \quad x = 1.5(t + \tfrac{3}{20}(e^{-20t/3} - 1))$$

Substituting $t = 3$ into this expression gives $x = 4.275$ metres. In 3 seconds, the spinner will have sunk to a depth of 4.3 metres.

(c) Substituting $t = 3$ into the expression for $v(t)$, after 3 seconds the spinner is almost travelling at its terminal speed of $1.5\,\mathrm{m\,s^{-1}}$.

Assuming that for the remaining distance of 10.725 metres the spinner is travelling at $1.5\,\mathrm{m\,s^{-1}}$,

$$t = 3 + \frac{10.725}{1.5} = 10.15$$

The time taken to sink 15 metres is 10.15 seconds. This gives an average speed of $1.48\,\mathrm{m\,s^{-1}}$, almost the terminal speed of the spinner.

Note that, for large enough t, you can use the approximation

$$x \approx 1.5(t - \tfrac{3}{20}) \quad (\text{as } e^{-20t/3} \to 0)$$

4.2 Exercise 1

In the following questions take $g = 10\,\mathrm{m\,s^{-2}}$.

1 A child lets go of a helium-filled balloon of mass 0.02 kg and it slowly rises. The equation of motion for the balloon is given by

$$1 - 0.5v = 0.02\frac{dv}{dt}$$

where $v\,\mathrm{m\,s^{-1}}$ is the speed of the balloon.

(a) State the forces acting on the balloon in this model and draw a force diagram. Find the magnitude of the upthrust force.

(b) Calculate the terminal speed of the balloon.

2 A tug boat is towing a ferry of mass 6000 tonnes by means of a single horizontal cable. The ferry experiences a resistance to motion given by $R = 12\,000v$ newtons, where $v\,\mathrm{m\,s^{-1}}$ is the speed of the ferry.

(a) Draw a diagram of the forces acting on the ferry.

(b) Find the tension in the cable when the ferry is pulled at a steady speed of $1.5\,\mathrm{m\,s^{-1}}$.

3 A small chick of mass 110 grams falls from a branch 12 metres above the ground. The chick's descent is slowed by air resistance, upthrust due to the air and the flapping of the chick's wings. The air resistance force is modelled by $R = 0.7v$ newtons, where $v\,\mathrm{m\,s^{-1}}$ is the speed of the chick and the upthrust force is 0.12 newtons.

(a) Write down an equation of motion for the chick's descent.

(b) Find the chick's terminal speed.

(c) By integrating twice, find an expression for the distance fallen in terms of time.

(d) Draw a graph of distance against time for the fall and hence find the time taken for the fall.

4 A feather and a marble are dropped at the same time from a 30-metre-high tower on a calm still day. The marble can be modelled as a particle of mass 0.5 kg for which air resistance is negligible. The feather is of mass 0.006 kg and the air resistance force is modelled as $R = 0.05v$ newtons where $v\,\mathrm{m\,s^{-1}}$ is the speed of the feather.

(a) Find an expression for the velocity of the feather after time t seconds. Hence deduce the terminal speed of the feather.

(b) Find the time taken for the feather to reach 99% of its terminal speed.

(c) Calculate the times taken for the marble and the feather to reach the ground.

(d) What are the speeds of the marble and the feather on impact?

4.2.2 Motion at high speeds

A sky-diver in free-fall is one example of motion at high speed, so the air resistance force is modelled by $R = kv^2$. You have already obtained a numerical solution to the equation of motion for a sky-diver using this model for air resistance. You can now find a general solution.

Problem

To find how the speed varies with time for the motion of a sky-diver.

Set up a model

The following assumptions are made.

- The sky-diver is a particle of mass m kilograms.
- She is in free-fall, with no cross-winds, and falls from rest.
- The model used for the resistance force at high speed is $R = kv^2$, where k is constant and v m s^{-1} is the speed of the sky-diver.
- Let w m s^{-1} be the terminal speed of the sky-diver.

Analyse the problem

Using Newton's second law,

$$mg - kv^2 = m\frac{dv}{dt}$$

At terminal speed,

$$mg = kw^2 \quad \Rightarrow \quad k = \frac{mg}{w^2}$$

$$\Rightarrow \qquad mg - \frac{mg}{w^2}v^2 = m\frac{dv}{dt}$$

$$\Rightarrow \qquad \frac{dv}{dt} = -\frac{g}{w^2}(v^2 - w^2)$$

$$\Rightarrow \qquad \int_0^v \frac{1}{v^2 - w^2}\, dv = \int_0^t \frac{-g}{w^2}\, dt$$

The left-hand integral is solved by writing the denominator as the difference of two squares and then expressing the fraction as partial fractions.

$$\int_0^v \frac{1}{v^2 - w^2}\, dv = \int_0^v \frac{dv}{(v - w)(v + w)}$$

$$= \int_0^v \left(\frac{1}{2w(v - w)} - \frac{1}{2w(v + w)} \right) dv$$

$$= \left[\frac{1}{2w}\ln|v - w| - \frac{1}{2w}\ln|v + w| \right]_0^v$$

$$= \left[\frac{1}{2w}\ln\left|\frac{v - w}{v + w}\right| \right]_0^v$$

$$= \frac{1}{2w}\ln\left(\frac{w - v}{w + v} \right) \qquad \text{since } w > v$$

Now, $\int_0^t \dfrac{-g}{w^2}\, dt = -\dfrac{gt}{w^2}$

so $-\dfrac{2gt}{w} = \ln\left(\dfrac{w-v}{w+v}\right)$

$\Rightarrow \quad \dfrac{w-v}{w+v} = e^{-2gt/w}$

$\Rightarrow \quad w - v = (w+v)\,e^{-2gt/w}$

$\Rightarrow \quad w(1 - e^{-2gt/w}) = v(1 + e^{-2gt/w})$

$\Rightarrow \quad v = w\left(\dfrac{1 - e^{-2gt/w}}{1 + e^{-2gt/w}}\right)$

This is a general solution for any object falling from rest under gravity, where the resistance force is modelled by $R = kv^2$.

The graph of speed against time shows how the speed approaches terminal speed, and that in this case the sky-diver almost reaches a terminal speed of $50\,\text{m s}^{-1}$ after about 15 seconds.

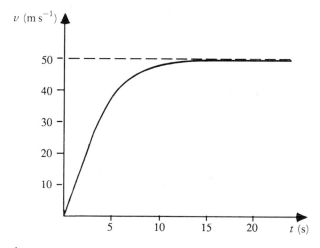

From the graph, as $t \to +\infty, \quad v \to 50 = w$

From the expression $v = w\left(\dfrac{1 - e^{-2gt/w}}{1 + e^{-2gt/w}}\right)$,

$v \to w$ (the terminal speed) because $e^{-2gt/w} \to 0$

When $t = \tfrac{1}{4}w$, $v \approx 0.99w$, so more than 99% of terminal speed is reached after 15 seconds.

To obtain a formula for distance fallen at time t, integrate the expression for v:

$$v = \frac{dx}{dt} = w\left(\frac{1 - e^{-2At}}{1 + e^{-2At}}\right) \quad \text{where } A = \frac{g}{w}$$

$$= w\left(\frac{e^{At} - e^{-At}}{e^{At} + e^{-At}}\right)$$

$$\int v \, dt = w \int \frac{e^{At} - e^{-At}}{e^{At} + e^{-At}} \, dt$$

$$x = \frac{w}{A}\ln\left|e^{At} + e^{-At}\right| + c$$

Equally, the problem could be solved numerically and a graph of the relationship plotted. The analytical and the numerical approach are compared below.

	Advantages	Disadvantages
Analytical method	Algebraic solutions are general and give exact answers. They facilitate interpretation.	It may be difficult or even impossible to find a solution for many possible models.
Numerical method	A numerical solution is always possible. A variety of models may be considered.	Only particular cases can be solved. Solutions are subject to inaccuracies.

The models used so far (resistance $\propto v$ and resistance $\propto v^2$) provide convenient analytic solutions to the problems and are attractive for this reason. Other models, such as resistance $\propto v^{1.2}$, may also be suitable, but here numerical solutions would be the only ones available.

 .2B

At some point, the sky-diver must end her free-fall and slow down before landing. She pulls the rip-cord and releases her parachute. Her speed is high even with the parachute open, so $R = kv^2$ is still an appropriate model for the air resistance force.

Problem

What is the least height at which the parachute can be opened in order to make a safe landing?

Set up a model

1 Make some simplifying assumptions about the sky-diver's motion, including her initial speed, U, before the parachute is opened; the terminal speed, W, with the parachute; and a reasonable 'safe' landing speed, V. Use $R = kv^2$ as the model for the air resistance force and let H metres be the least height at which the parachute could be opened.

2 Draw a diagram of the forces acting on the parachutist as she slows down, indicating the direction of the resultant force.

Analyse the problem

The problem is to find a value of H such that the increased air resistance force due to the parachute acts long enough to slow her down to a reasonable landing speed.

Since this is a problem involving speed and distance, a suitable equation of motion for the descent with a parachute is

$$mg - kv^2 = mv\frac{dv}{dx}$$

3 From your assumptions, substitute appropriate values into this equation and solve it to obtain a function for the distance fallen, x metres, in terms of the speed, $v\,\text{m s}^{-1}$.

4 At what height must the parachute be opened to give a 'safe' landing speed?

Interpret/validate

In tasksheet 1 of section 4.1 (page 365), the article stated that 610 metres was the lowest height at which the parachute should be opened.

5 Compare this height with the one you have calculated and comment on the validity of your model.

Example 2

A tennis ball of mass 0.1 kg is projected vertically upwards from a height of 1 metre with an initial speed of $12\,\text{m s}^{-1}$. The air resistance force is modelled as $R = 0.0025v^2$ newtons, where $v\,\text{m s}^{-1}$ is the speed of the ball. Find the time taken for the ball to reach its maximum height, that is, the height at which $v = 0$.

Solution

Using Newton's second law upwards,

$$-1 - 0.0025v^2 = 0.1\frac{dv}{dt}$$

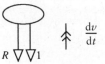

$$\Rightarrow \qquad -(400 + v^2) = 40\frac{dv}{dt}$$

Separating variables and integrating,

$$\int_0^t -\frac{1}{40}\,dt = \int_{12}^0 \frac{1}{400 + v^2}\,dv$$

$$\Rightarrow \qquad -\frac{t}{40} = 0 - \frac{1}{20}\tan^{-1}\left(\frac{12}{20}\right)$$

$$\Rightarrow \qquad t = 2\tan^{-1}(0.6) = 1.08$$

The time taken for the ball to reach its maximum height is 1.08 seconds.

Note that if air resistance is ignored, the time is $\dfrac{12}{g} \approx 1.2$ seconds.

4.2 Exercise 2

In the following questions take $g = 10\,\mathrm{m\,s^{-2}}$.

1 For the tennis ball in example 2,

    (a) calculate the maximum height above the ground that the ball reaches;

    (b) compare this with the maximum height it would reach if the resistance were zero.

2 A speed boat of mass 1200 kg is travelling at $30\,\mathrm{m\,s^{-1}}$ in calm water when the engine cuts out. When moving at $v\,\mathrm{m\,s^{-1}}$, the force due to water resistance on the boat is λv^2 newtons where λ is a constant.

    (a) Write down a differential equation of motion for the boat.

    (b) Show that the speed v at time t seconds after the engine cuts out is

$$v = \frac{1200}{\lambda t + 40}$$

    (c) It is observed that the speed slows down to $10\,\mathrm{m\,s^{-1}}$ in 5 seconds. Use this information to find the value of λ. Hence find how long it takes for the speed to slow to $5\,\mathrm{m\,s^{-1}}$.

3 A ski-jumper of mass 80 kg slides from rest down the smooth take-off ramp, inclined at 30° to the horizontal. The ramp is 85 metres long. The air resistance, R newtons, acting on the ski-jumper when on the ramp is modelled by $R = 0.64v^2$, where $v \, \text{m s}^{-1}$ is the speed of the ski-jumper.

(a) Find the speed of the ski-jumper at the end of the ramp.

(b) Comment on the change in the air resistance force when the jumper leaves the ramp.

4 A car of mass 1.8 tonnes is initially travelling at $28 \, \text{m s}^{-1}$. The engine is turned off and the car free-wheels to rest.

The horizontal force acting on the free-wheeling car has two components:

- a constant force of 144 newtons due to friction;
- a resistance of $36v^2$ newtons, where $v \, \text{m s}^{-1}$ is the speed of the car.

(a) Show that the differential equation of motion for the car is

$$\frac{dv}{dt} = \frac{-(4 + v^2)}{50}$$

(b) Find the time taken for the car to free-wheel to rest.

After working through section 4.2, you should:

1 be able to solve by analytical methods differential equations of the form

$$v \frac{dv}{dx} = f(v) \quad \text{or} \quad \frac{dv}{dt} = f(v)$$

2 be aware of a variety of situations which can be modelled using these differential equations;

3 be able to interpret graphical, algebraic and numerical solutions to problems in the context of resisted motion;

4 know the advantages and disadvantages of numerical and analytical methods.

4 Modelling with differential equations

.3 Variable mass and weight

4.3.1 The moon-lander

Suppose you are in a moon-lander, preparing to descend to the Moon. You are 50 000 metres above the surface with the module in line for descent when the fuel runs out! You have a problem!

Problem

Should you panic? How long before you crash-land? At what speed will the module crash onto the Moon?

> Set up a model

The assumptions are:

- the initial velocity of the lander is $0 \, \text{m s}^{-1}$;
- there is no air resistance;
- the gravitational acceleration is $1.62 \, \text{m s}^{-2}$ and is constant for the whole motion.

.3A

1 Solve the problem using the assumptions above.

2 Which of the assumptions would you want to change in order to obtain more realistic solutions?

In chapter 2, *Force and motion*, you saw that in some situations gravity should not be assumed to be constant. Over very large distances, the gravitational force of attraction changes significantly. This force was modelled by Isaac Newton when he proposed his law of gravitation.

Newton's law of gravitation
If two particles of masses m_1 and m_2 kilograms are a distance r metres apart, they will attract each other with a force of magnitude

$$F = \frac{Gm_1m_2}{r^2} \text{ newtons}$$

where $G = 6.67 \times 10^{-11} \text{ N m}^2 \text{ kg}^{-2}$ is the universal constant of gravitation.

At height h metres above the surface, the weight W newtons of the moon-lander is

$$W = \frac{GMm}{(R+h)^2} = mg_h$$

where g_h is the acceleration due to gravity h metres above the surface, m kilograms is the mass of the lander, M kilograms is the mass of the Moon, and R metres is the radius of the Moon. [The values of these and other constants are provided in Appendix 1, page 494.]

The acceleration due to gravity is therefore $g_h = \dfrac{GM}{(R+h)^2}$.

The graphs below show the acceleration due to gravity against height above the Moon's surface over three different ranges.

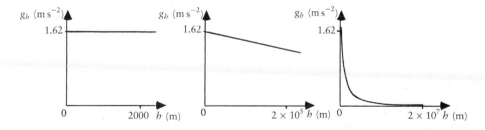

From the graphs, you can see that:

- From 0 to 2000 metres there is little variation in g_h. Over this range it is reasonable to assume that g_h is a constant equal to the gravitational acceleration at the surface (i.e. $1.62\,\mathrm{m\,s^{-2}}$ for the Moon).
- From 0 to 200 000 metres there is a small but noticeable decrease in g_h. It almost seems to be decreasing linearly with height over this range. For motion between the surface and a lunar orbit you might model gravity as a linear function.
- From 0 to 20 000 000 metres the acceleration due to the force of gravity begins to diminish noticeably. At 20 000 km away, $g_h = 0.35\,\mathrm{m\,s^{-2}}$ and will eventually become negligible as the height tends to infinity. For journeys over this range gravity should be modelled using Newton's law of gravitation.

A more accurate solution to the problem at the start of this section can be found by using Newton's law of gravitation to model the weight of the lander.

 .3B

The moon-lander has run out of fuel at a height of 50 km above the surface.

What is the speed on impact when it crash-lands?

Assume that the only force acting on the lander is its weight, which varies according to Newton's law of gravitation.

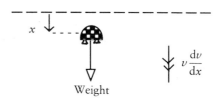

Weight

1 Show that the equation of motion for the lander of mass m kilograms can be written as

$$mv\frac{dv}{dx} = \frac{GMm}{(R + 50\,000 - x)^2}$$

where $v\,\mathrm{m\,s^{-1}}$ is the speed of descent after falling a distance x metres, M kilograms is the mass and R metres is the radius of the Moon.

2 Find an expression for the speed in terms of x, with initial conditions $v = 0$ and $x = 0$.

3 Calculate the impact speed of the lander.

4 Compare this value for the impact speed with the value calculated at the beginning of this section using a constant gravity model.

5 Show that a general expression for the impact speed, V_h, for an object falling from height h metres above the surface is

$$V_h = \sqrt{\left(\frac{2GMh}{R(R+h)} \right)}$$

6 (a) Sketch a graph of impact speed V_h against height h over the range $0 < h < 20\,000\,000$. Describe how the variation in weight affects the descent of the lander.

   (b) Superimpose the graph of impact speed calculated under the assumption of constant gravity, $g_m = 1.62\,\text{m s}^{-2}$. Comment on the difference between the two graphs.

7E Show that $V_h \approx \left(1 - \dfrac{h}{2R} \right) \sqrt{(2g_m h)}$ for an appropriate range of values of h.

The gravitational force of a planet acting on a particle can be assumed to be constant if the motion takes place over distances which are very small compared with the radius of the planet. Otherwise, Newton's law of gravitation is a more appropriate model for the gravitational force.

4.3.2 Escaping from the Earth

This is Michael Collins' commentary during the launch of Apollo 11, the first manned mission to land on the Moon.

This beast is best felt. Shake, rattle and roll! We are thrown left and right against our straps in spasmodic jerks. It is steering like crazy and I just hope it knows where it's going, because for the first ten seconds we are perilously close to the umbilical tower.

We started to burn at 100 miles altitude, and had reached only 180 miles at cut off, but we are climbing like a dingbat. In nine hours, when we are scheduled to make our first midcourse correction, we will be 57 000 miles out. At the instant of shutdown, Buzz recorded our velocity as 35 579 feet per second, more than enough to escape from the Earth's gravitational field. As we proceed outbound, this number will get smaller and smaller until the tug of the Moon's gravity exceeds that of the Earth's and then we will start speeding up again.

It's hard to believe that we are on our way to the Moon, at 1200 miles altitude now, less than three hours after lift-off, and I'll bet the launch-day crowd down at the Cape is still bumper to bumper.

Apollo expeditions to the Moon (NASA)

July 16th, 1969

The **escape speed** mentioned is the speed at which the projectile must be travelling in order to escape from the gravitational field of a planet, that is to avoid going into orbit or returning to the surface.

Modelling the launch of a rocket into space is not an easy task! There are a great many factors which need to be taken into account; some of these are discussed below.

Air resistance As the rocket moves higher and higher in the Earth's atmosphere and beyond, the resistance force will decrease.

Direction The first stage of the launch is usually to put the rocket into orbit about the Earth. From here, a fairly small amount of energy is needed to escape into space. It may be easier to consider a rocket as travelling directly away from the Earth, thus ignoring the trajectory required for orbit.

Gravity At the launch itself the distance travelled is relatively small so that gravity could be modelled as a constant. However, for motion into outer space the distances are so great that the variation in gravity would be significant.

Other bodies Once the rocket is far away from the Earth the gravitational attraction of other planets will become more significant than the attraction of the Earth. At some point, the rocket may be subject to significant attraction of two or even three bodies, such as the Moon, the Earth and the Sun.

Earth's rotation Since the rocket is travelling great distances over a rotating Earth it is subject to a force arising from the actual rotation. This force is known as the **Coriolis force** and will alter the path of the rocket slightly. To simplify matters this force will be ignored.

Rocket A Saturn V rocket was used in the Apollo space missions. This huge rocket consisted of three stages with a lunar module and a command module at the top of the stack. In total, the Saturn V rocket was 111 metres tall with a mass of about 3000 tonnes.

Fuel

The first stage of the Saturn V rocket burnt about 2100 tonnes of fuel in the first 160 seconds. The second stage burnt 450 tonnes in 6.5 minutes. In the final stage, 120 tonnes of fuel were burnt in two separate phases, the first (lasting 150 seconds) steering the rocket into Earth orbit and the second (lasting 345 seconds) altering the course to head towards the Moon.

Thrust

The initial thrust produced by the engines must be greater than the weight of the rocket or it would not take off.

Estimates of the thrust produced by each stage of the Saturn V rocket are:

- for the first stage, five F-1 engines producing a total of 33 million newtons of thrust;
- for the second stage, five J-2 engines producing a total of about 4.4 million newtons of thrust;
- for the third stage, a single J-2 engine producing about 0.9 million newtons of thrust.

In the following sections some of these factors will be considered to provide suitable models.

However, to simplify the problem, you can eliminate some of these factors from your model and concentrate on part of the problem, namely the escape speed required. Instead of modelling a rocket, which continues to accelerate after the launch, assume that it is a projectile on which the only force acting is gravity.

Problem

Find the speed of projection, $U \, \text{m s}^{-1}$, required for a projectile to escape from a planet.

Set up a model

The assumptions are:

- air resistance is negligible;
- the attraction of other bodies is negligible;
- the projectile is a particle of mass m kilograms, and its weight varies according to Newton's law of gravitation;
- the projectile has speed $v \, \text{m s}^{-1}$ and height h metres after t seconds;
- R metres is the radius and M kilograms the mass of the planet.

Analyse the problem

Using Newton's second law of motion and Newton's law of gravitation,

$$-\frac{GMm}{(R+h)^2} = mv\frac{dv}{dh}$$

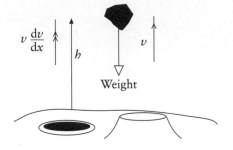

Separating variables and integrating,

$$\int v\,dv = -\int \frac{GM}{(R+h)^2}\,dh$$

$$\Rightarrow \qquad \frac{1}{2}v^2 = \frac{GM}{(R+h)} + \text{constant}$$

The initial conditions are
$h = 0, \quad v = U$, giving

$$\text{constant} = \frac{1}{2}U^2 - \frac{GM}{R}$$

$$\Rightarrow \qquad v^2 = U^2 - \frac{2GMh}{R(R+h)}$$

Interpret/validate

When $v = 0$, the projectile has reached its maximum height, H.

So $\qquad U = \sqrt{\left(\frac{2GMH}{R(R+H)}\right)}$

 .3c

1 Using a graph plotter, sketch the graph of U as a function of H for values of G, M, and R appropriate to the Moon.

2 Confirm that the value of the asymptote is $U = \sqrt{\left(\frac{2GM}{R}\right)}$.

3 What is significant about the asymptote?

For the projectile to escape from the planet its speed must always be greater than zero, i.e. the maximum height H is infinite.

$$U = \sqrt{\left(\frac{2GMH}{R(R+H)}\right)}$$

$$= \sqrt{\left(\frac{2GM}{R\left(\dfrac{R}{H}+1\right)}\right)} \rightarrow \sqrt{\left(\frac{2GM}{R}\right)} \quad \text{as } H \rightarrow +\infty$$

The escape speed of a projectile from the surface of a planet of mass M and radius R is

$$\sqrt{\left(\frac{2GM}{R}\right)}$$

Using $G = 6.67 \times 10^{-11}$, $M = 5.98 \times 10^{24}$ and $R = 6.378 \times 10^{6}$ in the formula gives the escape speed from the Earth as $11\,200\,\mathrm{m\,s}^{-1}$ (to 3 s.f.).

When setting up the model it was assumed that air resistance was negligible. However, travelling through Earth's atmosphere the air resistance would slow the projectile considerably. This would suggest that a greater speed of projection is required to escape.

In the description from *Apollo expeditions to the Moon* on page 293, the speed of the rocket at cut-off is given as $35\,579$ feet per second, which is approximately $10\,800\,\mathrm{m\,s}^{-1}$. This is comparable to the solution, although it is less than you might expect. In setting up the model it was assumed that the attraction of other bodies is negligible, but as you move farther away from the Earth, the Moon's attraction becomes more significant and effectively takes over. Furthermore, at cut-off the rocket is already at a height of 180 miles (288 km) above the Earth's surface so it would not need as great a speed to escape from this point.

Example 1
A space probe discovers a small dense meteor and lands on it to take measurements. The meteor is roughly spherical, of radius 17 metres and mass 10^{14} kg. On leaving, the probe runs out of fuel when it is only 25 metres up, travelling directly away from the meteor at $17\,\mathrm{m\,s}^{-1}$. Is this speed enough for the probe to escape?

Solution
Assume the probe is a particle of mass m kilograms and that there is no air resistance. Let h metres be the height of the probe above the meteor's surface and $v\,\mathrm{m\,s}^{-1}$ its speed.

Using Newton's second law away from the meteor and Newton's law of gravitation,

$$-\frac{G \times 10^{14} \times m}{(17+h)^2} = mv\frac{dv}{dh}$$

Separating variables and integrating,

$$\int_{17}^{v} v \, dv = \int_{25}^{h} -\frac{G \times 10^{14}}{(17+h)^2} \, dh$$

$\Rightarrow$

$$\left[\frac{v^2}{2}\right]_{17}^{v} = 6670 \left[\frac{1}{(17+h)}\right]_{25}^{h}$$

$\Rightarrow$

$$\frac{v^2}{2} - \frac{17^2}{2} = 6670 \left(\frac{1}{17+h} - \frac{1}{42}\right)$$

If probe is to escape, then $v > 0$ as $h \to +\infty$, and so

$$\frac{17^2}{2} + \frac{6670}{17+h} - \frac{6670}{42} > 0 \Rightarrow \frac{6670}{17+h} - 14.3 > 0$$

However, this expression is zero when $h = 449.1$. So the probe is not able to escape from the meteor and reaches a maximum height of 449 metres.

Solving the equation of motion for a projectile in a gravitational field with appropriate initial conditions gives

$$v^2 = u^2 + \left[\frac{2GM}{R+h}\right]_{h_1}^{h_2}$$

$v > 0$ for all $h_2 > h_1$, provided that

$$u > \sqrt{\left(\frac{2GM}{R+h_1}\right)}$$

which is the escape speed.

4.3 Exercise 1

Ignore the effects of air resistance.

1 Interpret the formula $U = \sqrt{\left(\frac{2GM}{R}\right)}$ for:

(a) different planets,

(b) a space station such as Skylab.

You might like to refer to Appendix 1 (page 494) for appropriate data.

2 A tiny meteor fragment of mass 0.3 kg enters the Earth's atmosphere. At 3000 km from the surface it is travelling directly towards the Earth at a speed of 10 m s^{-1}. Calculate its speed on impact.

3 (a) Calculate the distance from the Earth where the gravitational attraction of the Earth equals that of the Moon.

(b) Describe the motion of an unpowered craft passing through this point, travelling towards the Moon.

Earth

Moon

4 (a) In example 1, calculate the speed of impact of the probe after it falls back to the surface of the meteor.

(b) Calculate the minimum speed at which the probe needs to be travelling after 25 metres in order to be sure of escaping from the meteor.

5E What is the size of the biggest asteroid that you could jump off?

[Hint: make simplifying assumptions, for example, consider the asteroid to have the same mean density as the Earth. Estimate your maximum jumping speed on Earth and calculate the mass and radius of the asteroid for which this is sufficient speed for escape.]

4.3.3 Rocket propulsion

Sections 4.3.1 and 4.3.2 modelled the motion of bodies which were unpowered or projected by a single initial thrust. This section will develop the model for rocket-powered motion.

A common misconception about rockets is that they are propelled by the exhaust gases actually pushing against the ground, or the air. If this were the case, how would rockets be able to travel in space? The way a rocket engine produces thrust is investigated below.

.3D

Imagine standing on a trolley (or a skateboard) with a large bag of heavy balls. Suppose there is very little friction acting on the wheels of the trolley.

1 What will happen when a ball is thrown off the trolley?

2 Describe the effect each of the following will have on the trolley's motion:

    (a) the speed at which each ball is thrown;

    (b) the mass of each ball and the mass of the trolley;

    (c) the rate at which the balls are thrown.

It may be possible for you to verify some of these ideas if you have suitable equipment. You can set up a mathematical model for this motion by making some assumptions about the speeds and masses involved.

> **Set up a model**

The assumptions are as follows.

- The mass of you and your trolley is 60 kg.
- The mass of each ball is 2 kg.
- The speed of the balls is $10 \, \text{m s}^{-1}$ (relative to the trolley).
- The throwing rate is 1 per second.
- The initial number of balls is 100.
- The initial speed of the trolley is $0 \, \text{m s}^{-1}$.
- The speed of trolley at time t is $v \, \text{m s}^{-1}$.
- The air resistance and friction are negligible.

> **Analyse the problem**

3 Draw momentum diagrams before and after one ball has been projected.

4 Applying the principle of conservation of momentum to the trolley and the ball, show that the speed of the trolley after one ball has been thrown off (i.e. after one second) is $\frac{10}{129} \, \text{m s}^{-1}$.

5 Find the speed of the trolley over the next three seconds. (Note that when the trolley is moving forwards with speed v, the actual forwards speed of the ball relative to the ground is $v - 10 \, \text{m s}^{-1}$.)

It is possible to generalise the situation to calculate these small increases in speed using an iterative sequence.

6 Consider a trolley moving with initial speed v_0 m s^{-1}. The trolley has mass M kilograms and carries 100 balls, each of mass m kilograms. The balls are thrown from the trolley at a speed of C m s^{-1} relative to the trolley, at a rate of 1 per second. Let v_n m s^{-1} be the speed of the trolley after n balls have been thrown.

(a) Show that $v_1 = v_0 + \dfrac{mC}{M + 99m}$.

(b) Find a similar expression for v_2 in terms of v_1.

(c) Find an expression for v_n in terms of v_{n-1}.

7 Use your answers to question 6 to check your solutions to question 5.

8 v_n can be expressed as the sum of the sequence

$$v_n = \frac{mC}{M + (100 - n)m} + \cdots + \frac{mC}{M + 97m} + \frac{mC}{M + 98m} + \frac{mC}{M + 99m}$$

Using a program, calculate the speed of the original trolley after each 10 throws, plot the graph of speed against time for the trolley's motion and write down the final speed after 100 throws.

9 State the effect on the motion of the trolley of increasing:

(a) the mass of the balls,

(b) the speed of the throw,

(c) the throwing rate.

In a jet engine, the air around the aircraft is taken in, compressed, heated by combustion with the fuel, and the hot exhaust gases are ejected at high speed. A rocket engine operates by a similar principle but, for obvious reasons, it carries its own supply of oxygen to burn the fuel.

The aircraft's jet engines take air from outside, so consequently the decrease in mass is due only to the loss of fuel. The rocket, on the other hand, has a much greater change of mass because it carries both fuel and oxygen. This decrease in mass is a significant factor in modelling the motion of a rocket. The density and speed of the exhaust gas and the rate at which fuel is burnt are important in calculating the thrust produced.

Problem

Set up a differential equation to model a rocket's motion.

The assumptions are:

- the rocket burns fuel at a constant rate, μ kilograms per second;
- the rocket is in outer space, where no external forces are acting on it;
- the exhaust gas is ejected uniformly, at a constant speed of $C\,\mathrm{m\,s}^{-1}$ relative to the rocket;
- the initial mass of the rocket plus fuel is M_0 kilograms.

At time t the variables are:

- the speed of the rocket, $v\,\mathrm{m\,s}^{-1}$;
- the mass of the rocket and remaining fuel, M kilograms;
- the mass of fuel that has been ejected, m kilograms.

Therefore, $\quad M + m = M_0 \quad$ and $\quad \dfrac{\mathrm{d}M}{\mathrm{d}t} = -\dfrac{\mathrm{d}m}{\mathrm{d}t} = -\mu$

Consider a small interval of time, δt, during which time the mass of gas ejected is δm, resulting in an increase in speed of the rocket of δv.

Therefore $\delta m = \mu\,\delta t$ and the mass of the rocket at time t is $M(t) = M_0 - \mu t$.

Applying the principle of conservation of momentum,

At time t At time $t + \delta t$

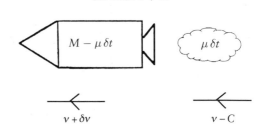

Total momentum at time t = Total momentum at time $t + \delta t$

$$Mv \approx (M - \mu\,\delta t)(v + \delta v) + \mu\,\delta t(v - C)$$

$\Rightarrow \qquad\qquad\qquad\qquad 0 \approx M\,\delta v - \mu\,\delta t\,\delta v - \mu\,\delta t\,C$

Since $\delta t\,\delta v$ is very small compared to other terms it can be ignored, giving

$$0 \approx M\,\delta v - \mu\,\delta t\,C$$

Dividing by δt leads (with $\delta t \to 0$) to

$$M\dfrac{\mathrm{d}v}{\mathrm{d}t} - \mu C = 0 \quad \text{or} \quad (M_0 - \mu t)\dfrac{\mathrm{d}v}{\mathrm{d}t} - \mu C = 0$$

where $\dfrac{dv}{dt}$ is the acceleration of the rocket and μ is the rate at which the fuel is ejected.

This equation of motion is known as the **rocket equation**. In this model, μ and C have been assumed to be constant. Note that M is the mass of the spacecraft at time t and so is not constant.

The equation of motion of the rocket is $\dfrac{dv}{dt} = \dfrac{\mu C}{M_0 - \mu t}$.

Separating variables,

$$\int_0^v dv = \int_0^t \frac{\mu C}{M_0 - \mu t}\, dt$$

$\Rightarrow \qquad v = \mu C \left[-\dfrac{1}{\mu}\ln|M_0 - \mu t| \right]_0^t$

$\Rightarrow \qquad v = C\ln\left| \dfrac{M_0}{M_0 - \mu t} \right|$

The rocket's speed increases from zero, the acceleration increasing as the burnt fuel is ejected.

For this equation, $v \to \infty$ as $t \to \dfrac{M_0}{\mu}$. In practice, however, the equation only holds while $t \leq \dfrac{M_1}{\mu}$, where $M_1(< M_0)$ is the initial mass of fuel.

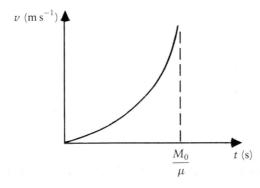

If the rate at which the fuel is ejected, μ, is doubled then the time before the fuel runs out is halved. Hence, although the rocket would accelerate at a different rate, its final speed would be the same. The final speed of the rocket would increase if the speed at which the fuel is ejected, C, is increased.

A similar equation can also be derived for a rocket taking off from the Earth.

Problem

Find the differential equation of motion for a rocket lifting off from the Earth

To analyse the motion, consider the changes in mass and velocity over a short interval of time δt.

The diagrams show the rocket and the exhaust gas ejected in the time interval of δt. M is the mass of the rocket at time t, $\mu \, \delta t$ is the mass of the ejected gas and C is the speed of the exhaust gas relative to the rocket.

1 At the start of the time interval, the rocket and exhaust gas have total mass M and velocity v and so have momentum Mv.

(a) Find the total momentum of the rocket and exhaust gas at the end of the time interval. Simplify your answer.

(b) Find the change in momentum during the time interval. By dividing by δt and considering the limit as $\delta t \to 0$, show that the rate of change of momentum is

$$M\frac{dv}{dt} - \mu C$$

2 Explain why the total external force acting on the rocket and exhaust gas is constant during the time interval. Hence show that the equation of motion for the rocket is

$$M\frac{dv}{dt} - \mu C = -Mg$$

3 In the diagram, T is the magnitude of the thrust on the rocket, the interaction force between the rocket and the gas.

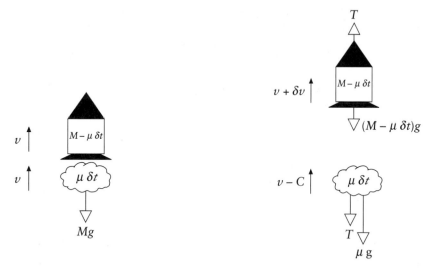

By considering just the rate of change of momentum of the gas, show that

$$T = \mu C$$

4 What condition on μ, C and M must be satisfied in order for lift-off to actually take place?

5E Show that if the initial mass of the rocket is M_0, where $M_0 \geq \dfrac{\mu C}{g}$, it will only lift off after time τ where

$$\tau = \frac{M_0}{\mu} - \frac{C}{g}$$

Interpret this equation for: (a) $\tau = 0$ (b) $\tau > 0$

You can obtain a model for the motion of a rocket by considering the change of momentum of the rocket and fuel in a time interval $(t, t + \delta t)$.

In deep space, the total rate of change of momentum is zero. In general, the total rate of change of momentum equals the resultant external force.

Example 2

An astronaut with a rocket pack is moving from a satellite back to his spacecraft at a speed of $2\,\mathrm{m\,s^{-1}}$. He fires the rockets for 5 seconds. The gas from the pack has an exhaust speed of $30\,\mathrm{m\,s^{-1}}$ and the fuel is burnt at a rate of $10\,\mathrm{kg\,s^{-1}}$. Initially, the total mass of the astronaut and pack is $200\,\mathrm{kg}$.

(a) Show that the equation of motion for the astronaut is

$$(20 - t)\frac{dv}{dt} = 30$$

(b) Calculate the speed of the astronaut after 5 seconds.

(c) Sketch a graph of v against t.

Solution

(a) At time t At time $t + \delta t$

Using the principle of conservation of momentum,

$$Mv = (M - 10\,\delta t)(v + \delta v) + 10\,\delta t(v - 30)$$

$$\Rightarrow \qquad 0 = M\,\delta v - 10\,\delta t\,\delta v - 300\,\delta t$$

Ignoring $\delta t \, \delta v$, dividing by δt and then letting $\delta t \to 0$,

$$M\frac{dv}{dt} = 300$$

Since $M = 200 - 10t$,

$$(200 - 10t)\frac{dv}{dt} = 300$$

$$\Rightarrow \qquad (20 - t)\frac{dv}{dt} = 30$$

(b) Separating variables,

$$\int_2^v dv = \int_0^t \frac{30}{20 - t} \, dt$$

$$\Rightarrow \qquad v - 2 = -30\ln\left|\frac{20 - t}{20}\right|$$

$$\Rightarrow \qquad v = 2 - 30\ln\left|\frac{20 - t}{20}\right|$$

Then $t = 5 \quad \Rightarrow \quad v = 10.63$

The speed of the astronaut at the end of the thrust is $10.6 \, \mathrm{m\,s^{-1}}$ (to 3 s.f.).

(c)

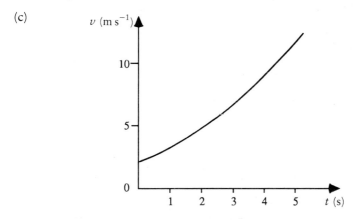

4.3 Exercise 2

Assume $g = 10 \, \mathrm{m\,s^{-2}}$ and ignore air resistance.

1 For the astronaut in example 2, explain what happens at $t = 20$.

2 A spacecraft is travelling initially at $250 \, \mathrm{m\,s^{-1}}$ in outer space. As the spacecraft approaches a space station its reverse thrust rockets are fired. The rockets eject fuel at $1000 \, \mathrm{m\,s^{-1}}$ relative to the craft and at a rate of $200 \, \mathrm{kg\,s^{-1}}$. Assume the attraction of the space station and other bodies to be negligible.

(a) Let M kilograms be the mass of the spacecraft at time t. Using the principle of conservation of momentum, show that

$$M\frac{dv}{dt} = -200\,000$$

(b) If initially the mass of the spacecraft is 9000 kg, show that the equation of motion for the spacecraft can be written as

$$(9000 - 200t)\frac{dv}{dt} = -200\,000$$

(c) Calculate the time taken for the spacecraft to stop.

3 A rocket of initial mass 10 000 kg is launched vertically upwards under gravity. The rate at which the rocket burns fuel is $50\,\mathrm{kg\,s^{-1}}$ and the burnt matter is ejected vertically downwards with a speed of $2000\,\mathrm{m\,s^{-1}}$ relative to the rocket. The burning ends after three minutes.

(a) Find the mass, M kg, of the rocket t seconds after the launch.

(b) The equation of motion for the rocket is

$$M\frac{dv}{dt} = -Mg + 100\,000$$

Calculate the speed of the rocket after three minutes.

4 The motion of a rocket during lift-off is modelled by the equation

$$M\frac{dv}{dt} - \mu C = -9.8M - kv^2$$

where $C\,\mathrm{m\,s^{-1}}$ is the speed of the exhaust gas relative to the rocket, $\mu\,\mathrm{kg\,s^{-1}}$ is the rate of decrease in mass of the rocket, M kilograms is the mass of the rocket at time t seconds and k is a constant.

(a) Describe the assumptions on which this model is based.

(b) Give two reasons why this model would only be valid for the launch stage of the rocket's motion.

5 A lunar lander of initial mass 1.8×10^4 kg fires its rockets to lift off from the Moon. The rockets burn fuel at a steady rate of $180\,\mathrm{kg\,s^{-1}}$. If the exhaust gas is ejected at $150\,\mathrm{m\,s^{-1}}$ relative to the lander, calculate the time taken before the lander begins to lift off.

After working through section 4.3, you should:

1 be able to model the motion of bodies subject to a variable gravitational force;

2 know what is meant by the term escape speed and be able to calculate it;

3 be able to model the motion of a body of variable mass such as a rocket;

4 be able to solve differential equations of the form

$$v\frac{\mathrm{d}v}{\mathrm{d}x} = \mathrm{f}(x) \quad \text{or} \quad \frac{\mathrm{d}v}{\mathrm{d}t} = \mathrm{f}(t)$$

5 be able to interpret graphical, analytical and numerical solutions to problems in variable weight and variable mass contexts.

4 Modelling with differential equations

.4 Simple harmonic motion

4.4.1 Vibrations everywhere

Vibrations and **oscillations** play a major part in everyday life. Everything you hear is vibrating! Some vibrations are useful, some are essential, some are irritating and some are even destructive.

In each vibration, a point can be identified which is moving about a fixed mean position, that is, it is oscillating. For example, each point on the baby in the baby-bouncer in the illustration is moving up and down about a mean position. Suitable functions to model this oscillating behaviour would be sine or cosine functions or a combination, that is,

$$x = a \cos \omega t \quad \text{or} \quad x = a \sin \omega t \quad \text{or} \quad x = a \cos \omega t + b \sin \omega t$$

where $a(t)$ is the **amplitude** of oscillation, which may grow, decay or be constant, and ω is the number of oscillations in 2π seconds, called the **angular velocity**.

The graph of $x = a \cos \omega t$ is as shown.

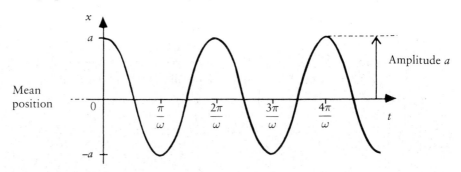

Example 1

A small child is placed in a baby-bouncer hung from a door frame. The height of the baby's bottom above the floor was measured as the baby bounced up and down. The results are plotted on the graph below.

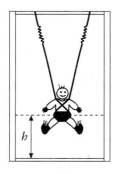
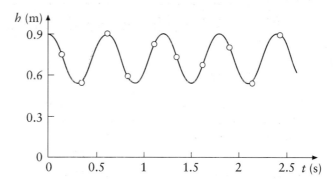

Describe the baby's motion:

(a) in words,   (b) by a suitable function, $h(t)$.

Solution

(a) The baby bounces up and down with a steady oscillation. In 2 seconds, approximately three and a half bounces are made, i.e. one bounce every 0.6 second. The baby's bottom reaches a maximum height of 0.9 m and a lowest height of about 0.54 m. The bounces all seem to have roughly the same amplitude.

(b) A cosine function of the type $h = a \cos \omega t + C$ seems to fit the data quite well. The time for one oscillation is 0.6 second, so in 2π seconds there will be $\dfrac{2\pi}{0.6} = 10.5$ oscillations. Therefore ω is 10.5, the amplitude a is 0.18 and the mean position is at $h = 0.72$.

So a suitable function to model these data would be

$$h = 0.18 \cos (10.5t) + 0.72$$

The fixed position about which a moving point oscillates is known as the **mean** or **equilibrium position**. The maximum displacement is called the **amplitude**, a.

The time for one complete oscillation is called the **time period**, τ (the Greek letter tau).

The number of oscillations in 2π seconds is called the **angular velocity**, ω, and so $\tau = \dfrac{2\pi}{\omega}$.

4.4 Exercise 1

1 Describe in words the motion of the following situations represented by the graphs, giving the time period and amplitude of oscillation. Suggest suitable functions for the graphs. In each case, $x(t)$ is the vertical displacement of an appropriate point.

(a) A seagull floating on the sea

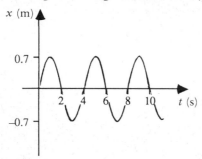

(b) A spin-drier with an uneven load

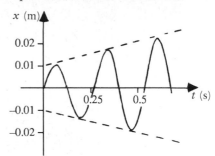

2 A piston is moving back and forth in a cylinder as shown in the diagram below.

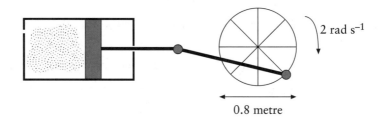

0.8 metre

(a) Sketch a graph representing the motion of a point in the piston's plunger over a suitable period of time.

(b) Suggest a possible function for your graph.

3 Hold a ruler over the edge of a table and strike it so that it vibrates. Try to model the vibration with a suitable function.

4.4.2 Simple harmonic motion

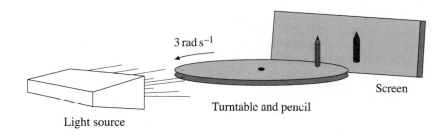

3 rad s^{-1}

Screen

Turntable and pencil

Light source

Consider the situation illustrated above. The pencil is fixed 20 cm from the centre of a turntable, rotating with constant angular speed 3 rad s^{-1}. The light projects the pencil's shadow on to a vertical screen.

A general model can be set up to describe the motion of the shadow.

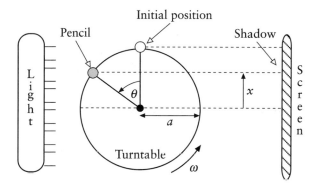

Initial position

Pencil   Shadow

Light

θ

x

a

Turntable

ω

Screen

Assume that the turntable is rotating with a constant angular speed of ω rad s^{-1}. The pencil is fixed at a distance a metres from the axis. Assume that the timing begins when the pencil's shadow is at its extreme position on the screen.

Let θ radians be the angle of displacement of the pencil at time t seconds and let x metres be the corresponding displacement of the shadow from the mean (central) position.

From the diagram, $x = a \cos \theta$.

The initial angle of displacement is zero (i.e. when $t = 0$, $\theta = 0$) $\Rightarrow \theta = \omega t$.

So the position of the shadow is given by $x = a \cos \omega t$.

The graph shows the shadow's displacement, x metres, with time t seconds.

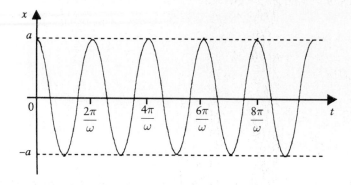

From the graph, the time period $\tau = \dfrac{2\pi}{\omega}$.

You may have already seen cosine and sine functions referred to as harmonic functions. Accordingly, the shadow's motion is an example of **simple harmonic motion** or **SHM**.

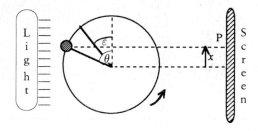

For general initial conditions, for example when $t = 0$, $\theta = \varepsilon$, then $\theta = \omega t + \varepsilon$.

The motion of the shadow is still called simple harmonic and the function describing its displacement is of the form

$$x = a\cos(\omega t + \varepsilon)$$

where a is the amplitude, ω is the angular velocity of oscillation and ε is a constant called the **phase constant**.

4 .4A

Show that $a\cos(\omega t + \varepsilon)$ is equivalent to $A\cos\omega t + B\sin\omega t$ and express the constants A and B in terms of a and ε.

In general, the displacement, velocity and acceleration of a body performing simple harmonic motion are given by:

- displacement $x = a \cos (\omega t + \varepsilon)$ ①
- velocity $\dot{x} = -a\omega \sin (\omega t + \varepsilon)$ ②
- acceleration $\ddot{x} = -a\omega^2 \cos (\omega t + \varepsilon)$ ③

Comparing equations ① and ③,

$$\ddot{x} = \frac{d^2x}{dt^2} = -\omega^2 x$$

The defining characteristic of simple harmonic motion is that the acceleration is proportional to the displacement of the body from the mean position, though it is always directed towards the mean position.

The equation for simple harmonic motion is

$$\ddot{x} + \omega^2 x = 0$$

This has the general solution

$$x = a \cos (\omega t + \varepsilon) \quad \text{or} \quad x = A \cos \omega t + B \sin \omega t$$

where a, ε, A and B are constants determined by the initial conditions.

4.4 Exercise 2

1 The displacement from the mean position of the shadow of a rotating pencil is given by $x = 0.2 \cos 3t$.

(a) Sketch, on the same set of axes, the graphs for the shadow's displacement, velocity and acceleration against time, for $0 \le t \le 12$ seconds.

(b) From the graphs, find the displacement of the shadow when:
    (i) its acceleration is zero;   (ii) its acceleration is maximum;
    (iii) its velocity is zero;   (iv) its velocity is maximum.

2 Show by substitution that the model for the baby-bouncer, $x = 0.18 \cos (10.5t)$, satisfies the SHM equation, $\ddot{x} + \omega^2 x = 0$, for some value of ω. (Note that in this case, x is the displacement from the mean position.)

3 Find the displacement, x, of the pencil's shadow, P, as a function of t given that P is at I when $t = 0$.

(a)   (b)

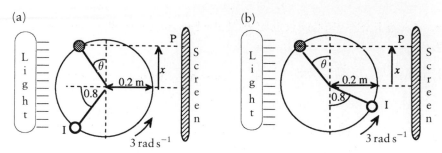

4 Show by substitution that $x = A \cos \omega t + B \sin \omega t$ is a general solution to the SHM equation

$$\frac{d^2 x}{dt^2} + \omega^2 x = 0$$

4.4.3 Modelling an oscillating body

Collecting data from oscillating bodies makes it possible to find a function that models the motion, as in the example of the baby-bouncer. However, this does not give any insight into how the bouncer would behave when a heavier or lighter baby uses it. To design a bouncer suitable for a range of different sized babies, you need to have an understanding of how the mass of the baby influences the period and amplitude of oscillation.

Problem

How does the period of oscillation of the baby-bouncer vary with the mass of the baby?

To set up a differential equation you will need to apply Newton's second law of motion. This requires a model for the forces involved.

Set up a model

Simplify the bouncer to a single spring of natural length l metres. Assume the tension in the spring can be modelled by Hooke's law. Assume also that the baby is a particle of mass m kilograms suspended from the spring so that it is never in contact with the floor. Ignore air resistance and assume the bouncer never goes slack.

When in equilibrium the spring is extended by a length, e metres. The baby is pulled down a further a metres and released.

Let x metres be the displacement of the baby beyond the equilibrium position at time t.

There are three positions to consider, as shown in the diagram below.

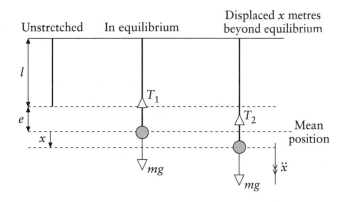

Analyse the problem

In the equilibrium position, $\quad mg = T_1$
and from Hooke's law, $\qquad T_1 = ke$
$\qquad\qquad \Rightarrow \qquad\quad mg = ke$

For a further vertical displacement, x, the new tension is $T_2 = k(e + x)$.

There will be a resultant force, $mg - T_2$.

So using Newton's second law vertically downwards, we obtain the second order linear differential equation describing the motion,

$$mg - k(e + x) = m\ddot{x}$$

Substituting $mg = ke$,

$$-kx = m\ddot{x} \quad \Rightarrow \quad \ddot{x} = -\frac{k}{m}x$$

This differential equation is the same as the equation for SHM,

$$\ddot{x} = -\omega^2 x$$

where the angular velocity $\omega = \sqrt{\left(\dfrac{k}{m}\right)}$.

.4B

1 For the baby-bouncer, use the initial conditions $t = 0$, $x = a$ and $\dfrac{dx}{dt} = 0$ to show that the solution to the differential equation is

$$x = a \cos\left(\sqrt{\left(\dfrac{k}{m}\right)}\,t\right)$$

2 For $k = 500$, $m = 10$ and $a = 0.6$, sketch the graph of the displacement x against time t for the oscillating baby.

3 Use the graph to estimate the time period of oscillation.

Interpret/validate

The initial problem was to find how the time period of oscillation varies with the mass of the baby. Using the graph it is possible to find the time period τ.

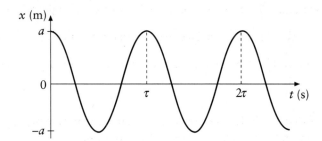

The first oscillation is complete when $t = \tau \quad \Rightarrow \quad \cos\left(\sqrt{\left(\dfrac{k}{m}\right)}\tau\right) = 1$

that is, when $\sqrt{\left(\dfrac{k}{m}\right)}\tau = 2\pi$.

So the time period of one oscillation is

$$\tau = \dfrac{2\pi}{\sqrt{\left(\dfrac{k}{m}\right)}} = 2\pi\sqrt{\left(\dfrac{m}{k}\right)}$$

(Alternatively, the formula $\tau = \dfrac{2\pi}{\omega}$ where $\omega = \sqrt{\left(\dfrac{k}{m}\right)}$ can be used to give this result.)

The time period increases as the mass on the spring increases, and is greater for springs with a low spring constant. Oscillations are less rapid for lower values of the spring constant k. Note that the period of oscillation does not depend on the amplitude of the oscillation.

It should now be possible to validate the solution with data from an experiment using different masses on strings and springs, or even a real baby in a baby-bouncer.

4.4 Tasksheet 1 – Validating the formula $T \propto \sqrt{m}$ (page 368)

Example 2

A metal block of mass 2 kg is attached to the end of a light spring of natural length 30 cm. The other end is fixed to a wall and the whole system is at rest on a smooth horizontal table, with the spring unstretched.

The block is struck so that it moves away from the wall with an initial speed of $2 \, \text{m s}^{-1}$. Assume the spring obeys Hooke's law (i.e. it is a Hookean spring) and has a spring constant of $800 \, \text{N m}^{-1}$.

(a) Show that the equation of motion can be written as $\dfrac{d^2x}{dt^2} = -400x$ where

x metres is the displacement of the block from its original position.

(b) Solve the equation for the displacement in terms of time, t.

(c) How close does the block get to the wall during the subsequent motion?

Solution

(a) Assume that the block is a particle, the air resistance is negligible and the spring obeys Hooke's law for the whole motion.

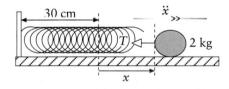

Using Newton's second law,

$$m \frac{d^2x}{dt^2} = -T$$

From Hooke's law,

$$T = 800x$$

$$\Rightarrow \quad 2 \frac{d^2x}{dt^2} = -800x \quad \Rightarrow \quad \frac{d^2x}{dt^2} = -400x$$

(b) This is an equation for SHM which has a solution in the form $x = a \cos(\omega t + \varepsilon)$, where $\omega^2 = 400$.

From the equation, $\omega = 20$. The initial conditions are $t = 0$, $x = 0$, $\dot{x} = 2$, so

$$x = a \cos \varepsilon = 0 \quad \Rightarrow \quad \varepsilon = \frac{\pi}{2} \quad \text{or} \quad \frac{3\pi}{2}$$

Substituting $\omega = 20$ and $\varepsilon = \frac{3\pi}{2}$ in the general solution gives

$$x = a \cos\left(20t + \frac{3\pi}{2}\right) \quad \text{or} \quad x = a \sin(20t)$$

Differentiating for velocity,

$$\dot{x} = 20a \cos(20t)$$

When $t = 0$, $\dot{x} = 2$, so

$$2 = 20a \cos 0 \quad \Rightarrow \quad a = 0.1$$

Therefore the displacement of the block is $x = 0.1 \sin 20t$.

(c) The amplitude is 0.1 metre, so the closest the block gets to the wall is 20 cm.

The SHM equation is an example of a second order linear differential equation (a differential equation with constant coefficients whose highest derivative is the second derivative) and can be solved by various methods without reference to the general solution. Another method of solution of the SHM equation is explored below.

 .4c

The equation for simple harmonic motion is the second order differential equation $\ddot{x} = -\omega^2 x$. It can be solved by separation of variables.

1 An alternative form of the SHM equation is

$$v \frac{dv}{dx} + \omega^2 x = 0, \quad \text{where } v = \dot{x}$$

Show, by separation of variables, that this has a solution

$$v^2 = -\omega^2 x^2 + \text{constant}$$

2 If the initial conditions are $x = a$ and $v = 0$, then show that

$$v = \pm \omega \sqrt{(a^2 - x^2)}$$

3 Sketch a graph of velocity against displacement and interpret it as x varies from $-a$ to a.

4 Show that separating variables once again gives

$$\int_0^t dt = \int_a^x \frac{\pm 1}{\omega\sqrt{(a^2 - x^2)}}\, dx$$

and find a solution for $x(t)$.

5 The equation of motion for the mass on a spring is

$$\ddot{x} = -\frac{k}{m}x$$

Find the solution for the initial conditions $t = 0$, $x = 0$, $\dot{x} = 9$. Suggest a possible physical situation that would have these initial conditions.

4.4 Exercise 3

Take $g = 10\,\mathrm{m\,s^{-2}}$.

1 A bob suspended on an elastic string is released from an initial displacement of 1.0 cm below its equilibrium position. The displacement from equilibrium of the bob, x metres, is given by a function of the form $x = a\cos\omega t$. The time for 10 oscillations is 8 seconds.

(a) Show that $a = \dfrac{1}{100}$ and $\omega = \dfrac{5\pi}{2}$.

(b) Calculate the maximum speed and maximum acceleration of the bob.

(c) State the displacement of the bob when these maxima occur.

2 A Hookean spring of natural length 30 cm doubles in length when a 100 g mass is hung on the end of it.

(a) Find a formula for the tension in the spring when the mass is x metres below the equilibrium position.

From the equilibrium position, the hanging mass is displaced a further 2 cm downwards and released so that it oscillates vertically.

(b) Calculate the initial acceleration of the mass.

(c) Find the time period of these small oscillations.

3 A particle of mass 0.3 kg is suspended from a vertical Hookean spring of length 0.6 metres and spring constant $15 \, \mathrm{N \, m^{-1}}$. The particle is pulled down until the spring is 0.9 metres long and then released from rest.

(a) Show that the equation of motion is

$$\frac{\mathrm{d}^2 x}{\mathrm{d}t^2} = 10 - 5x$$

where x metres is the extension of the spring.

(b) Verify by substitution that $x = 2 + \cos{(t\sqrt{5})}$ is a solution to the differential equation, satisfying the initial conditions.

(c) Show that the spring never actually compresses.

4 A particle of mass 1.2 kg is attached between two identical Hookean springs which rest on a smooth horizontal table. The other end of each spring is fixed to a support. The springs are unstretched until the particle is displaced to one side and then released.

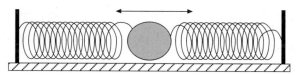

(a) Assuming that air resistance and friction are negligible, draw a diagram showing the forces on the particle when its displacement is x metres from the central position.

(b) If the spring constant of both springs is $24 \, \mathrm{N \, m^{-1}}$, write down the equation of motion of the particle and show that it performs SHM with angular velocity of $6.32 \, \mathrm{rad \, s^{-1}}$.

After working through section 4.4, you should:

1 understand and be able to use the terms equilibrium or mean position, amplitude, time period and angular velocity when applied to oscillations;

2 be able to recognise the equation for simple harmonic motion, $\ddot{x} + \omega^2 x = 0$, and write down its general solution;

3 be able to model the motion of a body oscillating on the end of a spring by applying Hooke's law;

4 be able to solve the SHM equation;

5 be able to interpret solutions to the SHM equation.

4 Modelling with differential equations

.5 Other oscillations

4.5.1 The pendulum

The first pendulum clock was invented in about 1657 by Christiaan Huygens. Up until the 1950s the most accurate clocks were pendulum clocks, the best being accurate to within a few thousandths of a second per day. To ensure such accuracy, it is essential to know how to modify the period of oscillation.

▶ 4.5 Tasksheet 1 – Pendulum clocks (page 369)

In the tasksheet, the effects of three factors on the time period were considered – the length, the mass of the bob and the initial angle of displacement. Before studying the theoretical analysis you should be familiar with the result that the tangential component of acceleration of a particle moving in a circle of radius r is $r\ddot{\theta}$. This was established in Chapter 3, *Towards circular motion*.

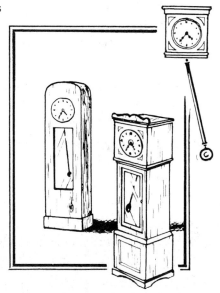

Problem

How is the time period of oscillation of a pendulum affected by varying the length, mass or initial angle of displacement?

Set up a model

To analyse the motion of a pendulum, a simple model is required. Assume that the pendulum consists of a bob on the end of an inextensible string or rod. The bob is assumed to be a particle of mass m kilograms and the string or rod is assumed to have no mass. The other end of the string is suspended from a fixed point so that the pendulum swings freely. The friction at the pivot and air resistance are assumed to be negligible. This is known as a **simple pendulum**.

Assume that the simple pendulum is of length l metres. Let it be displaced initially by a small angle, α radians, from the vertical, and then released. Let θ radians be the angle the string makes with the vertical at time t seconds.

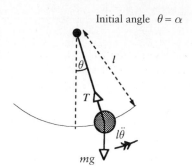

Initial angle $\theta = \alpha$

```
```

Analyse the problem

Using Newton's second law, taking the component along the tangent to the arc in the direction of increasing θ,

$$-mg \sin\theta = ml\frac{\mathrm{d}^2\theta}{\mathrm{d}t^2}$$

$$\ddot{\theta} = -\frac{g}{l}\sin\theta$$

Notice that m cancels out and so does not affect the rest of the analysis (in other words, the motion is independent of the mass of the bob).

If the initial angle of displacement is small then the approximation $\sin\theta \approx \theta$ can be made. So the equation of motion becomes

$$\ddot{\theta} = -\frac{g}{l}\theta$$

This is the SHM equation, with $\omega^2 = \frac{g}{l}$. The general solution is

$$\theta = a\cos\left(t\sqrt{\left(\frac{g}{l}\right)} + \varepsilon\right)$$

where a and ε are constants determined by the initial conditions. In this example, $\theta = \alpha$ and $\dot{\theta} = 0$ when $t = 0$ and so

$$\theta = \alpha\cos\left(t\sqrt{\left(\frac{g}{l}\right)}\right)$$

Interpret/validate

The time period is given by

$$\tau = \frac{2\pi}{\omega} = 2\pi\sqrt{\left(\frac{l}{g}\right)}$$

τ is independent of the mass of the bob and depends only on the length of the pendulum and the value of g. For a pendulum of length 1 metre, i.e. $l = 1$ and $g = 10$, the time period is $2\pi\sqrt{\left(\frac{1}{10}\right)} \approx 2.0$ seconds.

This model implies that the time period is independent of the initial angle α. However, experimental results suggest that this is not the case for larger amplitudes. In setting up the model it was assumed that the initial displacement was small, which allowed the small angle approximation $\sin\theta \approx \theta$ to be made.

The pendulum equation $\ddot{\theta} = -\frac{g}{l}\sin\theta$ can be solved numerically by a numerical method using

$$\theta_{n+1} = \theta_n + \dot{\theta}_n\,\delta t, \qquad \dot{\theta}_{n+1} = \dot{\theta}_n + \ddot{\theta}_n\,\delta t \quad \text{and} \quad \ddot{\theta}_n = -\frac{g}{l}\sin\theta_n$$

 .5A

1 For $l = 1$, $g = 10$ and $\alpha = 0.1$, use a time interval of 0.01 to find the time period of the pendulum.

2 Find the time period if α is changed to 1.5.

3 Explain how you should vary l to correct a pendulum clock which runs fast or slow.

The motion of a simple pendulum of length l metres, for small initial angle of displacement, can be modelled as simple harmonic motion, i.e.

$$\ddot{\theta} + \omega^2\theta = 0, \qquad \text{where} \quad \omega = \sqrt{\left(\frac{g}{l}\right)}$$

However, for larger amplitude oscillations the pendulum equation should be used.

$$\ddot{\theta} + \frac{g}{l}\sin\theta = 0$$

Example 1

The equation of motion of a pendulum consisting of a bar with a slide weight is $\ddot{\theta} + 0.64 \sin \theta = 0$, where θ radians is the displacement of the bar from the vertical. The pendulum is released from rest with an initial angle of displacement 0.1 radian.

(a) Find an expression for its subsequent displacement in terms of time t seconds.

(b) Calculate the approximate number of oscillations performed in one minute.

Solution

(a) Since the angle of displacement is small, the equation of motion becomes

$$\ddot{\theta} + 0.64\theta = 0$$

This is the SHM equation where $\omega = \sqrt{0.64} = 0.8$. Therefore the general solution is

$$\theta = a \cos(0.8t + \varepsilon)$$

The initial conditions are $t = 0$, $\theta = 0.1$

$$\Rightarrow \quad 0.1 = a \cos \varepsilon \qquad ①$$

Differentiating for angular velocity,

$$\dot{\theta} = -0.8a \sin(0.8t + \varepsilon)$$

Initially,

$$\dot{\theta} = 0 \quad \Rightarrow \quad 0 = -0.8a \sin \varepsilon$$

$$\Rightarrow \quad \sin \varepsilon = 0 \quad \Rightarrow \quad \varepsilon = 0$$

Substituting in ① gives $a = 0.1$.

So the angular displacement of the bar is $\theta = 0.1 \cos (0.8t)$.

(b) The time period $\tau = \dfrac{2\pi}{0.8} = 7.85$ seconds. So in 60 seconds there will be approximately seven and a half oscillations.

4.5 Exercise 1

Take $g = 10 \, \text{m s}^{-2}$.

1 A simple pendulum is hanging vertically at rest when it is gently struck and given an initial angular velocity of $0.2 \, \text{rad s}^{-1}$. The subsequent motion is described by the differential equation

$$\frac{\mathrm{d}^2\theta}{\mathrm{d}t^2} + \frac{25}{9}\theta = 0$$

where θ radians is the angle the string makes with the vertical.

(a) Solve the equation of motion, giving θ as a function of time, t seconds.

(b) Find the time period of the oscillations.

(c) State three main assumptions that have been made in setting up the differential equation.

2 A simple pendulum with a bob of mass 200 grams is displaced initially by an angle of 0.17 radian and released. The subsequent oscillations have a time period of 0.9 second.

(a) Estimate the length of the pendulum.

(b) Find the maximum angular speed of the bob.

3

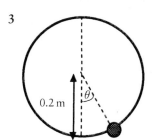

0.2 m

A smooth circular ring of wire, of radius 0.2 metre, is fixed in a vertical plane with a small bead of mass 15 grams threaded onto the wire, as shown in the diagram.

The bead oscillates to and fro about the lowest position.

(a) Set up a model for the motion of the bead, drawing a diagram of the forces acting on the bead when in the position shown in the diagram.

(b) Assuming that the amplitude of oscillation is small, show that the equation of motion is

$$\ddot{\theta} + 50\theta = 0$$

(c) Deduce the time period of oscillation of the bead.

4 (a) By differentiating the equation

$$\dot{\theta}^2 = \frac{2g}{l}\cos\theta + C, \quad \text{where } C \text{ is constant}$$

verify that

$$\dot{\theta} = \pm\sqrt{\left(\frac{2g}{l}\cos\theta + C\right)}$$

is a general solution to the pendulum equation, $\ddot{\theta} + \frac{g}{l}\sin\theta = 0$.

(b) For a simple pendulum of length 1 metre, released from rest when $\theta = \dfrac{\pi}{2}$ radians, show that the solution for $\dot\theta$ is

$$\dot\theta = \pm\sqrt{(20\cos\theta)}$$

(c) Explain why the time period of oscillation is

$$4\int_0^{\pi/2} \frac{d\theta}{\sqrt{(20\cos\theta)}}$$

Use a numerical method to evaluate this integral and compare your answer with the time period for oscillation of small amplitude.

4.5.2 Damping

So far, in setting up the model for the motion of an oscillating body the amplitude has been assumed to be constant. In reality, this may only be valid for a short time. For example, the amplitude of oscillation of a mass on the end of a spring gradually decreases. This is an example of **damping**.

In many systems, damping is deliberately introduced to reduce unwanted vibrations. Examples are the shock absorbers in a vehicle's suspension, damped restoring springs in doors, and control devices in gauges and meters to stop the needles or pointers oscillating.

For a mass oscillating at the end of a spring it is possible to make the following observations based on experimental evidence.

(a) The amplitude of oscillation for a spring remains reasonably constant, but over time the amplitude gradually decreases and at some point the oscillations will cease.

Possible graphs of amplitude against time are illustrated below.

(i)　　　　　　　　　　　　　　　　　　　(ii)

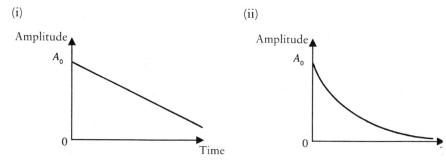

(b) Possible functions to describe how the amplitude varies with time could be:

(i) amplitude $= A_0 - \lambda t$ (ii) amplitude $= A_0 e^{-\lambda t}$

where A_0 is the initial amplitude and λ is a constant.

From experiment it is found that $A_0 e^{-\lambda t}$ is the more appropriate function for modelling the amplitude decay.

There are a number of possible damping forces causing the damping of the motion. Possible forces are:

- the air resistance due to the mass moving through air;
- the frictional force at the support;
- internal forces in the spring itself.

(You may like to investigate the decrease in amplitude experimentally, by finding the amplitude at intervals of, for example, 10 seconds.)

Problem

How does the amplitude of the mass–spring oscillator decay with time?

Set up a model

Consider a mass of m kilograms oscillating vertically on the end of a spring with spring constant k newtons per metre and natural length l metres. Assume that there is a damping force, R newtons, proportional to the speed of the mass and acting in the opposite direction to the motion.

Let e metres be the extension of the spring when the mass is in equilibrium and x metres be the displacement from equilibrium at time t seconds.

Analyse the problem

When the mass is in static equilibrium, $R = 0$. By Hooke's law,

$$T = mg$$

$$\Rightarrow \quad ke = mg$$

The damping force R is of the form

$$R = Cv$$

where $v\,\mathrm{m\,s^{-1}}$ is the speed of the mass and C is a constant, the **damping coefficient**.

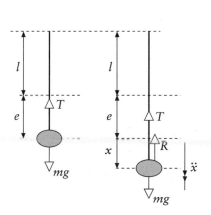

.5B

1 Using Newton's second law, show that the equation of motion for the mass is

$$m\ddot{x} + C\dot{x} + kx = 0 \qquad (1)$$

This is the equation for **damped SHM**. It is a second order linear differential equation and standard methods can be used for its solution. You will need to apply the following results.

The general solution of the equation

$$a\frac{d^2y}{dx^2} + b\frac{dy}{dx} + cy = f(x)$$

is the sum of the **complementary function** (a solution with two arbitrary constants of the related equation $a\dfrac{d^2y}{dx^2} + b\dfrac{dy}{dx} + cy = 0$, and a **particular integral**.

The equation

$$am^2 + bm + c = 0$$

is called the **auxiliary equation**. If the roots of the auxiliary equation are α and β, then the complementary function is

$$y = A\,e^{\alpha x} + B\,e^{\beta x} \qquad \text{if } \alpha \neq \beta$$

$$y = (A + Bx)\,e^{\alpha x} \qquad \text{if } \alpha = \beta$$

In equation (1) we have $f(x) = 0$ and so there is no particular integral. The solutions for this equation are considered in the following questions.

Consider a mass of m kilograms oscillating on the end of a spring with spring constant $k = 10\,\mathrm{N\,m^{-1}}$, with a damping coefficient $C = 20\,\mathrm{N\,m^{-1}\,s}$. The mass is released from rest with an initial displacement of 2 metres.

The equation of motion (1) for damped simple harmonic motion is

$$m\ddot{x} + C\dot{x} + kx = 0$$

2 Obtain the auxiliary equation by making the substitution $x = A\,e^{pt}$.

3 The auxiliary equation has two roots

$$p_1 = \frac{-C + \sqrt{(C^2 - 4mk)}}{2m} \qquad \text{and} \qquad p_2 = \frac{-C - \sqrt{(C^2 - 4mk)}}{2m}$$

Using the given values of k and C, show that there are three possible cases, giving a condition on the size of the mass for each case.

Case 1

If p_1 and p_2 are both real, then the general solution is $x = A\,e^{p_1 t} + B\,e^{p_2 t}$ where A and B are arbitrary constants.

4 Find the solution for a mass of 7.5 kg on the end of the spring. Sketch the graph of displacement against time and describe the motion of the mass.

In this case the motion is said to be **overdamped**.

Case 2

If $p_1 = p_2$, then the general solution is $x = (A + Bt)\,e^{-Ct/2m}$, where A and B are arbitrary constants.

5 Find the solution for a mass of 10 kg on the end of the spring. Sketch the graph of displacement against time and describe the motion of the mass.

Case 3

If p_1 and p_2 are complex, then the general solution is

$$x = A\,e^{-Ct/2m}\cos(nt + \varepsilon)$$

where $n = \dfrac{\sqrt{(4mk - C^2)}}{2m}$ and A and ε are arbitrary constants. (You could confirm this by substitution back into the equation of motion.)

6 Find the solution for a mass of 100 kg on the end of the spring. Sketch the graph of displacement against time and describe the motion of the mass.

In this case the motion is said to be **underdamped**.

7 In the underdamped case, the general solution has an oscillating factor $\cos(nt + \varepsilon)$ and a decay factor $e^{-Ct/2m}$. Describe what happens to the motion as $C \to 0$.

There are three possible types of solution to the damped SHM equation

$$m\ddot{x} + C\dot{x} + kx = 0$$

according to the values of m, C and k. They are:

- overdamping   when $C^2 > 4mk$
- critical damping   when $C^2 = 4mk$
- underdamping   when $C^2 < 4mk$

$C^2 > 4mk$

The auxiliary equation has real roots.
The mass does not complete an oscillation.

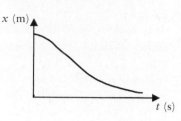

$C^2 = 4mk$

The auxiliary equation has equal roots.
As in the case of overdamping, the mass does
not complete an oscillation. In this
situation the amplitude decays to zero most
rapidly.

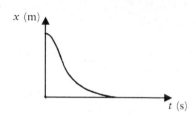

$C^2 < 4mk$

The auxiliary equation has complex roots. The
mass oscillates with decaying amplitude.

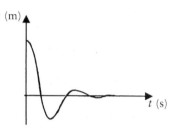

Example 2

The differential equation describing the motion of a shock absorbing device of
mass m kilograms is

$$m\ddot{x} + 18\dot{x} + 3x = 0$$

Find the mass for which the system is critically damped.

Solution

The auxiliary equation is $mp^2 + 18p + 3 = 0$

$$\Rightarrow \quad p = \frac{-18 \pm \sqrt{(324 - 12m)}}{2m}$$

For critical damping, the auxiliary equation must have equal roots, i.e.
$324 = 12m$.

The system is critically damped when the mass is 27 kg.

4.5 Exercise 2

Take $g = 10\,\text{m}\,\text{s}^{-2}$.

1 A mass on the end of a spring performs damped harmonic motion given by

$$x = 0.2\,e^{-0.5t} \sin 2t$$

where x metres is the displacement of the mass at time t seconds.

Sketch a graph of displacement against time for $0 < t < 8$ and interpret the graph.

2 A clock has a simple pendulum of length 20 cm with a bob of mass 180 grams. The air resistance force on the bob is of magnitude $3.6k$ times its speed.

(a) Draw a diagram showing the forces acting on the bob and indicating the direction of motion.

(b) Show that the differential equation for the motion of the bob, swinging freely with small amplitude, is

$$\ddot{\theta} + 20k\dot{\theta} + 50\theta = 0$$

where θ is the small angular displacement of the pendulum from the downward vertical.

(c) Find the condition on k for the pendulum to oscillate with underdamped harmonic motion.

3 A particle of mass 5 kg is suspended from a fixed support by means of a light spring of natural length 1.6 metres and spring constant $45\,\text{N}\,\text{m}^{-1}$, so that it hangs vertically.

(a) Find the equilibrium position of the particle below the support.

The particle is projected downwards from equilibrium with a speed of $2\,\text{m}\,\text{s}^{-1}$. When moving with speed $v\,\text{m}\,\text{s}^{-1}$ vertically, the motion is resisted by a damping force of magnitude $30v$ newtons.

(b) If x metres is the displacement of the particle below the equilibrium position at time t seconds, write down a differential equation in x and t to describe the particle's motion.

(c) Show that the motion is critically damped and find x in terms of t.

4E A Hookean spring of natural length 0.5 metre is used in a simple set of scales to measure the weights of objects placed on the pan. The pan of mass 0.5 kg rests on top of the spring and causes it to compress by 2 cm.

(a) Find the value of the spring constant k.

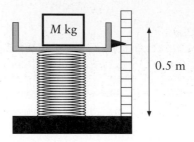

(b) A block of mass M kg is placed on the pan, causing the spring to oscillate. There is a damping force $R = 10v$ newtons, where v m s^{-1} is the speed of the pan. The equation of motion for the subsequent damped oscillations is

$$(M + 0.5)\ddot{x} + 10\dot{x} + kx = 0$$

Show that the general solution to the differential equation is of the form

$$x = A_0\, e^{-10t/(2M+1)} \cos{(nt + \varepsilon)}$$

where A_0 is the initial amplitude.

Hence find an expression for n in terms of M.

(c) Find, in terms of M, the time taken for the system to settle down to oscillations of only 25% of the initial amplitude.

(d) What effect would removing the damping force have on the system?

4.5.3 Forced oscillations

After its opening in July 1940, it was noticed that the Tacoma Narrows bridge in Washington, USA, oscillated in the wind. Taking a ride on the bridge became a popular attraction. The fun did not last long. In November 1940 the wind was strong, forcing the bridge to oscillate with increasing amplitude. After a few hours the strain on the structure was too great. The bridge began cracking and finally collapsed.

 .5c

1 Imagine you are pushing a child on a swing.

(a) For the best effect, when should you push the swing?

(b) What would happen if you pushed a little earlier or later?

2 Take a spring loaded with a few masses and try pulling upwards periodically to set up a forced oscillation. When should you apply a force to increase the amplitude?

In these examples, the key point to note is that to produce oscillations the force must be applied repeatedly at regular intervals in the direction of motion. This condition makes the force F dependent on time.

One way to model the external driving force is as a periodic function, for example $F = F_0 \cos pt$, where F_0 is its amplitude.

Consider the following experiment to investigate forced oscillations. A mass–spring oscillator is attached by a string to a peg on a rotating turntable.

As the peg at A rotates it causes the end B of the string, attached to the top of the spring, to move up and down. If the peg is fixed at a distance of b metres from the centre of a turntable, then the displacement, y metres, of the end of the string at B is in the range $-b \le y \le +b$. Let the turntable rotate with constant speed p rad s^{-1}. If the radius b is very small compared with the length AB, then the displacement y can be approximated by $y = b \cos pt$.

Problem

How does the rate of rotation of the peg affect the oscillations of the mass on the end of the spring?

Set up a model

Consider a spring of length l metres and spring constant k N m^{-1} attached to the string at B.

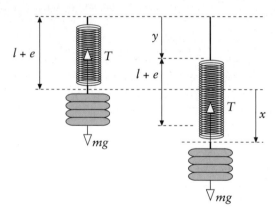

You can assume that:

- the spring obeys Hooke's law for the whole of the motion;
- air resistance is negligible;
- friction in the pulley can be ignored (i.e. assume there are no damping forces);
- the mass on the spring is a particle of mass m kg;
- the extension of the spring is e metres when the mass is in equilibrium;
- the displacement of the mass from the equilibrium position is x metres at time t;
- the displacement of the top of the spring is y metres where $y = b \cos pt$.

Analyse the problem

 4 .5D

1 Show that the tension T in the spring is

$$T = k(e + x - y)$$

2 Using Newton's second law of motion, show that

$$\ddot{x} + w^2 x = bw^2 \cos pt, \quad \text{where } w^2 = \frac{k}{m}$$

This is an example of an equation for **forced SHM**.

> The equation of motion for forced simple harmonic motion is of the form
>
> $$\frac{d^2 x}{dt^2} + w^2 x = F(t)$$
>
> The general solution is the sum of a complementary function (which is a solution of the *simple* SHM equation $\ddot{x} + w^2 x = 0$) and a particular integral.

3 For $p \neq w$, show that a *particular integral* is

$$x = \frac{bw^2}{w^2 - p^2} \cos pt$$

The general solution to the equation for forced oscillations considered above is

$$x = A \cos(wt + \varepsilon) + \frac{bw^2}{w^2 - p^2} \cos pt \qquad \text{if } p \neq w$$

Interpret/validate

This solution for the forced oscillation is the sum of two terms, the first representing the unforced oscillation of natural angular velocity w, and the second term having the angular velocity of the driving force, p. The graph overleaf shows an oscillation where $w = 8p$.

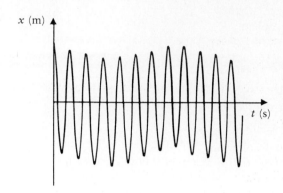

The graph shows the combination of the two oscillations. The curve oscillates with a period of approximately 1 second for the unforced oscillation. The peaks of the curve oscillate with a longer period of about 8 seconds, the time period of the driving force.

Note that when the angular velocity of the driving force, p, is very small compared with the angular velocity, ω, of the unforced oscillation, then the amplitude of the forcing term, $\dfrac{b\omega^2}{\omega^2 - p^2}$ is approximately equal to b and the time period is very long. Thus you observe the natural oscillations with only a slight variation due to the driving force.

As p increases for a fixed value of b, the amplitude of the forcing term increases and the time period shortens, hence the variation in the amplitude of the natural oscillation becomes more noticeable. When p is almost equal to ω the variation in amplitude is large. The amplitude of the forced oscillation rises and falls at regular intervals. This phenomenon is known as **beats**. The frequency of the beat is the difference between p and ω.

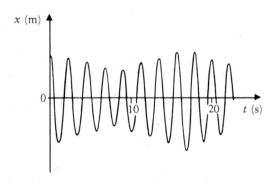

The graph shows the beats, where $\omega = 3$ and $p = 2.6$.

At the point where $p = \omega$, the amplitude of the forcing term tends to infinity. However, the solution is not valid since it was obtained on the assumption that $p \neq \omega$. If p is increased further then beats will be obtained once more. As p becomes very large, the amplitude of the forcing term tends to zero and has very little effect on the natural oscillation.

When $p = \omega$,

$$\ddot{x} + \omega^2 x = b\omega^2 \cos \omega t$$

Trying $x = At \sin \omega t$,

$$2A\omega \cos \omega t - A\omega^2 t \sin \omega t + A\omega^2 t \sin \omega t \equiv b\omega^2 \cos \omega t$$

$$\Rightarrow \quad A = \frac{b\omega}{2}$$

and the particular integral is

$$x = \frac{b\omega}{2} t \sin \omega t$$

Hence, the full solution is

$$x = A \cos (\omega t + \varepsilon) + \frac{b\omega}{2} t \sin \omega t$$

although the complementary function is less significant in this situation.

When $p = \omega$, the amplitude of the forced oscillations increases with time. This situation is known as **resonance**. The graph shows resonance when $A = 0$ (no complementary function), $b = 0.25$ and $\omega = 6$.

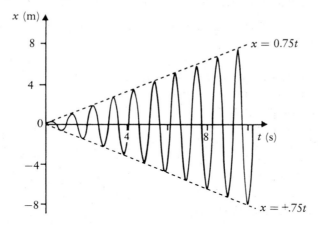

The mass oscillates with increasing amplitude. It seems as if the amplitude will continue to grow, but in reality this is unlikely. At some point the spring would either overstretch and break, or it would not be able to compress to less than its natural length. There is also likely to be damping in the system due to air resistance or friction, and this would restrict the increase in amplitude.

4.5 Exercise 3

1 (a) Suppose that $x = t \cos \omega t$ is a particular integral of an equation of motion for oscillations

$$\ddot{x} + \omega^2 x = F(t)$$

Find $F(t)$.

(b) Sketch the graph of displacement against time and interpret it.

2 The equation of motion of a particle at the end of a flag-pole oscillating from side to side on a windy day is modelled by

$$\frac{d^2 x}{dt^2} + 100x = 20 \cos pt$$

where p rad s^{-1} is the frequency of the gusts of wind and x metres is the horizontal displacement of the end of the flag-pole.

(a) Find the value of p for which resonance occurs.

(b) By substitution, or otherwise, show that the displacement of the particle when resonance occurs is given by $x = 0.05 \cos 10t + 10t \sin 10t$, where 0.05 m is the initial displacement when the particle is at rest.

(c) Sketch the graph of the displacement for $0 \le t \le 5$ seconds.

(d) Interpret the result and comment on its validity.

3 A baby of mass 12 kg is bouncing up and down in her baby-bouncer. She uses her legs to apply an upward force at the lowest point of each bounce. The oscillations are modelled by the equation

$$12\ddot{x} + 108x = 0.6 \sin 3t$$

where x metres is the displacement of her centre of gravity from its equilibrium position.

(a) Give two assumptions used to set up this model.

(b) Find the angular velocity of the unforced oscillations.

(c) Describe the subsequent motion of the baby and comment on the validity of the model.

After working through section 4.5, you should:

1 be able to recognise the damped and forced SHM equations and be able to find solutions by an appropriate method;

2 be able to set up a model for an oscillating body and apply Newton's second law to obtain equations as appropriate for:

- damped SHM,
- forced SHM;

3 be able to interpret solutions graphically and analytically;

4 be able to sketch graphs of displacement, velocity and acceleration against time for an oscillating body;

5 understand what is meant by the terms overdamped, critically damped and underdamped;

6 understand what is meant by resonance.

Modelling with differential equations

Miscellaneous exercise 4

Take $g = 10\,\mathrm{m\,s^{-2}}$.

1 (a) A parachutist falls freely from rest at $t = 0$. Ignoring air resistance, estimate his velocity when he pulls his rip-cord 8 seconds later, and sketch the velocity–time graph for this interval.

 (b) The air resistance to a parachutist is not a constant force but increases directly with velocity. Show that if air resistance is taken into account, a possible expression for the acceleration of the parachutist during free-fall might be

$$\frac{\mathrm{d}v}{\mathrm{d}t} = 10 - 0.2v$$

where the parachutist's velocity is $v\,\mathrm{m\,s^{-1}}$ vertically downwards after t seconds. Find the velocity when he pulls the rip-cord after 8 seconds in this case.

2 The motion of the parachutist after his parachute has opened is described by

$$\frac{\mathrm{d}v}{\mathrm{d}t} = 10 - 0.1v^2$$

If his velocity is initially $v = 15\,\mathrm{m\,s^{-1}}$ vertically downwards, what is his initial acceleration?

If at a later stage his velocity is almost constant, what is his acceleration then, and what is his velocity?

3 (a) A ball is thrown vertically upwards with velocity $8\,\mathrm{m\,s^{-1}}$. For how long will it rise if air resistance is negligible?

 (b) If, in fact, air resistance is taken into account, so that the velocity satisfies the equation

$$\frac{\mathrm{d}v}{\mathrm{d}t} = -(10 + 0.2v)$$

calculate the approximate time taken for the ball to reach its highest point.

4 A motor boat is travelling at 30 knots in still water when the engine cuts out. It is known that when moving at v knots, the boat experiences a retardation due to water resistance of λv^2 knots per second.

(a) Write a differential equation for the speed at a time t seconds after the engine cuts out, and solve it.

(b) It is observed that the speed drops to 10 knots in 15 seconds. Use this information to find the value of λ, and hence find how long it takes for the speed to drop to 5 knots.

5 A car initially travelling at $15 \, \mathrm{m\,s^{-1}}$ freewheels to rest. The retardation of the car has two components: one a constant $0.08 \, \mathrm{m\,s^{-2}}$ due to friction in the working parts and road resistance, and the other due to air resistance, of $0.02v^2 \, \mathrm{m\,s^{-2}}$, where v is the speed in $\mathrm{m\,s^{-1}}$. Find how long it takes for the car to freewheel to rest.

6 The acceleration of a sphere falling through a liquid is $(30 - 3v) \, \mathrm{cm\,s^{-2}}$, where v is its speed in $\mathrm{cm\,s^{-1}}$.

(a) If the sphere starts from rest, how fast will it be travelling at time t, and how far will it then have fallen?

(b) What is the maximum possible velocity? Is this ever reached?

7 A particle moves in a straight line with variable acceleration $\dfrac{k}{1+v} \, \mathrm{m\,s^{-2}}$, where k is a constant and $v \, \mathrm{m\,s^{-1}}$ is the speed of the particle when it has travelled a distance x m. Find the distance moved by the particle as its speed increases from 0 to $u \, \mathrm{m\,s^{-1}}$.

8 A mass of $2\,\mathrm{kg}$ is projected vertically upwards with speed $u \, \mathrm{m\,s^{-1}}$. If it experiences a resistive force of $kv^2 \, \mathrm{N}$, where $v \, \mathrm{m\,s^{-1}}$ is its speed, show that it reaches a maximum height of

$$\frac{1}{k} \ln \left(1 + \frac{ku^2}{2g}\right) \text{metres}$$

and find the time taken to reach this height.

9 A car is started from rest under a force which is proportional to the time against a resistance proportional to the velocity.

(a) Show that the differential equation is of the form $\dfrac{dv}{dt} + kv = \lambda t$.

(b) Solve this equation.

(c) Show that $v \approx \frac{1}{2}\lambda t^2$ for small values of t.
[Hint: you will need to use the series expansion of e^x.]

10 A bullet fired from a gun experiences a retardation due to air resistance of kv^2 m s^{-2}. If the bullet has an initial speed of 300 m s^{-1}, show that its speed after t seconds is

$$v = \frac{300}{1 + 300kt}$$

If the speed is halved after 1.5 seconds, find k.

11 A space vehicle in force-free space speeds up by ejecting propellant gases (formed by burning liquid fuels) backwards at a speed u relative to the vehicle. The mass of the vehicle including fuel is m_0 initially and fuel is burned at a constant rate α so that the total mass m at time t is such that
$$\frac{dm}{dt} = -\alpha.$$

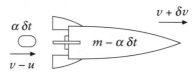

(a) If the speed of the vehicle is v at time t, by considering the conservation of linear momentum of the system, show that in a small interval of time δt the vehicle increases its speed by δv where

$$(m - \alpha\,\delta t)(v + \delta v) + \alpha\,\delta t(v - u) \approx mv$$

(b) By rearranging this equation and allowing δt to tend to zero, show that

$$\frac{dv}{dt} = \frac{\alpha u}{m}$$

(c) Show that $m = m_0 - \alpha t$ and hence that

$$v = v_0 - u\ln\left(1 - \frac{\alpha t}{m_0}\right)$$

where $v = v_0$ when $t = 0$.

12 A mass of 0.3 kg is attached to one end of a spring of stiffness 30 N m^{-1}, the other end of which is fixed to the ceiling. The mass is released when the spring is vertical and just unstretched. Find the amplitude and period of the ensuing oscillations and the position, velocity and acceleration of the mass after one second.

13 A spring performs 150 complete simple harmonic oscillations in a minute. If its greatest acceleration is 10 m s^{-2}, find its greatest speed.

14 A particle of mass 1 kg is suspended from an elastic string of natural length 1 m, the other end of which is attached at a point A. When the particle is in equilibrium the string is extended by 0.25 m. If the particle is allowed to fall from A, find the maximum extension of the string in the subsequent motion.

15 A particle of mass $4\,kg$ moves with SHM about a centre P. Initially the particle is at P, moving to the left at $5\,m\,s^{-1}$; when it first reaches a point Q, $1.5\,m$ to the left of P, its speed is $3\,m\,s^{-1}$.

   (a) Find the period and amplitude of the motion.

   (b) Calculate the work done by the forces producing the motion of the particle in moving it from Q (moving away from P) back to P.

16 A $1\,kg$ mass is suspended by a light elastic string of natural length $0.5\,m$ and spring constant $24g\,N\,m^{-1}$.

   (a) Find the extension of the string when the mass is in equilibrium.

   (b) The mass is pulled down a further distance y, and then released. If the mass just reaches the point of suspension of the string, find:

      (i) the value of y,
      (ii) the maximum speed and acceleration during the motion.

17 A particle of mass m is suspended by a light elastic string with spring constant $\dfrac{mg}{a}$ and natural length a. The particle is dropped from a point $\dfrac{a}{2}$ above its equilibrium position; as it passes through its equilibrium position it collides with and sticks to another, stationary particle of the same mass. Find the amplitude of the subsequent motion.

18 A mass of $7\,kg$ moves with SHM between points A and B. The mass returns to A at intervals of 1.5 seconds and passes through the midpoint of AB at a speed of $2\pi\,m\,s^{-1}$. Find:

   (a) the distance between A and B;

   (b) the force experienced by the mass at B;

   (c) the time taken for the mass to travel from A to a point $\frac{1}{3}$ of the way along AB.

19 Verify that $x = A\sin(\omega t + \varepsilon)$ is a solution of the equation
$$\ddot{x} + \omega^2 x = 0$$

   A particle performs SHM in a straight line about a point O; in doing so is passes a point P at times $t = 0$, 3 and 9 seconds. If $OP = 5\,cm$, find the period and amplitude of the oscillations.

20 A particle of mass m moves along the x-axis so that its motion satisfies the equation
$$\ddot{x} + \omega^2 x = \lambda\omega^2\cos 3\omega t$$

   When $t = 0$, the particle passes the origin at a velocity of $\frac{1}{2}\lambda\omega$ in the positive x-direction. Find an expression for the displacement x as a function of t.

21 A body moving in a straight line with displacement x from the origin O experiences an acceleration towards O of magnitude $13\omega^2$ times its distance from O, together with a retardation of 6ω times its speed. Find a differential equation which is satisfied by x, and use it to show that the general expression for x is

$$x = e^{-3\omega t}(A \cos 2\omega t + B \sin 2\omega t)$$

22 A particle of mass m moving along the x-axis is attracted towards the origin by a force of magnitude $m\omega^2 x$; its motion is also forced by a function $m\,f(t)$.

(a) Show that the particle's displacement x satisfies

$$\ddot{x} + \omega^2 x = f(t)$$

(b) Solve this equation when $f(t) = 0$.

(c) Suppose that $f(t) = p \cos \omega t$ and that at time $t = 0$, $x = \dot{x} = 0$. Find an expression for x as a function of t and sketch your solution, describing any significant features.

Experiments

1 *The bricklayer's lament*
(based on a story by Gerard Hoffnung)

Respected Sir

When I got to the top of the building I found that a lot of bricks were missing so I rigged up a beam and a pulley and hoisted up a couple of barrels of bricks. When I had finished there were a lot of bricks left over so I hoisted the barrel to the top again and secured the line at the bottom. I then filled the barrel with bricks and climbed down. I cast off the line but unfortunately the barrel of bricks was heavier than I was and before I knew what was happening the barrel started down jerking me off my feet. I decided to hang on. Halfway up I met the barrel coming down and received a severe blow to my shoulder. I continued up and hit my head on the beam. When the barrel reached the bottom, the bricks spilled out. I was now heavier than the barrel and started coming down again at high speed. Halfway down I met the barrel coming up and got another severe blow. When I hit the ground I must have lost my presence of mind for I let go of the line. The barrel then came down again hitting me on the head and putting me in hospital.

I respectfully request sick leave.

Find a model for the motion of the bricklayer and the barrel.

Hints

Set up the apparatus shown.

(a) Find the time taken for the 100-gram mass to hit the floor when it is released 60 cm above the floor.

(b) How long does it take when it is released 70 cm above the floor?

(c) Repeat for other distances.

(d) Make a table or a graph.

(e) Find a general rule and test it

(f) Where can you go from here?

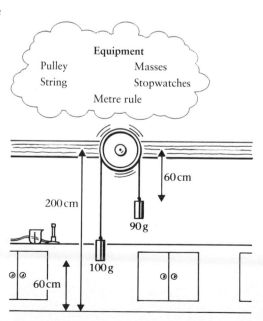

Equipment

Pulley   Masses
String   Stopwatches
Metre rule

200 cm

60 cm

90 g

100 g

60 cm

2 Find a model for the motion of a rolling ball.

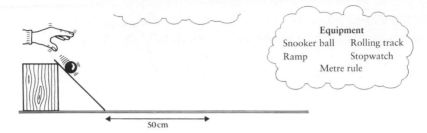

Equipment

Snooker ball   Rolling track

Ramp   Stopwatch

Metre rule

50 cm

Hints

(a) How long will the ball take to roll 50 cm along the track? How long will it take to roll 75 cm?

(b) Estimate how far it will travel in 1 second.

(c) Take careful measurements for several different distances.

(d) Plot a graph of distance against time. Find a general rule for the motion and test it.

(e) What happens if the ball rolls along a carpet or cloth? Repeat your experiment with a strip of ribbon or felt in the track. Remember to record your results carefully.

3 Find a model for the motion of a ball rolling across a sloping plane.

Equipment

Sugar paper   Water

Wooden blocks

Tape measure

Stopwatch   Ramp

Snooker ball or smooth hard rubber ball

Hints

(a) Roll the ball gently down the ramp so that it rolls onto the table.

(b) Adjust the height of release so that the ball traces a curve similar to that in the diagram.

(c) Now dampen the ball and release it from the same point on the ramp. Go over the path of the ball with a felt-tip pen.

(d) Using the same release point each time, find how long it takes for the ball to reach A, B, C and D. (A ruler placed as a stop will help you to time accurately.)

(e) Cut around the path and stick it onto squared paper. Mark your times on the graph.

(f) Find and test a general rule.

1.1 TASKSHEET 1

Jumping buses

Find a model for the motion of a motorbike jumping over buses.

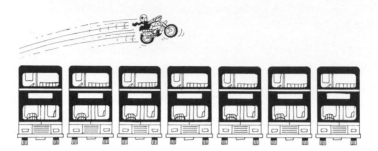

Hints:

- Use a small, thin stretchy rubber band and a ruler to simulate the bike and rider.
- Hook the rubber band on the ruler. Pull it back and then release it.
- Take care where you aim it.
- Use the same rubber band each time.

1 Place a target about 2 metres away. Aim your band from the same level, so that it lands on the target consistently. What angle are you firing at? Mark your ruler so you know how far to stretch the band for your given angle of projection.

2 Fire your band vertically upward using the same setting. How high does it travel?

3 Use this measurement, h, to calculate your speed of projection, u. Remember that v changes by $9.8 \, \text{m s}^{-1}$ each second.

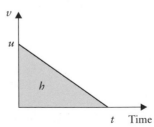

4 Using the same speed, u, alter your angle of projection. What do you notice about:

(a) the range,

(b) the maximum height,

(c) the time in the air?

2.2 TASKSHEET 1

Investigating forces

The students shown in the photographs are doing experiments to validate the following statements.

1 The resultant of two forces can be found by adding the forces as vectors, using a triangle of forces (or parallelogram of forces).

2 If a particle is in equilibrium then the vector sum of the forces acting on it is zero.

3 Three or more forces can be added by drawing a vector polygon.

Carry out your own experiments to validate one or more of the above. You may want to use some of the ideas shown or design your own experiment.

Using a rubber band

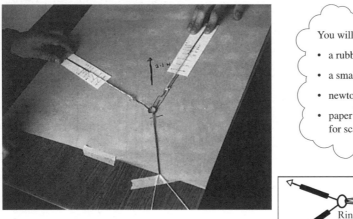

You will need:

• a rubber band

• a small ring

• newton meters

• paper and pencils for scale drawing

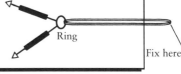

Hints:
- Loop one end of the rubber band around the ring and fix the other end to the table.
- Hook a couple of newton meters in the ring and use them to stretch the rubber band to a certain length.
- Draw line vectors on the paper to model, in magnitude and direction, the pulls of the newton meters on the ring.
- Now use a single newton meter to extend the rubber band to the same point.
- Draw a line vector representing the pull of the single newton meter on the ring.

What can you say about the three force vectors you have drawn?

Using pulleys and masses

You will need:

- two pulleys
- three sets of masses
- string
- paper and pencils for scale drawing

Hints:

- Tie three pieces of string together in a knot at A and put loops in the other ends of the strings.
- Suspend the masses on the pulleys in front of a sheet of paper as shown.
- Draw line vectors on the paper to model the forces acting on the knot at A.

What can you say about the three force vectors you have drawn?

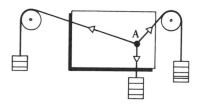

Using pieces of string

You will need:

- string
- newton meters
- paper and pencils for scale drawing

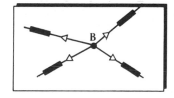

Hints:

- Tie four pieces of string together in a knot B. Put loops in their other ends.
- Hook a newton meter in each loop and pull them tight on a sheet of paper.
- Draw line vectors on the paper to model, in magnitude and direction, the pull of each of the newton meters on the knot B.

What can you say about the four force vectors you have drawn?

Modelling with force

Choose one of the situations A and B below.

Select a suitable standard model or models for the analysis from the lists of standard models at the end of the tasksheet. Test your solution using the apparatus suggested.

Prepare a report on your findings.

A How does the tension in a spring or elastic string vary with its extension?

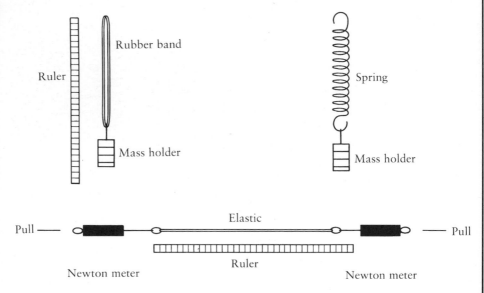

B What effect does the surface area of a balloon have on the resistance acting on it? Drop four identical balloons from a height 2 metres and measure the time they take to reach the ground.

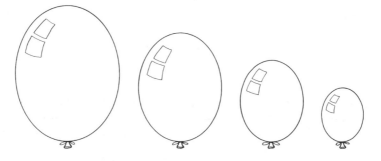

Four identical balloons blown up to different sizes

Standard models for tension
The simplest model for tension is that of a light inextensible string.

1 A light string or chain

T_1

T_2

If a string has negligible mass then the tension at one end of the string is assumed to be the same as that at the other end of the string even if the ends are pulled apart in a vertical line.

$$T_1 = T_2$$

2 An inextensible string or chain

If a string is 'inextensible' you can assume that it does not stretch. The tension T can take any value up to a breaking value T_B.

$$0 \le T \le T_B$$

Other models which may be appropriate are:

3 A heavy string or chain

T_1

T_2

If a heavy string or chain of mass m is hung vertically from one end then the tension in the string varies such that

$$T_1 = T_2 + mg$$

4 A light elastic spring or string

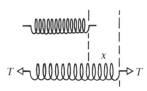

x

T T

If a string or spring can stretch under tension then the tension can be assumed to vary with the extension. Hooke's model states that, for a given range of extension x, $T = kx$ where k is the spring stiffness and depends on the length of the spring or string and the material it is made from. The tension has a fixed limit beyond which the string will break.

5 A pretensioned elastic string or spring

Some springs or strings require an initial tension before they will start to stretch. They then obey Hooke's model up to a breaking point.

$$T \le T_0 \quad \text{for } x = 0$$

$$T = T_0 + kx \quad \text{for } 0 < x \le x_0$$

Standard models for resistance to motion through a medium such as air or water

1 Negligible resistance

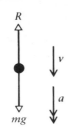

The resistive force is small compared to the other forces acting parallel to it and it may be ignored.

$$R = 0$$

2 $R = $ constant

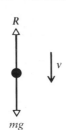

If the variation in resistance is small compared to the other forces acting – for example when a parachute is open and the parachute descends at nearly zero acceleration – then the resistance can be taken as constant and the body is said to travel at terminal velocity.

Other models which may be used are:

3 $R = kv$

In normal motion, the resistive force is proportional to the velocity of the object through the resistive medium.

4 $R = kv^2$

For motion at high speeds, the resistive force can be taken to be proportional to the square of the velocity of the object through the resistive medium.

5 $R = kA$

The resistive force at any velocity can be taken to be proportional to the area normal to the direction of motion relative to the resistive medium.

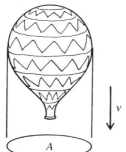

Satellites

In 1957, Sputnik I, a round sphere of metal, was blasted off into space by the USSR. It neither fell back to the ground nor disappeared into the depths of space. Instead it remained near the Earth, going round and round only a few hundred miles above the ground. It finally fell back to Earth three months later. Since then, many hundreds of satellites have been put into orbit, mostly around the Earth. Craft have been orbited around the Sun, Moon, Mars and other planets in the solar system but these are generally known as **space probes**.

The use of satellites has many practical benefits to humanity. The world's meteorological services depend increasingly on satellite photographs of cloud cover and on measurements made from space of atmospheric properties. They can also be used for pollution and pest control. The pictures that can be obtained are of such good resolution that the swarms of locusts travelling across Africa can be tracked and the information used to combat their menace. Communications satellites are of great importance, not just for relaying television transmissions but also for providing industry and government with the telephone and data links needed. The data gained from scientific satellites has greatly increased people's knowledge and understanding of their planet. The first space laboratory, the Skylab space station, launched in 1973, had a mass of 82 000 kg and a length of 36 metres. It orbited 434 km above the Earth. The drag of the atmosphere gradually slowed it down and in its 34 981st orbit it fell to Earth, burning up over Western Australia.

Many different types of orbit can be achieved depending on the mass of the satellite, the capability of the launch rocket and the angle of the orbit to the equator. The satellite must achieve a velocity of $8450 \, \text{m s}^{-1}$ to achieve a low orbit, and $11\,170 \, \text{m s}^{-1}$ to escape from the Earth's pull and go into deep space. By choosing a suitable combination of upward and horizontal thrust, the satellite can be put into any orbit from circular to highly elliptical. The greater the thrust, the higher the orbit. The greater the horizontal thrust, the more elliptical the orbit will be. Almost all the world's communications satellites are in circular orbits above the Earth's equator at a height of 35 900 km. A satellite in such an orbit circles the Earth at the same angular speed as the Earth and so it always lies above the same point on the Earth's surface. Not all satellites travel in orbit above the equator. A satellite launched at an angle to the equator will pass over most of the Earth's surface during its life. Satellites used to watch for pollution usually have such an orbit. Most satellites are launched from somewhere near the equator. This means that they can use the velocity of the Earth's surface to help them achieve their orbit.

2.3 TASKSHEET 1

Although a satellite in orbit should stay in space for ever, this is often not the case. If it is in orbit within a few hundred miles of the Earth's surface the atmosphere will eventually slow the satellite down and it will fall back to Earth. Many satellites are equipped with small booster rockets that can be used to increase their height above the Earth when it reaches a critical point and so extend the life of the satellite. In addition, the Space Shuttle programme has enabled some satellites to be repaired. In April 1984, George Nelson was one of a team of astronauts who jetted from the shuttle to repair the satellite Solar Max, in orbit at a height of 467 km above the Earth. They jokingly named themselves the Ace Satellite repair company.

Problem

George Nelson passed over Singapore as he was mending Solar Max. Assuming that the satellite travelled on an orbit above the equator, how many *more* times did he pass over Singapore in the following 24 hours that he stayed on the satellite?

1 Set up a simple mathematical model of the motion of George Nelson as he travelled around the Earth with Solar Max. You should draw a diagram and label it clearly, state any assumptions you make and define any variables you use, obtaining any appropriate constants from the data on the previous page or earlier in the text.

2 Use your model to find his speed and hence find out how many times he passed over Singapore in the 24-hour period.

Modelling the Fosbury flop

The 'average' human body may be modelled by a series of connected cylinders for the arms, legs and trunk, and a sphere for the head.

The relative proportions of the length and mass will vary considerably from person to person, but a reasonable model is shown.

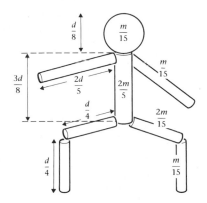

You will probably have seen athletes doing the Fosbury flop in international high-jump competitions. Although the movements through the air are complex, the path of the centre of gravity is parabolic and once the athlete has left the ground there is nothing he or she can do to alter it. The athlete's complicated movements are aimed at 'raising herself' above her centre of gravity as much as possible at the critical point of clearing the bar. It is interesting to investigate her position relative to her centre of gravity at this point in the jump.

Although the whole process is three-dimensional, you can gain a good idea of what is happening by looking at a two-dimensional model as shown in the diagram below. Sketch an enlargement of the drawing onto thick (stiff) card.

Use Blu-Tack to attach coins to the card along the legs and body and on the head to approximate the mass of the high jumper. 2p coins are suitable, with one coin per $\frac{1}{15}$th mass. Except for the head, you should balance the coins on either side of the card.

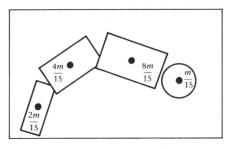

Pin the card to the board in such a way that it is free to swing about the pin. This is the pivot.

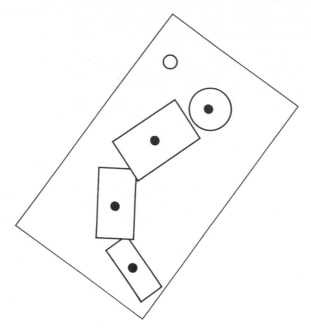

When the card is at rest the centre of gravity will be directly below the pivot. This is because when the line of action of the gravitational force passes through the pivot the moment of the force is zero, so there is no rotation about the pivot.

If you draw a line vertically down from the pivot, the centre of gravity must be somewhere on this line. If you repeat this process from different pivot points, the lines you draw will intersect at the centre of gravity. (The accuracy will depend on how accurate your vertical lines are.)

Once you have identified the position of the centre of gravity, what do you expect to happen if you pivot the card about an axis through this point? Try it and see.

On the other side of the card draw a model of someone, for example, bending down to touch her toes, doing a dive, or performing a gymnastic movement, and identify the position of the centre of gravity.

Which slides first?

Balance a long length of track on your fingers as shown, and gradually begin to draw your hands together. What happens?

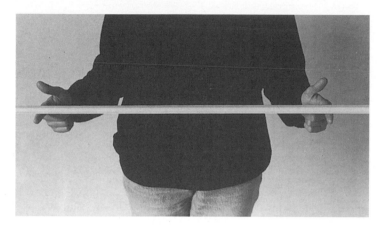

- Which finger slides first?
- What happens to the track?
- Where do your fingers finish?
- Do both your fingers slide at once?
- What happens if you use a pencil or a rubber instead of one of your fingers?

Model the situation mathematically and explain all the features observed.

Sporting collisions

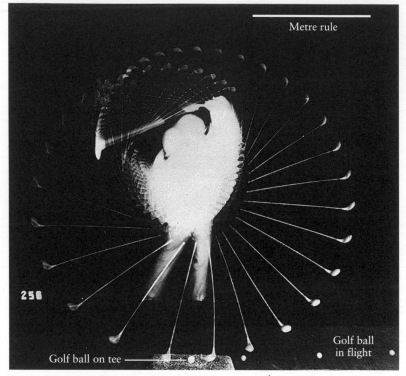

The picture shows strobe photographs, taken every $\frac{1}{100}$th of a second, of a golfer striking a golf ball.

1   Use measurements taken from the photograph to find the speed of the head of the golf club just before the collision and the speed of the golf ball after being struck.

The speed of the golf ball is less than twice the initial speed of the club. This initial speed of the club is determined by the golfer's technique and physique. It is important to know how this limits the speed of the golf ball.

You can model the striking of the golf ball by an elastic collision of a mass M with a stationary mass m.

$$(M) \xrightarrow{u} (m)$$

2   Comment upon whether these assumptions are reasonable. What, in your opinion, is the most significant difference between this mathematical model and reality?

After the collision the speeds are

$$\text{(M)} \rightarrow v - u \qquad \text{(m)} \rightarrow v$$

where

$$M(v - u) + mv = Mu$$

$$\Rightarrow \qquad (M + m)v = 2Mu$$

$$\Rightarrow \qquad \frac{v}{u} = \frac{2M}{M + m}$$

and so $\dfrac{v}{u}$ can never be greater than 2.

3 (a) Explain why the speeds after the collision can be taken to be v and $v - u$.

(b) Justify the equation $M(v - u) + mv = Mu$.

(c) Explain why $\dfrac{2M}{M + m}$ can never be greater than 2.

When a mass with speed u collides with a smaller stationary mass, the resulting speed of the small mass is limited to $2u$. This value is achieved approximately in golf and whenever the stationary mass is relatively very small.

As you have seen, golf is a sporting example of $\dfrac{v}{u}$ being maximised. You can also investigate what relative values of the masses will maximise the proportion of the initial kinetic energy which is transferred to the second object.

The initial kinetic energy is $\frac{1}{2}Mu^2$ and so the proportion transferred is

$$\frac{\frac{1}{2}mv^2}{\frac{1}{2}Mu^2} = \frac{m}{M}\left(\frac{v}{u}\right)^2 = \frac{m}{M}\left(\frac{2M}{M + m}\right)^2 = \frac{4m/M}{(1 + m/M)^2}$$

4 Let $x = \dfrac{m}{M}$ and show that the maximum value, for positive x, of the function $\dfrac{4x}{(1 + x)^2}$ is 1.

Find the value of x for which this maximum occurs, and state the relationship between m and M for which all the original kinetic energy is transferred.

5 Describe a sporting example of this situation.

3.4 TASKSHEET 1

Tension

You will need
- retort stand or clamp
- spring
- ruler
- mass holder and masses
- stop-watch

Hooke's experimental law states that the tension in a stretched spring is proportional to the extension of the spring beyond its natural length. (The constant of proportionality is called the **spring constant**.)

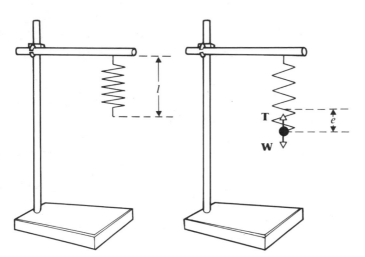

When the mass hangs at rest (equilibrium), the tension in the spring, T, is equal and opposite to the weight, W, of the mass.

Hooke's law states that

$$T = ke$$

1 Place various masses on the mass holder, record the extension of the spring in each case, and hence draw the (extension, tension) graph for the spring.

2 Use your graph to estimate k, the spring constant for your spring.

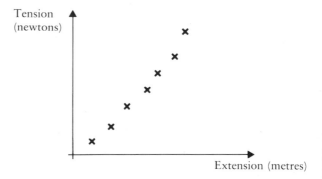

Tension (newtons)

Extension (metres)

Sky-diving

Read the following article carefully.

As a sky-diver stands at the door of an aeroplane nearly 12 000 ft. (3700 m) up, the Earth below is a patchwork of colour seen through patches of cloud, with houses almost too small to be picked out. The aeroplane arrives at the jump point and the sky-diver launches herself into space – arms and legs outstretched, body arched slightly backwards, head pulled up. Her speed increases for about eight seconds, reaching a 'terminal speed' of approximately 120 m.p.h. (190 km h^{-1}). This is the highest speed she will achieve in this position. Her altimeter tells her the height, second by second, as she plunges earthward, and she knows that to make a safe landing, she must open her parachute before she reaches 2000 ft. (610 m). So the free-fall will last less than one minute – a brief, floating interlude during which the parachutist carries out the acrobatics which are the real purpose of sky-diving. As she completes the sky-dive she opens her parachute and directs her approach to the landing spot by controlling the two steering lines.

Sky-divers use many different types of parachute, but the principles are much the same. The type of parachute used by beginners is the familiar circular canopy with two L-shaped gaps cut at the back. As air rushes through these gaps, it produces a forward thrust which enables the parachutist to steer to the landing place, otherwise she would drift with the wind. In still air, she travels forward at what, on land, would be a brisk walking speed. Whatever type of canopy is used – round or square – the jumper is suspended in a nylon harness. Four nylon strips called 'risers' connect the harness to the rigging lines of the canopy. Two steering lines from the canopy allow the jumper to steer left or right by pulling on them. The jumper also has an emergency parachute, in case the first should malfunction. Sky-divers always pack their own parachutes, initially under careful supervision.

For most jumps, a small, high-winged aircraft, such as the three-passenger Cessna 172, is used. If several sky-divers are jumping together, a larger aircraft, such as a Short's Sky Van, which carries up to 16 people, is needed. When the plane arrives above the chosen spot, an experienced parachutist dives through the open door. The free-fall time depends on the altitude at the time of exit, and can be as short as eight seconds or as long as one minute.

The first aerial gymnastics performed by beginners are usually simple somersaults and turns in the air. As sky-divers become more experienced, they advance to formation falls, joining up with other sky-divers to complete a series of rapidly changing patterns. These displays require great skill, as the divers are travelling at speed and may have to 'track' across the sky to join up with the other divers. To achieve this they must be almost vertical, with the body forming a slight curve. Arms must be held to the side and the legs together and extended. The 'lift' created by air passing over her curved body causes the parachutist to travel forward as well as down. The forward movement can be fast enough to cause injury if two sky-divers collide. So to break the speed, a parachutist brings her arms up, presenting a greater area to the air flow and slowing down her body. This skill must be mastered before she can join in formation jumps.

1 Draw a diagram showing the forces acting on the sky-diver.

2 Explain why the sky-diver reaches a maximum speed, called terminal speed.

3 How can the sky-diver increase or decrease her terminal speed?

4 From the text or your own experience, describe how the air resistance force is related to speed.

5 Sketch a possible graph of resistance against speed and suggest a suitable function for this relationship.

Resistance experiments

 Problem   To find an appropriate model for the resistance force in a practical situation.

1 Choose or design a simple experiment for which the resistance force is significant.

Some suggestions, shown in the picture, are:

- a falling ball with a sail;
- weights sinking in a long tube filled with water;
- a balloon (possibly filled with helium) with light weights (such as paper clips) attached;
- a parachute made from polystyrene, card or a carrier bag;
- a set of paper bun cases that can be stacked together to increase mass.

2 Collect data for the time taken to travel a range of distances.

3 Plot the graph of distance against time and use it to estimate the terminal speed of the object.

4 Vary the mass of the object, taking care not to alter its shape or size significantly, and find its new terminal speed.

5 Collect data to sketch a graph and find a relationship between terminal speed and mass.

6 Suggest an appropriate model for the resistance force.

4.4 TASKSHEET 1

Validating the formula $T \propto \sqrt{m}$

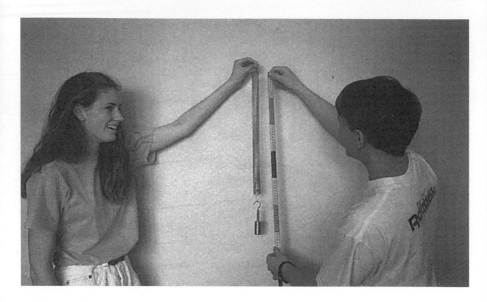

The objective is to validate the formula for a real spring.

> You will need a stopwatch, a ruler, some masses and a spring.

Before starting to take any measurements it is advisable to stretch the springs a few times to loosen them up. Take care not to overstretch the springs as this may cause them to break or, more likely, to deform.

1 Find the spring constant k of your spring, assuming that Hooke's law is valid.

2 Measure the time period for a suitable range of masses.

3 By plotting a graph of the time period τ seconds against the mass m kilograms, comment on the validity of the formula $\tau \propto \sqrt{m}$. Also comment on the validity of the specific solution

$$T = \frac{2\pi}{\sqrt{(k/m)}} = 2\pi \sqrt{\left(\frac{m}{k}\right)}$$

using the value of k found previously.

Pendulum clocks

Investigate how the time period of oscillation of a simple pendulum is affected by varying:

- the mass, m kilograms, of the bob;
- the length, l metres, of the pendulum;
- the initial angle of displacement, α radians.

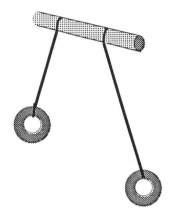

You will need a stop-watch, spring, some masses or weighted bobs, a ruler, a protractor and some means of supporting the pendulum.

4.5 TASKSHEET 1

1   Set up a simple pendulum and begin by making some qualitative observations of the effects that changing each of the variables, m, l and α, have on the time period of oscillation.

(Hint: You might try comparing the time period for a pendulum with a very heavy bob with that of a medium- or light-weight bob, or a long pendulum with a short one and so on.)

2   Choose one of the variables m, l or α, and set up an experiment to collect more detailed data.

3   By plotting a graph of the results, or otherwise, suggest a relationship between the time period and your chosen variable.

SOLUTIONS
1 NEWTON'S LAWS OF MOTION

1.1 Modelling motion
1.1.1 Introduction

1.1 A

You are *not* expected to provide the correct theoretical explanations at this stage. The point of these investigations is to direct your attention to the interesting questions you can ask about the world of mechanics and motion in which we live.

(a) If the small ball is on the top, it will rebound to a much greater height than it would if it were dropped on its own. The large ball hardly leaves the floor at all.

If the large ball is on top, the small ball stays near the ground, while the large ball bounces more or less normally.

(b) A full can takes the shorter time to roll down the slope. (However, a half-full can does not take a time halfway between those taken by the full and the empty cans.)

(c) The bicycle will roll backwards, but the pedal will rotate forwards. Try the experiment yourself.

(d) (i) The reading stays the same.
    (ii) The reading decreases.

Perpetual motion machines, the swirling of bathwater down a plughole and road banking angles are just a few of the many other interesting ideas you may have considered. Further examples are described in the following books:

Epstein, L. C., *Thinking Physics: Is Gedanken Physics*, Insight, San Francisco, 1983.
Walker, J., *The Flying Circus of Physics*, J. Wein, New York, 1975.

1.1 B

The aim of the experiment is to find the relationship between time taken and distance rolled. It is important at this stage to learn the art of good experimental practice! Some important points to remember are:

Consistency
It is important that each result is obtained by a set procedure, so that the experiment is repeatable. If a ball rolls 1 metre down the track in 2.2 seconds the first time, the experiment should be repeated to test how consistent this time is (within the degree of accuracy concerned). If the ball bounces from side to side, or if the measuring is done in a sloppy and inconsistent manner (for example, from the front of the ball one time and the middle the next), then you should expect inconsistent results.

The following points may help.

(a) Call out '3, 2, 1, go' as you release the ball and let the ball hit a brick at the end of its measured run.

(b) Use a brick to hold the ball in place at the start. This will help you to get the correct distance between the start and the finish.

Accuracy
What sources of inaccuracy are there? For example, in measuring time, there are delayed reactions. Can these cancel each other out at the beginning and end of the run?

The experiment should be set up to take at least 3 seconds for the ball to roll the full length of the track.

Consider the use of the mean, mode or median in choosing which measurement to use in your analysis.

Galileo had difficulty measuring time accurately and records show that he had to design a special time-piece; he used a large flat vessel of water from which water was allowed to drip, the weight of the water released being measured to give the time.

Repeatability
The data collected *must* be repeatable by other experimenters at other times. It is essential, therefore, to note all pertinent details, for example:

• type of track and ball,
• angle of slope,
• length of track,
• method of timing.

Analysis
Having collected the data, a graph can be drawn and a function fitted to it. The points should be joined by some type of curve. A function graph plotter can be used.

The ball starts from rest and travels with increasing speed down the track. The results should give an approximation to $d = kt^2$. The shape of the graph is indicated below. As the slope of the track is increased, k increases. However, if the angle of the track is too great then it becomes impossible to measure t with accuracy. (Any result using a value of t smaller than 0.5 second is suspect.)

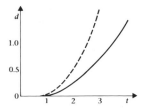

Interpretation and validation
The experiment should not stop here, but should be followed by:

- prediction of a given time for a roll of given distance, within the range of distances recorded (interpolation);
- validation of predictions by testing them practically.

1.2 Kinematics
1.2.1 Motion

1.2 Exercise 1

1 Distance covered in first 30 seconds
= 150 metres
Distance covered in second 30 seconds
= 60 metres
$$\text{Average speed} = \frac{150 + 60}{30 + 30} = 3.5 \text{ m s}^{-1}$$

2 $$\text{Average speed} = \frac{150 + 150}{30 + 75} = 2.9 \text{ m s}^{-1}$$

3 2.25 m s^{-1}

4 The total time for the journey was
$\frac{210}{42} = 5$ hours. The time for the first half of the journey's distance was $\frac{105}{30} = 3.5$ hours and so the average speed for the second half was $\frac{105}{1.5} = 70$ miles per hour (31.3 m s^{-1}).

5 $$\frac{30u + 30v}{60} = \frac{u + v}{2} \text{ m s}^{-1}$$

You can use the arithmetic average of the speeds if the jogger runs and walks for equal lengths of time.

6 Running: $30u$ metres in 30 seconds

Walking: $30u$ metres in $\dfrac{30u}{v}$ seconds

$$\text{Average speed} = \frac{30u + 30u}{30 + \dfrac{30u}{v}} = \frac{2uv}{u + v} \text{ m s}^{-1}$$

1.2.2 Distance–time and distance–speed graphs

1.2 A

1 There are many possible explanations of the shape of the graph. The actual journey was:

- a walk up a hill;
- a slow walk while waiting for a chance to cross a road;
- a brisk walk to the main road;
- a wait at a pedestrian crossing;
- a walk to the office, slightly slowed down by the large number of students on their way to lectures.

2

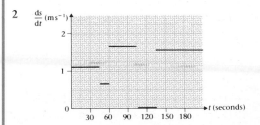

3 On the (t, s) graph, the total distance of 250 metres is the height of the final point.

On the $\left(t, \dfrac{ds}{dt}\right)$ graph it is the sum of the areas under the horizontal line segments.

4 The fact that the lecturer was stationary is represented by a horizontal line on the (t, s) graph and by the graph running along the t-axis on the $\left(t, \dfrac{ds}{dt}\right)$ graph.

5 The lecturer travelled most quickly in the interval from 60 to 105 seconds. The (t, s) graph has its steepest gradient, and the $\left(t, \dfrac{ds}{dt}\right)$ graph is highest, on this interval.

1.2 Exercise 2

1 Distance covered = 2250 m   (or 2.25 km)

A simple model would represent her stopping by a discontinuity (or break) in the (time, speed) graph at $t = 900$ as shown above. More realistically, the graph might be shaped as shown.

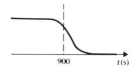

2 Running distance = $4.8 \times 60 = 288$ metres
Jogging distance = $3.0 \times 90 = 270$ metres

Total distance covered is
$20 \times (288 + 270) = 11\,160$ metres

3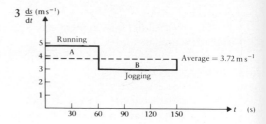

Note that area A and area B are equal.

4 (a)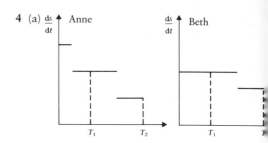

Anne set off quickly but soon slowed down and then finished the race at an even slower pace. Beth maintained a steady pace for most of the race (the same as Anne's middle pace) and then slowed down to a somewhat higher finishing pace than Anne. They finished the race together.

(b) At T_1, they have the same speed. The (t, s) graphs have equal gradients; the $\left(t, \dfrac{ds}{dt}\right)$ graphs have the same heights.

(c) At T_2, they have covered the same distance. The (t, s) graphs have equal heights; the areas under the $\left(t, \dfrac{ds}{dt}\right)$ graphs are equal.

5 Distance to motorway
= $11.4 \times 1.5 \times 3600 = 61\,560$ m
Distance on motorway
= $16.2 \times 2 \times 3600$ = $116\,640$ m
Distance after motorway
= $10.7 \times 45 \times 60$ = $28\,890$ m

Total distance = 207.09 km   (say 207 km)

6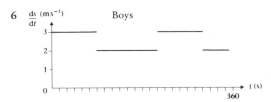

In 1 hour the boys completed 16 repetitions of
(2×270) m, i.e. 8640 m.

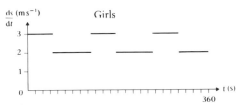

In 58 minutes 20 seconds the girls completed
28 repetitions of (2×150) m, i.e. 8400 m. In
the remaining 100 seconds the girls completed
the 150 m running phase and walked for
50 seconds at $2\,\mathrm{m\,s}^{-1}$, covering a further
250 m. The girls therefore won by 10 metres.

1.2.3 Speed

1.2 **B**

1 The ball's speed $\dfrac{ds}{dt}$ at that instant is
$0.64\,\mathrm{m\,s}^{-1}$. If its speed remained constant at
$0.64\,\mathrm{m\,s}^{-1}$, then its speed (t,s) graph would follow
the dashed tangent from 2 seconds onwards.

2

Time in seconds	0.5	1	1.5	2	2.5	3
Gradient	0.16	0.32	0.48	0.64	0.80	0.96

3 The $\left(t, \dfrac{ds}{dt}\right)$ graph is a straight line. The
speed of the ball increases by approximately
$0.32\,\mathrm{m\,s}^{-1}$ each second.

If you use your own data, a curve should be
drawn and the gradients found.

The $\left(t, \dfrac{ds}{dt}\right)$ points found using your gradients
may not lie exactly on a line but you should have
a set of points giving a good approximation to a
straight line through the origin.

1.2 Exercise 3

1 (a) The area under the curve between $t = 10$
and $t = 15$ is just less than 75 metres.
The speed is increasing, but not at a
steady rate.

(b) Between $t = 20$ and $t = 25$, the object
slows down at a constant rate until it is
stationary. The distance covered each
second decreases. A total distance of
50 metres is covered in this period.

2 Each 1 cm square represents 20 metres and
each small square represents $\frac{20}{25} = 0.8$ metres.
Estimates to 2 s.f. are:

(a) 130 metres

(b) 380 metres

3 B starts 2 seconds later than A from the same
point and walks in the same direction but at a
greater speed. B covers $3 \times 3 = 9$ metres.
A and B therefore meet 9 metres from the
start. A's speed is $\frac{9}{5} = 1.8\,\mathrm{m\,s}^{-1}$.

4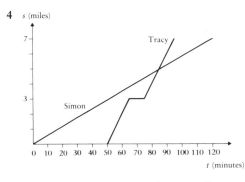

(a) Approximately 2 miles from Ceville

(b) $7 \div 46 = 0.152$ miles per minute
$0.152 \times 60 \approx 9.1$ m.p.h.

(c) $7 \div 2 = 3.5$ m.p.h.

[It is assumed that, when travelling, they both
maintain a constant speed.]

5 (a) From $t = 2$ to $t = 5$, speed increases uniformly from 2 to $8 \, \mathrm{m \, s^{-1}}$. Using areas,

when $t = 3$, $\dfrac{ds}{dt} = 4$ and

$s = 4 + \frac{1}{2}(2 + 4) = 7$

when $t = 4$, $\dfrac{ds}{dt} = 6$ and

$s = 7 + \frac{1}{2}(4 + 6) = 12$

when $t = 5$, $\dfrac{ds}{dt} = 8$ and

$s = 12 + \frac{1}{2}(6 + 8) = 19$

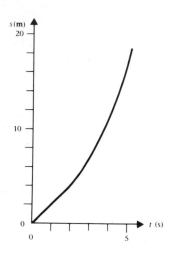

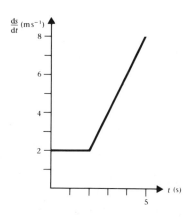

(b) The distance covered is 19 metres.

6 (a) A moves at constant speed.

(b) B moves with a constant rate of increase of speed, up to twice the speed of A.

(c) After 2 seconds

(d) After 4 seconds

1.2.4 Investigating speed

1.2 C

A 'two-second gap' means that if there is a gap of 50 metres, say, between the front of your car and the rear of the car in front, it should take you at least two seconds to cover that distance. This means that you should not be travelling at more than $25 \, \mathrm{m \, s^{-1}}$.

1.2 D

Set up a model

Assume:

- the car has length 5 m and is moving at a constant speed of $V \, \mathrm{m \, s^{-1}}$;
- the lorry has length 15 m and is moving with constant speed $U \, \mathrm{m \, s^{-1}}$;
- they obey the two-second rule;
- the car takes t seconds to overtake.

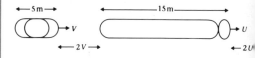

Analyse the problem

The car must travel $(5 + 2V + 15 + 2U) \, \mathrm{m}$ if the lorry is stationary. But the lorry will have travelled Ut metres in that time, so the total overtaking distance in metres is
$20 + 2(U + V) + Ut$.

But the car has travelled Vt metres, so

$$Vt = 20 + 2(U + V) + Ut$$

$$\Rightarrow \quad t(V - U) = 20 + 2(U + V)$$

$$\Rightarrow \quad t = \dfrac{20 + 2(U + V)}{V - U}$$

The distance travelled, s, is

$$s = Vt = \frac{2V(10 + U + V)}{(V - U)}$$

Interpret/validate

As $V - U$ increases, s decreases. The greater the difference in speed, the smaller the distance needed.

As V increases, the car must pull out earlier if it is not to break the two-second rule. However, the overall passing distance decreases unless V is much bigger than U.

The greater the combined speeds of the two, the greater the distance. If $U > V$ then s is negative, i.e. passing is impossible. If $U = 0$ then the distance is $20 + 2V$.

1.3 Vectors
1.3.1 Introduction

1.3 Exercise 1

(Answers are given to 1 decimal place where necessary.)

1 (a)

$$\overrightarrow{PQ} = \begin{bmatrix} 7\sin 60° \\ 7\cos 60° \end{bmatrix} \approx \begin{bmatrix} 6.1 \\ 3.5 \end{bmatrix}$$

(b)

$$\overrightarrow{RS} = \begin{bmatrix} -4.1 \\ -11.3 \end{bmatrix}$$

(c)

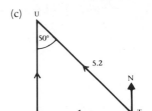

$$\overrightarrow{TU} = \begin{bmatrix} -4.0 \\ 3.3 \end{bmatrix}$$

2 (a) $AB = \sqrt{(5^2 + 12^2)} = 13$

$\tan \alpha = \frac{5}{12} \quad \Rightarrow \quad \alpha \approx 22.6°$

The bearing is $022.6°$.

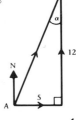

(b) $(22.6, 045°)$

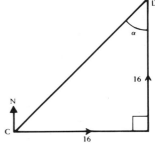

(c) $(10.1, 212.9°)$

(d) $(5, 143.1°)$

3 846 m east, 172 m south;   281°; there is no current.

4 57 cm at $-12°$ to the x-axis

1.3.2 Vectors and maps

1.3 A

1 033498,   016409 (taken at the middle)

2 Dairy,   The Bite

3 (2.4, 47.3),   (3.2, 50.5)

1.3 Exercise 2

1 (a) Distance from C to B
$$= \sqrt{(12.7^2 + 20.1^2)} \approx 23.8 \, \text{km}$$

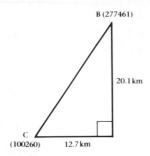

B (277461)

20.1 km

C
(100260) 12.7 km

(b) $\tan \alpha = \dfrac{6.3}{29.7} \quad \Rightarrow \quad \alpha \approx 12.0°$

The bearing of D from A is about 102°.

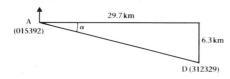

A
(015392) α 29.7 km

6.3 km

D (312329)

(c) $\overrightarrow{BD} = \begin{bmatrix} 8.5 \\ -13.2 \end{bmatrix}$

$\overrightarrow{BD}$ is 15.7 km on a bearing of 147.2°.

(d) The bearing of $\overrightarrow{DB}$ is
147.2° + 180° = 327.2°.

(e) $\overrightarrow{AB} = \begin{bmatrix} 21.2 \\ 6.9 \end{bmatrix}$

$\overrightarrow{CD} = \begin{bmatrix} 21.2 \\ 6.9 \end{bmatrix}$

Hence $\overrightarrow{AB} = \overrightarrow{CD} \quad \Rightarrow \quad AB = CD$, and AB is in the same direction as CD.

2 318358

3 Ayton is 14.0 km from Botton, on a bearing of 312° (both to 3 s.f.).

1.3.3 Adding vectors

1.3 B

1 (a) $\overrightarrow{XZ} = \begin{bmatrix} 18.5 - 2.6 \\ 49.6 - 10.2 \end{bmatrix} = \begin{bmatrix} 15.9 \\ 39.4 \end{bmatrix}$

$\overrightarrow{XY} = \begin{bmatrix} 10.8 \\ 5.2 \end{bmatrix}$

$\overrightarrow{YZ} = \begin{bmatrix} 5.1 \\ 34.2 \end{bmatrix}$

(b) The sum of the eastwards components of $\overrightarrow{XY}$ and $\overrightarrow{YZ}$ is 10.8 + 5.1 = 15.9, which equals the eastwards component of $\overrightarrow{XZ}$. Also the sum of the northwards components of $\overrightarrow{XY}$ and $\overrightarrow{YZ}$ is 5.2 + 34.2 = 39.4, which equals the northwards component of $\overrightarrow{XZ}$. Therefore you can write $\overrightarrow{XZ} = \overrightarrow{XY} + \overrightarrow{YZ}$.

(c) (i) XZ ≈ 42.5
$\alpha \approx 22.0°$

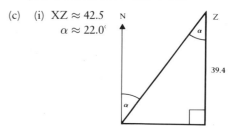

N

Z

α

39.4

α

X 15.9

In going from X to Z the helicopter flies a distance of 42.5 km in the direction 022.0°.

(ii) In going from X to Y it flies a distance of 12.0 km in the direction 064.3°.

(iii) In going from Y to Z it flies a distance of 34.6 km in direction 008.5°.

2 $\overrightarrow{AB} = \begin{bmatrix} 4 \\ -2 \end{bmatrix}$, $\overrightarrow{BC} = \begin{bmatrix} 2 \\ 6 \end{bmatrix}$, $\overrightarrow{AC} = \begin{bmatrix} 6 \\ 4 \end{bmatrix}$

Notice that $\overrightarrow{AB} + \overrightarrow{BC} = \begin{bmatrix} 4 \\ -2 \end{bmatrix} + \begin{bmatrix} 2 \\ 6 \end{bmatrix}$

$= \begin{bmatrix} 6 \\ 4 \end{bmatrix} = \overrightarrow{AC}$

3 $\overrightarrow{AD} = \overrightarrow{AB} + \overrightarrow{BC} + \overrightarrow{CD}$

$$= \begin{bmatrix} 2 \\ 2 \end{bmatrix} + \begin{bmatrix} 2 \\ 0 \end{bmatrix} + \begin{bmatrix} 3 \\ -4 \end{bmatrix} = \begin{bmatrix} 7 \\ -2 \end{bmatrix}$$

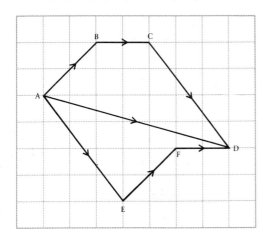

4 $\overrightarrow{AD} = \overrightarrow{AE} + \overrightarrow{EF} + \overrightarrow{FD}$

$$= \begin{bmatrix} 3 \\ -4 \end{bmatrix} + \begin{bmatrix} 2 \\ 2 \end{bmatrix} + \begin{bmatrix} 2 \\ 0 \end{bmatrix} = \begin{bmatrix} 7 \\ -2 \end{bmatrix}$$

Notice that the resultant is the same, irrespective of the order in which the vectors are added.

1.3 Exercise 3

1 $\begin{bmatrix} 3 \\ -1 \end{bmatrix} + \begin{bmatrix} -2 \\ 4 \end{bmatrix} = \begin{bmatrix} 1 \\ 3 \end{bmatrix}$

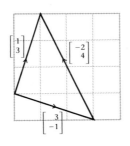

2 (a) $\mathbf{u} + \mathbf{v}$ (b) $\mathbf{u} + 2\mathbf{v}$ (c) $\mathbf{v} - \mathbf{u}$

3 $\begin{bmatrix} -2 \\ -3 \end{bmatrix} + \begin{bmatrix} 5 \\ -7 \end{bmatrix} + \begin{bmatrix} 16 \\ 4 \end{bmatrix} = \begin{bmatrix} 19 \\ -6 \end{bmatrix}$

Missing vector $= \begin{bmatrix} -9 \\ 4 \end{bmatrix}$

4 (a) D (115350)

(b) $\overrightarrow{AD} = \begin{bmatrix} 11.5 - 2.5 \\ 35 - 10.5 \end{bmatrix} = \begin{bmatrix} 9 \\ 24.5 \end{bmatrix}$

$\overrightarrow{BC} = \begin{bmatrix} 19.5 - 10.5 \\ 40 - 15.5 \end{bmatrix} = \begin{bmatrix} 9 \\ 24.5 \end{bmatrix}$

$\overrightarrow{AD} = \overrightarrow{BC}$

(c) AD = BC and AD is parallel to BC
⇒ ABCD is a parallelogram

1.3.4 Using vectors

1.3 Exercise 4

1 $\overrightarrow{PQ} = \begin{bmatrix} -100 \cos 45° \\ 100 \sin 45° \end{bmatrix} \approx \begin{bmatrix} -70.7 \\ 70.7 \end{bmatrix}$

$\overrightarrow{AQ} = \begin{bmatrix} 12.3 \\ 70.7 \end{bmatrix}$

$|\overrightarrow{AQ}| \approx 71.8$

Airport Q is closer to the aircraft by 11.2 km.

2 $\overrightarrow{PS} = \begin{bmatrix} 15.97 \\ -12.04 \end{bmatrix}$

$\overrightarrow{HS} \approx \begin{bmatrix} 10.97 \\ -12.04 \end{bmatrix}$

$|\overrightarrow{HS}| \approx 16.3$

$\theta \approx 47.7°$

The helicopter has to fly in the direction 137.7° for a distance of 16.3 km.

3 The displacement westwards of the boat is 9 sin 38° km each hour, and the time taken for its displacement westwards to be 4.7 km is

$$\frac{4.7}{9 \sin 38°} \approx 0.85 \text{ hour} = 51 \text{ minutes}$$

Hence it will be due north of Black Cap Light at 3:06 a.m.

4 The helicopter has to fly 24.6 km in the direction 279.9°.

5 The displacement of HMS *Battledore* from port at 15:00 is

$$\frac{2}{5} \begin{bmatrix} 15 \sin 61° \\ -15 \cos 61° \end{bmatrix} + \frac{7}{20} \begin{bmatrix} -15 \sin 17° \\ 15 \cos 17° \end{bmatrix}$$

$$= \begin{bmatrix} 6 \sin 61° - 5.25 \sin 17° \\ -6 \cos 61° + 5.25 \cos 17° \end{bmatrix}$$

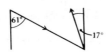

The displacement of HMS *Shuttlecock* from port at 15:00 is

$$\begin{bmatrix} -6 \sin 25° \\ -6 \cos 25° \end{bmatrix}$$

The displacement of HMS *Shuttlecock* from HMS *Battledore* is

$$\begin{bmatrix} -6.25 \\ -7.55 \end{bmatrix}$$

$$d \approx 9.80$$

So at 15:00 the ships are about 9.80 nautical miles apart.

Time taken to meet $\approx \dfrac{9.80}{20} = 0.49$ hour

$$= 29\tfrac{1}{2} \text{ min}$$

$$\tan \phi = \frac{6.25}{7.55}$$

$$\Rightarrow \quad \phi \approx 39.6°$$

HMS *Battledore* proceeds on bearing 219.6°.

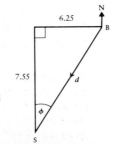

1.3.5 Position and displacement

1.3 C

This result is obvious in view of the fact that going from O to Q is simply the resultant of going from O to P to Q, i.e. $\overrightarrow{OQ} = \overrightarrow{OP} + \overrightarrow{PQ}$.

1.3 Exercise 5

1

	(a)	(b)	(c)	(d)
Original position vector	$\begin{bmatrix} 200 \\ 90 \end{bmatrix}$	$\begin{bmatrix} 7 \\ -7 \end{bmatrix}$	$\begin{bmatrix} -32 \\ 16 \end{bmatrix}$	$\begin{bmatrix} -88 \\ -262 \end{bmatrix}$
New position vector	$\begin{bmatrix} 326 \\ 81 \end{bmatrix}$	$\begin{bmatrix} 73 \\ -81 \end{bmatrix}$	$\begin{bmatrix} -15 \\ -4 \end{bmatrix}$	$\begin{bmatrix} -10 \\ -8 \end{bmatrix}$
Displacement	$\begin{bmatrix} 126 \\ -9 \end{bmatrix}$	$\begin{bmatrix} 66 \\ -74 \end{bmatrix}$	$\begin{bmatrix} 17 \\ -20 \end{bmatrix}$	$\begin{bmatrix} 78 \\ 254 \end{bmatrix}$

2 (a) The new position vector is

$$\begin{bmatrix} 5.7 \\ 2.6 \end{bmatrix} + \begin{bmatrix} 0.9 \\ 0.2 \end{bmatrix} + \begin{bmatrix} 1.4 \\ -0.7 \end{bmatrix} + \begin{bmatrix} 1.2 \\ 0.5 \end{bmatrix}$$

$$= \begin{bmatrix} 9.2 \\ 2.6 \end{bmatrix}$$

(b) The total displacement is $\begin{bmatrix} 3.5 \\ 0 \end{bmatrix}$.

(c) The boat has travelled

$$\sqrt{(0.9^2 + 0.2^2)} + \sqrt{(1.4^2 + 0.7^2)}$$
$$+ \sqrt{(1.2^2 + 0.5^2)}$$

$$= 0.922 + 1.565 + 1.3$$

$$= 3.79 \text{ km} \quad \text{(to 3 s.f.)}$$

1.4 Velocity

1.4.1 Speed or velocity?

1.4 A

(a) After slowing down to B, equal distances are covered in equal 10-second time intervals and so the speed is constant throughout the rest of the journey.

(b) For the velocity to be constant, the direction of motion has to be in the same straight line *and* the speed must be constant, throughout the journey. The part of the journey for which this holds is from E to F.

1.4 B

Average speed is obtained by dividing the distance travelled by the time taken to cover that distance. As the road winds from Southlea to Northaven, the distance *along the road* between them is more than 30 km and hence, travelling at $60 \, \mathrm{km \, h^{-1}}$, the car will take more than half an hour for the journey.

Average velocity is obtained by dividing the displacement between the start and finish of a journey by the time taken for the journey. The displacement between Southlea and Northaven is 30 km due north. Hence, if the average velocity of the second car is $60 \, \mathrm{km \, h^{-1}}$ due north, the time taken for the journey is half an hour.

Equivalent constant speed and equivalent constant velocity can only have the same magnitude if the motion is wholly in a straight line in a given direction.

1.4 Exercise 1

1 Time for outward journey $= \frac{20}{40} = 0.5$ hour

Time for return journey $\quad = \frac{20}{80} = 0.25$ hour

Time for total journey $\quad = 0.75$ hour

Total distance covered $\quad = 40 \, \mathrm{km}$

Average speed $= \frac{40}{0.75} \, \mathrm{km \, h^{-1}} \approx 53.3 \, \mathrm{km \, h^{-1}}$

2 Time taken over first stage $= 1$ hour

Time taken to travel $d \, \mathrm{km}$ of second stage $= \dfrac{d}{60}$ hours

Total length of journey $= (30 + d) \, \mathrm{km}$

Total time of journey $= \left(1 + \dfrac{d}{60}\right)$ hours

Hence

$$45\left(1 + \frac{d}{60}\right) = 30 + d$$

$$\Rightarrow d = 60$$

Length of second stage $= 60 \, \mathrm{km}$

3 Time taken to go from A to B
$= 30 + 20 + 10 = 60$ seconds

Total distance $= 120 \, \mathrm{m}$

Average speed $= \frac{120}{60} \, \mathrm{m \, s^{-1}} = 2 \, \mathrm{m \, s^{-1}}$

Total displacement $= 60 \, \mathrm{m}$ due north

Average velocity $= 1 \, \mathrm{m \, s^{-1}}$ due north

4 An object travelling at constant speed, for example a car moving around a curve, will change its direction of motion continuously and hence cannot have constant velocity. However, a train travelling along a straight portion of track with constant speed will have constant velocity since its direction of motion is unaltered.

An aircraft flying with constant velocity must be moving with constant speed in a fixed direction.

To sum up, an object travelling with constant speed is not travelling with constant velocity, unless the motion takes place in a straight line. On the other hand, a constant velocity means motion in a straight line in a given direction with constant speed; hence, constant velocity implies constant speed.

5 If the average velocity is $50 \, \mathrm{km \, h^{-1}}$ due east, the end of the journey, B, must be due east of the start A. Unless the car travels due east throughout the journey (when the average speed would be $50 \, \mathrm{km \, h^{-1}}$), the distance

travelled must be greater than the length of the straight line AB. Hence the average speed must be at least $50\,\mathrm{km\,h^{-1}}$.

6 (a) Taking $\pi \approx \frac{22}{7}$, the distance covered by the particle around the semicircular path is $\frac{22}{7} \times 7\,\mathrm{m} = 22\,\mathrm{m}$. If the speed increases uniformly with time, the average speed is

$$\frac{8+14}{2}\,\mathrm{m\,s^{-1}} = 11\,\mathrm{m\,s^{-1}}$$

Hence the time taken to complete the path is $\frac{22}{11} = 2$ seconds.

(b) The speed is increasing each second by $3\,\mathrm{m\,s^{-1}}$. Hence it takes 1 second to reach $11\,\mathrm{m\,s^{-2}}$.

If the distance covered in that one second is $d\,\mathrm{m}$, the average speed is $d\,\mathrm{m\,s^{-1}}$. So

$$d = \frac{8+11}{2} = 9\tfrac{1}{2}$$

The particle's speed is $11\,\mathrm{m\,s^{-1}}$ when the particle has travelled $9\tfrac{1}{2}\,\mathrm{m}$ along the path.

(c) The displacement in travelling from A to B is $14\,\mathrm{m}$ in the direction of $\overrightarrow{AB}$ and this takes 2 seconds. Hence, the average velocity is $7\,\mathrm{m\,s^{-1}}$ in the direction of $\overrightarrow{AB}$.

7 As the length of the track is not given in the question you should choose a suitable numerical value; $40\,\mathrm{km}$ is recommended. The graphical solutions are easiest.

(a) Distance (km)

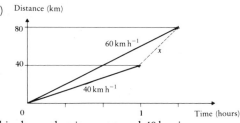

This shows that it must travel $40\,\mathrm{km}$ in 20 minutes.

The speed required is thus $120\,\mathrm{km\,h^{-1}}$.

(b)

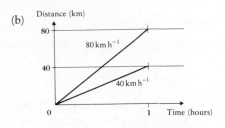

Clearly it is impossible to travel $40\,\mathrm{km}$ in no time at all. Therefore an average speed of $80\,\mathrm{km\,h^{-1}}$ or greater is impossible to achieve.

1.4.2 Straight line motion

1.4 C

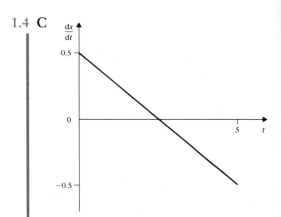

1 The graphs show that the furthest distance the ball travels from the bottom of the ramp is $62\,\mathrm{cm}$. The ball is momentarily at rest when $t = 2.5$ seconds. The maximum speed of $0.5\,\mathrm{m\,s^{-1}}$ occurs when $t = 0$ and $t = 5$. The velocity changes from $0.5\,\mathrm{m\,s^{-1}}$ to $-0.5\,\mathrm{m\,s^{-1}}$.

2 The area under the $\left(t, \dfrac{dx}{dt}\right)$ graph represents the displacement.

3 If the area is underneath the t-axis, then the ball is rolling down the ramp.

4 (a) $0.3\,\mathrm{m\,s^{-1}}$ (b) $-0.3\,\mathrm{m\,s^{-1}}$

5 (a) $0.6 - 0.4 = 0.2\,\mathrm{m\,s^{-1}}$ (b) $0\,\mathrm{m\,s^{-1}}$

1.4 Exercise 2

1 (a) From the (t, x) graph, after 9 seconds, the displacement $= 0$.

From the $\left(t, \dfrac{dx}{dt}\right)$ graph for the first

T seconds, displacement $= 4T$ metres and for the next $(9 - T)$ seconds, displacement $= -2(9 - T)$ metres.

The total displacement is

$4T - 2(9 - T) = 6T - 18 = 0 \Rightarrow T = 3$.

(b) When $t = 3$, $x = 12$

so the distance travelled after 9 seconds is $2 \times 12 = 24$ metres.

(c) The displacement after 9 seconds is 0 metres.

2 (a) For the motion,

$$x = 6t - 5t^2 \Rightarrow \frac{dx}{dt} = 6 - 10t$$

When $t = 0.25$, $\dfrac{dx}{dt} = 3.5$

When $t = 2$, $\dfrac{dx}{dt} = -14$

The velocity of the ball after 0.25 seconds is $3.5 \, \text{m s}^{-1}$ vertically upwards, and after 2 seconds is $14 \, \text{m s}^{-1}$ vertically downwards.

Alternatively, the (t, x) graph could be drawn and the gradient measured to find $\dfrac{dx}{dt}$ (the answers then would only be approximate).

(b) The displacement after the first 3 seconds is -27 metres.

Average velocity $= \dfrac{-27}{3} = -9 \, \text{m s}^{-1}$

3 (a)

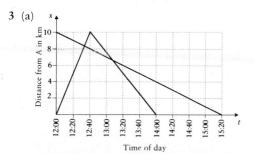

Time of day

(b) Pass at $t_1 = 12{:}33$, distance from A $\approx 8.3 \, \text{km}$

Pass at $t_2 = 13{:}07$, distance from A $\approx 6.7 \, \text{km}$

(c) From t_1 to 12:40, the distance apart increases. From 12:40 to t_2, the distance apart decreases. The time when they are the greatest distance apart is 12:40.

4 (a) By calculating gradients it can be established that $\dfrac{dy}{dt} = -10t$ from $t = 0$ to $t = 1.4$.

Between $t = 1.4$ and $t = 3.6$, the graph is symmetrical about $t = 2.5$. You can calculate that $\dfrac{dy}{dt} = 11$ just after $t = 1.4$, and that the graph of $\left(t, \dfrac{dy}{dt}\right)$ is a straight line of gradient -10.

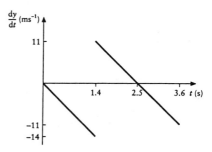

(b) At $t = 1.4$ seconds, the ball hits the ground with a speed of $14 \, \text{m s}^{-1}$ (velocity $-14 \, \text{m s}^{-1}$) and rebounds with a speed of $11 \, \text{m s}^{-1}$ (velocity $11 \, \text{m s}^{-1}$).

(c)

(d) When $t = 1$, ball's speed $= 10 \, \text{m s}^{-1}$

1.4.3 Change in velocity

1.4 D

1 *Car A* The car moves 30 cm every second, relative to the mat, while the mat is simultaneously moving 40 cm every second in the same direction. Hence the velocity of car A is $(40 + 30)\,\text{cm s}^{-1} = 70\,\text{cm s}^{-1}$ in the direction of the motion of the mat.

Car B The car moves 30 cm every second, relative to the mat, in a direction opposite to that of the motion of the mat. The mat is simultaneously moving 40 cm every second.

Hence the velocity of car B is $(40 - 30)\,\text{cm s}^{-1} = 10\,\text{cm s}^{-1}$ in the direction of the motion of the mat.

Car C Every second the car moves 30 cm relative to the mat, perpendicular to the direction of the motion of the mat. The mat is simultaneously moving 40 cm every second.

The magnitude of the velocity of car C is $50\,\text{cm s}^{-1}$.

$$\tan\theta = \frac{30}{40} \quad \Rightarrow \quad \theta \approx 36.9°$$

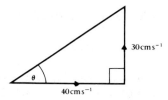

That is, the velocity of car C is $50\,\text{cm s}^{-1}$ making an angle of 36.9° with the direction of the motion of the mat.

2 The change in velocity for each car is $40\,\text{cm s}^{-1}$ in the direction of motion of the mat.

3 In each case,

> Initial velocity + Change in velocity = Final velocity

For example, for car A

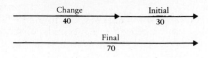

1.4 Exercise 3

1 (a) $13\,\text{m s}^{-1}$ due west   (b) $13\,\text{m s}^{-1}$ due east

(c)

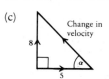

$$\sqrt{(8^2 + 5^2)} = 9.43 \quad \text{(to 3 s.f.)}$$

$$\tan\alpha = \tfrac{8}{5} \quad \Rightarrow \quad \alpha = 58.0°$$

The change in velocity is $9.43\,\text{m s}^{-1}$ in direction 328°.

2

The change in velocity is $7.2\,\text{km h}^{-1}$ in direction 079°.

3 Resultant velocity of aeroplane

$$= \begin{bmatrix} 200 \\ 10 \end{bmatrix} + \begin{bmatrix} -30 \\ 40 \end{bmatrix} \text{km h}^{-1}$$

$$= \begin{bmatrix} 170 \\ 50 \end{bmatrix} \text{km h}^{-1}$$

The resultant velocity of the aeroplane is $177.2\,\text{km h}^{-1}$ in direction 073.6°.

4 Change in velocity $= \begin{bmatrix} 6 \\ 6 \end{bmatrix} \text{m s}^{-1}$

Its magnitude is $8.5\,\text{m s}^{-1}$. Its direction is 045°

5 Velocity of the wind $\approx 14.0\,\text{km h}^{-1}$ in direction 142°

1.4.4 Resultant velocity

1.4 Exercise 4

1 By Pythagoras' theorem, her speed is

$$\sqrt{(8^2 + 2^2)} = 8.25 \text{ m s}^{-1} \quad \text{(to 3 s.f.)}$$

2 $\cos\theta \approx \dfrac{1}{1.5} \quad \Rightarrow \quad \theta \approx 48°$

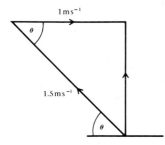

The girl should point her canoe upriver making an angle of 48° with the bank.

Resultant speed $= \sqrt{(1.5^2 - 1^2)} \text{ m s}^{-1}$

Time taken to cross river $= \dfrac{100}{\text{Resultant speed}}$

≈ 89 seconds

Assumptions made:

- she can paddle immediately with speed 1.5 m s^{-1};
- she can maintain both this speed and the direction throughout the motion;
- the speed of the river is the same throughout its width.

3 He should swim at an angle of 48° to the bank. The resultant speed will be 3.7 km h^{-1}.

4 Sketch

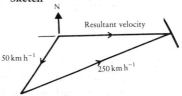

The wind blows at 50 km h^{-1} from a bearing of 030°. Draw this vector first.

The plane flies at a speed of 250 km h^{-1} but you do not know its direction. Draw a circle of radius 250.

The resultant must also be due east. Draw a vector from the start due east. This completes your vector triangle.

Scale drawing   *Scale* $1 \text{ cm} : 50 \text{ km h}^{-1}$

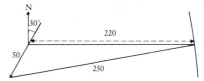

By measurement, the resultant velocity is about 220 km h^{-1} due east. The plane must head on a bearing of 080°.

The plane must cover 100 km so the time taken is $\dfrac{100}{220} = 0.4545$ hour.

This is approximately 27 minutes.

5 75 m;   25 seconds

6 You should point the canoe into the current at an angle of 41.4° to the bank. It will take 8 seconds to cross.

7 This is best tackled by writing the vectors in component form.

$$V_{\text{canoe}} = \begin{bmatrix} -4\cos 45° \\ 4\sin 45° \end{bmatrix} \quad V_{\text{river}} = \begin{bmatrix} 3 \\ 0 \end{bmatrix}$$

$$V_{\text{resultant}} = \begin{bmatrix} -4\cos 45° \\ 4\sin 45° \end{bmatrix} + \begin{bmatrix} 3 \\ 0 \end{bmatrix} = \begin{bmatrix} -0.17 \\ 2.83 \end{bmatrix}$$

The canoe takes $\dfrac{100}{2.83} = 35.4$ seconds to cross the river.

It will end up approx. 6.1 m upstream on the other bank.

1.4.5 A modelling exercise

1.4 E

Set up a model

Let the wind speed be $v\,\mathrm{m\,s^{-1}}$ south.

Analyse the problem

The resultant speed out is $(150 - v)\,\mathrm{m\,s^{-1}}$.
The resultant speed back is $(150 + v)\,\mathrm{m\,s^{-1}}$.

$$\frac{d}{150 - v} + \frac{d}{150 + v} = 14\,400$$

$$\Rightarrow \quad d = 48(150^2 - v^2)$$

Drawing a graph of d against v gives

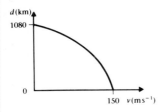

Interpret/validate

When $v = 0$, then $d = 1080$ as in model 1.

The value of d is not altered if v is replaced by $-v$. Thus the result is the same whether the wind blows south or north. (Sketch the appropriate graph.)

If the velocity is greater than $150\,\mathrm{m\,s^{-1}}$ then d is negative and the aeroplane can never return to base!

As v increases then d decreases, slowly at first and then more rapidly.

1.5 Changes in motion
1.5.1 Momentum – the 'quantity of motion'

1.5 A

Experiment 1

1 (a) The faster the snooker ball is rolled, the harder it is to stop and the more effect it has on the block which it hits.

  (b) This also occurs with the table tennis ball.

  (c) However, at any given speed, the table tennis ball is much easier to stop than the snooker ball and has much less effect on the block.

Experiment 2

2 (a), (b) You should be able to feel a definite difference in the effort needed to stop the balls as they fall farther. The farther they fall, the greater their velocity.

  (c) As a result of the experiments, the important factors of the quantity of motion are seen to be the mass and the velocity of the moving object.

    A reasonable way of combining these would be by multiplying the two together, since the quantity of motion appears to increase with both mass and velocity.

3 If mass and velocity are multiplied for the lorry, the quantity of motion would be $4000 \times 1\,\mathrm{kg\,m\,s^{-1}}$. For the car the quantity of motion is $800 \times 5 = 4000\,\mathrm{kg\,m\,s^{-1}}$.

Thus the car and the lorry would have the same quantity of motion.

1.5 B

A rough idea of speeds can be gained without any detailed measurement or timing, although a ruler and watch can be used to improve accuracy a little. There is no need for more sophisticated timing methods in these experiments.

Initially, random selections of masses can be made. After a few attempts, the outcome of an experiment should be predicted *before* the experiment is performed. Conclusions can then be confirmed with a systematic choice of masses.

Results can be recorded easily in a simple table of possibilities and outcomes.

Experiment 3

When the two trucks are of equal mass, the moving one will stop and the initially stationary truck will move away. The speed with which the trucks separate can be seen to be roughly equal to the speed of approach.

When the moving truck is more massive than the stationary one, the moving truck will have its speed reduced and the initially stationary truck will move away with a greater speed than the initial speed of approach. The speed with which the trucks separate is again equal to the speed of approach, although this result may not be as apparent as in the case when the masses are equal.

When the moving truck is less massive than the stationary one, the trucks will move off in opposite directions after the collision. The direction of motion of the initially moving truck will therefore be reversed. The speed of separation is again roughly equal to the speed of approach.

Experiment 4

When the trucks have equal mass, it can be observed that the resultant speed of the joined trucks is roughly half of the moving truck's original speed. In general, if the two trucks have masses a and b then the resultant speed of the joined trucks is $\dfrac{a}{a+b}$ of the original speed of the moving truck of mass a, although this will be difficult to observe.

1.5 Exercise 1

1 (b) and (c) have the same momentum, which is $15 \, \text{kg m s}^{-1}$ eastwards. (a) is in a different direction.

2 $70 \times \begin{bmatrix} 3 \\ 4 \end{bmatrix} = \begin{bmatrix} 210 \\ 280 \end{bmatrix} \text{kg m s}^{-1}$

which has magnitude
$70 \times \sqrt{(3^2 + 4^2)} = 70 \times 5 = 350 \, \text{kg m s}^{-1}$ in the direction making angle $\tan^{-1} \frac{3}{4}$ with north, i.e. bearing 037°.

3 (a)

The car has three times the speed of the truck but only one tenth of its mass.

(b)

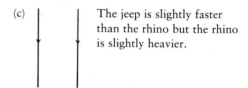

The speedboat has a greater speed than the ferry but a much smaller mass.

(c)

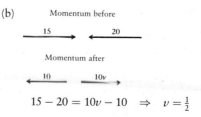

The jeep is slightly faster than the rhino but the rhino is slightly heavier.

1.5.2 Conservation of momentum

1.5 Exercise 2

1 (a) Momentum before   Momentum after

20   10v

$20 = 10v \quad \Rightarrow \quad v = 2$

The velocity of B has magnitude $2 \, \text{m s}^{-1}$.

(b)   Momentum before

15   20

Momentum after

10   10v

$15 - 20 = 10v - 10 \quad \Rightarrow \quad v = \frac{1}{2}$

The velocity of B has magnitude $\frac{1}{2} \, \text{m s}^{-1}$.

(c)

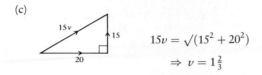

$$15v = \sqrt{(15^2 + 20^2)}$$
$$\Rightarrow v = 1\tfrac{2}{3}$$

This is a velocity of $1\tfrac{2}{3}\,\mathrm{m\,s}^{-1}$ at an angle of $\tan^{-1}\tfrac{3}{4}$ to the original direction of the motion of A.

2 $19\,\mathrm{m\,s}^{-1}$ (to 2 s.f.)

3 $3\,\mathrm{m\,s}^{-1}$

4 $2\,\mathrm{kg}$

5

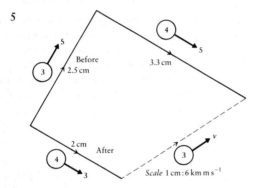

The final velocity of the 3 kg mass is $\tfrac{17}{3} \approx 5.7\,\mathrm{m\,s}^{-1}$ on bearing 058°.

1.5.3 Change in momentum

1.5 C

For the puck of mass 0.1 kg, the momentum changes from $0.2\,\mathrm{kg\,m\,s}^{-1}$ towards the right to $0.1\,\mathrm{kg\,m\,s}^{-1}$ towards the left: a total change of momentum, towards the left, of

$$0.1 - (-0.2) = 0.3\,\mathrm{kg\,m\,s}^{-1}$$

For the puck of mass 0.3 kg, the momentum change is from zero to $0.3\,\mathrm{kg\,m\,s}^{-1}$ towards the right.

So the momentum changes for the two pucks are equal in size and opposite in direction. You can conclude that the 'hit' experienced by one is equal and opposite to the 'hit' experienced by the other. The two changes in momentum cancel each other out if you look at the total momentum of both pucks. This is the law of conservation of momentum.

1.5 Exercise 3

1 The speed increases from $18.05\,\mathrm{m\,s}^{-1}$ to $33.3\,\mathrm{m\,s}^{-1}$. The initial momentum is $180\,556\,\mathrm{kg\,m\,s}^{-1}$ and the final momentum is $333\,333\,\mathrm{kg\,m\,s}^{-1}$.

The change in momentum is $152\,777\,\mathrm{kg\,m\,s}^{-1}$
$= 153\,000\,\mathrm{kg\,m\,s}^{-1}$ to 3 significant figures

2 (a) Initial momentum $= 30\,000\,\mathrm{kg\,m\,s}^{-1}$
New momentum $= 15\,000\,\mathrm{kg\,m\,s}^{-1}$

The new speed is $7.5\,\mathrm{m\,s}^{-1}$.

  (b) Initial momentum $= 150\,000\,\mathrm{kg\,m\,s}^{-1}$
New momentum $= 135\,000\,\mathrm{kg\,m\,s}^{-1}$

The new speed is $13.5\,\mathrm{m\,s}^{-1}$.

3

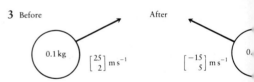

$$\text{Momentum before} = \begin{bmatrix} 2.5 \\ 0.2 \end{bmatrix}\,\mathrm{kg\,m\,s}^{-1}$$

$$\text{Momentum after} = \begin{bmatrix} -1.5 \\ 0.5 \end{bmatrix}\,\mathrm{kg\,m\,s}^{-1}$$

  (a) The change in momentum is
$\begin{bmatrix} -4.0 \\ 0.3 \end{bmatrix}\,\mathrm{kg\,m\,s}^{-1}$.

  (b) If the change in momentum is
$\begin{bmatrix} -2.0 \\ 0.15 \end{bmatrix}\,\mathrm{kg\,m\,s}^{-1}$, then

the new momentum is $\begin{bmatrix} 0.5 \\ 0.35 \end{bmatrix}\,\mathrm{kg\,m\,s}^{-1}$.

The new velocity would be $\begin{bmatrix} 5 \\ 3.5 \end{bmatrix}\,\mathrm{m\,s}^{-1}$.

1.6 Force
1.6.1 Newton's first and second laws of motion

1.6 A

1 Your graph should have the general shape of the graph shown.

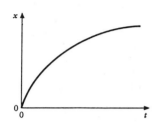

2 Your results will only be approximate but should show that the velocity decreases by about $40 \, \text{cm s}^{-1}$ every second.

1.6 Exercise 1

1 $mu + Ft = mv$, $\quad F = 20 \, \text{N}$ in the direction of motion, $\quad m = 2 \, \text{kg}$

$t = 0, \quad u = 0 \quad\quad 2 \times 0 + 20 \times 1 = 2v$

$t = 1, \quad v = ? \quad\quad\quad\quad \Rightarrow v = 10 \, \text{m s}^{-1}$

$t = 2, \quad\quad\quad\quad\quad\quad v = 20 \, \text{m s}^{-1}$

$t = 3, \quad\quad\quad\quad\quad\quad v = 30 \, \text{m s}^{-1}$

$t = 4, \quad\quad\quad\quad\quad\quad v = 40 \, \text{m s}^{-1}$

The speed is increased by a constant amount each second.

2 $mu + Ft = mv \quad\quad t = 5, \quad m = 0.2$, take north as positive.

$0.2 \times (-1.5) + F \times 5 = 0.2 \times 2$

$\Rightarrow \quad\quad\quad\quad F = 0.14$

A force of $0.14 \, \text{N}$ is needed, acting due north.

3 The time taken is 4.8 seconds.

4 A force of $5250 \, \text{N}$ is required.

5 The speed is $2.25 \, \text{m s}^{-1}$.

1.6.2 Newton's third law of motion

1.6 B

The skateboard experiment may be carried out practically. Subject to effects such as differences in the two skateboards themselves, you could expect:

(a) the interaction forces of the two students to be equal in magnitude and opposite in direction;

(b) their momenta to be equal in magnitude and opposite in direction, at least initially.

The two students still exert the same force on each other, even if one is twice the weight of the other. Because their momenta are the same in magnitude, the heavier student will move off with half the speed of the lighter. (Note that if two skateboarders have a rope, they can pull towards one another in the same manner.)

1.6 Exercise 2

1 The weight of the apple is the gravitational force due to the attraction of the Earth. Thus the 'other body' is the Earth. The total momentum of the Earth and the apple is conserved. This implies that the Earth moves towards the apple as well as the apple moving towards the Earth. This does, in fact, happen but the mass of the Earth is so much greater than that of the apple that the effect is far too small to measure.

2

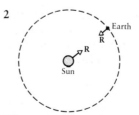

There is a gravitational force exerted by the Sun on the Earth and a force, equal in magnitude and opposite in direction, exerted by the Earth on the Sun. Once again, the total momentum of the system is conserved.

However, the mass of the Sun is far greater than that of the Earth and so the effect on the Earth's velocity is much greater than the effect on the velocity of the Sun.

The pull of the Sun causes a change in the Earth's velocity but not its speed. This motion must, of course, satisfy Newton's second law.

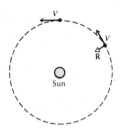

3 (a)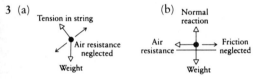

(b)

(c) (d) (e)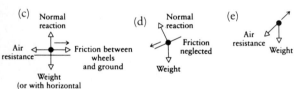

1.6.3 Weight and change of momentum

1.6 C

1 A set of scales registers the same weight for the golf ball no matter at what height it is used. The pull on the golf ball is therefore the same throughout its motion and so its momentum changes at a constant rate. The (time, velocity) graph will therefore be linear.

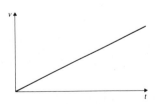

2 Contrary to what many people believe, the speed at which an object falls does not depend upon its mass. (You may have seen a film of the experiment performed on the Moon where, in the absence of air resistance, a feather falls at the same rate as a stone.) Air resistance has a negligible effect on the golf and cricket balls and so they have the same speed at any time.

Since the balls have the same speed at any time, their changes in momenta are in proportion to their masses. By Newton's second law, the resultant forces acting on them must be in proportion to their masses. The weight of an object is therefore a fixed multiple of its mass.

3 (a) The velocity can be found by estimating the gradient of the (time, displacement) graph. Your estimates should be close to those shown in the table below.

Time t (seconds)	0	0.5	1.0	1.5	2.0
Velocity v (m s^{-1})	0	-5	-10	-15	-20

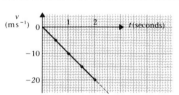

The (time, velocity) graph is shown above. The linear relationship shows that the magnitude of the velocity (the speed) is increasing at a steady $10 \, \text{m s}^{-1}$ each second. The velocity is negative because the direction is downwards.

(b) During the first second the momentum of the shot changes from 0 to $-10 \, \text{kg m s}^{-1}$, and during the next second the momentum changes from -10 to $-20 \, \text{kg m s}^{-1}$. The change in momentum is therefore $-10 \, \text{kg m s}^{-1}$ during each second.

(c) You should expect the change in momentum to continue to be $-10 \, \text{kg m s}^{-1}$ per second.

(d) According to Newton's second law, the change in momentum each second is a measure of the resultant force acting on the shot, so it would seem that there is a constant force of −10 newtons pulling the shot down. (The force is negative simply because it is acting in what has been taken to be the negative direction.) This is clearly the force of gravitational attraction.

It is interesting to note that if a second shot with a mass of 0.5 kg had been released simultaneously with the 1 kg shot, it would have had the same velocity and so its change in momentum would only have been $-5\,\mathrm{kg\,m\,s^{-1}}$ per second. The force of gravitational attraction on a 0.5 kg mass would therefore be −5 N. The force of gravitational attraction would appear to be a constant −10 N per kilogram.

Change in momentum during the 2nd second is $1\,\mathrm{kg\,m\,s^{-1}}$.
Change in momentum during the 3rd second is $1\,\mathrm{kg\,m\,s^{-1}}$.
Change in momentum during the 4th second is $1\,\mathrm{kg\,m\,s^{-1}}$.
Change in momentum during the 5th second is $1\,\mathrm{kg\,m\,s^{-1}}$.

(d) The change in momentum during each second is the same; $1\,\mathrm{kg\,m\,s^{-1}}$ downwards. The same constant rate of change of momentum is seen when a ball (or an apple) falls vertically downwards. It is caused by its weight, i.e. the force due to the gravitational attraction of the Earth.

4 (a)

Time	Velocity
1	$\begin{bmatrix} 10 \\ 20 \end{bmatrix}$
2	$\begin{bmatrix} 10 \\ 10 \end{bmatrix}$
3	$\begin{bmatrix} 10 \\ 0 \end{bmatrix}$
4	$\begin{bmatrix} 10 \\ -10 \end{bmatrix}$
5	$\begin{bmatrix} 10 \\ -20 \end{bmatrix}$

(b)

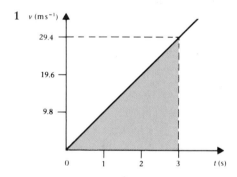

The velocity can be expressed as a column vector.

(c) The tip of each momentum vector lies on the same vertical line. Therefore the horizontal component of momentum is the same in each case, and so the speed of the ball along the horizontal direction remains constant.

The change in momentum in each second is in the downward vertical direction.

1.6 Exercise 3

1

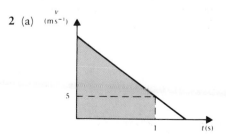

(a) When $t = 3$, $v = 29.4\,\mathrm{m\,s^{-1}}$

(b) The distance fallen is the area under the graph, 44.1 metres.

(c) When $t = 3.5$, $v = 9.8 \times 3.5$
$s = \frac{1}{2}vt = 60$ metres
The cliff is 60 metres high.

2 (a)

(b) The graph shows that after 1 second the ball will have slowed to $5\,\mathrm{m\,s^{-1}}$.

The distance travelled is given by the area under the graph, $s = 9.9$ metres. The conker can be 9.9 metres above the ground.

3 (a)

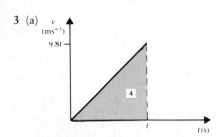

(b) $4 = \dfrac{9.8t \times t}{2} \quad \Rightarrow \quad t = 0.90$ seconds

The velocity with which the tin hits the ground is $8.9\,\mathrm{m\,s^{-1}}$.

4 $s = 0.5gt^2$ so $t = 1.01$ seconds

Both have a velocity of $9.9\,\mathrm{m\,s^{-1}}$. The girl has momentum of $247\,\mathrm{kg\,m\,s^{-1}}$ and her father has momentum of $742\,\mathrm{kg\,m\,s^{-1}}$.

5 The momentum is $16\,000\,\mathrm{kg\,m\,s^{-1}}$ so the velocity is $8\,\mathrm{m\,s^{-1}}$.

$t = 8 \div 9.8 = 0.82$ seconds

Then $s = 0.5 \times 8 \times 0.82 = 3.3$ metres (to 2 s.f.)

Miscellaneous exercise 1

1 (a)

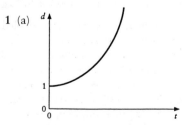

(b) $4\,\mathrm{cm\,s^{-1}}$

(c) (i) 1 cm   (ii) 3 cm

2 (a) $v = 3t^2 - 2t$; $8\,\mathrm{m\,s^{-1}}$

(b) $t = 0$ and $t = \frac{2}{3}$ seconds

(c) (i) $v = -0.25\,\mathrm{m\,s^{-1}}$;   it is moving from right to left.

(ii) $v = 0.32\,\mathrm{m\,s^{-1}}$;   it is moving from left to right.

3 (a) $\begin{bmatrix} 3.0 \\ 1.9 \end{bmatrix}$ (b) $\begin{bmatrix} -4.0 \\ -6.2 \end{bmatrix}$ (c) $\begin{bmatrix} -7.5 \\ 9.2 \end{bmatrix}$

4 Jane is 1.5 km and Nicola is 2.45 km from the *George and Dragon*. They are 1.96 km apart.

5 (a) 36 km,   034°   (b) 25 km,   037°

(c) 11 km,   207°   (d) 11 km,   027°

6 087080

7 B is 43 km from A. The bearing of A from B is 157°.

8 14.5 km;   no, if both are affected equally.

9 (a) $3.5\,\mathrm{m\,s^{-1}}$ (b) 5 s, $5\,\mathrm{m\,s^{-1}}$

10 (a) $2\,\mathrm{m\,s^{-1}}$ (b) 0.94 m   (c) after 2.5 s

11 (a)

t (s)	0	1	2	3	4	5
y (cm)	50	45	34	23	18	25
v (cm s^{-1})	0	−9	−12	−9	0	15

(b) 18 cm, when the velocity changes from negative to positive

(c) $12\,\mathrm{cm\,s^{-1}}$

12 (a) $-3\,\mathrm{m\,s^{-1}}$ ($3\,\mathrm{m\,s^{-1}}$ downwards)

(b) Velocity $= 0\,\mathrm{m\,s^{-1}}$ when it lands

13 (a) 52.1 m   (b) $13\frac{1}{3}$ seconds

14 (a) 234°, 23 minutes

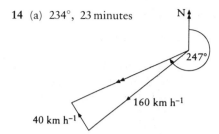

(b) 074°, 35 minutes

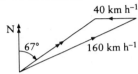

15 $\frac{2}{3}$ m s^{-1}

16 0.141 kg

17 (a) $\begin{bmatrix} 1 \\ 0 \end{bmatrix}$ (b) $\begin{bmatrix} 3 \\ 0 \end{bmatrix}$ (c) 4

18

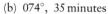

2.5 × 10⁷ m s⁻¹	8.55 × 10⁶ m s⁻¹ 2.35 × 10⁷ m s⁻¹
Before	After

19 1.97 m s^{-1}, 1.18 m s^{-1}

20 24 N

21 0.3 m s^{-1}

22 25 s, 62.5 m

23 Still 0.2 m s^{-1}

24 13.5 m s^{-1}, 16.7 m

2 FORCE AND MOTION

2.1 Projectiles

2.1.1 Weight

2.1 **A**

1 In chapter 1, *Newton's laws of motion*, you saw that

> On a mass of m kg at the Earth's surface, the Earth exerts a downwards force of approximately mg newtons.

$\frac{F}{m}$ is therefore equal to g, the acceleration due to gravity. An approximate value for this is 9.8 m s^{-2}.

This is easy to obtain from a measurement of the time an object takes to fall a given distance.

2 The gravitational force on a mass of m kg is approximately $9.8m$ newtons.

$$F = \frac{GmE}{r^2}$$

$$\Rightarrow \quad \frac{GE}{r^2} \approx 9.8$$

$$\Rightarrow \quad E \approx \frac{9.8 \times (6.4 \times 10^6)^2}{6.673 \times 10^{-11}}$$

$$\approx 6 \times 10^{24} \text{ kg}$$

[A more precise value is 5.983×10^{24} kg.]

Knowing the mass of the Earth enabled astronomers to calculate the mass of the Sun, Moon and planets from observations of their gravitational effects on each other. By measuring the attraction of lead balls, Cavendish, in effect, measured the mass of the Earth and the other bodies in the solar system.

2.1 B

Assumptions include the following:

1 The weights are assumed to be parallel, acting vertically downwards towards the centre of the Earth.

2 The distance of the skier from the centre of the Earth is the same for each position of the skier, so that the magnitude of the force is the same.

3 The Earth is assumed to be a particle.

Assumption 1 is valid as long as the skier's movement across the surface of the Earth is not great compared to the radius of the Earth. The radius of the Earth is approximately 6380 km, so a difference in distance of 10 km would mean a change in angle of 0.0016 radians or 0.09°.

Assumption 2 is valid as long as the skier's distance from the centre of the Earth does not vary much compared to the radius of the Earth. If the skier moved to the top of Mount Everest then the magnitude of his weight would be multiplied by a factor of 0.996. This effect is highly significant for rocket motion.

Assumption 3 works as long as the skier is not too near a large mountain or geological irregularity. It can be proved that the gravitational force of attraction of a uniform, spherical planet is exactly the same as that of a particle of the same mass situated at the centre of the planet.

2.1 Exercise 1

All answers are given to 3 significant figures.

1 $F = \dfrac{Gm_1m_2}{r^2} = \dfrac{6.67 \times 10^{-11} \times 1 \times 1.5}{1}$ N

$= 1.00 \times 10^{-10}$ N

They do not accelerate towards one another because the force of attraction is opposed by friction forces.

2 (a) $F = 9.8m = 39.2$ N

Change in momentum each second is 39.2 kg m s^{-1}
Change in momentum after 3 s is $3 \times 39.2 = 117.6 \text{ kg m s}^{-1}$

(b) The Earth's change in momentum $= 117.6 \text{ kg m s}^{-1}$

Therefore its change in velocity

$$= \frac{117.6}{5.98 \times 10^{24}}$$

$= 1.97 \times 10^{-23} \text{ m s}^{-1}$ (to 3 s.f.)

which is negligible.

3 (a) Momentum after t seconds
$= 5 \times 49 = 245 \text{ kg m s}^{-1}$
Change in momentum after t seconds
$= 245 \text{ kg m s}^{-1}$

(b) Force $= 5g = 5 \times 9.8 = 49$
Change in momentum produced by the force in t seconds $= 49t \text{ kg m s}^{-1}$

$245 = 49t \quad \Rightarrow \quad t = 5$ seconds

(c) Distance fallen

$=$ area under a (velocity, time) graph

$$= \frac{5 \times 49}{2} = 122.5 \text{ metres}$$

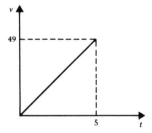

4 Change in momentum in 4 seconds
$= 78.4 \text{ kg m s}^{-1}$
Force $= mg = 9.8m$ N

$\Rightarrow$ Change in momentum in 4 seconds
$= 4 \times 9.8m = 39.2m \text{ kg m s}^{-1}$

$\Rightarrow \quad 78.4 = 39.2m$

$\Rightarrow \quad m = 2 \text{ kg}$

Change in momentum
= final momentum − initial momentum

$$\Rightarrow \quad 78.4 = mv - mu$$

$$\Rightarrow \quad 78.4 = 2v - 0$$

$$\Rightarrow \quad v = 39.2 \, \text{m s}^{-1}$$

5 (a) (i) Since the radius of the Earth is only to 4 significant figures, i.e. to the nearest kilometre, the weight at the top of the Eiffel Tower is the same as at the Earth's surface, 9.80 N to 3 s.f.

   (ii) At the top of Mount Everest, the distance from the centre of the Earth is

$$d = 6.387 \times 10^6 \text{ metres}$$

So weight $= \dfrac{GMm}{d^2}$

$$= \frac{6.673 \times 10^{-11} \times 5.974 \times 10^{24}}{6.387^2 \times 10^{12}}$$

$$= 9.77 \text{ newtons}$$

   (iii) At height 928 km, the distance from the centre of the Earth is

$$d = (6.378 + 0.928) \times 10^6$$

$$= 7.31 \times 10^6 \text{ metres}$$

So weight $= \dfrac{GMm}{d^2}$

$$= \frac{6.673 \times 10^{-11} \times 5.974 \times 10^{24}}{7.31^2 \times 10^{12}}$$

$$= 7.46 \text{ newtons}$$

(b) Let r be the radius of the Earth.

$$\text{Weight} = \frac{GMm}{(2r)^2} = \frac{9.8}{4} = 2.45 \text{ N}$$

(c)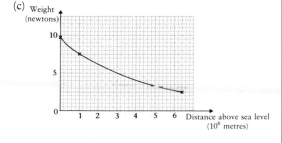

6 Defining upwards as positive,
change in momentum in t_1 seconds
$= -117.6 \text{ kg m s}^{-1}$

Force $= -3g = -3 \times 9.8 = -29.4 \text{ kg m s}^{-1}$
Change in momentum in t_1 seconds $= -29.4t_1$

$$\Rightarrow \quad -29.4t_1 = -117.6$$

$$\Rightarrow \quad t_1 = 4 \text{ seconds}$$

For the second instant, $t_2 = 6$ seconds.

7E $F = 257 \text{ N}$ (to 3 s.f.)

2.1.3 Velocity

2.1 C

$$\begin{bmatrix} x \\ y \end{bmatrix} = \begin{bmatrix} 30t \\ 9t - 5t^2 \end{bmatrix}$$

2.1 D

1 $\mathbf{v} = \dfrac{d\mathbf{r}}{dt}$ and for small δt, $\delta \mathbf{r} = \begin{bmatrix} \delta x \\ \delta y \end{bmatrix}$,

so $\dfrac{d\mathbf{r}}{dt} = \begin{bmatrix} \dfrac{dx}{dt} \\ \dfrac{dy}{dt} \end{bmatrix}$

2 If $\mathbf{r} = \begin{bmatrix} 30t \\ 9t - 5t^2 \end{bmatrix}$, $\mathbf{v} = \begin{bmatrix} 30 \\ 9 - 10t \end{bmatrix}$

3 $t = 0.7$, $\mathbf{v} = \begin{bmatrix} 30 \\ 2 \end{bmatrix}$; $t = 0.9$, $\mathbf{v} = \begin{bmatrix} 30 \\ 0 \end{bmatrix}$;

$t = 1.1$, $\mathbf{v} = \begin{bmatrix} 30 \\ -2 \end{bmatrix}$

4 The bike lands when $t = 1.8$ and $\mathbf{v} = \begin{bmatrix} 30 \\ -9 \end{bmatrix}$,

so its speed is $\sqrt{(30^2 + 9^2)} = 31.3 \text{ m s}^{-1}$.

5 This can be interpreted as follows.

The take-off speed and landing speed are the same, that is $31.3 \text{ m s}^{-1} = 113 \text{ km h}^{-1}$. The horizontal component of velocity is always the same, 30 m s^{-1}, but the vertical component is steadily decreasing from 9 m s^{-1} on take-off, to zero after 0.9 seconds, to -9 m s^{-1} on landing.

In the absence of any real data on speeds and velocities, these results are validated simply by common sense. 113 km h^{-1} is a reasonable speed. You can expect the vertical component of velocity to decrease because of the weight. The effect of air resistance seems to have been negligible in the 1.8 seconds of the flight. However, the actual motion could be studied on a video, frame by frame.

2.1 Exercise 2

1 If $\mathbf{r} = \begin{bmatrix} 10t \\ 30t - 5t^2 \end{bmatrix}$ then $\mathbf{v} = \begin{bmatrix} 10 \\ 30 - 10t \end{bmatrix}$

(a) $\dfrac{dy}{dt} = 0$ when $t = 3$

(b) When $t = 3$, $\mathbf{v} = \begin{bmatrix} 10 \\ 0 \end{bmatrix}$ and $\mathbf{r} = \begin{bmatrix} 30 \\ 45 \end{bmatrix}$

so the maximum height = 45 metres

(c) When $t = 6$, $\mathbf{r} = \begin{bmatrix} 60 \\ 0 \end{bmatrix}$

so the range = 60 metres

2 (a) At $t = 0$, $\mathbf{v} = \begin{bmatrix} 30 \\ 9 \end{bmatrix}$

so speed $= \sqrt{(30^2 + 9^2)} = 31.3 \text{ m s}^{-1}$

(b) When $t = 0.9$, $\mathbf{v} = \begin{bmatrix} 30 \\ 0 \end{bmatrix}$

so speed $= 30 \text{ m s}^{-1}$

3 $\mathbf{r} = \begin{bmatrix} 10t \\ 9t - 5t^2 + 2 \end{bmatrix}$

(a) Height of the net above the ground $= 2 \text{ m}$
When $y = 2$, $9t - 5t^2 + 2 = 2$
$\Rightarrow \quad 9t - 5t^2 = 0$
$\Rightarrow \quad t = 0$ or $t = \frac{9}{5}$
When $t = \frac{9}{5}$, $x = 10t = 18 \text{ m}$

The net should be placed with its centre at $\begin{bmatrix} 18 \\ 2 \end{bmatrix}$.

(b) $\mathbf{v} = \begin{bmatrix} 10 \\ 9 - 10t \end{bmatrix}$

When $t = \dfrac{9}{5}$, $\mathbf{v} = \begin{bmatrix} 10 \\ -9 \end{bmatrix}$

The speed is 13.5 m s^{-1} to 3 significant figures.

4 $\mathbf{r} = \begin{bmatrix} 10t \\ 2 + 10t - 5t^2 \end{bmatrix}$

(a) $\dfrac{d\mathbf{r}}{dt} = \begin{bmatrix} 10 \\ 10 - 10t \end{bmatrix}$

$\Rightarrow$ velocity of projection $= \begin{bmatrix} 10 \\ 10 \end{bmatrix}$

$\Rightarrow$ magnitude $= 10\sqrt{2} \text{ m s}^{-1}$,
direction $= 45°$ to the horizontal

(b) $t = 0$, $\mathbf{r} = \begin{bmatrix} 0 \\ 2 \end{bmatrix}$

The height of release above ground is 2 metres.

(c) The shot hits the ground when
$2 + 10t - 5t^2 = 0$
i.e. $t = 2.18$ seconds   (to 2 d.p.)
Length $= 21.8 \text{ m}$

(d) $\dfrac{d\mathbf{r}}{dt} = \begin{bmatrix} 10 \\ 10 - 10t \end{bmatrix} = \begin{bmatrix} 10 \\ -11.8 \end{bmatrix}$

on striking the ground.

(e) It is moving horizontally when
$10 - 10t = 0$

It moves horizontally when $t = 1$ second.
It is then at its maximum height.

(f) Height $= 2 + 10t - 5t^2 = 7 \text{ m}$ when $t = 1$

5 $r = \begin{bmatrix} 0.5 + 10t \\ 0.75 + 2.8t - 5t^2 \end{bmatrix}$

(a) Initial velocity $= \begin{bmatrix} 10 \\ 2.8 \end{bmatrix} \mathrm{m\,s}^{-1}$

(b) $t = 0$ on take-off, $r = \begin{bmatrix} 0.5 \\ 0.75 \end{bmatrix}$ metres

i.e. the centre of gravity is in front of the take off board.

(c) On landing, $0.75 + 2.8t - 5t^2 = 0.75$

$\Rightarrow t(2.8 - 5t) = 0$

$\Rightarrow t = 0$ or $t = \dfrac{2.8}{5} = 0.56$ seconds

Length of jump $= 0.5 + 10 \times 0.56$ seconds

$= 6.1$ metres

2.1.4 Acceleration under a constant force

2.1 E

1 Force $\times$ time = change in momentum

$\Rightarrow$ force $= \dfrac{\text{change in momentum}}{\text{time}}$

$= \text{mass} \times \dfrac{\text{change in velocity}}{\text{time}}$

$= \text{mass} \times \text{acceleration}$

or

$Ft = mv - mu$

$F = \dfrac{mv - mu}{t}$

$= m\left(\dfrac{v - u}{t}\right)$

$= ma$

Note that it has been assumed that acceleration is constant and so equals the change in velocity divided by time.

2 Weight = mass $\times$ acceleration

$\Rightarrow$ acceleration $= \dfrac{\text{weight}}{\text{mass}}$

or

$W = ma$

$a = \dfrac{W}{m} = g$

g is the weight per unit mass.

2.1 Exercise 3

1 $v = \begin{bmatrix} 5 \\ 6 - 10t \end{bmatrix} \mathrm{m\,s}^{-1}$

$a = \begin{bmatrix} 0 \\ -10 \end{bmatrix} \mathrm{m\,s}^{-2}$

2 $v = \begin{bmatrix} 9 - 2t \\ 2 - 2t \end{bmatrix} \mathrm{m\,s}^{-1}$

$a = \begin{bmatrix} -2 \\ -2 \end{bmatrix} \mathrm{m\,s}^{-2}$

$F = ma \Rightarrow F = \begin{bmatrix} -0.2 \\ -0.2 \end{bmatrix}$ newtons

3    $v = \begin{bmatrix} 5 - 2t \\ 5 - 2t \end{bmatrix}$

$a = \begin{bmatrix} -2 \\ -2 \end{bmatrix}$

$\Rightarrow F = ma = 70 \begin{bmatrix} -2 \\ -2 \end{bmatrix} = \begin{bmatrix} -140 \\ -140 \end{bmatrix}$ N

4 $v = \begin{bmatrix} 6t \\ 8t \end{bmatrix}$ $a = \begin{bmatrix} 6 \\ 8 \end{bmatrix}$

$\Rightarrow F = 0.5 \begin{bmatrix} 6 \\ 8 \end{bmatrix} = \begin{bmatrix} 3 \\ 4 \end{bmatrix}$

$\Rightarrow F = 5\,\mathrm{N}$ at an angle $\tan^{-1}\frac{4}{3}$ to the x-axis

5 (a) $\mathbf{a} = \begin{bmatrix} 0 \\ 2 \end{bmatrix}$

$\mathbf{a} = \begin{bmatrix} 0 \\ 2 \end{bmatrix}$ when $t = 2$

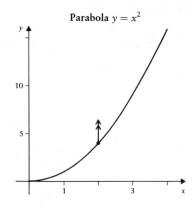

Parabola $y = x^2$

(b) $\mathbf{a} = \begin{bmatrix} 0 \\ 8t^{-3} \end{bmatrix}$

$\mathbf{a} = \begin{bmatrix} 0 \\ 1 \end{bmatrix}$ when $t = 2$

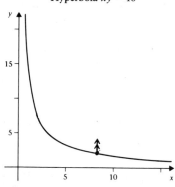

Hyperbola $xy = 16$

(c) $\mathbf{a} = \begin{bmatrix} -\cos t \\ -\sin t \end{bmatrix}$

$\mathbf{a} = \begin{bmatrix} 0.42 \\ -0.91 \end{bmatrix}$ when $t = 2$

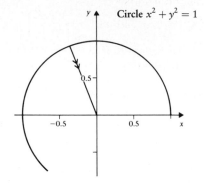

Circle $x^2 + y^2 = 1$

(d) $\mathbf{a} = \begin{bmatrix} 0 \\ 0 \end{bmatrix}$

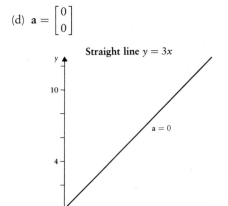

Straight line $y = 3x$

$\mathbf{a} = 0$

2.1.5 Projectile motion

2.1 **F**

1 Given $\mathbf{v}(t) = \begin{bmatrix} 3.81 \\ 2.2 - 10t \end{bmatrix}$

then $\mathbf{r}(t) = \begin{bmatrix} 3.81t + c_1 \\ 2.2t - 5t^2 + c_2 \end{bmatrix}$

But $\mathbf{r}(0) = \begin{bmatrix} 0 \\ 0 \end{bmatrix} \Rightarrow c_1 = c_2 = 0$

So $\mathbf{r}(t) = \begin{bmatrix} 3.81t \\ 2.2t - 5t^2 \end{bmatrix}$

2 (a) $(2.2 - 5t)t = 0$

$\Rightarrow \quad t = 0 \text{ or } t = \dfrac{2.2}{5} = 0.44$

(b) When $t = 0.44$, $\mathbf{r}(t) = \begin{bmatrix} 3.81 \times 0.44 \\ 0 \end{bmatrix}$

$\qquad \approx \begin{bmatrix} 1.7 \\ 0 \end{bmatrix}$

So the range is $R \approx 1.7$ metres.

3 You can conclude that the elastic band will land about 170 cm away, after about 0.44 seconds. During flight its highest point is about 25 cm off the ground.

4 It is clear that there is a degree of inaccuracy in these predictions. Problems arise because it is very difficult to measure accurately less than one second even with a stopwatch.

It is possible to measure the range (or even the height) and so validate the theory. Sources of error are:

- the point of projection may not be exactly at the end of the table;
- the angle of projection may not be exactly 30°;
- the velocity of projection will not be exactly $4.4 \, \text{m s}^{-1}$;
- the elastic band is not a particle.

2.1 Exercise 4

1 Initial velocity $= \begin{bmatrix} 7 \\ 5 \end{bmatrix} \text{m s}^{-1}$

$\Rightarrow$ displacement $= \begin{bmatrix} 7t \\ 5t - 5t^2 \end{bmatrix}$ metres

2 $\mathbf{a} = \begin{bmatrix} 0 \\ -g \end{bmatrix} = \begin{bmatrix} 0 \\ -10 \end{bmatrix}$

$\Rightarrow \mathbf{v} = \begin{bmatrix} 3 \\ 5 - 10t \end{bmatrix}$

$\Rightarrow \mathbf{r} = \begin{bmatrix} 3t \\ 1 + 5t - 5t^2 \end{bmatrix}$

At maximum height, $\quad 5 - 10t = 0$

$\qquad\qquad\qquad\qquad \Rightarrow t = 0.5$

Maximum height $= 2.25$ m

3 $\mathbf{a} = \begin{bmatrix} 0 \\ -g \end{bmatrix} = \begin{bmatrix} 0 \\ -10 \end{bmatrix}$

$\mathbf{v} = \begin{bmatrix} 21\cos 40° \\ 21\sin 40° - 10t \end{bmatrix} = \begin{bmatrix} 16.1 \\ 13.5 - 10t \end{bmatrix}$

$\mathbf{r} = \begin{bmatrix} 16.1t \\ 2 + 13.5t - 5t^2 \end{bmatrix}$

For length of throw,

$2 + 13.5t - 5t^2 = 0 \;\Rightarrow\; t = 2.84$ seconds

The length of the throw is 45.7 m.

4E (a) $\mathbf{v} = \begin{bmatrix} 4 \\ 5 - gt \end{bmatrix} = \begin{bmatrix} 4 \\ 5 - 10t \end{bmatrix}$

$\mathbf{r} = \begin{bmatrix} 4t \\ 5t - 5t^2 \end{bmatrix}$

When $t = 2$, $\mathbf{r} = \begin{bmatrix} 8 \\ -10 \end{bmatrix}$ and the cannon-ball is at A. Furthermore, when

$t = 2$, $\mathbf{v} = \begin{bmatrix} 4 \\ -15 \end{bmatrix}$

(b) Let the rebound velocity be **V**. The momentum is conserved.

So $8 \times \begin{bmatrix} 4 \\ -15 \end{bmatrix} = 8 \times \mathbf{V} + 48 \times \begin{bmatrix} 0 \\ -3 \end{bmatrix}$

$\Rightarrow \mathbf{V} = \begin{bmatrix} 4 \\ -15 \end{bmatrix} - 6 \times \begin{bmatrix} 0 \\ -3 \end{bmatrix} = \begin{bmatrix} 4 \\ 3 \end{bmatrix}$

(c) After a further t seconds, the ball's velocity is $\mathbf{v} = \begin{bmatrix} 4 \\ 3 - 10t \end{bmatrix}$

and $\mathbf{r} = \begin{bmatrix} 8 \\ -10 \end{bmatrix} + \begin{bmatrix} 4t \\ 3t - 5t^2 \end{bmatrix}$

Now $3t - 5t^2 = -2$ when $5t^2 - 3t - 2 = 0$ or $t = 1$ or -0.4

so when $t = 1$, $\mathbf{r} = \begin{bmatrix} 12 \\ -12 \end{bmatrix}$

This takes the cannon-ball clear of the water hazard.

5E (a) $\mathbf{v} = \begin{bmatrix} 3 \\ 4 \\ -10t \end{bmatrix}$

(b) At $t = 0$, $\quad \mathbf{v} = \begin{bmatrix} 3 \\ 4 \\ 0 \end{bmatrix}$

There is no upward velocity, so the missile travels horizontally at first, on a bearing of 127°.

(d) $10\sqrt{5}$ m (e) $t = 10\sqrt{6}$ s

(f) $\mathbf{a} = \begin{bmatrix} 0 \\ 0 \\ -10 \end{bmatrix}$ m s^{-2}

Only gravitational force is acting on the rocket, so it is not powered.

2.1.6 The general case

2.1 G

1 (a) When $t = \dfrac{2u \sin \phi}{g}$,

$\mathbf{r} = \begin{bmatrix} \dfrac{2u \sin \phi \times u \cos \phi}{g} \\ \dfrac{2u \sin \phi \times u \sin \phi}{g} - \dfrac{g(2u \sin \phi)^2}{2g^2} \end{bmatrix}$

$= \begin{bmatrix} \dfrac{2u^2 \sin \phi \cos \phi}{g} \\ 0 \end{bmatrix} = \begin{bmatrix} \dfrac{u^2 \sin 2\phi}{g} \\ 0 \end{bmatrix}$

(b) When $y = 0$, $x = \dfrac{u^2 \sin 2\phi}{g}$. This is called the range, R. Interpreting this, you will find that R increases from 0 to $\dfrac{u^2}{g}$ as ϕ increases from 0° to 45°. Once ϕ has passed 45° then sin 2ϕ starts to decrease again. Because $\sin 2\phi = \sin 2(90° - \phi)$, the same horizontal distance can be gained by firing either at an angle ϕ or its complementary angle.

The range varies as the square of the velocity for any angle of projection. So if you double the velocity of projection, you multiply the range by 4.

2 (a) $\mathbf{v} = \begin{bmatrix} u \cos \phi \\ u \sin \phi - gt \end{bmatrix}$

At the highest point, $t = \dfrac{u \sin \phi}{g}$,

i.e. $\mathbf{v} = \begin{bmatrix} u \cos \phi \\ 0 \end{bmatrix}$

This is half of the total flight time – the projectile's flight is symmetrical.

(b) $\mathbf{r} = \begin{bmatrix} \dfrac{u^2 \sin 2\phi}{2g} \\ \dfrac{u^2 \sin^2 \phi}{2g} \end{bmatrix}$

and the greatest height reached $= \dfrac{u^2 \sin^2 \phi}{2g}$

(c) As the speed of projection increases so does the maximum height gained. As the angle of projection increases so does the maximum height gained. This reaches its highest value when the object is thrown vertically upwards.

2.1 Exercise 5

1 They all land on the floor at the same time. In fact they always have the same height. The range increases as the horizontal speed of projection is increased.

2 $\mathbf{v} = \begin{bmatrix} 15 \\ 20 - 10t \end{bmatrix}$ $\quad \mathbf{r} = \begin{bmatrix} 15t \\ 20t - 5t^2 \end{bmatrix}$

(a) When $t = 2$, $\mathbf{v} = \begin{bmatrix} 15 \\ 0 \end{bmatrix}$ and

$\mathbf{r} = \begin{bmatrix} 30 \\ 20 \end{bmatrix}$ so it rises to a height of 20 metres.

(b) When $t = 4$, $\mathbf{r} = \begin{bmatrix} 60 \\ 0 \end{bmatrix}$ and it bounces 60 m away.

3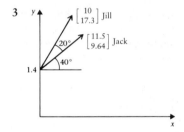

Jill's stone has velocity and displacement

$$\mathbf{v} = \begin{bmatrix} 10 \\ 17.3 - 10t \end{bmatrix}$$

$$\mathbf{r} = \begin{bmatrix} 10t \\ 17.3t - 5t^2 + 1.4 \end{bmatrix}$$

Jack's stone has velocity and displacement

$$\mathbf{v} = \begin{bmatrix} 11.5 \\ 9.64 - 10t \end{bmatrix}$$

$$\mathbf{r} = \begin{bmatrix} 11.5t \\ 9.64t - 5t^2 + 1.4 \end{bmatrix}$$

(a) When Jill's stone is at its highest point,

$$\mathbf{v} = \begin{bmatrix} 10 \\ 0 \end{bmatrix} \Rightarrow t = 1.73$$

Her stone rises to $t(17.3 - 5t) = 15$ metres.

(b) Jill: Her stone lands when
$1.4 + 17.3t - 5t^2 = 0$
$t = 3.54$ or -0.08 so Jill's stone lands after 3.54 seconds.

Jack: His stone lands when
$1.4 + 9.64t - 5t^2 = 0$
$t = 2.06$ or -0.13 so his stone lands after 2.06 seconds.

Jack's stone lands first.

(c) Jill: Horizontal distance
$= 10t = 35.4$ metres
Jack: Horizontal distance
$= 11.5t = 23.7$ metres

Jill's stone lands further away.

4 (a) Set up the model:
Ignore air resistance.
Let the trees be d metres away.

Analyis:
The velocity of the package is
$$\begin{bmatrix} 30 \\ -10t \end{bmatrix} \text{m s}^{-1}$$
so $$\begin{bmatrix} x \\ y \end{bmatrix} = \begin{bmatrix} 30t \\ 210 - 5t^2 \end{bmatrix}$$

After T seconds, $30T = d$ and
$210 - 5T^2 = 30$
$T = 6$ and $d = 180$

(b) Let the package land D metres from the release point after T seconds.
Then $30T = D$ and $210 - 5T^2 = 0$
$T \approx 6.48$ and $D = 194.4$
The package lands 14.4 metres beyond the trees.

5 The initial velocity is $\begin{bmatrix} 16 \\ 24.5 \end{bmatrix} \text{m s}^{-1}$.

6 The maximum range for a projectile occurs when the angle of projection is $45°$.

You should look this up yourself. You could try the *Guinness Book of Records*.

Substituting your value for the distance into the equation $u^2 = g \times \text{distance}$ will allow you to check your estimation. Remember, however, that this is still just an approximation as the ball did not leave the cricketer's hand at ground level, nor at $45°$ to the horizontal.

7 Let initial speed of the ball be V.

So $\mathbf{v} = \begin{bmatrix} V \cos 40° \\ V \sin 40° - 10t \end{bmatrix}$

$\mathbf{r} = \begin{bmatrix} Vt \cos 40° \\ Vt \sin 40° - 5t^2 \end{bmatrix}$

so $\begin{bmatrix} Vt \cos 40° \\ Vt \sin 40° - 5t^2 \end{bmatrix} = \begin{bmatrix} 12 \\ 4 \end{bmatrix}$

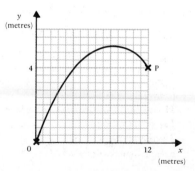

$$Vt \cos 40° = 12$$

$$\Rightarrow \quad t = \frac{15.7}{V}$$

$$Vt \sin 40° - 5t^2 = 4$$

Substituting for t, $\quad 10.1 - \dfrac{1227}{V^2} = 4$

$$\Rightarrow \quad 6.1V^2 = 1227$$

$$\Rightarrow \quad V = 14 \, \text{m s}^{-1}$$

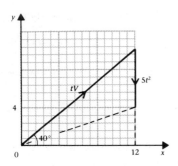

Or using a vector diagram, if the ball is kicked at 40°, then

$$5t^2 = 6.1 \quad \Rightarrow \quad t = 1.10 \text{ seconds}$$

and $V = \dfrac{12}{t \cos 40°} = 14 \text{ m s}^{-1}$

2.2 Forces
2.2.1 Contact forces

2.2 Exercise 1

1 (a) **A** is the normal contact force;
   B is the friction on the sledge;
   C is the weight of the sledge.

   (b) **D** is the lift force of air on the plane;
   E is the drag force of air resistance on the plane;
   F is the weight of the plane;
   G is the forward thrust of the jet (of air) on the plane due to the jet engines.

   (c) **H** is the normal contact force on the toy;
   I is its weight;
   J is the friction;
   K is the push of the child.

(d) **L** is the tension force of the cable on the climber;
   M is the weight of the climber;
   N is the friction force of the ice face on the climber;
   O is the normal contact force of the ice face on the climber.

(e) **P** is the friction force of the bat on the ball;
   Q is the weight of the ball;
   R is the normal contact force of the bat on the ball.

(f) **S** is the upward lift force on the balloon due to the hot air/cold air pressure differences;
   U is the force of the wind on the balloon;
   V is the weight of the balloon.

2 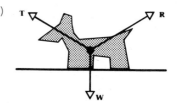 **T** is the tension in the rope;
   F is the friction;
   N is the normal contact force;
   W is the weight.

3 (a)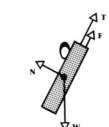

   T is the tension in the rope;
   R is the contact force;
   W is the weight.

   (b)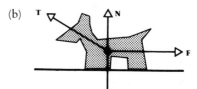

   T is the tension in the rope;
   N is the normal contact force;
   W is the weight;
   F is the friction force.

4 (a)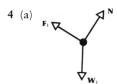

(b)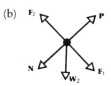

(c)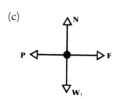

(d)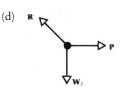

(e)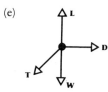

(f) or (g)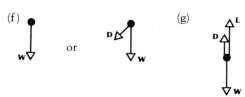

In the diagrams,

N is the normal contact force;
W is the weight;
P is push; **R** is contact force;
L is upthrust due to water;
D is the force due to air resistance or water;
F is the friction force;
F_1 is the friction between girl and sledge;
F_2 is the friction between sledge and ground;
T is tension.

2.2.2 Adding forces

2.2 A

(a) The tension in each rope is just more than half the weight of the object.

(b) The tension increases.

(c) The tension becomes very large.

The strings can never be horizontal because there would be no upward force to balance **W** downwards.

2.2 Exercise 2

1 (a) 6.4 N at 39° to the force of 5 N.

(b) 1.3 N, 88° above the force of 0.8 N.

2 900 N (898 N to 3 s.f.) at an angle of 13° or 14° (13.6° to 3 s.f.) to the force of 420 N.

3 Between 112 000 and 113 000 N in the direction of the ship.

4 215 N at an angle of 22° to the vertical.

5 The angle between the forces is 63°.

6 (a) **P** = 4.5 N at an angle of 117° to the force of 2 N.

(b) **Q** = 11.7 N at an angle of 149° to the force of 10 N.

(c) **F** = 5.4 N at an angle of 112° to the force of 2 N.

(d) **T** = 4 N at an angle of 120° to the force of 4 N.

7 The force required is 98 N.

To estimate the least angle ϕ, first estimate the largest force the two people can apply, say $T = 200$ N, then draw the triangle with sides 200, 200, 150, and measure the acute angle, which is 2ϕ.

For $T = 200$, the angle is 22°. In general,

$$\phi = \sin^{-1}\frac{75}{T}.$$

2.2.3 Resolving forces

2.2 Exercise 3

1 (a) $\begin{bmatrix} 43.3 \\ 25.0 \end{bmatrix}$

(b) The components are:
49.2 N up the slope;
8.68 N perpendicular to the slope.

(c) The components are:
32.1 N down the slope;
38.3 N perpendicular to the slope.

2 (a)

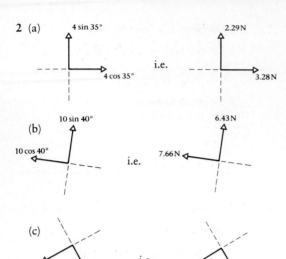

4 sin 35°

4 cos 35°

i.e.

2.29 N

3.28 N

(b)

10 sin 40°

10 cos 40°

i.e.

6.43 N

7.66 N

(c)

7 cos 60°

7 sin 60°

i.e.

3.5 N

6.06 N

(d)

100 cos 65°

100 sin 65°

i.e.

42.3 N

90.6 N

3 (a) Force diagram

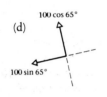

N   F

θ   θ

10g

Equivalent set of forces

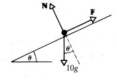

N   F

10g sin θ   10g cos θ

For equilibrium, the resultant force is zero.

i.e. $\begin{bmatrix} N - 10g\cos\theta \\ F - 10g\sin\theta \end{bmatrix} = \begin{bmatrix} 0 \\ 0 \end{bmatrix}$

Thus $F = 10g\sin\theta = 10g\sin 20° = 33.5\,\text{N}$

(b) $F = 10g\sin\theta$ newtons and
$N = 10g\cos\theta$ newtons

$$\Rightarrow \quad \frac{F}{N} = \tan\theta$$

4 If you consider directions parallel to and perpendicular to the 11 newton force, then

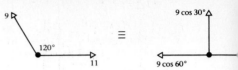

9

120°

11

9 cos 30°

9 cos 60°

$\equiv$

The sum of the forces

$$= \begin{bmatrix} 11 - 9\cos 60° \\ 9\cos 30° \end{bmatrix} = \begin{bmatrix} 6.5 \\ 7.79 \end{bmatrix}$$

The resultant force is 10.1 newtons at an angle of 39.8° to the 11 newton force.

5 (a) $\mathbf{R} = \begin{bmatrix} 2.60 \\ 1.50 \end{bmatrix} + \begin{bmatrix} -1.00 \\ 1.73 \end{bmatrix} + \begin{bmatrix} -1.97 \\ -0.347 \end{bmatrix}$

$$= \begin{bmatrix} -0.37 \\ 2.88 \end{bmatrix}$$

This has magnitude 2.91 N, making an angle of 82.7° clockwise from the leftward horizontal.

(b) Take the x-axis parallel to the top right 2 N force.

$$\mathbf{R} = \begin{bmatrix} 2 \\ 0 \end{bmatrix} + \begin{bmatrix} -1 \\ 1.73 \end{bmatrix} + \begin{bmatrix} -2 \\ 0 \end{bmatrix} + \begin{bmatrix} 1.29 \\ -1.53 \end{bmatrix}$$

$$= \begin{bmatrix} 0.29 \\ 0.20 \end{bmatrix}$$

This has magnitude 0.35 N and cuts the 120° angle into 35° and 85°, reading anticlockwise.

6 $\mathbf{R} = \begin{bmatrix} 34.6 \\ 20 \end{bmatrix} + \begin{bmatrix} -35 \\ 0 \end{bmatrix} + \begin{bmatrix} 0 \\ -20 \end{bmatrix} = \begin{bmatrix} -0.4 \\ 0 \end{bmatrix}$

It will move in the direction of the 35 N force.

7 Let the tensions be T_1 and T_2, in newtons.

(a) $\begin{bmatrix} T_2\sin 60° \\ T_2\cos 60° \end{bmatrix} + \begin{bmatrix} -T_1\sin 50° \\ T_1\cos 50° \end{bmatrix} + \begin{bmatrix} 0 \\ -600 \end{bmatrix}$

$$= \begin{bmatrix} 0 \\ 0 \end{bmatrix}$$

$\Rightarrow \quad T_2 \sin 60° = T_1 \sin 50°$

$\Rightarrow \quad T_2 \cos 60° + T_1 \cos 50° = 600$

$\Rightarrow \quad \dfrac{T_1 \sin 50°}{\sin 60°} \times \cos 60° + T_1 \cos 50° = 600$

$\Rightarrow \quad T_1 = 553\,\text{N}$

and $T_2 = \dfrac{T_1 \sin 50°}{\sin 60°} = 489\,\text{N}$

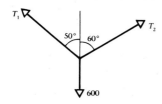

(b) Taking axes parallel and perpendicular to T_2,

$$\begin{bmatrix} T_2 \\ 0 \end{bmatrix} + \begin{bmatrix} -T_1 \sin 20° \\ T_1 \cos 20° \end{bmatrix} + \begin{bmatrix} -600 \sin 30° \\ -600 \cos 30° \end{bmatrix}$$

$$= \begin{bmatrix} 0 \\ 0 \end{bmatrix}$$

$\Rightarrow \quad T_2 - T_1 \sin 20° - 600 \sin 30° = 0$

and $\quad T_1 \cos 20° - 600 \cos 30° = 0$

$\Rightarrow \quad T_1 = \dfrac{600 \cos 30°}{\cos 20°} = 553\,\text{N}$

$\quad T_2 = T_1 \sin 20° + 600 \sin 30° = 489\,\text{N}$

8 $m = \dfrac{3\sqrt{2}}{100}\,\text{kg} = 42\,\text{grams}$

9 Let the tensions in the strings be T_1 and T_2 as shown.

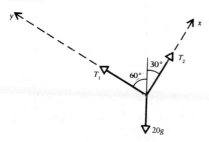

By Newton's second law,

$$\begin{bmatrix} T_2 \\ 0 \end{bmatrix} + \begin{bmatrix} 0 \\ T_1 \end{bmatrix} = \begin{bmatrix} 200 \cos 30° \\ 200 \sin 30° \end{bmatrix}$$

$T_2 = 100\sqrt{3}\,\text{newtons}$

$T_1 = 100\,\text{newtons}$

2.2.4 Force and acceleration

2.2 Exercise 4

1 $N = 11.5\,\text{N}$

The acceleration of the block

$$a = \dfrac{15 \sin 40° - 2}{1.5}$$

$$a = 5.1\,\text{m s}^{-2}$$

2 The acceleration of the trolley is $0.58\,\text{m s}^{-2}$.

3 The resultant force $\mathbf{R} = 650 - 540 = 110\,\text{N}$ downwards, giving an acceleration of $1.7\,\text{m s}^{-2}$.

If the rope breaks, she will start to accelerate at $g = 10\,\text{m s}^{-2}$.

4 The air resistance is 4 newtons.

5 (a) If the woman is travelling with constant speed, she is in equilibrium so the contact force between her and the lift is 600 newtons.

(b) If she moves upward with acceleration $1.5\,\text{m s}^{-2}$ then, if the normal contact force is R,

$$R - 600 = 60 \times 1.5$$

$$R = 690\,\text{newtons}$$

(c) If she moves downward with acceleration $1.5\,\text{m s}^{-2}$ then, if the normal contact force is R,

$$600 - R = 60 \times 1.5$$

$$R = 510\,\text{newtons}$$

2.2.5 Models of static friction

2.2 B

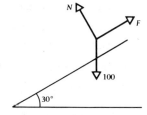

When no one pushes the crate there is no friction force. As P increases, F increases in order to maintain equilibrium. At any time, $P = F$.

When the fifth person helps, the crate accelerates from rest and so $P > F$. So there seems to be a maximum possible value for F.

The magnitude of the friction force therefore equals the magnitude of P, until F reaches its maximum value.

The maximum value of F is likely to depend upon such things as:

- the types of material in contact;
- the weight of the crate;
- the area of contact.

2.2 Exercise 5

All answers are to 2 s.f.

1 (a) Let F be the friction force and N the normal contact force. The crate is in equilibrium, so by Newton's second law,

$$F = 100 \sin 30° = 50 \text{ newtons}$$

and

$$N = 100 \cos 30° = 87 \text{ newtons}$$

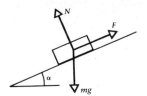

(b) But the crate is about to slip, so $F = \mu N$.
$$\Rightarrow 50 = 86.6\mu$$
$$\Rightarrow \mu = 0.58$$

2 The rubber is on the point of slipping so $F = 0.7N$. But by Newton's second law along and perpendicular to the slope,

$$F = mg \sin \alpha \quad \text{and} \quad N = mg \cos \alpha$$

so $\tan \alpha = 0.7$
$$\alpha = 35°$$

The table can be tilted to $35°$.

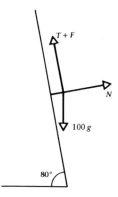

3 (a) The greatest angle of slope is $50°$.

  (b) The friction force is 500 newtons.

4 (a) $T = 840 \text{ N}$

  (b) $T = 880 \text{ N}$

5 The climber is in equilibrium, so $F \leq \mu N$.

$$N = 1000 \cos 80° = 173.6 \text{ newtons}$$

and $T + F = 1000 \sin 80° = 984.8 \text{ newtons}$

Now $F \leq 0.9N = 156.2$

but F can act either up or down the slope depending on which way the body is trying to move, so

$$1141 \geq T \geq 828.6$$

The tension in the rope lies approximately between 830 newtons and 1140 newtons.

2.2.6 Models of sliding friction

.2 C

1 A suitable value of u of the first 20 metres is the average speed $\dfrac{20}{11.9} = 1.68\,\mathrm{m\,s^{-1}}$.

2 (a) For the first few seconds, the standard model $F = 0$ provides a reasonable fit to the experimental data and is therefore satisfactory.

   (b) For $t > 10$ seconds, the model is not satisfactory and must be modified.

3 (a) Using a graphic calculator a curve can be fitted to the data. A reasonable fit is obtained by using the curve $x = 2.05t - 0.03t^2$. Hence a value of 0.06 for $\dfrac{F}{m}$ would appear to give a good model.

   (b) Constant resistive force seems to be a good model. It is interesting to note that the estimated initial speed of the stone is greater in this model than in the simple model.

.2 Exercise 6

1 Let μ be the coefficient of sliding friction between the block and table.

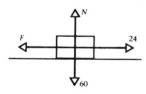

The block is in equilibrium so by Newton's second law

$$F = 24 \quad \text{and} \quad N = 60$$

But the block is sliding so $F = \mu N$

$$\Rightarrow \quad 24 = 60\mu$$

$$\mu = 0.4$$

2 The puck is sliding freely so $F = 0.02\mathrm{N}$

$$\Rightarrow \quad F = 0.02$$

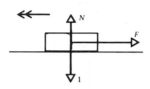

By Newton's second law, $\quad -F = ma$

$$\Rightarrow \quad -0.02 = 0.1a$$

$$a = -0.2$$

The initial speed is $10\,\mathrm{m\,s^{-1}}$
so $v = 10 - 0.2t \qquad t = 20$

$$v = 6\,\mathrm{m\,s^{-1}} \text{ after 20 seconds}$$

3 $F = 0.3\mathrm{N} = 3$ newtons, but by Newton's second law,

$$0 - F = ma \qquad a = -3$$

Initial speed is $5\,\mathrm{m\,s^{-1}}$, so $v = 5 - 3t$
so when $v = 0, \quad t = \frac{5}{3}$

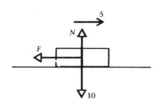

Now $s = ut + \frac{1}{2}at^2$

$$= 5 \times \tfrac{5}{3} + \tfrac{1}{2} \times -3 \times \tfrac{25}{9}$$

$$= \tfrac{25}{6} \text{ metres}$$

4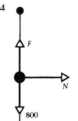

The normal contact force N must be horizontal.

Let all the mass of the gymnast be taken by his hands.

The gymnast is in equilibrium,

$$\Rightarrow \quad F = 800$$

but $F = \mu N \quad \Rightarrow \quad N = \dfrac{800}{0.3}$

so $N = \dfrac{8000}{3}$ newtons

5E If the particle is sliding down the slope, F acts up the slope.

$P + F = mg \sin \phi$ and $N = mg \cos \phi$ by Newton's second law,

but $F = \mu N$

so $P + \mu mg \cos \phi = mg \sin \phi$

$P = mg(\sin \phi - \mu \cos \phi)$

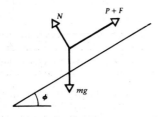

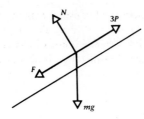

If the particle is sliding up the slope at constant speed, F acts down the plane,

so $3P - F = mg \sin \phi$ and $N = mg \cos \phi$

$\Rightarrow \quad 3P = mg(\sin \phi + \mu \cos \phi)$

but $P = mg(\sin \phi - \mu \cos \phi)$

$\Rightarrow \quad 3(\sin \phi - \mu \cos \phi) = \sin \phi + \mu \cos \phi$

$\Rightarrow \quad 2 \sin \phi = 4\mu \cos \phi$

$\tan \phi = 2\mu$

2.3 Acceleration and circular motion

2.3.1 The motion of the Moon

2.3 Exercise 1

1 (a) Gravitational force

$$= \frac{GMm}{r^2}$$

$$= \frac{6.67 \times 10^{-11} \times 7.34 \times 10^{22} \times 5.98 \times 10}{(3.8 \times 10^8)^2}$$

$$= 2.02 \times 10^{20} \text{ N} \quad \text{(to 3 s.f.)}$$

(b) The acceleration of the Moon is

$$\frac{2.02 \times 10^{20}}{7.34 \times 10^{22}} \text{ m s}^{-2}$$

$$= 2.8 \times 10^{-3} \text{ m s}^{-2} \quad \text{(to 2 s.f.)}$$

It acts towards the centre of the Earth.

2 (a) Using $R = \dfrac{GMm}{r^2}$,

$R = 3.55 \times 10^{22}$ newtons

The acceleration is $5.93 \times 10^{-3} \text{ m s}^{-2}$ towards the Sun.

(b) If $r = 1.52 \times 10^{11}$, $\quad \dfrac{R_1}{R} = \dfrac{1.5^2}{1.52^2}$

$\Rightarrow \quad R_1 = 0.974R$

$$= 3.46 \times 10^{22} \text{ newtons}$$

If $r = 1.47 \times 10^{11}$,
$R_2 = 3.70 \times 10^{22}$ newtons
The range is from 3.46×10^{22} to 3.70×10^{22} newtons.

3 Assume Skylab is a particle of mass 82 000 kg a distance $(434 + 6378)$ km from the Earth's centre.

Using Newton's law of gravitation,

$$R = \frac{GMm}{r^2}$$

$$= \frac{6.67 \times 10^{-11} \times 8.2 \times 10^4 \times 5.98 \times 10^{24}}{6.812^2 \times 10^{12}}$$

The force of attraction is 7.05×10^5 newtons

2.3.2 Angular speed and velocity

2.3 A

1 The angular speed is 2 radians per second.

The angular speed in r.p.m. is $\dfrac{2 \times 60}{2\pi} = 19.1$ r.p.m. to 3 s.f.

2 The penny travels $2\pi r$ metres in $\dfrac{2\pi}{2}$ seconds, giving a speed of $2r = 0.12\,\mathrm{m\,s^{-1}}$.

3 The velocity of the penny is $0.12\,\mathrm{m\,s^{-1}}$ tangentially.

4 (a) If the speed is to be half that of the first penny then $v = 0.06$. ω is constant no matter where the penny is, so $0.06 = 2r$, hence $r = 0.03$ metres. The penny must be 3 cm from the centre.

   (b) The penny must be anywhere on the disc 12 cm from the centre.

   (c) The directions of motion must be the same so the penny must lie 12 cm from the centre on the line joining the centre of the turntable to the centre of the penny.

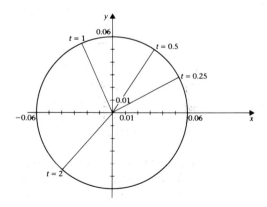

5 The turntable has turned through $\tfrac{1}{2}\pi$ radians

so the time taken is $\dfrac{\tfrac{1}{2}\pi}{2} = 0.785$ seconds to 3 s.f.

6

t	0	0.25	0.5	1	2
r	$\begin{bmatrix} 0.06 \\ 0.00 \end{bmatrix}$	$\begin{bmatrix} 0.053 \\ 0.029 \end{bmatrix}$	$\begin{bmatrix} 0.032 \\ 0.05 \end{bmatrix}$	$\begin{bmatrix} -0.025 \\ 0.055 \end{bmatrix}$	$\begin{bmatrix} -0.039 \\ -0.045 \end{bmatrix}$

7 The coordinates after t seconds are
$\mathbf{r} = (0.06\cos 2t, 0.06\sin 2t)$.

2.3 B

1

t	0.5	1	1.5	2	2.5	3
r	$\begin{bmatrix} 0.054 \\ 0.084 \end{bmatrix}$	$\begin{bmatrix} -0.042 \\ 0.091 \end{bmatrix}$	$\begin{bmatrix} -0.099 \\ 0.014 \end{bmatrix}$	$\begin{bmatrix} -0.065 \\ -0.076 \end{bmatrix}$	$\begin{bmatrix} 0.028 \\ -0.096 \end{bmatrix}$	$\begin{bmatrix} 0.096 \\ -0.028 \end{bmatrix}$
v	$\begin{bmatrix} -0.17 \\ 0.11 \end{bmatrix}$	$\begin{bmatrix} -0.18 \\ -0.08 \end{bmatrix}$	$\begin{bmatrix} -0.03 \\ -0.20 \end{bmatrix}$	$\begin{bmatrix} 0.15 \\ -0.13 \end{bmatrix}$	$\begin{bmatrix} 0.19 \\ 0.06 \end{bmatrix}$	$\begin{bmatrix} 0.06 \\ 0.19 \end{bmatrix}$

2 The velocity is of constant magnitude. The direction is always perpendicular to the radius. The acceleration is of constant magnitude. The direction is always towards the centre.

2.3 Exercise 2

1 $50\,\text{r.p.m.} = \dfrac{50 \times 2\pi}{60}\,\mathrm{rad\,s^{-1}}$

Speed of tip is $\dfrac{4 \times 50 \times 2\pi}{60}\,\mathrm{m\,s^{-1}} = 21\,\mathrm{m\,s^{-1}}$ (to 2 s.f.)

2 Angular speed,

$\omega = \dfrac{v}{r} = \dfrac{1}{0.1}\,\mathrm{rad\,s^{-1}} = 10\,\mathrm{rad\,s^{-1}}$

3 $500\,\text{r.p.m.} = \dfrac{500 \times 2\pi}{60}\,\mathrm{rad\,s^{-1}} \approx 52\,\mathrm{rad\,s^{-1}}$

$1000\,\text{r.p.m.} \approx 105\,\mathrm{rad\,s^{-1}}$

The speed of a point on the drum varies between $\dfrac{500 \times 2\pi \times 0.6}{60}\,\mathrm{m\,s^{-1}}$ and double this, i.e. between 31.4 and $62.8\,\mathrm{m\,s^{-1}}$.

4 (a) $v = r\omega = \dfrac{6.37 \times 10^{6} \times 2\pi}{24 \times 60 \times 60}\,\mathrm{m\,s^{-1}}$

   $\approx 464\,\mathrm{m\,s^{-1}}$

   (b) The speed at the north pole is zero.

5 (a) Angular speed $= 3 \, \text{rad s}^{-1}$
$= 3 \div 2\pi$ revolutions per second

Time for one revolution $= \dfrac{2\pi}{3}$ seconds

(b) Angular speed $= \omega \, \text{rad s}^{-1}$
$= \dfrac{\omega}{2\pi}$ revolutions per second

Time for 1 revolution $= T = \dfrac{2\pi}{\omega}$

6E The cotton on the outside of the reel unwinds at $3 \, \text{m s}^{-1}$.

The angular speed is $\dfrac{3}{0.02} = 150 \, \text{rad s}^{-1}$.

When the reel is nearly empty the angular speed is $\dfrac{3}{0.01} \, \text{rad s}^{-1} = 300 \, \text{rad s}^{-1}$.

After 25 minutes half the cotton will have gone, but the diameter of the reel will be greater than 1.5 cm, so the angular speed is less than $200 \, \text{rad s}^{-1}$.

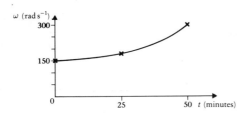

2.3.3 Circular motion

2.3 C

1 $\mathbf{v} = \begin{bmatrix} -r\omega \sin \omega t \\ r\omega \cos \omega t \end{bmatrix}$

$v = \sqrt{(r^2\omega^2 \sin^2 \omega t + r^2\omega^2 \cos^2 \omega t)} = r\omega$

The direction of PO is $\begin{bmatrix} -\cos \omega t \\ -\sin \omega t \end{bmatrix}$

so the direction of the velocity is perpendicular to the radius.

2 $\mathbf{v} = \begin{bmatrix} -r\omega \sin \omega t \\ r\omega \cos \omega t \end{bmatrix}$

$\Rightarrow \mathbf{a} = \begin{bmatrix} -r\omega^2 \cos \omega t \\ -r\omega^2 \sin \omega t \end{bmatrix} = -\omega^2 \mathbf{r}$

so $a = r\omega^2 = r\left(\dfrac{v}{r}\right)^2 = \dfrac{v^2}{r}$

The direction is towards the centre of the circle.

2.3 Exercise 3

1 (a) One revolution in 27.32 days is
$$\dfrac{2\pi}{27.32 \times 24 \times 3600} \, \text{rad s}^{-1}$$
$$\approx 2.7 \times 10^{-6} \, \text{rad s}^{-1}$$

(b) Acceleration $= \dfrac{3.8 \times 10^8 \times (2\pi)^2}{(27.32 \times 24 \times 3600)^2} \, \text{m s}^{-}$
$$\approx 2.7 \times 10^{-3} \, \text{m s}^{-2}$$

(c) Allowing for inaccuracy of data, the answers are the same.

2 $120 \, \text{km h}^{-1} = \dfrac{120 \times 1000}{3600} \, \text{m s}^{-1}$

The acceleration $\dfrac{v^2}{r} = 30 \, \text{m s}^{-2}$,

so the radius is $\left(\dfrac{120}{3.6}\right)^2 \div 30 \, \text{m} \approx 37$ metres

3 $10 \, \text{r.p.m.} = 1.05 \, \text{rad s}^{-1}$

(a) Her speed is $1 \times 1.05 \, \text{m s}^{-1} \approx 1.1 \, \text{m s}^{-1}$

Her acceleration is $1 \times \left(\dfrac{\pi}{3}\right)^2 \approx 1.1 \, \text{m s}^{-2}$

(b) Her speed is $2.1 \, \text{m s}^{-1}$ and her acceleration is $2.2 \, \text{m s}^{-2}$ (to 2 s.f.).

At 1 metre from the centre, the force towards the centre is $30 \times 1.1 \, \text{N}$ or $33 \, \text{N}$.

At 2 metres from the centre the force is doubled to 66 N.

4

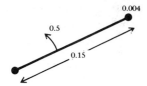

The acceleration is $0.5^2 \times 0.15 = 0.0375 \text{ m s}^{-2}$ towards the centre of the circle.

$F = 0.004 \times 0.0375 = 0.000\,15 \text{ N}$

This force is towards the centre of the turntable and is due to friction.

$$\frac{F}{N} \leq \mu \Rightarrow \frac{0.000\,15}{0.04} \leq \mu$$

$$\Rightarrow \mu \geq 0.003\,75$$

The coefficient of friction is greater than or equal to 0.003 75.

5 Let the block have mass m kilograms and be modelled as a particle 0.2 metres from the axis of rotation. Let the angular speed be $\omega \text{ rad s}^{-1}$.

Acceleration $= \omega^2 \times 0.2$ towards the centre, force $= 0.2m\omega^2$

In limiting friction, $F = \mu N = 0.3mg$

$0.2m\omega^2 = 0.3mg$

$$\Rightarrow \quad \omega = 3.87 \text{ rad s}^{-1} \text{ (to 3 s.f.)}$$

The turntable must spin with an angular speed of over 3.87 rad s^{-1} for the block to slide off.

6E 1 revolution in 6 seconds $= \dfrac{2\pi}{6} \text{ rad s}^{-1}$

$$= 1.05 \text{ rad s}^{-1}$$

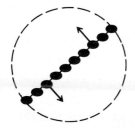

Set up a model

Assume that each skater is 0.8 metre from elbow to elbow. You can model the skater as a particle halfway along this 80 cm length.

Assume that the mass of each skater is 65 kg.

Analyse the problem

(a) The furthest skater makes a circle of radius 3.6 metres and the central skaters make circles of radius 0.4 metres.

The speeds of the outside skaters are therefore 3.8 m s^{-1} and those of the central skaters are 0.42 m s^{-1}.

Interpret/validate

(b) The acceleration of the outside pair is 3.96 m s^{-2} radially inwards.

(c) Now $F = ma$ so the force is 257 newtons to 3 s.f. (Remember this is the resultant force. What do you think the force on each arm of the central skaters will be?)

2.3.4 Acceleration

2.3 Exercise 4

1 (a)

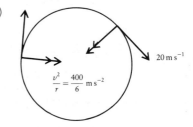

(b) The velocity is not constant since its direction is changing as the skater moves around the circle.

(c) The acceleration has constant magnitude but its direction changes as the skater moves around the circle. It is always perpendicular to the velocity.

2 $100 \text{ r.p.m.} = \dfrac{100 \times 2\pi}{60} \text{ rad s}^{-1} = \dfrac{10\pi}{3} \text{ rad s}^{-1}$

The radius is $\dfrac{27}{2}$ cm or $\dfrac{0.27}{2}$ m.

The acceleration of the object is

$$r\omega^2 = \dfrac{0.27}{2} \times \left(\dfrac{10\pi}{3}\right)^2 = 15 \text{ m s}^{-2}$$

directed towards the centre of the drum.
Using Newton's second law, $F = ma$

$$F = 0.2 \times 15 = 3$$

The resultant force is 3 newtons towards the centre of the circle.

3 (a)

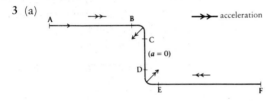

(b) Rate of change of speed:

AB : rate of change of speed = |acceleration|
BC : rate of change of speed = 0
CD : rate of change of speed = 0 = |acceleration|
DE : rate of change of speed = 0
EF : rate of change of speed = −|acceleration|

4

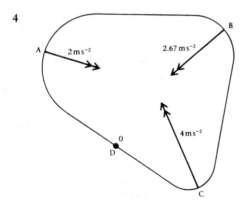

5E (a) $\mathbf{v} = \begin{bmatrix} 2t \times -10 \sin t^2 \\ 2t \times 10 \cos t^2 \end{bmatrix}$

$$= 20 \begin{bmatrix} -t \sin t^2 \\ t \cos t^2 \end{bmatrix} = 20t \begin{bmatrix} -\sin t^2 \\ \cos t^2 \end{bmatrix}$$

The velocity has magnitude $20t$, and is a *variable*. In fact, the speed is increasing and the motion is *not* uniform.

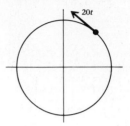

The direction of the velocity $\begin{bmatrix} -\sin t^2 \\ \cos t^2 \end{bmatrix}$ is still tangenial to the circle.

$$\mathbf{a} = 20 \begin{bmatrix} -\sin t^2 - 2t^2 \cos t^2 \\ \cos t^2 - 2t^2 \sin t^2 \end{bmatrix}$$

$$= 20 \begin{bmatrix} -\sin t^2 \\ \cos t^2 \end{bmatrix} - 40t^2 \begin{bmatrix} \cos t^2 \\ \sin t^2 \end{bmatrix}$$

(b) The acceleration has two parts,

$$20 \begin{bmatrix} -\sin t^2 \\ \cos t^2 \end{bmatrix} \quad \text{and} \quad -40t^2 \begin{bmatrix} \cos t^2 \\ \sin t^2 \end{bmatrix}$$

The first part has magnitude 20 m s^{-2} and is tangential. The second part has magnitude $40t^2 \text{ m s}^{-2}$ and is towards the centre of the circle.

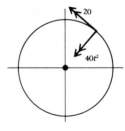

(c) The acceleration is *in general* not towards the centre of the circle. There is often, as in this case, a tangential component. If the angular speed is constant (the speed is constant), then the tangential component is zero and the acceleration *is* directed towards the centre. This special case is uniform circular motion.

2.4 Rigid bodies
2.4.1 Rotating bodies – moments

2.4 Exercise 1

1 Total moment about A $= 50 \times 4 + 100 \times 6$
   $= 800\,\mathrm{N\,m}$ anticlockwise

2 The moment of **P** about O is $5 \times 6 = 30\,\mathrm{N\,m}$
   anticlockwise.
   The moment of **Q** about O is
   $8 \times \sin 30° \times 7 = 28\,\mathrm{N\,m}$ clockwise.
   The moment of **R** about O is zero.

3 The moment of the force **W** about O is
   $Wa \sin \phi\,\mathrm{N\,m}$ clockwise.
   The moment of the force **P** about O is
   $2Pa \cos \phi\,\mathrm{N\,m}$ anticlockwise.

4 (a) The moment of the 10 newton force about O
        $= 10 \times 0.24 \times \sin 50° = 1.84\,\mathrm{N\,m}$
        clockwise.
        The moment of the 6 newton force about O
        $= 1.84\,\mathrm{N\,m}$ anticlockwise.
        The moment of the 16 newton force about O
        $= 16 \times 0 = 0$

   (b) The moment of the 10 newton force about A
        $= 10 \times 0 = 0$
        The moment of the 6 newton force about A
        $= 2.94\,\mathrm{N\,m}$ anticlockwise.
        The moment of the 16 newton force about A
        $= 2.94\,\mathrm{N\,m}$ clockwise.

5 The moment of the force **T** about $O = Tl \sin \phi$
   but $\sin \phi$ is a maximum when $\phi = 90°$,
   so the turning effect will be greatest when
   $\sin \phi = 1$. She should pull vertically upwards.

6 The wheel of the wheelbarrow acts as a pivot.
   If the wheelbarrow handles are three times as
   far from the wheel as the centre of the barrow
   part is, then Carole's lifting force is
   approximately 300 N.

7E

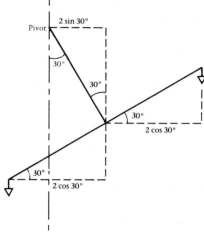

The line of action of Winston's weight will
be $2 \cos 30° + 2 \sin 30°$ metres from the pivot,
so Winston's weight will produce a
clockwise moment of

$$200(2 \cos 30° + 2 \sin 30°) = 546\,\mathrm{N\,m}$$

Josie's weight will be $2 \cos 30° - 2 \sin 30°$
metres from the pivot and will produce an
anticlockwise moment of

$$600(2 \cos 30° - 2 \sin 30°) = 439\,\mathrm{N\,m}$$

Winston's weight has the greater turning
effect.

8E (a) Assume that the plank is weightless, that
        they sit right at the ends of the plank,
        and that Josie is x metres from the pivot.
        The moment of Josie about the pivot is
        $600x$ anticlockwise. The moment of
        Winston is $200(3 - x)$ clockwise. These
        must balance, so

        $$600x = 600 - 200x \implies x = 0.75$$

        Josie must be 0.75 metres from the pivot.

   (b) The plank would provide an extra
        clockwise moment and the pivot would
        therefore be slightly farther away from
        Josie than the 0.75 metres calculated in
        part (a).

2.4.2 Equilibrium

2.4 A

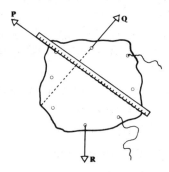

3 newtons

1 newton   2 newtons

1 (a) The force diagram is shown above. You would expect the spring balance to show 3 newtons plus a small amount for the rod.

(b) The spring balance acts as a pivot. To balance the 200-gram mass, the 100-gram mass would have to be twice as far away from the pivot as the 200-gram mass. (The moment of the rod itself would be zero as it is suspended from its 'point of balance'.)

(c) The resultant force is zero and the resultant moment is zero.

Experiment
The card should be sufficiently stiff to enable the strings to be pulled without deforming the card. The string should be passed through a hole and knotted on the underneath so that it can swivel freely. It should not be tied in a loop around the card.

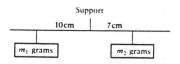

Several students should pull the strings while one student draws the line of action of each force on the card by holding a ruler along the edge of each string as a guide. Each set of forces can be marked in a different colour.

2 (a) Yes; it is possible for the body to be in equilibrium under the action of three parallel forces. The force in the middle must act in a direction opposed to the two outside forces.

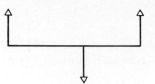

(b) Yes; it is possible for the lines of action of three forces acting on the body to pass through a point.

(c) No; the three forces must always line in a plane.

(d) No; either (a) or (b) must be true.

3 If there are four or more forces acting on the body which is in equilibrium then the forces may be parallel, they may pass through a point but they may do neither. They do not have to lie in a plane.

2.4 Exercise 2

1 The weight of the ruler acts through its midpoint, the point of support. For equilibrium, the total moment about the support is zero.

The force due to the m_1 gram mass is $0.001m_1g$ downwards. That due to the m_2 mass is $0.001m_2g$.

Taking moments about the support,

Support

10cm   7cm

m_1 grams m_2 grams

For equilibrium,

$$0.001m_1g \times 0.1 - 0.001m_2g \times 0.07 = 0$$

so $m_1 = 0.7m_2$; when $m_1 = 49$, $m_2 = 70$
The second mass is 70 grams.

2 Taking moments about A, the body is in equilibrium, so the sum of the moments is zero.

$$T \times 2a = Wa \cos\theta$$

so $\quad T = 0.5W \cos\theta$

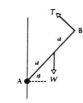

3 If the string makes an angle of 60° then

$$T \times 2a \sin 60° = Wa \cos\theta$$

so $T = 0.577W \cos\theta$, which is greater than before.

4 (a) The moments of the component about the origin are 3×2 clockwise and 4×5 anticlockwise.

The sum is $-6 + 20 = 14\,\text{N m}$ anticlockwise.

(b) The resultant force is 5 newtons in the direction shown.

Its moment about the origin $= 5 \times ON$

But $ON = 3.5 \sin\phi$ where $\sin\phi = 0.8$

$$ON = 2.8$$

The moment of the resultant force about the origin is $5 \times 2.8 = 14\,\text{N m}$ anticlockwise.

5 Assuming the weight is equally distributed over the box and its interior (which is not very likely), the diagram represents the situation.

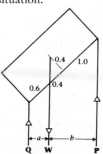

From the diagram,

$$a = 0.6 \cos 45°$$

$$b = 1.4 \cos 45°$$

Taking moments about the bottom corner,

$$a \times 750 = (a + b)P$$

$$\Rightarrow P = 225 \text{ newtons}$$

Resolving vertically,

$$P + Q = 750 \quad \Rightarrow \quad Q = 525 \text{ newtons}$$

The stronger man needs to be at the bottom. (However, the top position is more difficult and uncomfortable in practice.)

Each hand should provide half the required lift so the supporting force provided by each hand is 262.5 newtons from the man at the bottom and 112.5 newtons from the man at the top.

6 (a)

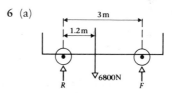

Assume the load on each of the front wheels is the same.

Assume that the load on each of the rear wheels is the same.

Assume that the contact force between the wheels and the road is normal to the road surface.

Taking moments about the rear axle,

$$3 \times F = 1.2 \times 6800$$

$$\Rightarrow \quad F = 2720 \text{ newtons}$$

$$R + F = 6800 \text{ newtons}$$

so $\quad R = 4080 \text{ newtons}$

The total reaction at each front wheel is 1360 newtons.

The total reaction at each rear wheel is 2040 newtons.

(b) Each rear wheel carries 2220 N and each front wheel carries 1480 N.

(c) With the luggage in the boot the forces acting are as shown.

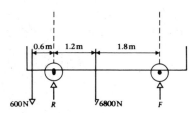

Considering moments about the front axle,

$$R \times 3 = 600 \times 3.6 + 6800 \times 1.8$$

$$\Rightarrow \quad R = 4800 \text{ newtons}$$

Considering moments about the rear axle,

$$F \times 3 + 600 \times 0.6 = 6800 \times 1.2$$

$$\Rightarrow \quad F = 2600 \text{ newtons}$$

Each rear wheel will carry 2400 newtons. Each front wheel will carry 1300 newtons.

7

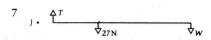

With the notation in the figure, taking moments about J,

$$T \times 0.02 = 27 \times 0.13 + W \times 0.3$$

(a) When $W = 0$, $\qquad T = 175.5$
The tension is about 180 newtons.

(b) When $W = 45$, $\qquad T = 850.5$
The tension is about 850 newtons.

This is, of course, a very greatly simplified model of the real situation.

8E

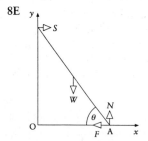

Taking axes with the origin at O, since the ladder is in equilibrium,

$$\begin{bmatrix} S \\ 0 \end{bmatrix} + \begin{bmatrix} -F \\ 0 \end{bmatrix} + \begin{bmatrix} 0 \\ N \end{bmatrix} + \begin{bmatrix} 0 \\ -W \end{bmatrix} = 0$$

$$\Rightarrow S = F, \qquad W = N$$

Taking moments about A, the foot of the ladder,

$$S \times 4 \sin\theta - W \times 2 \cos\theta = 0$$

$$\Rightarrow \quad S \tan\theta = \tfrac{1}{2} W$$

$$\Rightarrow \quad F \tan\theta = \tfrac{1}{2} W$$

For equilibrium, $\quad F \le \mu N$

i.e. $\quad \tfrac{1}{2} W \tan\theta \le \tfrac{1}{2} W$

$$\Rightarrow \qquad \tan\theta \ge 1$$

$$\Rightarrow \qquad \theta \ge 45°$$

The ladder must be inclined at an angle of at least 45° to the horizontal.

9E $\mu \ge 1.73$

2.4.3 Centre of gravity

2.4 **B**

The centre of gravity is a fixed point for a given body. Its position does not depend on where you choose to take the pivot in order to calculate it.

2.4 **Exercise 3**

1 (a) Taking moments about the centre of the 3 N weight, C, as the pivot,

$$2 \times 0.4 + 2 \times 0.8 = 7X$$

where X is the distance of the centre of gravity from C.

$$X = 0.343 \text{ metres}$$

The centre of gravity is 34.3 cm from the 3 newton weight (to 3 s.f.).

(b) Taking moments about the unweighted end of the rod, A,

$$0.5 \times 2 + 1 \times 3 = 5X$$

$$X = 0.8 \text{ metres}$$

The centre of gravity is 80 cm from the unweighted end of the rod. Notice that it divides the distance between the weights in the ratio $3:2$.

2

Movement	Displacement in the direction of the		
	x-axis	y-axis	z-axis
(a)	zero	zero	positive
(b)	zero	positive	negative
(c)	positive	negative	zero
(d)	positive	zero	negative

2.4.4 Centre of mass

2.4 C

1 The lamina will balance along any line through the point shown at $(2.5, 3.65)$. This is its centre of gravity (or centre of mass).

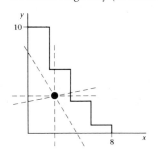

2 $\bar{y} = \dfrac{10 \times 5 + 6 \times 3 + 3 \times 1.5 + 1 \times 0.5}{10 + 6 + 3 + 1}$

$= 3.65$

3 The centre of gravity of the lamina lies on the mean of the histogram. It is, in effect, the mean position of the mass.

Notice that a line through the centre of gravity does not necessarily divide the area of the lamina into two equal parts.

Exercise 4

1 Assume that the centres of gravity of the spheres are at their geometric centres. The total mass of the toy is 100 grams.

Taking the axes shown, if the centre of gravity of the toy is at $(\bar{x}, \bar{y})$ and taking moments about A,

$$1 \times \bar{x} = 0.2 \times 60$$

$$\Rightarrow \quad \bar{x} = 12$$

Similarly $\bar{y} = 20$

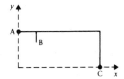

Hence the pin must be a fixed distance 12 cm along the rod from the centre of the large sphere and must be 5 cm long.

2 (a)

$(\bar{x}, \bar{y}) = (2, 1\frac{2}{3})$

(b)

$(\bar{x}, \bar{y}) = (2\frac{1}{6}, 1\frac{1}{2})$

(c)

$(\bar{x}, \bar{y}) = (2.1, 1.1)$

(d)

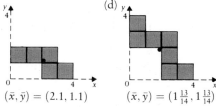

$(\bar{x}, \bar{y}) = (1\frac{13}{14}, 1\frac{13}{14})$

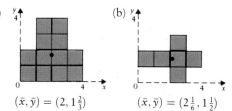

3 The Earth and Moon can be replaced by point masses of 5.98×10^{24} kg and 7.34×10^{22} kg, a distance of 384 000 km apart (average value). Their joint centre of mass therefore lies 4660 km from the Earth's centre (to 3 s.f.), approximately 1700 km below the Earth's surface.

2.4.5E Solid shapes

2.4 Exercise 5E

1 The volume of each slice $= \pi y^2 \, \delta x$
The mass of each slice $= \rho \pi y^2 \, \delta x$,
where ρ is the mass per unit volume.

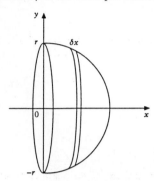

Let the centre of mass be at $(\bar{x}, 0)$.
Then taking moments about $0y$,

$$\bar{x} \sum_{x=0}^{r} \rho \pi y^2 \, \delta x = \sum_{x=0}^{r} x \rho \pi y^2 \, \delta x$$

$\rho \pi$ is constant, so in the limit,

$$\bar{x} \int_0^r y^2 \, dx = \int_0^r x y^2 \, dx$$

But $x^2 + y^2 = r^2$, so

$$\bar{x} \int_0^r (r^2 - x^2) \, dx = \int_0^r x(r^2 - x^2) \, dx$$

$$\bar{x} \left[r^2 x - \frac{x^3}{3} \right]_0^r = \left[\frac{r^2 x^2}{2} - \frac{x^4}{4} \right]_0^r$$

$$\Rightarrow \quad \tfrac{2}{3} r^3 \bar{x} = \tfrac{1}{4} r^4$$

$$\Rightarrow \quad \bar{x} = \tfrac{3}{8} r$$

2 (a)

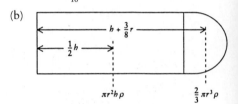

Mass of the cone $= \tfrac{1}{3} \pi r^2 h \rho$
where ρ = mass per unit volume.
Centre of mass of the cone is $\tfrac{3}{4} h$ from the vertex.

Mass of cylinder $= \pi r^2 h \rho$

The centre of mass is $\tfrac{1}{2} h$ from the circular end, i.e. $\tfrac{3}{2} h$ from vertex of cone.

Then the centre of mass is at $(\bar{x}, 0)$, where axes are as shown.

$$\left(\tfrac{1}{3} \pi r^2 h \rho + \pi r^2 h \rho \right) \bar{x}$$

$$= \tfrac{1}{3} \pi r^2 h \rho \times \tfrac{3}{4} h + \pi r^2 h \rho \times \tfrac{3}{2} h$$

$$\tfrac{4}{3} \bar{x} = \tfrac{1}{4} h + \tfrac{3}{2} h$$

$$\bar{x} = \tfrac{21}{16} h$$

(b)

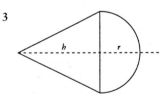

Use the same notation and method as in (a).

Taking moments about the free face of the cylinder,

$$\left(\pi r^2 h \rho + \tfrac{2}{3} \pi r^3 \rho \right) \bar{x}$$

$$= \pi r^2 h \rho \times \tfrac{1}{2} h + \tfrac{2}{3} \pi r^3 \rho \times (h + \tfrac{3}{8} r)$$

$$(h + \tfrac{2}{3} r) \bar{x} = \tfrac{1}{2} h^2 + \tfrac{2}{3} r(h + \tfrac{3}{8} r)$$

$$\Rightarrow \quad \bar{x} = \frac{6h^2 + 8rh + 3r^2}{4(3h + 2r)}$$

3

From example 7,

$$\bar{x} = \frac{3h^2 + 8rh + 3r^2}{4(h + 2r)}$$

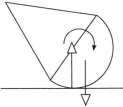

The centre of gravity must be in the hemisphere if the toy is to return to the upright position. So,

$$\frac{3h^2 + 8rh + 3r^2}{4(h + 2r)} > h$$

$$\Rightarrow \quad 3h^2 + 8rh + 3r^2 > 4h^2 + 8rh$$

$$\Rightarrow \qquad\qquad 3r^2 > h^2$$

$$\Rightarrow \qquad\qquad h < r\sqrt{3}$$

4
 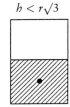 

As the level of cola initially drops, the centre of mass also drops, though not as quickly. By the end of the evening, the centre of mass is back in the centre of the can, so there is a position in which the centre of mass is just in the surface of the liquid remaining.

To consider this position, you might find it easiest to imagine the cola as a solid and then tip the can on its side and balance it at its centre of mass.

If more liquid is added, the can will rotate clockwise. If some liquid is removed, this makes it lighter on the left so the can will again rotate clockwise. In both cases, the centre of mass moves to the right.

Hence the centre of mass is at its lowest point when it is just in the surface of the liquid. Making some assumptions about relative densities of cola and aluminium, can you confirm this argument?

Miscellaneous exercise 2

1 $14\,000\,\text{N}$; $\quad 1400\,\text{kg}$

2 $6.66 \times 10^{-11}\,\text{N m}^2\,\text{kg}^{-2}$

3 $99\,\text{N}$

4 (a) $\sqrt{2}$ at $45°$ to the horizontal;
    2 vertically downwards

  (b) $t = 1$ (c) $t = \frac{3}{2}$ (d) yes

5 (a) $\begin{bmatrix} 1 \\ 4 \end{bmatrix} \text{m s}^{-2}$

  (b) Displacement $= \begin{bmatrix} 27.5 \\ 40 \end{bmatrix} \text{m}$

  which is in the same direction as $\begin{bmatrix} 11 \\ 16 \end{bmatrix}$

6 $\begin{bmatrix} \frac{1}{2}t^2 - t \\ \frac{1}{3}t^3 + 9 \\ t - \frac{1}{2}t^2 + \frac{1}{2} \end{bmatrix} \text{m}$; $\quad \begin{bmatrix} 1 \\ 2t \\ -1 \end{bmatrix} \text{m s}^{-2}$; $\quad \sqrt{6}\,\text{m s}^{-2}$

7 (a) $\begin{bmatrix} 7 \\ 1 - t \\ 4 - 10t \end{bmatrix}$

  (b) $\begin{bmatrix} 7 \\ 0 \\ -6 \end{bmatrix}$; $\quad 9.22$; $\quad \begin{bmatrix} 7 \\ 0.5 \\ 1 \end{bmatrix}$

8 (a) $2\,\text{m s}^{-2}$ (b) $\frac{2}{3}\,\text{m s}^{-2}$

  (c) $30\,\text{s}$ (d) $30\,\text{m s}^{-1}$

9 $2.5\,\text{s}$; $\quad 30.6\,\text{m}$

10 $0.54\,\text{m}$ below the centre, at $18.3\,\text{m s}^{-1}$

11 $1.71\,\text{s}$; $\quad 40.2\,\text{m}$; $\quad 3.66\,\text{m}$

12 $2\,\text{s}$; $\quad 2.2\,\text{m s}^{-1}$; $\quad 0.33\,\text{m}$

13 $\begin{bmatrix} 2 \\ 6 \end{bmatrix}$ N

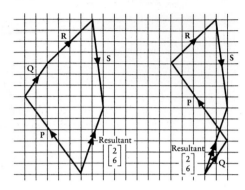

14 18 N making 119° with the x-axis

15 40 N along the x-axis

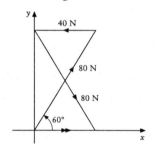

16 (a) $\mu \geq 0.18$ (b) 21.8° (c) 0.75 m s^{-2}

17 (a) 39.2 N (b) 6.08 m s^{-2}
(c) 1.08 m s^{-2}

18 $\mu = 0.84$

19 $\mu = 0.58$ (a) 9.3 N (b) 0.99 N

20 5600 m s^{-1}

21 8.5×10^4 N

22 42 000 km

23 480 N

24 $T = 0.11$ N; $\omega = 4.8$ rad s^{-1}

25 4.7 m s^{-1}; 4.4 m s^{-2} towards the centre

26 $\mu \geq 0.53$

27 $\mu = 0.80$

28 $\left(5, 3\frac{1}{3}\right)$

29 $(1, 2)$

30 If the long sides of the remaining piece lie along the positive x- and y-axes, the centre of mass is at $\left(\dfrac{5p}{6}, \dfrac{5p}{6}\right)$.

31 $\left(\frac{4}{7}, \frac{26}{7}\right)$

32 12 cm

3 TOWARDS CIRCULAR MOTION

3.1 Circular motion

3.1.1 Modelling horizontal circular motion

3.1 A

1 As $\sin\theta \neq 0$, $T = ml\omega^2$,

But $\qquad T\cos\theta = mg$

$\Rightarrow \qquad ml\omega^2 \cos\theta = mg$

$\Rightarrow \qquad \cos\theta = \dfrac{g}{l\omega^2} \quad$ as $m \neq 0$

2 The relationship between the angle, length and angular speed, $\cos\theta = \dfrac{g}{l\omega^2}$, is independent of mass, so θ does not depend on the mass of the bob. Therefore, the heavier bob should swing out at the same angle as the lighter bob.

3 (a)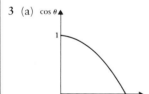

$\cos\theta = \dfrac{g}{l\omega^2}$

so if l is constant, as ω increases, $\cos\theta$ decreases
$\Rightarrow \theta$ increases
So as ω increases, θ will also increase.

(b) $\cos\theta = \dfrac{g}{l\omega^2}$

No matter how much you increase ω or l, the expression $\dfrac{g}{l\omega^2}$ is always positive; it can never reach zero. It follows that θ can only get very close to $90°$ and can never reach (or go beyond) $90°$.

(c) For constant angular speed,

$l\cos\theta = \dfrac{g}{\omega^2}$, 'a constant'.

So as l increases, $\cos\theta$ decreases and therefore θ increases.

(d) $l\cos\theta = \dfrac{g}{\omega^2}$ and $h = l\cos\theta \;\Rightarrow\; h = \dfrac{g}{\omega^2}$

This relationship is independent of mass and length so you would expect h to be the same for both bobs.

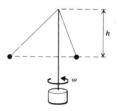

4 If $\omega < \sqrt{\left(\dfrac{g}{l}\right)}$, the string remains vertical.

The bob will not start to swing out until the angular speed exceeds $\sqrt{\left(\dfrac{g}{l}\right)}$.

If you refer back to the analysis section of the problem (page 172), you will notice that the equation $T\sin\theta = ml\omega^2 \sin\theta$ has two possible solutions: $T = ml\omega^2$ and $\sin\theta = 0$. If $\sin\theta = 0$, then the string is vertical.

Notice that the angular speed at which a bob starts to swing out is inversely proportional to $\sqrt{l}$. When you tie two bobs to the same spindle with different lengths of string, you will find that the bob on a long string will swing out before the bob on the short string, as the angular speed increases from zero.

5 The main difference is that the 'bob' on a chair-o-plane is suspended some distance from the axis of rotation. An analysis of the chair-o-plane will have to take this into account.

3.1 Exercise 1

1 $v = 120 \, \text{km h}^{-1} = 33.\dot{3} \, \text{m s}^{-1}$

$$a = \frac{v^2}{r}$$

So $30 = \dfrac{33.3^2}{r} \quad \Rightarrow \quad r = 37.0 \, \text{metres}$

2

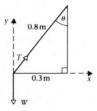

Newton's second law gives

$$\begin{bmatrix} T \sin\theta \\ T \cos\theta \end{bmatrix} + \begin{bmatrix} 0 \\ -0.5g \end{bmatrix} = \begin{bmatrix} 0.5 \times v^2/0.3 \\ 0 \end{bmatrix}$$

$\sin\theta = \dfrac{0.3}{0.8} \quad \Rightarrow \quad \theta = 22.02°$

$T \cos 22.02° = 0.5 \times 9.8 \quad \Rightarrow \quad T = 5.29 \, \text{newtons}$

$5.29 \sin 22.02° = 0.5 \times \dfrac{v^2}{0.3} \quad \Rightarrow \quad v = 1.09 \, \text{m s}^{-1}$

3 $\omega < 3.87 \, \text{rad s}^{-1}; \qquad \theta < 49.2°$

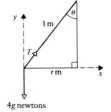

4 $\qquad\qquad\qquad \omega = 2.21 \, \text{rad s}^{-1}$

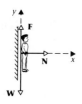

5 $\qquad\qquad v = 7.52 \, \text{m s}^{-1}$

3.2 Work and kinetic energy
3.2.1 Areas under graphs

3.2 A

1

t (s)	1	3	7
v (m s^{-1})	$\frac{15}{4}$	$\frac{80}{9}$	$\frac{428}{25}$
(a) mv (N s)	3000	7111	13 696
(b) a (m s^{-1})	$\frac{-10t+20}{4}$	$\frac{-14t+70}{9}$	$\frac{-16t+160}{25}$
	$\frac{10}{4}$	$\frac{28}{9}$	$\frac{48}{25}$
(c) ma (N)	2000	2489	1536

2 (a) The (time, momentum) graph is the same as the (time, velocity) graph with a vertical scale of 0 to 24 000 N s replacing the scale of 0 to 30 m s^{-1}.

(b)

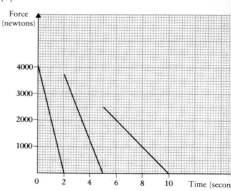

3 The area under the (time, force) graph is 16 000 N s. It represents the increase in momentum of the car during the 10 seconds. Notice that when $t = 10$, $v = 20$ and the momentum is $800 \times 20 = 16\,000$ N s

3.2 Exercise 1

1 The change in momentum is

$$\frac{90}{1000} \times 8 + \frac{90}{1000} \times 6 = 1.26 \, \text{N s}$$

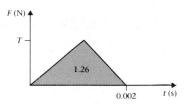

The maximum force T satisfies

$$T \times 0.001 = 1.26$$

$$\Rightarrow \quad T = 1260 \, \text{newtons}$$

2 Using the trapezium rule, the total impulse is approximately

$$10 \times (850 + 565 + 370 + 215 + 150 + 105)$$

$$= 22\,550 \, \text{N s}$$

The final speed is therefore approximately $23 \, \text{m s}^{-1}$.

3 Initial momentum $= \begin{bmatrix} 4 \\ 2 \end{bmatrix}$

Final momentum $= \begin{bmatrix} 2 \\ 3 \end{bmatrix}$

Impulse = change in momentum

$$= \begin{bmatrix} -2 \\ 1 \end{bmatrix} \text{kg m s}^{-1}$$

4 (a) $\displaystyle\int_0^{0.5} 42\,000 \sin{(2\pi t)} \, dt \approx 13\,400 \, \text{N s}$

(b) The force is perpendicular to the barrier and so the change in momentum must also be perpendicular to the barrier.

(c) $1200 \times 20 = 24\,000 \, \text{N s}$ at $30°$ to the barrier.

(d)

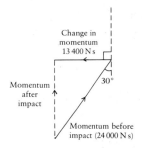

A scale drawing shows that the momentum after impact is approximately $21\,000 \, \text{N s}$ at $4°$ to the barrier.

(e) The velocity is approximately $18 \, \text{m s}^{-1}$ at $4°$ to the barrier.

3.2.2 Speed and distance

3.2 B

1 Plotting a (u, x) graph with these values produces a shape as shown.

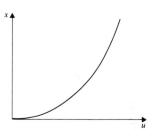

When u is doubled (from 40 to 80), x is multiplied by 4 (from 9 to 36). This suggests that x is proportional to u^2.

Trying pairs of values for u and x shows that the relationship appears to be

$$x = \frac{u^2}{180}$$

When $u = 120$, $x = 80$.

For an initial speed of $120 \, \text{km h}^{-1}$, the skid marks may be expected to be of length 80 metres.

$$2 \quad x = \left(\frac{u+v}{2}\right)t$$

So $\quad Fx = Ft\left(\dfrac{u+v}{2}\right)$

$$= (mv - mu)\left(\frac{u+v}{2}\right)$$

$$= \tfrac{1}{2}mv^2 - \tfrac{1}{2}mu^2$$

3.2 Exercise 2

1 The kinetic energy
$\tfrac{1}{2}mv^2 = \tfrac{1}{2} \times 1500 \times (150 \times \tfrac{1000}{3600})^2\,\mathrm{J} = 1.3 \times 10^6\,\mathrm{J}$

The retarding force, F newtons, is given by

$F \times 100 = \tfrac{1}{2} \times 1500 \times 0^2 - 1.3 \times 10^6$

$\Rightarrow \quad F = -1.3 \times 10^4$

The retarding force has magnitude 1.3×10^4 newtons.

2 The resistive force, F newtons, is given by

$F \times 0.02 = \tfrac{1}{2} \times 0.015 \times 300^2 - \tfrac{1}{2} \times 0.015 \times 500^2$

$\Rightarrow \quad F = -6 \times 10^4$

The resistive force has magnitude 6×10^4 newtons.

3 The accelerating force, F newtons, is given by

$F \times 15 = 1000 \times 108 \times \tfrac{1000}{3600}$

$\Rightarrow \quad F = 2000$

The accelerating force is 2000 newtons.

The distance travelled while accelerating, x metres, is given by

$2000x = \tfrac{1}{2} \times 1000 \times \left(108 \times \tfrac{1000}{3600}\right)^2$

$\Rightarrow \quad x = 225$

The distance travelled while slowing down, y metres, is given by

$-500y = \tfrac{1}{2} \times 1000 \times 0^2 - \tfrac{1}{2} \times 1000$

$\qquad\qquad \times \left(108 \times \tfrac{1000}{3600}\right)^2$

$\Rightarrow \quad y = 900$

The total distance travelled is 1125 metres.

4 The speed attained is $20\,\mathrm{m\,s^{-1}}$. In reality, the force would vary in each gear.

5 $50\,\mathrm{km\,h^{-1}} = 13.89\,\mathrm{m\,s^{-1}}$

The initial sliding speed of the van, $u\,\mathrm{m\,s^{-1}}$, is given by

$-2 \times 10^4 \times 32 = \tfrac{1}{2} \times 2250 \times 13.89^2$

$\qquad\qquad\qquad\qquad - \tfrac{1}{2} \times 2250 \times u^2$

$\Rightarrow \quad u = 27.6$

The initial sliding speed of the van was around $27.6\,\mathrm{m\,s^{-1}}$.

$27.6 \times \tfrac{3600}{1000} = 99.4\,\mathrm{km\,h^{-1}}$

The type of skid test described would be extremely unreliable and potentially inaccurate.

6 Circumference of (assumed circular) orbit

$= 2 \times \pi \times 1.5 \times 10^8 \times 10^3$ metres

$= 3\pi \times 10^{11}$ metres

Speed of the Earth relative to the Sun

$$= \frac{3\pi \times 10^{11}}{365 \times 24 \times 60 \times 60}\,\mathrm{m\,s^{-1}}$$

$\approx 29.9 \times 10^3\,\mathrm{m\,s^{-1}}$

Kinetic energy of the Earth

$= \tfrac{1}{2} \times 6.04 \times 10^{24} \times 29.9^2 \times 10^6\,\mathrm{J}$

$\approx 3 \times 10^{33}\,\mathrm{J} \quad$ (to 1 s.f.)

3.2.3 Work done by a variable force

3.2 C

1 Assume, as a reasonable approximation, that the force is 3800 N during the first 10 metres, 3675 N during the next 10 metres, and so on. The work done in each 10-metre interval is then as follows.

Distance travelled (m)	0–10	10–20	20–30	30–40	40–50
Work done (J)	38 000	36 750	35 000	32 750	30 000
Total work done (J)	38 000	74 750	109 750	142 500	172 500

The additional kinetic energy equals the total work done and is 38 000 joules in the first 10 metres.

$$38\,000 = \tfrac{1}{2} \times 1000 \times v^2 - \tfrac{1}{2} \times 1000 \times 0^2$$

$$\Rightarrow v^2 = 76$$

The speed is approximately $8.7\,\mathrm{m\,s^{-1}}$. Similarly, the speeds after 20, 30, 40 and 50 metres are 12.2, 14.8, 16.9 and $18.6\,\mathrm{m\,s^{-1}}$. The additional kinetic energy has been obtained by adding the areas under the step graph.

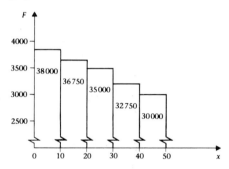

2 You might expect a better approximation to be obtained by drawing a continuous curve through the known points and finding the area under the graph.

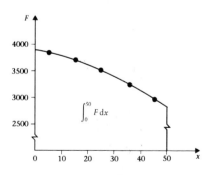

The general result is $\displaystyle\int F\,\mathrm{d}x = \tfrac{1}{2}mv^2 - \tfrac{1}{2}mu^2$.

3.2 Exercise 3

1

Distance (m)	0		1		2		3		4
Force (N)	400		300		240		210		190
Average force over interval (N)		350		270		225		200	
Kinetic energy* (J)			350		620		845		1045
Velocity (m s^{-1})			8.4		11.1		13.0		14.5

Distance (m)	4		5		6		7		8
Force (N)	190		160		130		80		0
Average force over interval (N)		175		145		105		40	
Kinetic energy* (J)	1045		1220		1365		1470		1510
Velocity (m s^{-1})	14.5		15.6		16.5		17.1		17.4

* For instance, the energy after 2 m is $(350 \times 1 + 270 \times 1)$ joules

2 Kinetic energy acquired

$$= \int_0^{50} (4000 - 22.5x - 0.25x^2)\,\mathrm{d}x$$

$$= \left[4000x - \frac{22.5x^2}{2} - \frac{0.25x^3}{3} \right]_0^{50}$$

$$= 161\,500\ \mathrm{J}$$

Speed, $v\,\mathrm{m\,s^{-1}}$, is given by

$$161\,500 = \tfrac{1}{2} \times 1400 \times v^2$$

$$\Rightarrow v = 15.2$$

After 50 metres, the van is travelling at $15\,\mathrm{m\,s^{-1}}$ (about $55\,\mathrm{km\,h^{-1}}$).

3

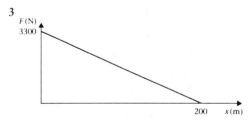

The (distance, force) graph is as shown. The kinetic energy acquired equals the area under this graph over the appropriate interval.

By inspection,

$$F - 3300 = \frac{3300x}{200} = 3300 - 16.5x$$

The kinetic energy (J) acquired during the first x metres is

$$\int_0^x (3300 - 16.5x)\, \mathrm{d}x = 3300x - 8.25x^2$$

Distance (m)	0	50	100	150	200
Kinetic energy (J)	0	144 400	247 500	309 400	330 000
Speed (m s^{-1})	0	17.0*	22.2	24.9	25.7

* $144\,400 = \frac{1}{2} \times 1000 \times v^2$ gives $v = 17.0$

The shape of the (distance, speed) graph is illustrated.

$4\ v = 30\,\mathrm{m\,s}^{-1}, \qquad h = 45\,\mathrm{m}$

3.2.4 Collisions

3.2 D

1 In all three collisions, the momentum before collision is $mu + m \times 0 = mu$.
The kinetic energy before the collision is
$$\tfrac{1}{2}mu^2 + \tfrac{1}{2}m \times 0^2 = \tfrac{1}{2}mu^2$$

Collision (i)
The momentum after the collision is

$$m \times 0 + mu = mu$$

The momentum is conserved.
The KE after the collision is

$$\tfrac{1}{2}m \times 0^2 + \tfrac{1}{2}mu^2 = \tfrac{1}{2}mu^2$$

KE is conserved.

Collision (ii)
The momentum after the collision is

$$m \times \frac{u}{2} + m \times \frac{u}{2} = mu$$

The momentum is conserved.
The KE after the collision is

$$\tfrac{1}{2}m\left(\frac{u}{2}\right)^2 + \tfrac{1}{2}m\left(\frac{u}{2}\right)^2 = \tfrac{1}{4}mu^2$$

KE is not conserved.

Collision (iii)
The momentum after the collision is

$$m \times \frac{u}{4} + m \times \frac{3u}{4} = mu$$

The momentum is conserved.
The KE after the collision is

$$\tfrac{1}{2}m\left(\frac{u}{4}\right)^2 + \tfrac{1}{2}m\left(\frac{3u}{4}\right)^2 = \tfrac{5}{16}mu^2$$

KE is not conserved.

2 (i) In the case where the trucks couple together, they will move with the same velocity.
It follows that collision (ii) is the case of the trucks coupling.

(ii) Where spring buffers are used, the left-hand truck will be slowed most dramatically (to rest, in fact).
It follows that collision (i) is the case with the spring buffers.

(iii) Collision (iii) must, therefore, be the case with the cork buffers.

3 Kinetic energy is conserved in collision (i) only.

3.2 Exercise 4

1			Before collision	After collision
(a)	(i)		mu	mu
	(ii)		$\tfrac{1}{2}mu^2$	$\tfrac{1}{2}mu^2$
	(iii)		Speed of approach $= u$	Speed of separation $= u$
(b)	(i)		$2mu$	$\tfrac{2}{3}mu + \tfrac{4}{3}mu$ $= 2mu$
	(ii)		mu^2	$\tfrac{1}{9}mu^2 + \tfrac{8}{9}mu^2$ $= mu^2$
	(iii)		u	$\tfrac{4}{3}u - \tfrac{1}{3}u = u$
(c)	(i)		mu	$-\tfrac{1}{3}mu + \tfrac{4}{3}mu$ $= mu$
	(ii)		$\tfrac{1}{2}mu^2$	$\tfrac{1}{18}mu^2 + \tfrac{4}{9}mu^2$ $= \tfrac{1}{2}mu^2$
	(iii)		u	$\tfrac{2}{3}u - \left(-\tfrac{1}{3}u\right) = u$

2 (a) Let the speed of one truck after the collision be w.

Before collision   **After collision**

$\boxed{m} \!\!\to\! v \quad v \!\leftarrow\! \boxed{m} \qquad \boxed{m} \!\!\to\! w \quad \boxed{m} \!\!\to\! w + 2v$

Speed of separation = speed of approach
$$= 2v$$

So the speed of the other truck after the collision is $w + 2v$.

Since momentum is conserved,
$$mv - mv = mw + m(w + 2v)$$
$$\Rightarrow \quad 0 = w + w + 2v$$
$$\Rightarrow \quad w = -v$$
$$\Rightarrow \quad w + 2v = -v + 2v = v$$

The velocities of the two trucks after collision are as shown.

$v \!\leftarrow\! \boxed{m} \quad \boxed{m} \!\!\to\! v$

The speed of each truck is v.

(b) Speed of approach $= u + v$
$$\Rightarrow \quad \text{speed of separation} = u + v$$

So after collision, the trucks have speeds w and $w + u + v$.

By conservation of momentum,
$$mu - mv = mw + mw + mu + mv$$
$$\Rightarrow \quad w = -v$$

So the velocities are $-v$ and u.

(c) In (a), the total kinetic energy before the collision is
$$\tfrac{1}{2}mv^2 + \tfrac{1}{2}mv^2 = mv^2$$

Since the speed of each truck is unaltered after the collision, the total kinetic energy after the collision is mv^2 also.

In (b), the total kinetic energy before the collision is
$$\tfrac{1}{2}mu^2 + \tfrac{1}{2}mv^2$$

The total kinetic energy after the collision is also $\tfrac{1}{2}mu^2 + \tfrac{1}{2}mv^2$.

3.3 Using scalar products
3.3.1 Work done in two dimensions

3.3 A

(a) If $\mathbf{u} = \begin{bmatrix} 10 \\ 0 \end{bmatrix}$, $\mathbf{r} = \begin{bmatrix} 10t \\ -5t^2 \end{bmatrix}$ and $u = 10$

The belt hits the water when
$$-5t^2 = -20 \quad \Rightarrow \quad t = 2$$

Hence $\mathbf{r} = \begin{bmatrix} 20 \\ -20 \end{bmatrix}$ and $\mathbf{v} = \begin{bmatrix} 10 \\ -20 \end{bmatrix}$

$$\Rightarrow \quad v = \sqrt{500}$$

Initial KE $= 150\,\text{J}$ and final KE $= 750\,\text{J}$
The change in KE is 600 joules.

(b) If $\mathbf{u} = \begin{bmatrix} 20 \\ 0 \end{bmatrix}$, $\mathbf{r} = \begin{bmatrix} 40 \\ -20 \end{bmatrix}$

and change in KE $= 1200 - 600$
$$= 600 \text{ joules}$$

(c) If $\mathbf{u} = \begin{bmatrix} 30 \\ 0 \end{bmatrix}$, $\mathbf{r} = \begin{bmatrix} 60 \\ -20 \end{bmatrix}$

and change in KE $= 1950 - 1350$
$$= 600 \text{ joules}$$

(d) If $\mathbf{u} = \begin{bmatrix} u \\ 0 \end{bmatrix}$, $\mathbf{r} = \begin{bmatrix} 2u \\ -20 \end{bmatrix}$

and change in KE $= \dfrac{3u^2}{2} + 600 - \dfrac{3u^2}{2}$
$$= 600 \text{ joules}$$

The work done is independent of the horizontal distance travelled.
The work done by gravity is
$3g \times 20 = 600\,\text{J}$.

3.3 Exercise 1

1 Gravitational force (weight) $= 750\,\text{N}$

Work done by this force $= 750 \times 35\cos 55°$

$$= 15\,056\,\text{J}$$

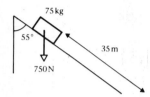

2 Work done by tension $= 100 \times \dfrac{5}{\sin 25°}$

$$= 1183\,\text{J}$$

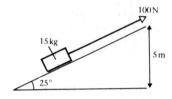

3 $\qquad\qquad$ Work done $= Fr\cos\phi$

$\Rightarrow \qquad\qquad 500 = 100 \times 25 \times \cos\phi$

$\Rightarrow \qquad\qquad\qquad \phi = 78.5°$

$\Rightarrow \qquad$ angle of slope $= 90° - 78.5°$

$$= 11.5°$$

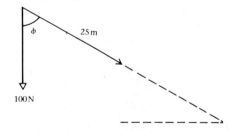

4 Work done $= Fr\cos 120°$

$$= -25\,000\,\text{J}$$

Work done against gravity $= 25\,000\,\text{J}$.

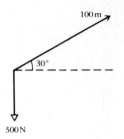

3.3.2 The scalar product

3.3 **B**

1 (a) Work done $= 200 \times 4$
$\qquad\qquad\qquad\quad = 800\,\text{J}$

(b) Work done $= 200 \times 4\cos 30°$
$\qquad\qquad\qquad\quad = 400\sqrt{3}\,\text{J}$

(c) Work done $= 400\,\text{J}$

2 Both forms give the correct answer for the scalar product because $\cos\theta = \cos(360° - \theta)$ for any angle, and so $\cos 60° = \cos 300°$. The angle must be measured between the two vectors drawn from a common point. The vectors must therefore be thought of as

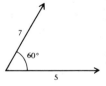

and not as

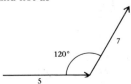

3 (a) **R** is perpendicular to the displacement so the work done is $R \times 5 \times \cos 90° = 0$.

(b) Work done by the weight
$$= 35 \times 5 \times \cos 120°$$
$$= -87.5 \, J$$

4 (a) Work done by the force $= 30 \times 2 = 60 \, J$

(b) Work done by the force $= 30 \times 2 = 60 \, J$

(c) In each case the force is in the same direction as the displacement and so the work done is positive.

(d) $(-\mathbf{p}) \cdot (-\mathbf{q}) = (-p) \times (-q) \times \cos \theta$
$$= pq \cos \theta$$
$$= \mathbf{p} \cdot \mathbf{q}$$

5 (a) Work done $= 7 \times 7$
$$= 49 \, J$$

(b) $\mathbf{p} \cdot \mathbf{p} = p \times p \times \cos 0° = p^2$, the square of the vector's magnitude

6 (a) Work done by the force $= 1057 \, J$

(b) The new distance is $15 \, m$.
Work done by the force $= 3171 \, J$
Three times as much work is done.

(c) The new force $= 1000 \, N$
The work done $= 1000 \times 5 \sin 25°$
$$= 2 \times 1057 \, J$$
i.e. the work done is doubled.

(d) The work done is six times as great.

(e) $(k\mathbf{p}) \cdot (l\mathbf{q}) = kp \times lq \times \cos \theta$
$$= klpq \cos \theta$$
$$= kl(\mathbf{p} \cdot \mathbf{q})$$

7 Total work done
$$= 100 \times 4 \sin 25° + 100 \times 6 \sin 10°$$
$$= 273 \, J$$

8 (a) From the diagram in question 7 it follows that
$$x = 6 \cos 10° + 4 \cos 25° = 9.53 \, m$$
$$y = 2.73 \, m$$
$$\Rightarrow \quad r = 9.91 \, m$$
and $\theta = \tan^{-1} \dfrac{y}{x} = 16.0°$

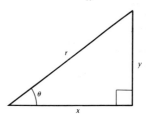

(b) $Wr \cos (90° - \theta) = 100 \times 9.91 \times \cos 74°$
$$= 273 \, joules$$

(c) The work done by gravity in question 7 is the same as in (b) above. This shows that
$$\mathbf{W} \cdot \mathbf{r}_1 + \mathbf{W} \cdot \mathbf{r}_2 = \mathbf{W} \cdot \mathbf{r}$$
$$= \mathbf{W} \cdot (\mathbf{r}_1 + \mathbf{r}_2)$$

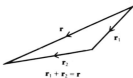

9 Work done by force up the ramp 5 m long
$$= 1250 \, J$$
Work done by force up the ramp 4 m long
$$= 1500 \, J$$
The difference in the work done by the force is $1500 - 1250 = 250 \, J$.

3.3 **Exercise 2**

1 (a) Work done $= 5 \times 4 \times \cos 60° = 10 \, J$

(b) Work done $= 5 \times 4 \times \cos 120°$
$$= -10 \, J$$

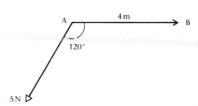

2 (a) Scalar product $= 8 \times 3 \times \cos 64°$
$= 10.5$

(b) Scalar product $= -16.3$

(c) Scalar product $= -16.3$

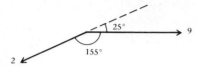

3 (a) Work done $= 100 \cos 20° \times 7$
$= 658 \text{ J}$

(b) Work done $= 658 \text{ J}$

4 Approximately 188 kJ
Notice in your working that the mass of the barge is irrelevant (as long as its speed is constant).

3.3.3 Using column vectors

3.3 Exercise 3

(a) $\mathbf{F} \cdot \mathbf{r} = 24 - 16 = 8 \text{ J}$

(b) $\mathbf{F} \cdot \mathbf{r} = -3 - 8 = -11 \text{ J}$

2 Force $= \begin{bmatrix} 3 \\ -5 \end{bmatrix}$, displacement $= \begin{bmatrix} 5a \\ 12a \end{bmatrix}$

$\Rightarrow \quad 90 = \begin{bmatrix} 3 \\ -5 \end{bmatrix} \cdot \begin{bmatrix} 5a \\ 12a \end{bmatrix} = 15a - 60a$

$\Rightarrow \quad 90 = -45a$

$\Rightarrow \quad a = -2$

The displacement is $\begin{bmatrix} -10 \\ -24 \end{bmatrix}$ and the distance travelled is 26 metres.

3 Resultant $= \begin{bmatrix} 12 \\ 12 \end{bmatrix}$, displacement $= \begin{bmatrix} 12a \\ 12a \end{bmatrix}$

$120 = 144a + 144a$

$\Rightarrow \quad a = \frac{5}{12}$

The displacement is $\begin{bmatrix} 5 \\ 5 \end{bmatrix}$ metres.

4 Taking axes along and perpendicular to the slope,

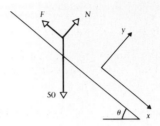

(a) Force due to gravity $= \begin{bmatrix} 50 \times \frac{3}{5} \\ -50 \times \frac{4}{5} \end{bmatrix}$

$= \begin{bmatrix} 30 \\ -40 \end{bmatrix}$ newtons

Work done $= \begin{bmatrix} 30 \\ -40 \end{bmatrix} \cdot \begin{bmatrix} 12 \\ 0 \end{bmatrix} = 360 \text{ J}$

(b) Normal contact force $= \begin{bmatrix} 0 \\ N \end{bmatrix}$

Work done $= \begin{bmatrix} 0 \\ N \end{bmatrix} \cdot \begin{bmatrix} 12 \\ 0 \end{bmatrix} = 0 \text{ J}$

5 The expression is correct for diagram (a). The angle marked θ in diagram (b) is not the angle between the force and the displacement. Here

$\mathbf{F} \cdot \mathbf{r} = Fr \cos(\pi - \theta) = -Fr \cos \theta$

3.3.4 Work done by several forces

3.3 C

1 (a) Work done by the force of
$\begin{bmatrix} 2 \\ 3 \end{bmatrix}$ newtons is $\begin{bmatrix} 2 \\ 3 \end{bmatrix} \cdot \begin{bmatrix} 5 \\ 7 \end{bmatrix} = 31 \text{ J}$

Work done by the force of
$\begin{bmatrix} 4 \\ -1 \end{bmatrix}$ newtons $= 13 \text{ J}$

Work done by the force of
$\begin{bmatrix} -3 \\ -2 \end{bmatrix}$ newtons $= -29 \text{ J}$

(b) The resultant of the three forces is

$$\begin{bmatrix} 3 \\ 0 \end{bmatrix} \text{ newtons.}$$

(c) Work done by the resultant is 15 J.

(d) The total work done by all the forces is equal to the work done by the resultant force.

2 The work done by the resultant should be equal to the sum of the work done by each of the component forces.

3 (a) $\begin{bmatrix} 3 \\ 2 \end{bmatrix} \cdot \begin{bmatrix} 6 \\ -3 \end{bmatrix} = 12\,\text{J}$

$$\begin{bmatrix} 4 \\ -8 \end{bmatrix} \cdot \begin{bmatrix} 6 \\ -3 \end{bmatrix} = 48\,\text{J}$$

$$\begin{bmatrix} 2 \\ -6 \end{bmatrix} \cdot \begin{bmatrix} 6 \\ -3 \end{bmatrix} = 30\,\text{J}$$

$$\begin{bmatrix} 3 \\ 6 \end{bmatrix} \cdot \begin{bmatrix} 6 \\ -3 \end{bmatrix} = 0\,\text{J}$$

(b) The resultant force

$$= \begin{bmatrix} 3 \\ 2 \end{bmatrix} + \begin{bmatrix} 4 \\ -8 \end{bmatrix} + \begin{bmatrix} 2 \\ -6 \end{bmatrix} + \begin{bmatrix} 3 \\ 6 \end{bmatrix}$$

$$= \begin{bmatrix} 12 \\ -6 \end{bmatrix} \text{ newtons}$$

$$\text{Work done} = \begin{bmatrix} 12 \\ -6 \end{bmatrix} \cdot \begin{bmatrix} 6 \\ -3 \end{bmatrix} = 90\,\text{J}$$

This equals the total work done by all the forces acting:

$$12 + 48 + 30 + 0 = 90$$

(c) It is perpendicular to the displacement.

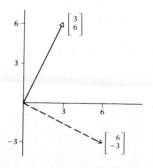

4 The resultant force is

$$\begin{bmatrix} 22 \\ -4 \end{bmatrix} + \begin{bmatrix} -6 \\ -8 \end{bmatrix} = \begin{bmatrix} 16 \\ -12 \end{bmatrix} \text{ newtons.}$$

The magnitude of the vector $\begin{bmatrix} 4 \\ -3 \end{bmatrix}$ is 5 units.

Therefore the displacement $= 6\begin{bmatrix} 4 \\ -3 \end{bmatrix}$ cm

$$= \frac{6}{100}\begin{bmatrix} 4 \\ -3 \end{bmatrix} \text{ metres}$$

The work done $= \dfrac{6}{100}\begin{bmatrix} 4 \\ -3 \end{bmatrix} \cdot \begin{bmatrix} 16 \\ -12 \end{bmatrix}$

$$= 6 \text{ joules}$$

3.3 Exercise 4

1 Assume there is no friction.

(a) Work done from A to B $= 800 \times 5 = 4000\,\text{J}$
Work done from B to C $= 8000\,\text{J}$
Work done from C to D $= 1600\,\text{J}$

(b) Total work done $= 13\,600\,\text{J}$

(c) Since the initial velocity is zero and the work done equals the change in kinetic energy,

$$\tfrac{1}{2}mv^2 = 13\,600$$

$$\tfrac{1}{2} \times 80 \times v^2 = 13\,600$$

$$v^2 = 340$$

$$v = 18.4\,\text{m s}^{-1}$$

2 (a) The 100 N force is the force provided by the cyclist.

(b) Work done by 100 N force

$$= \begin{bmatrix} 100 \\ 0 \end{bmatrix} \cdot \begin{bmatrix} 50 \\ 0 \end{bmatrix}$$

$$= 5000\,\text{J}$$

Work done by normal reaction

$$= \begin{bmatrix} 0 \\ R \end{bmatrix} \cdot \begin{bmatrix} 50 \\ 0 \end{bmatrix}$$

$$= 0$$

Work done by weight

$$= \begin{bmatrix} -800\cos 80° \\ -800\cos 10° \end{bmatrix} \cdot \begin{bmatrix} 50 \\ 0 \end{bmatrix}$$

$$= -6946\,\text{J}$$

Total work done $= 5000 - 6946 = -1946\,\text{J}$

(c) Work done equals change in kinetic energy and so

$$\tfrac{1}{2}mv^2 - \tfrac{1}{2}mu^2 = -1946$$

Hence the speed is decreasing.

3 (a)

$$\mathbf{R} = \begin{bmatrix} 0 \\ R \end{bmatrix}$$

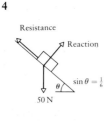

$$\mathbf{W} = \begin{bmatrix} 0 \\ -300 \end{bmatrix}$$

(b) Work done by weight $= \begin{bmatrix} 0 \\ -300 \end{bmatrix} \cdot \begin{bmatrix} 80 \\ 0 \end{bmatrix} = 0$

Work done by reaction $= \begin{bmatrix} 0 \\ R \end{bmatrix} \cdot \begin{bmatrix} 80 \\ 0 \end{bmatrix} = 0$

4

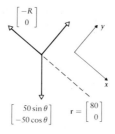

Work done by weight

$$= \begin{bmatrix} 50\sin\theta \\ -50\cos\theta \end{bmatrix} \cdot \begin{bmatrix} 80 \\ 0 \end{bmatrix} = 667\,\text{joules}$$

Work done by resistance

$$= \begin{bmatrix} -R \\ 0 \end{bmatrix} \cdot \begin{bmatrix} 80 \\ 0 \end{bmatrix} = -80R\,\text{joules}$$

Total work done equals change in kinetic energy.

$$667 - 80R = \tfrac{1}{2}mv^2$$

$$= \tfrac{1}{2} \times 5 \times 10^2$$

$$R = 5.2\,\text{newtons} \quad \text{(to 1 d.p.)}$$

5 Initial kinetic energy $= \tfrac{1}{2} \times 0.01 \times (4^2 + 16^2)$
$$= 1.36\,\text{J}$$

Final kinetic energy $= 2.32\,\text{J}$

Work done $= 0.96\,\text{J}$

6 Force down the slope is
$(10\cos 60° - F)$ newtons.

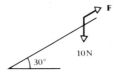

Work done is $(5 - F) \times 5$ joules.

Gain in kinetic energy $= \tfrac{1}{2} \times 1 \times 4^2 - 0$
$$= 8\,\text{joules}$$

$\Rightarrow \quad 25 - 5F = 8$

$$5F = 17$$

$\Rightarrow \quad F = 3.4\,\text{newtons}$

7E Initial KE $= \tfrac{1}{2} \times 6.5 \times 4^2$
$$= 52\,\text{joules}$$

$$\mu = \tfrac{2}{3}, \quad \sin\theta = \tfrac{5}{13}$$

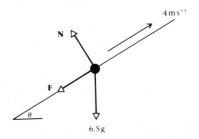

(a) Work done by gravity $= -6.5g\sin\theta \times d$
$$= -6.5 \times 10 \times \tfrac{5}{13} \times d$$
$$= -25d\,\text{joules}$$

(b) Work done by friction $= -Fd$

Since the block is sliding, $F = \mu N = \frac{2}{3}N$

There is no acceleration perpendicular to the plane, so

$N = 6.5g \cos \theta = 65 \times \frac{12}{13} = 60 \, \text{newtons}$

Work done by friction $= -\frac{2}{3} \times 60 \times d$

$= -40d \, \text{joules}$

Total work done by the forces

$= -65d \, \text{joules}$

The kinetic energy is reduced by 52 joules, and so

$65d = 52$

$d = 0.8 \, \text{metres}$

8E (a)

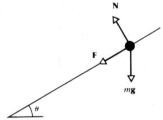

Total work done by friction

$= -Fd + -Fd$

$= -2Fd$

Since the body is sliding, $\quad F = \mu N$

There is no acceleration perpendicular to the plane, so

$N = mg \cos \theta$

Total work done by friction

$= -2\mu mgd \cos \theta$

(b) Work done by gravity $= -mgd \sin \theta$

Work done by the normal contact force $= 0$

Total work done by forces from P to Q

$= -mgd \sin \theta - \mu mgd \cos \theta$

$= -mgd(\sin \theta + \mu \cos \theta)$

Work done $=$ change in KE

$-mgd(\sin \theta + \mu \cos \theta) = 0 - \frac{1}{2}mu^2$

$\Rightarrow \quad u = \sqrt{(2gd(\sin \theta + \mu \cos \theta))}$

(c) Consider the path from Q to P.

Total work done by the forces

$= mgd \sin \theta - \mu mgd \cos \theta$

Let the speed of the body be v.

Then $\frac{1}{2}mv^2 - 0 = mgd \sin \theta - \mu mgd \cos \theta$

$v = \sqrt{(2gd(\sin \theta - \mu \cos \theta))}$

3.3.5 Variable forces

3.3 D

1 The work done is $\begin{bmatrix} 0 \\ -700 \end{bmatrix} \cdot \begin{bmatrix} x \\ -y \end{bmatrix} = 700y.$

This has a maximum when y is a maximum, i.e. $y = 7$.

2 If $g = 9.81 \, \text{N kg}^{-1}$

$\mathbf{W} = \begin{bmatrix} 0 \\ -70 \times 9.81 \end{bmatrix} = \begin{bmatrix} 0 \\ -686.7 \end{bmatrix}$

$\begin{bmatrix} 0 \\ -686.7 \end{bmatrix} \cdot \begin{bmatrix} x \\ -7 \end{bmatrix} = \frac{70v^2}{2}$

$\Rightarrow \quad 4806.9 = \frac{70v^2}{2}$

$\Rightarrow \quad v = 11.7 \, \text{m s}^{-1}$

So it does not make a big difference to the answer.

3 $\mathbf{W} \cdot \mathbf{r} = \begin{bmatrix} 0 \\ -mg \end{bmatrix} \cdot \begin{bmatrix} x \\ -7 \end{bmatrix} = \frac{mv^2}{2}$

$7mg = \frac{mv^2}{2}$

$v^2 = 14g$

Hence her maximum speed is the same as the man's.

3.3 Exercise 5

1 (a) $\mathbf{W} = \begin{bmatrix} 0 \\ -400 \end{bmatrix}, \quad \mathbf{W} \cdot \mathbf{r} = \frac{mv^2}{2} - \frac{mu^2}{2}$

$\begin{bmatrix} 0 \\ -400 \end{bmatrix} \cdot \begin{bmatrix} x \\ -1 \end{bmatrix} = \frac{40v^2}{2} - \frac{40 \times 3^2}{2}$

$400 = 20v^2 - 180$

$v^2 = 29$

$v = 5.4 \, \text{m s}^{-1} \, (\text{to 1 d.p.})$

(b) Maximum height occurs when $v = 0$

$$\begin{bmatrix} 0 \\ -400 \end{bmatrix} \cdot \begin{bmatrix} x \\ y \end{bmatrix} = -\frac{mu^2}{2}$$

$$-400y = -\frac{40}{2} \times 3^2$$

$$y = \frac{9}{20} = 0.45 \text{ metre}$$

Hence her maximum height above the ground is $2 + 0.45 = 2.45$ metres.

(c) No, you do not need to know her mass.

$$\begin{bmatrix} 0 \\ -10m \end{bmatrix} \cdot \begin{bmatrix} x \\ y \end{bmatrix} = -\frac{mu^2}{2}$$

$$-10my = -\frac{mu^2}{2} \quad \left(\begin{array}{c} m \text{ cancels} \\ \text{on each side} \end{array} \right)$$

$$y = \frac{u^2}{20}$$

2 (a) Assume the Scout starts from rest and that $g = 10 \, \text{N} \, \text{kg}^{-1}$.
Assume that there is no friction.

$$\mathbf{W} \cdot \mathbf{r} = \frac{mv^2}{2}$$

$$\begin{bmatrix} 0 \\ -mg \end{bmatrix} \cdot \begin{bmatrix} x \\ -8 \end{bmatrix} = \frac{mv^2}{2}$$

$$8mg = \frac{mv^2}{2}$$

$$v^2 = 160$$

$$v = 12.6 \, \text{m} \, \text{s}^{-1}$$

(b) $v = 11.0 \, \text{m} \, \text{s}^{-1}$

(c) $11.0 \, \text{m} \, \text{s}^{-1}$ is the same as $39.6 \, \text{km} \, \text{h}^{-1}$.
The final speed is too great for the runway to be safe.

3 (a) Displacement of bead $= \begin{bmatrix} 9 \\ 8 \end{bmatrix} - \begin{bmatrix} 6 \\ 7 \end{bmatrix}$

$$= \begin{bmatrix} 3 \\ 1 \end{bmatrix}$$

Work done by the force $= \begin{bmatrix} 3 \\ 1 \end{bmatrix} \cdot \begin{bmatrix} 2 \\ 5 \end{bmatrix}$

$$= 6 + 5$$

$$= 11 \text{ joules}$$

(b) Work done = change in KE
Initial KE = 0,   final KE = 11

$$\tfrac{1}{2} \times 0.1 \times v^2 = 11$$

$$v^2 = 220$$

$$v = 14.8 \, \text{m} \, \text{s}^{-1}$$

4 (a) Displacement $= \begin{bmatrix} 10 \\ 12 \end{bmatrix} - \begin{bmatrix} 6 \\ 7 \end{bmatrix} = \begin{bmatrix} 4 \\ 5 \end{bmatrix}$

Work done $= \begin{bmatrix} 4 \\ 5 \end{bmatrix} \cdot \begin{bmatrix} 6 \\ 5 \end{bmatrix}$

$$= 24 + 25 = 49 \text{ joules}$$

The change in KE is 49 joules.

(b) The force was not in the direction of motion so the velocity of the ball at A wa[s] not parallel to either the force or the displacement.

3.4 Potential energy
3.4.1 Gravitational potential energy

3.4 A

1 The pencil is stationary at both positions, so there is no change in KE.
Thus the total work done is zero.

2 The forces acting on the pencil are the conta[ct] force between you and the pencil and the gravitational force (weight) acting downwards.

3 Work done by the weight $= -mgh$

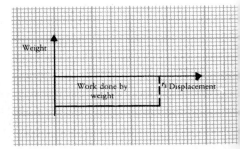

The total work done is zero.
So work done by the hand = mgh

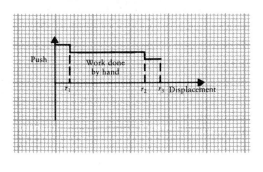

3.4 Exercise 1

1 The height above the ground is 2 metres.
⇒ gravitational potential energy relative
to the ground = $5 \times 10 \times 2$
= 100 joules

2 Height of the child above the ground
= $5 \sin 36° = 2.94$ metres
Gravitational PE relative to the ground
= 882 joules

3 Let the potential energy at B be zero.
The height of A above B is 7 metres.
Gravitational PE at A relative to B
= $70 \times 10 \times 7 = 4900$ joules
Change in PE
= $0 - 4900 = -4900$ joules
If the PE is measured relative to a point
h metres below B,

$$\text{PE at A} = 70 \times 10 \times (7 + h)$$

$$\text{PE at B} = 70 \times 10 \times h$$

Change in PE = $700h - 700h - 4900$

$$= -4900 \text{ joules}$$

4 (a)

(i) Height of top of ramp = $34.4 \sin 5°$
= 3.00 metres

Work done by gravity = -500×3.00
= -1500 joules

(ii) Height of top of ramp = $8.0 \sin 22°$
= 3.00 metres

Work done by gravity = -500×3.00
= -1500 joules

(b) The height the hod is lifted through is the
same in each case.

5

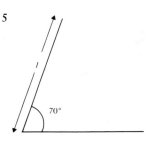

Height of top of ladder above ground
= $l \sin 70°$

Increase in PE = $50 \times 10 \times l \sin 70°$

But the increase = 4300

⇒ $500l \sin 70° = 4300$

$l = 9.15$ metres

3.4.2 Conserving energy

3.4 B

1 Work done = change in kinetic energy
If you assume that the weight is the only force
to do work, then the work done each metre as
the ball rises is $-mg \times 1$.
Work done = -0.5 J
Initial KE = $\frac{1}{2}mv^2 = 0.025 \times 10^2 = 2.5$

Height above point of projection (metres)	KE (joules)	PE relative to point of projection (joules)
0	2.5	0
1	2.0	0.5
2	1.5	1.0
3	1.0	1.5
4	0.5	2.0
5	0	2.5

2 The kinetic energy of the ball is zero when it has risen 5 metres. Its velocity is zero, so it will not rise any higher.

3 The sum of the potential and kinetic energies is 2.5 J. Energy appears to be conserved, given the initial assumptions.

4 As the kinetic energy decreases, the potential energy increases.

5 If a tennis ball is used, some work will be done *against* air resistance. The total work done each metre that the ball rises is −0.625 J.

Height above point of projection (metres)	KE (joules)	PE (joules)	KE + PE (joules)
0	2.500	0	2.500
1	1.875	0.5	2.375
2	1.250	1.0	2.250
3	0.625	1.5	2.125
4	0	2.0	2.000

6 Mechanical energy is converted into heat and sound energy.

3.4 Exercise 2

1 (a) PE relative to initial
position $= 0.2 \times 3$

$= 0.6 \, \text{J}$

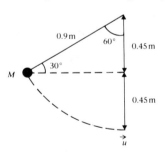

15 m s⁻¹ _replaced_

(b) KE at the start $= \frac{1}{2} \times 0.02 \times 15^2 = 2.25 \, \text{J}$

PE at the start $= 0$

PE + KE at start $=$ PE + KE after 3 metres

$\Rightarrow \quad \frac{1}{2}mv^2 + 0.6 = 2.25 + 0$

$v = 12.8 \, \text{m s}^{-1}$

(c) At the highest point of its path, the kinetic energy of the ball is zero.
By conservation of energy,

PE at the highest point $+ 0 = 2.25 + 0$

$\qquad$ PE $= 2.25 \, \text{joules}$

2

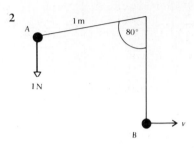

PE at A relative to B

$= 0.1 \times 10 \times 1(1 - \cos 80°)$

$= 0.826 \, \text{joule}$

KE at A $= 0$

But KE + PE at A $=$ KE + PE at B

$\Rightarrow \quad 0.826 + 0 = \frac{1}{2} \times 0.1 \times v^2 + 0$

$\qquad v = 4.07 \, \text{m s}^{-1}$

3 (a) Assume conservation of mechanical energy
as the lighter ball bearing swings down.

$\Rightarrow \quad$ KE gained $=$ PE lost

$\Rightarrow \qquad \frac{1}{2}Mu^2 = Mgh$

$\qquad \frac{1}{2}u^2 = 10 \times 0.45$

$\Rightarrow \qquad u^2 = 9$

$\Rightarrow \qquad u = 3 \, \text{m s}^{-1}$

(b) The collision is *not* perfectly elastic so you can only assume conservation of momentum. Mechanical energy is *not* conserved.

Before impact   After impact

M   2M   3M

The momentum is $3M + 0 = 3Mv$

$$\Rightarrow \quad v = 1\,\mathrm{m\,s}^{-1}$$

(c) Assume conservation of mechanical energy as the combined mass swings up.

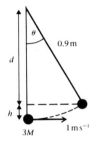

KE lost = PE gained

$$\Rightarrow \quad \tfrac{1}{2} \times 3M \times 1^2 = 3M \times 10 \times h$$
$$\Rightarrow \quad h = 0.05 \text{ metre}$$
$$\Rightarrow \quad d = 0.85 \text{ metre}$$
$$\Rightarrow \quad \theta = \cos^{-1}\left(\frac{0.85}{0.9}\right)$$
$$= 19°$$

3.4.3 Elastic potential energy

3.4 Exercise 3

1 (a) Work done $= \dfrac{kx^2}{2}$

$$= \frac{100 \times 0.05^2}{2}$$
$$= 0.125 \text{ joules}$$

(b) 1.125 joules

2 Let the spring constant be k.

$$0.2 = \frac{k \times 0.1^2}{2}$$
$$k = 40\,\mathrm{N\,m}^{-1}$$

3 (a) Work done when spring is compressed 5 cm

$$= \frac{500 \times 0.05^2}{2} = 0.625 \text{ joules}$$

(b) Work done when spring is compressed 10 cm
= 2.5 joules
So work done to compress the spring a further 5 cm
= 2.5 − 0.625 = 1.875 joules

3.4.4 Conserving mechanical energy

3.4 C

The spring constant is $8\,\mathrm{N\,m}^{-1}$. This means that a force of 8 N would extend the spring by 1 m, or 1 N extends it by $\frac{1}{8}$ m. Since the mass (0.2 kg) applies a force of 2 N to the spring, the extension is $\frac{2}{8} = 0.25$ m.

3.4 Exercise 4

1 (a) Let the spring constant be k.

$$1 = k \times 0.1$$
$$\Rightarrow \quad k = 10\,\mathrm{N\,m}^{-1}$$

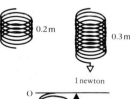

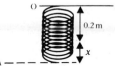

Let the gravitational potential energy be measured relative to O.

$$KE = \tfrac{1}{2}mv^2$$

$$PE = -mg(0.2 + x) = -(0.2 + x)$$

$$EPE = \frac{10 \times x^2}{2}$$

At the point of release,

$$KE = 0 \quad PE = -0.4 \quad EPE = \frac{10 \times 0.2^2}{2}$$

When the spring is 0.3 m long,

$$KE = \tfrac{1}{2}mv^2 \quad PE = -0.3 \quad EPE = \frac{10 \times 0.1^2}{2}$$

But total mechanical energy is conserved.

$$0 - 0.4 + 0.2 = 0.05v^2 - 0.3 + 0.05$$

$$\Rightarrow \quad 0.05v^2 = 0.05$$

$$v = 1\,\text{m s}^{-1}$$

(b) Its elastic potential energy is greatest at the point of release.

2 (a) $T = kx \quad \Rightarrow \quad 20 = 500x$

Its extension is 0.04 metre.

(b) Let the unstretched position be O.

Initial $PE = -2 \times 10 \times 0.1$

Initial $KE = 0$

Initial $EPE = \tfrac{1}{2} \times 500 \times 0.1^2$

Final $PE = 0$

Final $KE = \tfrac{1}{2} \times 2 \times v^2$

Final $EPE = 0$

Total mechanical energy is converved, so

$$-2 + 0 + 2.5 = 0 + v^2 + 0$$

$$v^2 = 0.5$$

$$v = 0.707\,\text{m s}^{-1}$$

3 Let the tension in the string, T newtons, be given by $T = kx$, where x metres is the extension.

$$4 = k \times 0.5 \quad \Rightarrow \quad k = 8$$

$$KE\ \text{at}\ B = 0$$

$$EPE\ \text{at}\ B = \tfrac{1}{2} \times 8 \times 0.5^2$$

$$PE = 0$$

$$KE\ \text{at}\ O = \tfrac{1}{2}mv^2$$

EPE at O = 0 (string is unstretched)

$$PE = 0$$

Total mechanical energy is conserved.

$$\Rightarrow \quad 0 + 1 + 0 = 0.025v^2 + 0 + 0$$

$$\Rightarrow \quad\quad v^2 = 40$$

$$v = 6.32\,\text{m s}^{-1}$$

The speed of the mass as it passes O is $6.32\,\text{m s}^{-1}$.

4 (a) PE lost by stunt actor $= 76 \times 10 \times 200$

$$= 152\,000\,\text{J}$$

Extension of rope

$$= \text{height} - \text{unstretched length}$$

$$= 200 - 100 = 100\,\text{m}$$

Spring constant, $k = 30\,\text{N m}^{-1}$

EPE gained by rope $= \dfrac{kx^2}{2}$

$$= \frac{30 \times 100^2}{2}$$

$$= 150\,000\,\text{J}$$

(b) The energy of the 'system' is conserved.

Initial $(PE + EPE + KE)$

$$= \text{Final}\ (PE + EPE + KE)$$

$$\Rightarrow \quad 152\,000 + 0 + 0 = 0 + 150\,000 + KE$$

$$\Rightarrow \quad \text{Final } KE = 2000\,\text{J}$$

$$\tfrac{1}{2}mv^2 = 2000$$

$$\Rightarrow \quad v^2 = \frac{2 \times 2000}{76}$$

$$\Rightarrow \quad v = 7.25\,\text{m s}^{-1}$$

(See note (iii).)

Notes (i) This speed is 'estimated' since the energy conservation equation which was used only dealt with mechanical energy. No account was taken of the energy lost as heat because of friction with the air and internal friction in the rope. This would reduce the KE remaining, and the final speed slightly.

(ii) The zero level for gravitational PE has been taken as ground level.

(iii) You may like to consider whether a speed of 7.25 m s^{-1} is likely to cause injury. From what height of wall would you have to jump to reach the ground at that speed?

5 Extension = final length − original length
= −0.04 metre
(negative because the spring is compressed)

EPE stored in spring when compressed = $\dfrac{kx^2}{2}$

= 0.8 J

The energy of the system is conserved.

Initial (PE + EPE + KE)

= Final (PE + EPE + KE)

$0 + 0.8 + 0 = \text{PE} + 0 + 0$

$\text{PE} = mgh = 0.8$

$\Rightarrow\quad h = \dfrac{0.8}{0.02 \times 10}$

Estimated height = 4 metres

NB: KE is zero initially at ground level and zero momentarily at the maximum height reached.

3.5 Modelling circular motion
3.5.1 Changing speed, changing energy

3.5 A

1 For the conker, some energy will be lost due to the effects of air resistance and friction at the support where the string is held. If both of these effects are small, then it is reasonable to assume that energy is conserved.

For the marble, you would expect the effect of air resistance to be negligible. Furthermore, no energy is lost because of friction, provided the marble 'rolls without slipping'. Negligible energy is therefore lost when the marble rolls around the cylinder. When the marble goes around the loop, some slipping does occur on the steep parts of the loop and therefore some energy is lost. Additional energy is lost when the marble goes over joins in the track. However, the total energy loss is likely to be sufficiently small for conservation of energy to be a reasonable assumption.

2 When the marble is released from rest it has potential energy but no kinetic energy. As it rolls down the track its kinetic energy increases at the expense of its potential energy and kinetic energy reaches its maximum value at the bottom of the loop. When climbing the loop its potential energy increases and kinetic energy decreases.

3 When a car is used there are additional friction losses due to the presence of internal friction acting on the axles. Your experiments should show that the energy lost is far greater than for the marble and that it is *not* reasonable to assume that energy is conserved.

3.5.2 Acceleration

3.5 B

1 (a) The forces acting on the conker are its weight, mg, and the tension, T, in the string (assuming that air resistance is negligible).

(b) The resultant force is not directed towards the centre of circular motion unless $\theta = 0°$ or 180°.

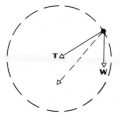

2 $\overrightarrow{OP} = \begin{bmatrix} r\cos\theta \\ r\sin\theta \end{bmatrix} = r\begin{bmatrix} \cos\theta \\ \sin\theta \end{bmatrix}$

$\begin{bmatrix} \cos\theta \\ \sin\theta \end{bmatrix}$ is therefore in the direction $\overrightarrow{OP}$.

Its length is $\sqrt{(\sin^2\theta + \cos^2\theta)} = 1$.

3 $\mathbf{r} = r\begin{bmatrix} \cos\theta \\ \sin\theta \end{bmatrix}$

$\mathbf{v} = \dfrac{d\mathbf{r}}{dt} = r\begin{bmatrix} \dfrac{d}{dt}\cos\theta \\[2mm] \dfrac{d}{dt}\sin\theta \end{bmatrix} = r\begin{bmatrix} \dfrac{d}{d\theta}\cos\theta \times \dot\theta \\[2mm] \dfrac{d}{d\theta}\sin\theta \times \dot\theta \end{bmatrix}$

$= r\begin{bmatrix} -\sin\theta \times \dot\theta \\ \cos\theta \times \dot\theta \end{bmatrix} = r\dot\theta\begin{bmatrix} -\sin\theta \\ \cos\theta \end{bmatrix}$

$\begin{bmatrix} -\sin\theta \\ \cos\theta \end{bmatrix}$ is a unit vector

and so $\mathbf{v}$ has magnitude $r\dot\theta$.

4 (a) Acceleration $\mathbf{a} = \dfrac{d\mathbf{v}}{dt}$

$= r\begin{bmatrix} -\sin\theta \times \ddot\theta - \cos\theta \times \dot\theta^2 \\ \cos\theta \times \ddot\theta - \sin\theta \times \dot\theta^2 \end{bmatrix}$

$\Rightarrow\ \mathbf{a} = -r\dot\theta^2\begin{bmatrix} \cos\theta \\ \sin\theta \end{bmatrix} + r\ddot\theta\begin{bmatrix} -\sin\theta \\ \cos\theta \end{bmatrix}$

(b) $\begin{bmatrix} -\sin\theta \\ \cos\theta \end{bmatrix}$ has length $\sqrt{(\sin^2\theta + \cos^2\theta)} = 1$

and

$\begin{bmatrix} \cos\theta \\ \sin\theta \end{bmatrix} \cdot \begin{bmatrix} -\sin\theta \\ \cos\theta \end{bmatrix}$

$= -\cos\theta\sin\theta + \cos\theta\sin\theta = 0$

Therefore $\begin{bmatrix} -\sin\theta \\ \cos\theta \end{bmatrix}$ is a unit vector in a

direction perpendicular to OP.

(c) Acceleration in the radial direction is directed towards O and has magnitude

$$r\dot\theta^2 = \frac{(r\dot\theta)^2}{r} = \frac{v^2}{r}$$

3.5 Exercise 1

1 (a) The maximum velocity will occur at the bottom of the bowl.

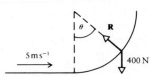

Assuming no energy is lost and $g = 10\,\text{N}\,\text{kg}^{-1}$, the maximum height occurs when $v = 0$.

By conservation of energy,

$$\tfrac{1}{2}mv^2 - 0 = mgh \quad\Rightarrow\quad h = \tfrac{25}{20} = 1.25\,\text{m}$$

(b) By Newton's second law radially,

$$R - 400\cos\theta = 40a$$

At the highest point,

$$a = \frac{v^2}{r} = 0 \quad \text{(since } v = 0\text{)}$$

$$\Rightarrow\quad R = 400\cos\theta \text{ where } \cos\theta = \frac{2 - 1.25}{2}$$

$$\Rightarrow\quad R = 150 \text{ newtons}$$

2 (a)

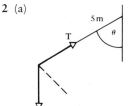

Let the tension in the rope be T newtons and the velocity be $v\,\text{m}\,\text{s}^{-1}$.

Assume $\cos\theta = \tfrac{4}{5}$ when $v = 0$, and $g = 10\,\text{N}\,\text{kg}^{-1}$.

By conservation of energy, when $\theta = 0$,

$$\tfrac{1}{2}mv^2 = mg \times 1$$

$$\Rightarrow\quad v^2 = 20 \quad\Rightarrow\quad v = 2\sqrt{5}\,\text{m}\,\text{s}^{-1}$$

(b) By Newton's second law radially,

$$T - 400 \cos \theta = \frac{40v^2}{5}$$

$$T = \frac{40v^2}{5} + 400 \cos \theta \qquad \text{①}$$

Substituting $v^2 = 20$ in ①:

$$T = \frac{40 \times 20}{5} + 400$$

$$= 560 \text{ newtons at the bottom of the swing}$$

(c) At the top of the swing, $v = 0$ and

$$\cos \theta = \tfrac{4}{5}$$

$$\Rightarrow \quad T = 320 \text{ newtons}$$

3

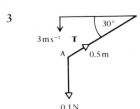

Let the velocity at A be $v \, \text{m s}^{-1}$ and take the PE to be zero at the start.

Assume energy is conserved and $g = 10 \, \text{N kg}^{-1}$.

(a) $\tfrac{1}{2} \times 0.01 \times 9$

$$= \tfrac{1}{2} \times 0.01 \times v^2 - 0.01 \times 10 \times 0.5 \sin 30°$$

$$\Rightarrow \quad v^2 = 9 + 5$$

$$\Rightarrow \quad v = \sqrt{14} \, \text{m s}^{-1}$$

(b) By Newton's second law radially,

$$T - 0.1 \cos 60° = \frac{mv^2}{0.5}$$

$$T = \frac{0.01 \times 14}{0.5} + \frac{0.1 \times 1}{2}$$

$$T = 0.33 \text{ newton}$$

3.5.3 Losing contact

3.5 **C**

1 Assumptions should include:

- Air resistance is negligible.
- The marble can be modelled as a particle, ignoring its rotation as it rolls.
- Forces acting on the particle are gravity, mg, and the normal contact force, N.
- The particle has speed v at P and angle AOP is θ.

2 Equating the two expressions for v^2 gives

$$gr \cos \theta = 2gr(1 - \cos \theta)$$

$$\Rightarrow \quad \cos \theta = \tfrac{2}{3}$$

$$\theta = \cos^{-1} \left(\tfrac{2}{3} \right)$$

3 The marble will lose contact when $\cos \theta = \tfrac{2}{3}$, i.e. $\theta = \cos^{-1} \left(\tfrac{2}{3} \right)$. The position P is a distance below A of

$$(r - r \cos \theta) = r(1 - \tfrac{2}{3}) = \tfrac{1}{3} r$$

4E When the marble leaves the tin,
$u = \sqrt{(gr \cos \theta)} = 2.58 \sqrt{r}$ tangentially.

$$\mathbf{u} = \begin{bmatrix} 2.58\sqrt{r} \cos \theta \\ 2.58\sqrt{r} \sin \theta \end{bmatrix} = \begin{bmatrix} 1.72\sqrt{r} \\ 1.92\sqrt{r} \end{bmatrix}$$

The marble travels as a projectile from P and hits the table at

$$\begin{bmatrix} x \\ -\tfrac{5}{3}r \end{bmatrix} \quad \text{(taking P as the origin).}$$

$$\mathbf{r} = \begin{bmatrix} 1.72t\sqrt{r} \\ 1.92t\sqrt{r} - 5t^2 \end{bmatrix}$$

$$\Rightarrow \quad 5t^2 - 1.92t\sqrt{r} - \tfrac{5}{3}r = 0$$

$$\Rightarrow \quad t = 0.80\sqrt{r}$$

$$\Rightarrow \quad x \approx 1.38r \text{ metres}$$

P is $r \sin \theta = 0.75r$ to the right of A; so in theory, the marble should hit the table approximately $2.13r$ metres from the point of contact of the tin and the table.

3.6E Rotation and energy
3.6.1 Rotational energy

3.6 Exercise 1

1 $\omega = 78$ r.p.m. $= \dfrac{78 \times 2\pi}{60}$ rad s^{-1}

Rotational KE $= \frac{1}{2}I\omega^2$

$\qquad = \dfrac{0.05 \times (78 \times 2\pi)^2}{60^2}$

$\qquad = 3.34$ joules

2 Work done $=$ change in rotational KE

$\qquad = \frac{1}{2} \times 0.05 \times 40^2 - 0$

$\qquad = 40$ joules

3 Initial rotational KE $= \frac{1}{2}I \times 10^2$

$\qquad = 50I$

Final rotational KE $= \frac{1}{2}I \times 5^2$

$\qquad = 12.5I$

But $50I - 12.5I = 1000$

$\qquad \Rightarrow \quad I = 26.7$ kg m^2

4 The rod has no mass so its moment of inertia is zero. The rotational KE of each particle is $\frac{1}{2}m(r\omega)^2$.

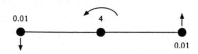

Total KE $= \left[\frac{1}{2} \times 0.01 \times (1 \times 4)^2\right] \times 2$

$\qquad = 0.16$ joule

5 (a) Assuming that the mass of cotton that unwinds can be ignored,

$\qquad F = 2, \quad r = 0.05, \quad \theta = 2\pi$

$\qquad$ Work done $= 2 \times 0.05 \times 2\pi$

$\qquad\qquad\qquad = 0.628$ joule

The initial KE is zero so the KE after 1 revolution is 0.628 joule.

(b) KE $= \frac{1}{2}I\omega^2 \quad \Rightarrow \quad 0.628 = \frac{1}{2} \times 0.0003 \times \omega^2$

$\qquad\qquad\qquad \omega = 64.7$ rad s^{-1}

6E (a)

Total KE $= \dfrac{1}{2}\dfrac{m}{3}\left(\dfrac{d\omega}{2}\right)^2 + \dfrac{1}{2}\dfrac{m}{3}(d\omega)^2$

$\qquad = \dfrac{1}{2}\dfrac{m}{3}d^2\omega^2\left[\dfrac{1}{4}+1\right]$

$\qquad = \dfrac{5md^2\omega^2}{24}$

(b)

Total KE $= \dfrac{1}{2}\dfrac{m}{5}\left(\dfrac{d\omega}{4}\right)^2 + \dfrac{1}{2}\dfrac{m}{5}\left(\dfrac{2d}{4}\omega\right)^2$

$\qquad + \dfrac{1}{2}\dfrac{m}{5}\left(\dfrac{3d}{4}\omega\right)^2 + \dfrac{1}{2}\dfrac{m}{5}(d\omega)^2$

$\qquad = \dfrac{md^2\omega^2}{10}\left[\left(\dfrac{1}{4}\right)^2 + \left(\dfrac{2}{4}\right)^2 \right.$

$\qquad \left. + \left(\dfrac{3}{4}\right)^2 + \left(\dfrac{4}{4}\right)^2\right]$

$\qquad = \dfrac{3}{16}md^2\omega^2$

(c)

Total KE $= \dfrac{1}{2}\dfrac{m}{101}\left(\dfrac{d\omega}{100}\right)^2 + \ldots$

$\qquad = \dfrac{md^2\omega^2}{2\,020\,000} \times (1^2 + 2^2 + \ldots + 100^2)$

$1^2 + 2^2 + \ldots + 100^2$

$= \frac{1}{6} \times 100 \times 101 \times 201$

The total KE is $0.1675md^2\omega^2$.

You will notice in the answers to (a), (b) and (c) a decreasing sequence of coefficients, $\frac{5}{24}$, $\frac{3}{16}$ and 0.1675.

As n increases, this sequence converges; you may like to find its limiting value.

3.6.2 Moment of inertia

3.6 Exercise 2

1 (a) Moment of inertia

$$= 1 \times 0^2 + 1 \times \left(\frac{\sqrt{3}}{2}\right)^2 \times 2 = \frac{3}{2} \, \text{kg m}^2$$

(b) Moment of inertia

$$= 1 \times 0^2 + 1 \times 1^2 + 1 \times 1^2 = 2 \, \text{kg m}^2$$

(c) Moment of inertia

$$= 1 \times 0^2 + 1 \times 0^2 + 1 \times \left(\frac{\sqrt{3}}{2}\right)^2 = \frac{3}{4} \, \text{kg m}^2$$

2 Each element of the cylinder is a distance r from the axis.

Moment of inertia $= Mr^2$

3 (a)

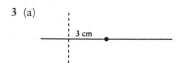

Mass per unit length is $\dfrac{0.010}{0.1}$

$= 0.1 \, \text{kg per metre}$.

Moment of inertia $= \displaystyle\int_{-0.02}^{0.08} 0.1x^2 \, dx$

$$= \left[\frac{0.1x^3}{3}\right]_{-0.02}^{0.08}$$

$$= 1.73 \times 10^{-5} \, \text{kg m}^2$$

(b)

Moment of inertia of small rod about right-hand end is $\frac{4}{3} \times 0.002 \times 0.01^2$.

Moment of inertia of long rod about left-hand end is $\frac{4}{3} \times 0.008 \times 0.04^2$.

Moment of inertia of combined rod

$$= \tfrac{4}{3} \times 0.002 \times 0.01^2 + \tfrac{4}{3} \times 0.008 \times 0.04^2$$

$$= 1.73 \times 10^{-5} \, \text{kg m}^2$$

4 Moment of inertia of a solid sphere about an axis through its centre is $\frac{2}{5}Mr^2$.

Moment of inertia $= \frac{2}{5} \times 5 \times (0.2)^2$

$$= 0.08 \, \text{kg m}^2$$

5 Moment of inertia of each rod $= \frac{4}{3}Ml^2$

Total moment of inertia $= \frac{8}{3}Ml^2$

3.6.3 Conservation of mechanical energy

3.6 A

1 For each particle which is $x \sin \theta$ above the zero level of potential energy and has potential energy

$$\frac{Mg}{n} x \sin \theta,$$

there will be a matching particle below the level of zero potential energy with potential energy

$$-\frac{Mg}{n} x \sin \theta.$$

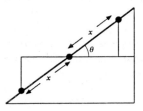

Summing, you can see that the total potential energy of the rod is

$$\sum \left(\frac{Mg}{n} x \sin \theta - \frac{Mg}{n} x \sin \theta \right) = 0$$

2 The potential energy is zero regardless of the value of θ. Thus the orientation does not alter its potential energy.

3.6 Exercise 3

1 The moment of inertia of the pencil is

$$\tfrac{4}{3} m \times 0.075^2 = 0.0075m$$

Initial PE $= mg \times 0.075$

Initial KE $= 0$

Final PE $= 0$

Final KE $= \tfrac{1}{2} I \omega^2$

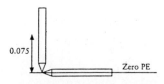

Since mechanical energy is conserved,

$$0.075mg = \frac{0.0075m\omega^2}{2}$$

$$\Rightarrow \quad \omega^2 = 20g \approx 200$$

$$\Rightarrow \quad \omega \approx 14.1 \text{ rad s}^{-1}$$

2 The barrier can be modelled as two rods of lengths 4 metres and 1 metre and masses 16 k and 4 kg, pivoted at their ends. The moment of inertia of the combined barrier about the pivot is therefore

$$\tfrac{4}{3} \times 16 \times 2^2 + \tfrac{4}{3} \times 4 \times \left(\tfrac{1}{2} \right)^2 = \tfrac{260}{3} \text{ kg m}^2$$

Initially, the centre of gravity is 1.5 m above the pivot.

Initial PE $= 20 \times 1.5g$ Final PE $= 0$

Initial KE $= 0$ Final KE $= \tfrac{1}{2} I \omega^2$

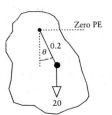

Assuming that no energy is lost at the pivot against air resistance,

$$30g = \tfrac{130}{3} \omega^2$$

$$\omega = 2.63 \text{ rad s}^{-1}$$

3 Let the moment of inertia of the body about the axis of rotation be I.

Initial PE $= -20 \times 0.2 \cos \theta$ Initial KE $= 0$

Final PE $= -20 \times 0.2$ Final KE $= \tfrac{1}{2} I\omega$

$$\tfrac{1}{2} I \omega^2 = 20 \times 0.2(1 - \cos \theta)$$

$$I = \frac{8(1 - \cos \theta)}{\omega^2} \qquad \qquad ①$$

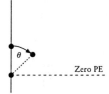

Zero PE

The energy equation for the particle is

$$\tfrac{1}{2} \times 2 \times \omega^2 \times 0.3^2 = 20 \times 0.3(1 - \cos\theta)$$

$$\Rightarrow \quad \omega^2 = \frac{20(1 - \cos\theta)}{0.3}$$

Substituting this value of ω^2 into ①,

$$I = \frac{8(1 - \cos\theta) \times 0.3}{20(1 - \cos\theta)} = 0.12 \,\text{kg m}^2$$

4 (a) Initial PE $= 2000 \times 10 \times 25$

Initial KE $= 0$

Final PE $= 0$

Final KE $= \tfrac{1}{2} I \omega^2$

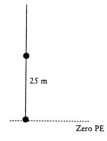

25 m

Zero PE

If the tree is modelled as a rod,

$$I = \tfrac{4}{3} \times 2000 \times 25^2$$

$$= \tfrac{5\,000\,000}{3}$$

By conservation of mechanical energy,

$$\tfrac{1}{2} \times \tfrac{5\,000\,000}{3} \times \omega^2 = 500\,000$$

$$\Rightarrow \quad \omega \approx 0.775 \,\text{rad s}^{-1}$$

(b) $v = \omega r \approx 38.7 \,\text{m s}^{-1}$

(c) A tree may be either heavier at the bottom than at the top, for example a fir tree, or heavier at the top than at the bottom, for example an oak tree.

Taking the first case and exaggerating the model so that the tree is modelled as a particle 10 m from the base of the tree,

$$2000 \times 10 \times 10 = \tfrac{1}{2} \times 2000 \times (10\omega)^2$$

$$\Rightarrow \qquad \omega^2 = 2$$

$$\Rightarrow \qquad \omega = 1.4 \,\text{rad s}^{-1}$$

The true value would lie between 0.775 and 1.4, so the answer in (a) is an underestimate.

In the second case you might model the tree as a particle at the topmost point.

$$2000 \times 10 \times 50 = \tfrac{1}{2} \times 2000 \times (50\omega)^2$$

$$\Rightarrow \qquad \omega^2 = \tfrac{20}{50}$$

$$\Rightarrow \qquad \omega = 0.63 \,\text{rad s}^{-1}$$

In this case the answer in (a) would be an overestimate.

5 Model the rope as a rod. Then its moment of inertia about an axis through one end is

$$\tfrac{4}{3} \times 20 \times 5^2 = \tfrac{2000}{3} \,\text{kg m}^2$$

When the rope is vertical,

$$\omega = \frac{v}{r} = \tfrac{6}{10} = 0.6 \,\text{rad s}^{-1}$$

Zero PE

Suppose that the greatest angle attained with the vertical is θ.

Initial KE $= \tfrac{1}{2} \times \tfrac{2000}{3} \times 0.6^2 + \tfrac{1}{2} \times 25 \times 6^2$

$$= 120 + 450 = 570 \,\text{joules}$$

Gain in PE $= 20g(5 - 5\cos\theta)$

$$+ 25g(10 - 10\cos\theta)$$

$$= 3500(1 - \cos\theta)$$

Final KE $= 0$

$$570 = 3500(1 - \cos\theta)$$

$$1 - \cos\theta = \tfrac{570}{3500} \quad \Rightarrow \quad \theta \approx 33°$$

3.6.4 Parallel axis theorem

3.6 Exercise 4

1 (a) Moment of inertia of a hollow sphere about a diameter $= \frac{2}{3}Mr^2$ kg m^2.

Moment of inertia of the given sphere
$$= \frac{2}{3} \times 10 \times 0.15^2$$
$$= 0.15 \text{ kg m}^2$$

Moment of inertia about an axis 1 metre from its centre
$$= 0.15 + 10 \times 1^2$$
$$= 10.15 \text{ kg m}^2$$

(b) Moment of inertia about diameter
$$= \frac{2}{5}Mr^2$$
$$= \frac{2}{5} \times 10 \times 0.15^2 = 0.09 \text{ kg m}^2$$

Moment of inertia about axis 1 metre away
$$= 0.09 + 10 \times 1^2 = 10.09 \text{ kg m}^2$$

2 Moment of inertia about axis through centre
$$= \frac{1}{2}Mr^2 = \frac{1}{8} \text{ kg m}^2$$

Moment of inertia about axis through point on circumference
$$= \frac{1}{8} + 1 \times \left(\frac{1}{2}\right)^2$$
$$= \frac{3}{8} \text{ kg m}^2$$

3 (a) Moment of inertia of a sphere about its centre is
$$\frac{2}{5}Mr^2 = \frac{2}{5} \times 0.1 \times 0.05^2 = 0.0001 \text{ kg m}^2$$

Moment of inertia of sphere about O is

$0.0001 + 0.1 \times 0.55^2 = 0.030\,35 \text{ kg m}^2$

Moment of inertia of rod about O is

$\frac{1}{3} \times 0.1 \times 0.5^2 = 0.008\,33 \text{ kg m}^2$

Moment of inertia of baton is

$0.030\,35 + 0.030\,35 + 0.008\,33 = 0.069 \text{ kg m}^2$

(b) Using the parallel axis theorem, the moment of inertia of the baton about a point through the centre of a sphere is

$0.069 + 0.3 \times 0.55^2 = 0.160 \text{ kg m}^2$

4 (a) Moment of inertia of disc about its centre is

$$\frac{1}{4}Mr^2 = \frac{1}{4} \times 0.2 \times 0.03^2$$
$$= 0.000\,045 \text{ kg m}^2$$

Moment of inertia of disc about O is

$0.000\,09 + 0.2 \times 0.8^2 \approx 0.128 \text{ kg m}^2$

Moment of inertia of rod about axis through O is

$\frac{4}{3} \times 0.1 \times 0.5^2 \approx 0.033 \text{ kg m}^2$

Moment of inertia of system about axis through O is

$0.128 + 0.033 = 0.161 \text{ kg m}^2$

(b) As the disc moves nearer O, the moment of inertia decreases.

5 Moment of inertia about the axis is 5.5 kg m^2.

Moment of inertia about a parallel axis through the centre is

$5.5 - 12 \times 0.5^2 = 2.5 \text{ kg m}^2$

Moment of inertia about parallel axis 20 cm from centre is

$2.5 + 12 \times 0.2^2 = 2.98 \text{ kg m}^2$

3.6.5 Perpendicular axes theorem

3.6 A

(a) Moment of inertia of the ring about a diameter is $\frac{1}{2}Mr^2$.

Moment of inertia of the ring about a perpendicular diameter is $\frac{1}{2}Mr^2$.

So the moment of inertia of the ring about an axis through the centre perpendicular to the ring should be

$$\tfrac{1}{2}Mr^2 + \tfrac{1}{2}Mr^2 = Mr^2$$

(b) Moment of inertia of square of side $2a$ about an axis in the plane through the centre is $\frac{1}{3}Ma^2$.

Moment of inertia of square of side $2a$ about a perpendicular axis in the plane through the centre is $\frac{1}{3}Ma^2$.

Moment of inertia of square about an axis through the centre perpendicular to the lamina should be $\frac{2}{3}Ma^2$.

3.6 Exercise 5

1 Moment of inertia about AD is $\frac{1}{3}Ma^2$.

Moment of inertia about AB is $\frac{1}{3}Mb^2$.

So the moment of inertia about an axis through A perpendicular to the lamina is

$$\tfrac{1}{3}Ma^2 + \tfrac{1}{3}Mb^2 = \tfrac{1}{3}M(a^2 + b^2)$$

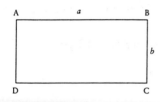

2 Moment of inertia of a disc with radius r about an axis through its centre perpendicular to the disc is $\frac{1}{2}Mr^2$.

The whole disc from which the quadrant is cut has mass $4 \times 3 = 12\,\text{kg}$, so its moment of inertia would be

$$\tfrac{1}{2} \times 12 \times (0.4)^2 = 0.96\,\text{kg m}^2$$

Hence the moment of inertia of the quadrant about the same axis is

$$\tfrac{1}{4} \times 0.96 = 0.24\,\text{kg m}^2$$

If the moment of inertia of the quadrant about a straight edge is $I\,\text{kg m}^2$, then by the perpendicular axes theorem

$$2I = 0.24$$

so $I = 0.12$.

[Note that the question can be answered more simply using the formula for the moment of inertia of a disc about a diameter.]

3 Area of outside circle $= \pi \times 2^2 = 4\pi$

Area of inside circle $= \pi \times 1^2 = 1\pi$

Mass of complete disc $= \dfrac{4M}{3}$

Mass of disc cut out $= \dfrac{M}{3}$

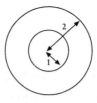

Moment of inertia of complete disc about a perpendicular axis through its centre is

$$\frac{1}{2} \times \frac{4M}{3} \times 2^2 = \frac{8M}{3}$$

Moment of inertia of disc removed about same axis is

$$\frac{1}{2} \times \frac{M}{3} \times 1^2 = \frac{M}{6}$$

Moment of inertia of turntable is

$$\frac{8M}{3} - \frac{M}{6} = \frac{5}{2}M$$

If the moment of inertia of the turntable about a diameter is I, then $\frac{5}{2}M = I + I$ by the perpendicular axes theorem. Hence the moment of inertia of the turntable about a diameter is $\frac{5}{4}M$.

[Again, the question can be solved without using the perpendicular axes theorem.]

4 (a) Moment of inertia of disc about the axis is

$$\frac{1}{2} \times 0.03 \times 0.08^2 + 0.03 \times 0.18^2 = 0.001\,068$$

Moment of inertia of rod about the axis is

$$\frac{4}{3} \times 0.03 \times 0.05^2 = 0.0001$$

Total moment of inertia $= 0.001\,168\,\text{kg}\,\text{m}^2$

Initial PE $= 0.03 \times 10 \times 0.18$

$$+ 0.03 \times 10 \times 0.05 = 0.069$$

Final PE $= 0$

Initial KE $= 0$ Final KE $= \frac{1}{2}I\omega^2$

Assuming mechanical energy is conserved,

$$0.069 = \frac{1}{2} \times 0.001\,168\omega^2$$

$$\Rightarrow \quad \omega^2 = 118.15$$

$$\Rightarrow \quad \omega = 10.9\,\text{rad}\,\text{s}^{-1}$$

(b) Moment of inertia of disc about the axis is

$$\frac{0.03}{4} \times 0.08^2 + 0.03 \times 0.18^2 - 0.001\,02\,\text{kg}\,\text{m}^2$$

Moment of inertia of rod about the axis
$$= 0.0001\,\text{kg}\,\text{m}^2$$

Total moment of inertia $= 0.001\,12\,\text{kg}\,\text{m}^2$

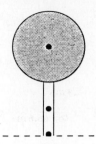

Assuming mechanical energy is conserved,

$$0.069 = \frac{1}{2} \times 0.001\,12\omega^2$$

$$\Rightarrow \quad \omega^2 = 123.2$$

$$\Rightarrow \quad \omega = 11.1\,\text{rad}\,\text{s}^{-1}$$

The bat should fall faster when allowed to fall in this way. However, air resistance will not be negligible in this case and so the model would need to be modified.

Miscellaneous exercise 3

1 Components in newtons are
   $(0, 360)$, $(0, 1110)$, $(375, 735)$, $(-375, 735$

2 (a) 27 N   (b) 64°

3 26°

4 (a) 28.6°   (b) 2320 N

5 (a) 0.083 rad s^{-1} (b) 2.08 m s^{-2}

6 4.17 m s^{-1}

7 Let initial speed $= \begin{bmatrix} 4 \times 10^{-5} \\ 0 \end{bmatrix}$,

   final speed $= \begin{bmatrix} 0 \\ 6 \times 10^{-5} \end{bmatrix}$

   (a) $10^{-25} \begin{bmatrix} -4 \\ 6 \end{bmatrix}$ (b) 10^{-19} J

8 (a) 9.65×10^7 J   (b) 4.82×10^5 N

9 19 m s^{-1}

10 2.6 m s^{-1},   600 J

11 (a) $4.93 \, \text{m s}^{-1}$, $74.7 \, \text{J}$, $913 \, \text{N}$

    (b) $1870 \, \text{J}$, $4 \, \text{cm}$

12 (a) $12.6 \, \text{kN}$ (b) $37 \, \text{cm}$

13 $4.9 \times 10^4 \, \text{J}$, $4.4 \, \text{m s}^{-1}$

14 (a) $6.32 \, \text{m s}^{-1}$ (b) $66.6 \, \text{m s}^{-1}$

15 $4 \, \text{m s}^{-1}$

16 $240 \, \text{J}$

17 (a) $\begin{bmatrix} -30 \\ 40 \\ 20 \end{bmatrix} \, \text{N}$ (b) $\begin{bmatrix} 1 \\ 4 \\ 1 \end{bmatrix} \, \text{m s}^{-1}$

18 (a) $-2 \, \text{J}$ (b) $13 \, \text{J}$ (c) $-3 \, \text{J}$

    (d) Work done by weight $= 353 \, \text{J}$;
    work done by $\mathbf{R} = 0 \, \text{J}$

19 $14 \, \text{m s}^{-1}$

20 (a) $125\,000 \, \text{J}$ (b) $\approx 110\,000 \, \text{N}$

21 $33.1 \, \text{cm}$

22 (a) $v = \sqrt{(u^2 - 2gh)}$ (b) $T = \dfrac{m}{l}(u^2 - 5gl)$

23 (a) $T \approx 1600 \, \text{N}$ (b) $h \approx 6.5 \, \text{m}$

24 $0.855 \, \text{m s}^{-1}$, $1.25 \, \text{m s}^{-1}$, $1.53 \, \text{m s}^{-1}$,
    $1.77 \, \text{m s}^{-1}$, $1.98 \, \text{m s}^{-1}$
    If the marble were to stay in contact with
    the bowl, $R = 0.0078 \, \text{N}$, $-0.0039 \, \text{N}$,
    $-0.016 \, \text{N}$, $-0.027 \, \text{N}$, $-0.039 \, \text{N}$.
    But R cannot be negative, so the marble
    flies off when R first reaches $0 \, \text{N}$ and R
    then remains at $0 \, \text{N}$.
    For the bead on a wire, the negative values
    above now apply, since R can be directed
    inwards.

25 (a) Thrust $= 665 \, \text{N}$,   tension $= 3450 \, \text{N}$

    (b) Thrust $= 602 \, \text{N}$,   tension $= 3510 \, \text{N}$

    (c) $2.86 \, \text{rad s}^{-1}$, $4120 \, \text{N}$

26E $0.35 \, \text{J}$

27E (a) $103\,200 \, \text{kg m}^2$ (b) $1.88 \, \text{m}$ (c) $1.84 \, \text{m}$

4 MODELLING WITH DIFFERENTIAL EQUATIONS

4.1 Modelling resisted motion

4.1.1 Resistance to motion

4.1 A

1 The ball of paper falls to the ground more
   quickly. The sheet of paper tends to glide
   from side to side.

   Assuming the ball of paper is made from a
   single sheet, then both objects have the same
   weight acting vertically downwards.
   However, the greater cross-sectional area of
   the sheet of paper means that there is a
   greater resistance to its motion through the
   air.

2 At high speed you would feel a substantial
   force pushing back on your hand. The force
   increases as the car's speed increases.

3 The force is called air resistance or drag and
   arises from movement through the air.

4 The drag force increases as either the area of
   the object or its speed increases.

4.1 Exercise 1

1 (a) A sky-diver free-falling.

   (b) The person and the rhinoceros using
       parachutes. The parachute has such a
       large cross-sectional area that the models
       for air resistance would have virtually the
       same value for k.

2 Assume that resistance is proportional to surface area.

For A: surface area $= 8\,\text{m}^2$
resistance $= 16v$ newtons

For B: surface area $= 2\,\text{m}^2$
resistance $= 4v$ newtons

3 Though the cross-sectional areas are the same, the shape of the object affects the resistance to motion. The cone falling point first is more aerodynamic and would experience a smaller resistance to motion.

4.1.2 Modelling a sky-diver's descent

4.1 B

1

Direction of motion

600

2 By Newton's second law,

$$600 - Kv = 60\,\frac{dv}{dt}$$

At terminal speed,

$$\frac{dv}{dt} = 0$$

$$\Rightarrow \quad 600 = K \times 50$$

$$\Rightarrow \quad K = 12$$

3 Substituting K into the equation of motion,

$$600 - 12v = 60\,\frac{dv}{dt}$$

$$\Rightarrow \quad 10 - \frac{12}{60}v = \frac{dv}{dt}$$

$$\Rightarrow \quad \frac{dv}{dt} = 10 - 0.2v$$

4.1 C

1 Assumptions are:

- the sky-diver is a particle of mass 60 kg;
- her terminal speed is $50\,\text{m s}^{-1}$;
- gravity is constant and $g = 10\,\text{m s}^{-2}$;
- let $v\,\text{m s}^{-1}$ be her speed and h metres the height at time t.

kv^2

Direction of motion

mg

Using Newton's second law downwards,

$$mg - kv^2 = m\,\frac{dv}{dt}$$

At terminal speed,

$$mg = kv^2 \quad \Rightarrow \quad k = \frac{mg}{v^2}$$

Using $m = 60$, $g = 10$ and $v = 50$

$$\Rightarrow \quad k = 0.24$$

Substituting values into the equation of motion,

$$60\,\frac{dv}{dt} = 600 - 0.24v^2$$

$$\Rightarrow \quad \frac{dv}{dt} = 10 - 0.004v^2$$

2

Time	Velocity	Acceleration	Height
t_n	v_n	a_n	h_n
0	0	10	3700
0.1	1.00	10.000	3700.0
0.2	2.00	9.996	3699.9
0.3	3.00	9.984	3699.7
0.4	4.00	9.964	3699.4
0.5	4.99	9.936	3699.0
0.6	5.99	9.900	3698.5
0.7	6.98	9.857	3697.9
0.8	7.96	9.805	3697.2
0.9	8.94	9.746	3696.4
1.0	9.92	9.680	3695.5
...	...	...	...

3

Time t_n	Velocity v_n	Acceleration a_n	Height h_n
2.0	19.19	8.66	3681.3
3.0	27.21	7.20	3658.4
4.0	33.69	5.61	3628.2
5.0	38.64	4.16	3592.1
...	...	...	...
10.0	48.48	0.62	3367.5
15.0	49.82	0.08	3120.8
20.0	49.98	0.01	2871.2
25.0	50.00	0	2621.2
30.0	50.00	0	2371.2
35.0	50.00	0	2121.2
40.0	50.00	0	1871.2
45.0	50.00	0	1621.2
50.0	50.00	0	1371.2
55.0	50	0	1121.2
60.0	50	0	871.2
65.0	50	0	621.2
65.2	50	0	611.2

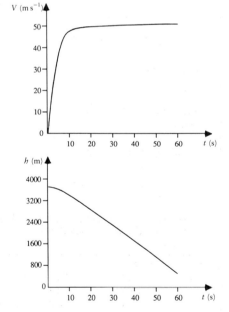

4 The sky-diver is almost at terminal speed from about 15 seconds onwards.

5 The parachute is opened at 610 metres, so the sky-diver has had about 65 seconds of free-fall.

6 In the article, the free-fall time is at most one minute long, which is just under the value calculated. In the model, a terminal speed of

$50\,\mathrm{m\,s^{-1}}$ was used, which is slightly slower than the speed in the text. Using this higher speed in the calculation would give a shorter free-fall time.

The time to reach terminal speed is given as approximately 8 seconds. In the model, terminal speed is not reached until after approximately 15 seconds. However, after 8 seconds the sky-diver is falling at $46.5\,\mathrm{m\,s^{-1}}$ which is approaching her terminal speed.

7E A smaller step size will increase the accuracy. As the step size tends to zero, the solution should tend to a limit.

4.1 Exercise 2

1 (a) By Newton's second law,

$$0.45 - 0.3v = 0.045\,\frac{\mathrm{d}v}{\mathrm{d}t}$$

$$\Rightarrow\quad 10 - \tfrac{300}{45}v = \frac{\mathrm{d}v}{\mathrm{d}t}$$

$$\Rightarrow\quad \frac{\mathrm{d}v}{\mathrm{d}t} = 10 - \tfrac{20}{3}v$$

(b) Using the relations

$$t_{n+1} = t_n + 0.01 \qquad v_{n+1} = v_n + 0.01a_n$$
$$a_{n+1} = 10 - \tfrac{20}{3}v_n \qquad h_{n+1} = h_n - 0.01v_n$$

you should produce the table below:

Time t_n	Speed v_n	Acceleration a_n	Height h_n
0	0	10	12
0.01	0.1	10.0	12.0
0.02	0.2	9.3	12.0
0.03	0.3	8.7	12.0
0.04	0.4	8.0	12.0
...	...	...	...
8.13	1.5	0.0	0.015
8.14	1.5	0.0	0.000
8.15	1.5	0.0	−0.015

The time taken for the mouse to fall 12 metres is approximately 8.14 seconds.

(c) The mouse's speed on impact is $1.5\,\mathrm{m\,s^{-1}}$.

(d) $\delta t = 0.005$ gives a time of 8.145 seconds; $\delta t = 0.001$ gives a time of 8.149 seconds.

(Note that if you assumed the mouse falls with a constant speed of $1.5\,\mathrm{m\,s^{-1}}$, this would give a time of fall of 8 seconds.)

2 (a)

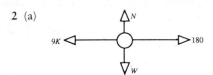

(b) At maximum speed,

$$9K = 180 \quad \Rightarrow \quad K = 20$$

(c) By Newton's second law,

$$180 - 20v = 60\,\frac{dv}{dt}$$

$$\Rightarrow \quad 9 - v = 3\,\frac{dv}{dt}$$

3 (a) The main assumptions are,

- the skier is a particle;
- the resistance is modelled as $R = kv^2$;
- the gradient of the slope is constant.

(b) At terminal speed,

$$\frac{dv}{dt} = 0 \quad \Rightarrow \quad 65g\sin 20^\circ - 0.5v^2 = 0$$

$$\Rightarrow \quad v \approx 21$$

The terminal speed is $21\,\mathrm{m\,s^{-1}}$ ($76\,\mathrm{km\,h^{-1}}$).

4 (a)

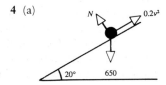

By Newton's second law along the slope,

$$650\sin 20^\circ - 0.2v^2 = 65\,\frac{dv}{dt}$$

At terminal speed,

$$0.2v^2 = 650\sin 20^\circ$$

$$\Rightarrow \quad v = 33.3$$

The new terminal speed is $33.3\,\mathrm{m\,s^{-1}}$ (approximately $120\,\mathrm{km\,h^{-1}}$).

(b) Use a step-by-step method with

$$a = 10\sin 20^\circ - \frac{v^2}{325}, \quad v + a\,\delta t \to v$$

and $h + v\,\delta t \to h$.

A step size of 0.1 gives $h = 2500$ at time 81.8 seconds.

4.1.3 Terminal speed

4.1 D

1 $R = Kv$

At terminal speed,

$$mg = Kw \quad \Rightarrow \quad w = \frac{mg}{K}$$

$R = kv^2$

At terminal speed,

$$mg = kw^2 \quad \Rightarrow \quad w^2 = \frac{mg}{k}$$

$$\Rightarrow \quad w = \sqrt{\left(\frac{mg}{k}\right)}$$

2 The terminal speed increases with mass and gravity but decreases as K or k increases. If the model is $R = Kv$, then terminal speed is directly proportional to the mass. However, if the model is $R = kv^2$, then the terminal speed increases more and more slowly as mass increases.

For a mouse, a small increase in mass, for example 10 grams, will have a large effect on its terminal speed. A similar increase in a sky-diver's mass has very little effect on her terminal speed.

3 A sky-diver can change her terminal speed by altering her position as she falls, so that more or less surface area is presented to the oncoming air, and by making her shape more aerodynamic. These adjustments would alter the value of k in the resistance model.

4 The parachute has a much greater area than the sky-diver, so that k is much greater. A large value of k, with m and g unchanged, results in a slower terminal speed.

5 On the Moon, gravity is less than on Earth. However, there is no air on the Moon so k is approximately zero in the model. Hence the terminal speed is very large, and in practice the speed on impact would depend on the initial altitude.

6 When two sky-divers link up, the resulting 'body' has double the mass and double the surface area. Since $\dfrac{m}{k}$ remains constant there should be no change in terminal speed.

4.1 Exercise 3

1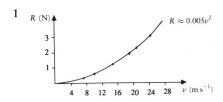

2 (a)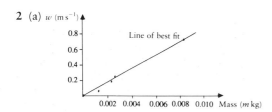

(b) $w = 85m$ seems to fit the data best. This suggests that the most appropriate model is $R = Kv$.

(c) At terminal speed,

$$mg = Kw \implies w = \frac{g}{K}m$$

$$\implies \frac{g}{K} = 85$$

$$\implies K \approx 0.118$$

3 (a) 2 A4 sheets: Double the mass,
  the same area
  Terminal speed $= 2w$

(b) A3 sheet: Double the mass,
  double the area
  Terminal speed $= w$

(c) $\frac{1}{2}$ A4 sheet: Half the mass,
  half the area
  Terminal speed $= w$

(d) Folded A4 sheet: The same mass,
  half the area
  Terminal speed $= 2w$

In practice, the sheets do not fall vertically but glide from side to side and are tilted at an angle to the horizontal. The results above are therefore only rough approximations to what would happen.

4 (a) Speed of car relative to headwind is $(v + 10)$. So the equation of motion is now

$$T - K(v + 10) = m\,\frac{dv}{dt}$$

(b) The car's maximum speed will be $10\,\mathrm{m\,s^{-1}}$ less than it would be in still air.

(c) The car in the slipstream experiences reduced air resistance, so it is possible to accelerate in the slipstream to a greater speed than the car in front. The rear car can then pull out to overtake before the air resistance slows it down.

4.1.4 Another force – upthrust

4.1 E

1 Upthrust depends on the volume of the airship, the density of air and the value of g. Assuming the airship has a fixed envelope of gas and is not an inflatable or hot air balloon, then the volume would remain reasonably constant. (If this were not the case the volume would increase as the pressure of the surrounding air decreases.) As the airship rises, the surrounding air becomes considerably less dense. At 18 km above the Earth's surface, the gravitational attraction will be only slightly smaller than near the surface. The result will be that the upthrust force will decrease as the airship rises, and at some point will equal the weight of the airship.

2 The upthrust is equal to the weight of air displaced. The density of a cannon-ball made of iron is approximately $8000 \, \text{kg m}^{-3}$, over 6000 times denser than the displaced air. Thus the upthrust is about $\frac{1}{6000}$ of the weight of the cannon-ball and can be ignored.

The density of helium in the balloon is approximately $0.18 \, \text{kg m}^{-3}$. The weight of the displaced air is greater than the combined weight of the balloon and the helium inside it, so the upthrust force is greater than the weight and cannot be ignored.

4.1 Exercise 4

1 (a) Volume of sphere,
$$V = \tfrac{4}{3}\pi \times \tfrac{1}{1000} \, \text{m}^3$$

Weight of lead sphere
$$= 11\,000Vg = \tfrac{440}{3}\pi \, \text{newtons}$$

Weight of iron sphere
$$= 8000Vg = \tfrac{320}{3}\pi \, \text{newtons}$$

Weight of water displaced
$$= 1000Vg = \tfrac{40}{3}\pi \, \text{newtons}$$

$$W - R - U = m\,\frac{dv}{dt}$$

For the lead sphere,

$$\tfrac{440}{3}\pi - 16v - \tfrac{40}{3}\pi = \tfrac{44}{3}\pi\,\frac{dv}{dt}$$

$$\Rightarrow \quad \tfrac{400}{3}\pi - 16v = \tfrac{44}{3}\pi\,\frac{dv}{dt}$$

For the iron sphere,

$$\tfrac{320}{3}\pi - 16v - \tfrac{40}{3}\pi = \tfrac{32}{3}\pi\,\frac{dv}{dt}$$

$$\Rightarrow \quad \tfrac{280}{3}\pi - 16v = \tfrac{32}{3}\pi\,\frac{dv}{dt}$$

(b) At terminal speed, $\dfrac{dv}{dt} = 0$

For the lead sphere,

$$\tfrac{400}{3}\pi = 16v \quad \Rightarrow \quad v = 26.18$$

The terminal speed is $26.18 \, \text{m s}^{-1}$.

For the iron sphere,

$$\tfrac{280}{3}\pi = 16v \quad \Rightarrow \quad v = 18.33$$

The terminal speed is $18.33 \, \text{m s}^{-1}$.

2 Assume that your body can be approximated to a cylinder.

For example,

volume = height × area of cross-section
$$= 1.70 \times \pi \times 0.12 \times 0.12$$
$$= 0.077 \, \text{m}^3$$

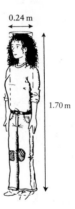

0.24 m

1.70 m

(a) $0.077 \times 10 \times 1.29 \approx 1 \, \text{newton}$

(b) When you are floating you are in equilibrium, so the upthrust force is equal to your weight. For example, if your mass is 60 kg, then the upthrust is 600 newtons.

(c) $0.077 \times 10 \times 1000 = 770 \, \text{newtons}$

3 (a) $U = 2200 \times 10 \times 1.29 = 28\,380 \, \text{newtons}$

(b)

$$U - W - R = m\,\frac{dv}{dt}$$

$$\Rightarrow \quad 820 - R = 2756\,\frac{dv}{dt}$$

Initially the balloon is at rest, so the air resistance $R = 0$.

$$\Rightarrow \quad \frac{dv}{dt} = \frac{820}{2756} = 0.2975$$

The initial acceleration is $0.3 \, \text{m s}^{-2}$ upwards.

(c) As the balloon rises, the resistance will increase. Eventually the resistance force and weight of the balloon will equal the upthrust. The balloon will continue to rise with constant speed.

(d) The upthrust will decrease as the balloon rises and the density of air decreases and so the balloon will eventually reach an equilibrium height.

4.2 Analytical methods
4.2.1 Motion at low speeds

4.2 A

1

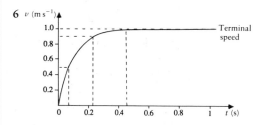

By Newton's second law,

$$m\frac{dv}{dt} = mg - Kv$$

At terminal speed, $Kw = mg$

$$\Rightarrow \quad K = \frac{mg}{w}$$

2 $m\dfrac{dv}{dt} = mg - Kv \quad \Rightarrow \quad m\dfrac{dv}{dt} = mg - \dfrac{mg}{w}v$

$$\Rightarrow \quad \frac{dv}{dt} = g\left(1 - \frac{v}{w}\right)$$

3 (a) $v < w$ The feather is falling more slowly than terminal speed. However,

$$\frac{dv}{dt} > 0$$

so the feather is accelerating downwards. As its speed increases the acceleration decreases to zero.

(b) $v = w$ The feather is falling at terminal speed and so there is no acceleration.

(c) $v > w$ The feather is moving faster than its terminal speed. Since

$$\frac{dv}{dt} < 0$$

the feather is decelerating. It will slow down until it is moving at its terminal speed.

4 $\dfrac{dv}{dt} = \dfrac{g}{w}(w - v)$

Separating variables,

$$\int_0^v \frac{1}{w - v}\, dv = \int_0^t \frac{g}{w}\, dt$$

$$\Rightarrow \quad -\ln|w - v| + \ln|w| = \frac{gt}{w}$$

$$\Rightarrow \quad \ln\left|\frac{w - v}{w}\right| = -\frac{gt}{w}$$

$$\Rightarrow \quad \frac{w - v}{w} = e^{-gt/w}$$

$$\Rightarrow \quad v = w(1 - e^{-gt/w})$$

5 As $t \to +\infty$, then the limit of $e^{-gt/w}$ is 0. Thus the limit of the feather's speed v as $t \to \infty$ is the terminal speed w. However, this is never achieved exactly in finite time.

6

The time taken to reach:

(a) 50% is 0.07 second,

(b) 90% is 0.23 second,

(c) 99% is 0.46 second.

7 The results show how quickly the feather approaches terminal speed. In less than 0.5 second it has reached 99% of its terminal speed. However, this is twice the time taken to reach 90%.

In practice, it is not reasonable to discuss the speed of a feather to very great accuracy since it will vary considerably according to air disturbances not accounted for in this simple model.

8 (a) By the chain rule,

$$\frac{dv}{dt} = \frac{dv}{dx} \times \frac{dx}{dt}$$

$$\Rightarrow \quad \frac{dv}{dt} = \frac{dv}{dx} \times v = v\frac{dv}{dx}$$

(b) $v\dfrac{dv}{dx} = g\left(1 - \dfrac{v}{w}\right)$

9 $\dfrac{v}{v-w} = \dfrac{v-w}{v-w} + \dfrac{w}{v-w} = 1 + \dfrac{w}{v-w}$

$$v\frac{dv}{dx} = \frac{-g}{w}(v-w)$$

$$\Rightarrow \quad \int \frac{v}{v-w}\,dv = \int \frac{-g}{w}\,dx$$

$$\Rightarrow \quad \int\left(1 + \frac{w}{v-w}\right)dv = -\frac{gx}{w} + C$$

$$\Rightarrow \quad v + w\ln|v-w| = -\frac{gx}{w} + C$$

Initial conditions are

$$v = 0, \quad x = 0 \quad \Rightarrow \quad C = w\ln|w|$$

Then

$$v + w\ln|v-w| = -\frac{gx}{w} + w\ln|w|$$

$$\Rightarrow \quad v + w\ln\left|\frac{v-w}{w}\right| = -\frac{gx}{w}$$

$$\Rightarrow \quad x = \frac{-w}{g}\left(v + w\ln\left|\frac{v-w}{w}\right|\right)$$

10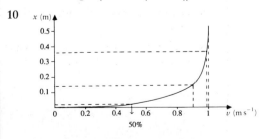

11 From the graph, the distance taken to reach:

(a) 50% of terminal speed is 0.02 m;

(b) 90% of terminal speed is 0.14 m;

(c) 99% of terminal speed is 0.36 m.

4.2 Exercise 1

1 (a) The forces are upthrust, weight and air resistance.

By Newton's second law,

$$U - W - R = m\frac{dv}{dt}$$

$$U - 0.2 - 0.5v = 0.02\frac{dv}{dt}$$

The upthrust force is 1.2 N.

(b) $\dfrac{dv}{dt} = 0 \quad \Rightarrow \quad 1 - 0.5v = 0$

The terminal speed is $2\,\mathrm{m\,s^{-1}}$.

2 (a)

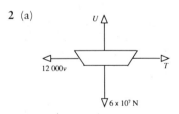

U is the upthrust.

T is the tension in the cable.

(b) At a constant speed, $T = 12\,000v$

When $v = 1.5$, the tension in the cable is 18 000 N.

3 (a)

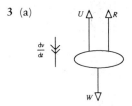

By Newton's second law,

$$W - R - U = m \frac{dv}{dt}$$

$$\Rightarrow \quad 1.1 - 0.7v - 0.12 = 0.11 \frac{dv}{dt}$$

$$\Rightarrow \qquad \frac{dv}{dt} = \frac{98 - 70v}{11}$$

(b) $\frac{dv}{dt} = 0 \Rightarrow v = 1.4$

The terminal speed is $1.4 \, \text{m s}^{-1}$.

(c) $\int_0^v \frac{1}{98 - 70v} \, dv = \int_0^t \frac{1}{11} \, dt$

$$\Rightarrow \quad \ln \left| \frac{98 - 70v}{98} \right| = -\frac{70}{11} t$$

$$\Rightarrow \qquad\qquad v = 1.4(1 - e^{-70t/11})$$

Integrating again,

$$x = \int_0^t 1.4(1 - e^{-70t/11}) \, dt$$

$$= 1.4(t + \tfrac{11}{70} e^{-70t/11} - \tfrac{11}{70})$$

(d) Using a graphical calculator, the value of t for which $x = 12$ can be found to be approximately 8.7. The chick therefore takes 8.7 seconds to fall to the ground.

4 (a) By Newton's second law,

$$0.06 - 0.05v = 0.006 \frac{dv}{dt}$$

$$\Rightarrow \qquad \frac{dv}{dt} = \frac{10}{6}(6 - 5v)$$

$$\int_0^v \frac{1}{6 - 5v} \, dv = \int_0^t \frac{10}{6} \, dt$$

$$\Rightarrow \quad -\tfrac{1}{5} \ln \left| \frac{6 - 5v}{6} \right| = \frac{10t}{6}$$

$$\Rightarrow \qquad\qquad v = 1.2(1 - e^{-25t/3})$$

As $t \to +\infty$, $v \to 1.2$

The terminal speed of the feather is $1.2 \, \text{m s}^{-1}$.

(b) $1 - e^{-25t/3} = 0.99$

$$\Rightarrow \quad t = 0.5526$$

The time taken is 0.55 second.

(c) For the marble,

$$30 = \tfrac{1}{2} \times 10 \times t^2$$

The marble takes 2.45 seconds.

For the feather,

$$x = \int_0^t 1.2(1 - e^{-25t/3}) \, dt$$

$$x = 1.2(t + \tfrac{3}{25} e^{-25t/3} - \tfrac{3}{25})$$

In the first 0.55 second the feather falls 0.52 m. The feather falls the remaining distance at approximately $1.2 \, \text{m s}^{-1}$ and so the time taken to fall 30 m is

$$0.55 + \frac{30 - 0.52}{1.2} = 25.12 \text{ seconds}$$

(d) The speed of the marble on impact is $24.5 \, \text{m s}^{-1}$.

The speed of the feather on impact is its terminal speed, $1.2 \, \text{m s}^{-1}$.

4.2.2 Motion at high speeds

4.2 **B**

1 Possible assumptions are:

- the sky-diver is a particle of mass 60 kg;
- there is no wind;
- the sky-diver is travelling initially with speed $50 \, \text{m s}^{-1}$;
- the parachute opens instantaneously;
- the terminal speed with the parachute is $5 \, \text{m s}^{-1}$;
- a safe landing speed is $5.5 \, \text{m s}^{-1}$ (equivalent to jumping from a height of 1.5 metres).

2

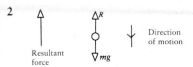

3 At terminal speed,

$$mg = kW^2 \quad \Rightarrow \quad k = \frac{mg}{W^2}$$

Then

$$mg - mg\frac{v^2}{W^2} = mv\frac{dv}{dx}$$

$$\Rightarrow \int_U^v \frac{v}{g(1 - v^2/W^2)}\,dv = \int_0^x dx$$

$$\Rightarrow \frac{W^2}{g}\int_U^v \frac{v}{W^2 - v^2}\,dv = \frac{-W^2}{2g}\Big[\ln|W^2 - v^2|\Big]_U^v$$

$$= x$$

$$\Rightarrow \quad x = \frac{-W^2}{2g}\ln\left|\frac{W^2 - v^2}{W^2 - U^2}\right|$$

4 For a safe landing speed of V, the distance fallen is

$$H = \frac{-W^2}{2g}\ln\left|\frac{W^2 - V^2}{W^2 - U^2}\right|$$

Using the values $W = 5$, $V = 5.5$, $g = 10$ and $U = 50$, the least height at which the parachute can be opened is found to be 7.7 metres.

5 The value obtained is considerably lower than that suggested as a safe height. In practice, time must be allowed for the parachute to open. Furthermore, there must be a safety margin to allow time for the first parachute to fail to open and for a reserve parachute to be used. Even at a height of 610 m, the sky-diver has only 12 seconds before impact when travelling at $50\,\mathrm{m\,s^{-1}}$.

4.2 Exercise 2

1 (a)
$$-1 - 0.0025v^2 = 0.1v\frac{dv}{dx}$$

$$\Rightarrow \quad -400 - v^2 = 40v\frac{dv}{dx}$$

$$\int_{12}^0 \frac{40v}{400 + v^2}\,dv = \int_1^H -1\,dx$$

$$\Rightarrow \quad \Big[\tfrac{40}{2}\ln(400 + v^2)\Big]_{12}^0 = -H + 1$$

The maximum height is 7.15 metres.

(b) When $R = 0$,
$$144 = 2g(H - 1) \quad \Rightarrow \quad H = 8.2$$

The air resistance reduces the maximum height by more than a metre.

2 (a) $-\lambda v^2 = 1200\dfrac{dv}{dt} \quad \Rightarrow \quad \dfrac{dv}{dt} = -\dfrac{\lambda}{1200}v^2$

(b) Separating variables,

$$\int_{30}^v \frac{1}{v^2}\,dv = \int_0^t -\frac{\lambda}{1200}\,dt$$

$$\Big[-\frac{1}{v}\Big]_{30}^v = \Big[-\frac{\lambda t}{1200}\Big]_0^t \quad \Rightarrow \quad v = \frac{1200}{\lambda t + 40}$$

(c) Substituting $t = 5$, $v = 10 \quad \Rightarrow \quad \lambda = 16$
For speed $v = 5$,

$$5 = \frac{1200}{40 + 16t} \quad \Rightarrow \quad t = 12.5$$

The boat takes 12.5 seconds to slow down to $5\,\mathrm{m\,s^{-1}}$.

3 (a) By Newton's second law,

$$800\sin 30° - 0.64v^2 = 80v\frac{dv}{dx}$$

$$\Rightarrow \quad v\frac{dv}{dx} = 5 - 0.008v^2$$

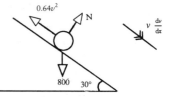

Separating variables,

$$\int_0^v \frac{v}{5 - 0.008v^2}\,dv = \int_0^{85} 1\,dx$$

$$\Rightarrow \quad \frac{-1}{0.016}\Big[\ln(5 - 0.008v^2)\Big]_0^v = 85$$

$$\Rightarrow \quad v = 21.55$$

The speed of the jumper at the end of the ramp is $21.6\,\mathrm{m\,s^{-1}}$.

(b) As the jumper leaves the ramp, the skis tilt and the area presented to the oncoming air increases. The air resistance is likely to increase.

4 (a) By Newton's second law,

$$-36v^2 - 144 = 1800 \frac{dv}{dt}$$

$$\Rightarrow \quad \frac{dv}{dt} = \frac{-(4 + v^2)}{50}$$

(b) Separating variables,

$$\int_{28}^{0} \frac{1}{4 + v^2} \, dv = \int_{0}^{t} -\frac{1}{50} \, dt$$

$$\Rightarrow \quad \left[\frac{1}{2} \tan^{-1}\left(\frac{v}{2} \right) \right]_{28}^{0} = \left[-\frac{1}{50} t \right]_{0}^{t}$$

$$\Rightarrow \quad t = 37.49$$

The time taken to free-wheel to rest is 37.5 seconds.

4.3 Variable mass and weight
4.3.1 The moon-lander

1

50 000 m

1.62 m s^{-2}

The acceleration $v \dfrac{dv}{dx} = 1.62$

$$\Rightarrow \quad \int_{0}^{v} v \, dv = \int_{0}^{50\,000} 1.62 \, dx$$

$$\Rightarrow \quad \frac{v^2}{2} = \left[1.62x \right]_{0}^{50\,000}$$

$$\Rightarrow \quad v^2 = 162\,000$$

The impact speed v is 402.5 m s^{-1}.

To obtain the time to impact, integrate $\dfrac{d^2x}{dt^2} = 1.62$ with respect to t, twice.

Then $50\,000 = \frac{1}{2} 1.62t^2 \quad \Rightarrow \quad t = 248.5$

The time until impact is 248.5 seconds.

2 In the model, the only assumption likely to change is that the gravitational attraction does not remain constant for the whole motion. It is smaller at 50 km from the Moon and increases as the lander gets nearer the surface. Thus the initial acceleration is smaller, and increases as the lander falls.

4.3 **B**

1 Using Newton's law of gravitation and second law towards the surface,

$$mv \frac{dv}{dx} = \frac{GMm}{r^2}$$

where r is the distance of the lander from the centre of mass of the Moon.

So $r = R + 50\,000 - x$ where R is the radius of the Moon.

Substituting for r,

$$mv \frac{dv}{dx} = \frac{GMm}{(R + 50\,000 - x)^2}$$

2 Separating variables and integrating,

$$\int_{0}^{v} v \, dv = \int_{0}^{x} \frac{GM}{(R + 50\,000 - x)^2} \, dx$$

$$\Rightarrow \quad \frac{1}{2}v^2 = \left[\frac{GM}{(R + 50\,000 - x)} \right]_{0}^{x}$$

$$= GM \left(\frac{1}{(R + 50\,000 - x)} \right.$$

$$\left. - \frac{1}{(R + 50\,000)} \right)$$

$$\Rightarrow \quad v^2 = \frac{2GMx}{(R + 50\,000 - x)(R + 50\,000)}$$

$$\Rightarrow \quad v = \sqrt{\left(\frac{2GMx}{(R + 50\,000 - x)(R + 50\,000)} \right)}$$

3 When $x = 50\,000$,

$$v = \sqrt{\left(\frac{2GM \times 50\,000}{R(R + 50\,000)} \right)} \approx 397$$

The impact speed is 397 m s^{-1}.

4 If gravity is modelled using Newton's law of gravitation, the initial acceleration of the lander is smaller, but this increases as the lander moves closer to the surface.

However, the impact speed found using the constant gravity model is 402.5 m s^{-1}, which is only slightly faster. For motion from a height of 50 km the two models give solutions that are similar.

5 If the initial height is h, then the speed after falling x metres becomes

$$v = \sqrt{\left(\frac{2GMx}{(R + h - x)(R + h)}\right)}$$

On impact, the distance fallen $x = h$, so the impact speed is

$$V_h = \sqrt{\left(\frac{2GMh}{R(R + h)}\right)}$$

6 (a)

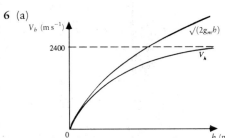

When the lander is at a very great distance from the Moon, its weight is very small, almost negligible. As the lander falls towards the Moon, initially it accelerates very slowly.

As the lander gets nearer the Moon, its weight increases and it begins to accelerate more rapidly.

From the graph, it is clear there is a limit to the impact speed.

From the formula,

$$V_h \to \sqrt{\left(\frac{2GM}{R}\right)} \approx 2400 \text{ m s}^{-1}$$

as $h \to \infty$.

(b) The superimposed graph shows that $v = \sqrt{(2GMh/R^2)} = \sqrt{(2g_m h)}$ (for $g_m = 1.62$) is a good approximation for small h.

7E $g_m = \dfrac{GM}{R^2} \quad \Rightarrow \quad V_h = \sqrt{\left(\dfrac{2g_m hR}{R + h}\right)}$

$$= \left(1 + \frac{h}{R}\right)^{-\frac{1}{2}} \sqrt{(2g_m h)}$$

$$\Rightarrow \quad V_h \approx \left(1 - \frac{h}{2R}\right)\sqrt{(2g_m h)}$$

$$\text{if } \frac{h}{R} \text{ is small}$$

4.3.2 Escaping from the Earth

4.3 C

1 $G = 6.67 \times 10^{-11}$, and for the Moon, $M = 7.35 \times 10^{22}$ and $R = 1.74 \times 10^6$.

The graph of U against H is shown below.

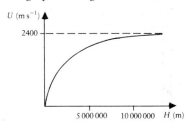

2 From the graph, the asymptote for the values of G, M and R given above is around $U = 2400$ which is approximately

$$\sqrt{\left(\frac{2GM}{R}\right)} \text{ for the Moon.}$$

3 The asymptote gives the value of U at which the maximum height reached by the projectile tends to infinity. Hence the asymptote is at the speed at which the projectile escapes.

4.3 Exercise 1

1 (a) Since G is a universal constant, the escape speed

$$U \propto \sqrt{\left(\frac{M}{R}\right)}$$

For planets of the same density, $M \propto R^3$ and $U \propto R$.

(b) Skylab has a mass of only 82 000 kg. If you were any distance greater than a few centimetres from the centre of mass then your escape speed would be extremely small. It would be wise for astronauts to secure themselves with a safety cable when on the outside of space stations in space.

2 Let M be the mass and R the radius of the Earth. Using Newton's second law towards the Earth,

$$mv\frac{dv}{dx} = \frac{GMm}{(R + 3\,000\,000 - x)^2}$$

$$\int_{10}^{v} v\,dv = \int_{0}^{3\times10^6} \frac{GM\,dx}{(R + 3\,000\,000 - x)^2}$$

$$= \left[\frac{GM}{(R + 3\,000\,000 - x)}\right]_0^{3\times10^6}$$

$$\Rightarrow \quad \tfrac{1}{2}v^2 - 50 = \frac{GM}{R} - \frac{GM}{R + 3\,000\,000}$$

Substituting $R = 6.378 \times 10^6$ and $M = 5.98 \times 10^{24}$ gives $v = 6325.5$.

The impact speed of the meteor is $6325\,\text{m s}^{-1}$ (approximately $22\,770\,\text{km h}^{-1}$).

3 (a)

Earth   Moon

Let $d = 3.84 \times 10^8$ m represent the distance between the Earth and the Moon. Let R metres be the distance from the Earth of the position where the resultant gravitational attraction is zero and r metres be the distance from the Moon.

Therefore $\dfrac{GE}{R^2} = \dfrac{GM}{r^2}$, where E is the mass of the Earth and M is the mass of the Moon.

Substituting $r = d - R$,

$$\frac{E}{R^2} = \frac{M}{(d-R)^2}$$

$$\Rightarrow \quad d - R = R\sqrt{\left(\frac{M}{E}\right)}$$

$$\Rightarrow \quad R = \frac{d}{1 + \sqrt{(M/E)}}$$

Substituting in values for d, M and E gives $R = 3.46 \times 10^8$.

The gravitational attraction of Earth equals that of the Moon at 3.46×10^8 metres from the centre of the Earth.

(b) The craft slows down as it moves away from the Earth until it passes through this point and then begins to accelerate towards the Moon.

4 (a) Using Newton's second law towards the meteor,

$$mv\frac{dv}{dx} = \frac{G \times 10^{14} \times m}{(17 + 449 - x)^2}$$

Separating variables, where U is the impact speed,

$$\int_0^U v\,dv = \int_0^{449} \frac{6670}{(466 - x)^2}\,dx$$

$$\Rightarrow \quad \tfrac{1}{2}U^2 = \left[\frac{6670}{(466 - x)}\right]_0^{449} = \frac{6670}{17} - \frac{6670}{466}$$

$$\Rightarrow \quad U^2 = 756$$

$$\Rightarrow \quad U = 27.5$$

The impact speed of the probe is $27.5\,\text{m s}^{-1}$.

(b) The equation of motion for the probe is

$$v\frac{dv}{dh} = -\frac{G \times 1 \times 10^{14}}{(17 + h)^2}$$

Integrating gives

$$\tfrac{1}{2}v^2 - \tfrac{1}{2}V^2 = 6670\left(\frac{1}{17 + h} - \frac{1}{42}\right)$$

where V is the escape speed required.

To escape, $v > 0$ as $h \to \infty$, so

$$\tfrac{1}{2}V^2 \geq \tfrac{6670}{42} \quad \Rightarrow \quad V \geq 17.82$$

In order to escape, the probe should be travelling faster than $17.82\,\text{m s}^{-1}$ when it reaches 25 metres.

5E To estimate your jump speed, $U\,\text{m s}^{-1}$, you could find the maximum height, H metres, you can jump off the Earth's surface and use the formula $U = \sqrt{(2gH)}$. Typical values for U would be between $2\,\text{m s}^{-1}$ and $4\,\text{m s}^{-1}$.

If the asteroid is assumed to be a sphere of radius R and density ρ then its mass is $M = \frac{4}{3}\pi R^3 \rho$. You can therefore escape if

$$U \geq \sqrt{\left(\frac{2GM}{R}\right)} = \sqrt{\left(\frac{8}{3}\pi R^2 \rho G\right)}$$

The maximum radius is $R = \sqrt{\left(\dfrac{3U^2}{8\pi\rho G}\right)}$

For an asteroid of the same density as the Earth (i.e. $\rho = 5520 \, \text{kg m}^{-3}$) the maximum radius is $R = 569.4U$.

For jumping speeds in the range $2 \, \text{m s}^{-1} < U < 4 \, \text{m s}^{-1}$ this gives asteroids with radii in the range 1139 metres $< R <$ 2278 metres that one could jump off.

There are known asteroids in the solar system with radii between 1000 and 2000 metres but their mass is not known. It is feasible that you could land on a small asteroid, walk around carefully and jump off!

An asteroid smaller than 1 km radius would be difficult to stay on, whereas it would be safe to walk on one with a radius greater than 2.5 km even though your weight would be very small.

4.3.3 Rocket propulsion

4.3 D

1 In theory you and the trolley should roll the other way, though this will depend on the friction in the wheel bearings.

2 (a) The greater the speed of the balls the more momentum they have, and since momentum is conserved the trolley will move the opposite way with greater speed.

   (b) More massive balls have greater momentum and the effect on the trolley will be the same in as (a) above.

   (c) Each time a ball is thrown there is an exchange of momentum and the mass of the trolley with the remaining balls

decreases. The rate at which the balls are thrown affects the acceleration of the trolley; the quicker the rate, the greater the average acceleration.

3   Before

$$0 \leftarrow \boxed{60 + 198 + 2}$$

          After

$$v_1 \, \text{m s}^{-1} \leftarrow \boxed{60 + 198} \quad ② \rightarrow 10 \, \text{m s}^{-1}$$

4 Applying conservation of momentum,

$$0 = (60 + 198)v_1 - 20$$

$$\Rightarrow \quad v_1 = \tfrac{10}{129}$$

The speed of the trolley is $\frac{10}{129} \, \text{m s}^{-1}$.

5   Before

$$v_1 \, \text{m s}^{-1} \leftarrow \boxed{60 + 198}$$

          After

$$v_2 \, \text{m s}^{-1} \leftarrow \boxed{60 + 196} \quad ② \rightarrow (10 - v_1) \, \text{m s}^{-1}$$

$$258 \times \tfrac{10}{129} = 256v_2 + 2(\tfrac{10}{129} - 10)$$

$$\Rightarrow \quad v_2 = 0.156 \, \text{m s}^{-1}$$

$$256 \times 0.156 = 254v_3 + 2(0.156 - 10)$$

$$\Rightarrow \quad v_3 = 0.234 \, \text{m s}^{-1}$$

$$254 \times 0.234 = 252v_4 + 2(0.234 - 10)$$

$$\Rightarrow \quad v_4 = 0.314 \, \text{m s}^{-1}$$

6 (a) Applying the principle of conservation of momentum,

$$(M + 100m)v_0 = (M + 99m)v_1$$
$$+ m(v_0 - C)$$

$$\Rightarrow \quad (M + 99m)v_0 = (M + 99m)v_1 - mC$$

$$\Rightarrow \quad v_0 = v_1 - \frac{mC}{M + 99m}$$

$$\Rightarrow \quad v_1 = v_0 + \frac{mC}{M + 99m}$$

   (b) $v_2 = v_1 + \dfrac{mC}{M + 98m}$

   (c) $v_n = v_{n-1} + \dfrac{mC}{M + (100 - n)m}$

7 Substituting $m = 2$, $M = 60$ and $C = 10$ into the relations given in question 6, gives solutions which are the same as those obtained in question 5.

$$v_0 = 0 \, \mathrm{m \, s^{-1}}, \quad v_1 = 0.078 \, \mathrm{m \, s^{-1}},$$

$$v_2 = 0.156 \, \mathrm{m \, s^{-1}}, \quad v_3 = 0.234 \, \mathrm{m \, s^{-1}},$$

$$v_4 = 0.314 \, \mathrm{m \, s^{-1}}$$

8 Using a program, the following speeds after each set of ten throws are obtained by substituting $m = 2$, $M = 60$ and $C = 10$ into the sum

$$v_n = \frac{20}{60 + 2(100 - n)} + \ldots + \frac{20}{60 + 2 \times 97}$$
$$+ \frac{20}{60 + 2 \times 98} + \frac{20}{60 + 2 \times 99}$$

Balls thrown	0	10	20	30	40	50
Speed (m s^{-1})	0	0.80	1.68	2.64	3.70	4.88

Balls thrown		60	70	80	90	100
Speed (m s^{-1})		6.22	7.78	9.62	11.88	14.80

The final speed of the trolley is $14.80 \, \mathrm{m \, s^{-1}}$.

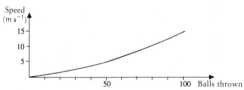

From the graph, you can see that the acceleration increases with time. As more balls are thrown from the trolley, the actual mass of you, the trolley and the remaining balls is decreasing. The increase in momentum due to an ejected ball results in a greater increase in the trolley's speed as it is becoming lighter.

9 Increasing any of these three variables increases the rate of change of the momentum of the ejected mass and hence the rate of change of the forward momentum of the trolley.

4.3 **E**

1 (a) $(M - \mu \, \delta t)(v + \delta v) + \mu \, \delta t(v - C)$
$$= Mv + M \, \delta v - \mu C \, \delta t - \mu \, \delta v \, \delta t$$

(b) Change in momentum
$$= M \, \delta v - \mu C \, \delta t - \mu \, \delta v \, \delta t$$

$$\frac{\text{Change of momentum}}{\delta t}$$

$$= M \frac{\delta v}{\delta t} - \mu C - \mu \, \delta v$$

As $\delta t \to 0$, $\delta v \to 0$ and so

$$\text{rate of change of momentum} = M \frac{dv}{dt} - \mu C$$

2 The only external force is the total weight of the rocket and fuel. This is Mg downwards throughout the time interval.

Applying Newton's second law,

$$-Mg = M \frac{dv}{dt} - \mu C$$

$$\Rightarrow \quad M \frac{dv}{dt} = \mu C - Mg$$

3 Applying Newton's second law,

$$-T - \mu \, \delta t \, g \approx \frac{\mu \, \delta t(v - C) - \mu \, \delta t \, v}{\delta t} = -\mu C$$

Let $\delta t \to 0$, then $T = \mu C$.

4 The thrust must be greater than Mg, i.e. $\mu C > Mg$.

5E Lift-off can only occur when $M = \dfrac{\mu C}{g}$

$$\Rightarrow \qquad M_0 - \mu \tau = \frac{\mu C}{g}$$

$$\Rightarrow \qquad \tau = \frac{M_0}{\mu} - \frac{C}{g}$$

(a) When $\tau = 0$, $\mu C = g M_0$

The rocket lifts off immediately. The rate at which fuel is burnt and the exhaust speed together provide just enough thrust to balance the initial weight of the rocket.

(b) When $\tau > 0$, $\mu C < g M_0$.

The rocket's weight is greater than the thrust. If the rocket is on the launch pad then there must be an additional reaction force R on the rocket such that $R + T - Mg = 0$. Time is taken while fuel is burnt and ejected, decreasing the weight of the rocket until R is zero and the thrust is sufficient for lift-off.

In practice, the exhaust speed and the rate of burn take time to reach their maximum, i.e. μ and C are not constant initially.

4.3 Exercise 2

1 At $t = 20$, the mass becomes zero and v becomes infinite. In reality this does not happen because the fuel runs out before this, leaving the astronaut moving at constant speed.

2

At time t At time $t + \delta t$

(a) Applying the conservation of momentum,

$$Mv = (M - 200\,\delta t)(v + \delta v)$$
$$+ 200\,\delta t(v + 1000)$$

$$\Rightarrow \quad 0 = M\,\delta v + 1000 \times 200\,\delta t,$$
since the $\delta v\,\delta t$ term is negligible

$$\Rightarrow \quad M\frac{dv}{dt} = -200\,000$$

(b) At time t, $\quad M = 9000 - 200t$

$$\Rightarrow \quad (9000 - 200t)\frac{dv}{dt} = -200\,000$$

(c)
$$\int_{250}^{0} dv = \int_{0}^{t} \frac{-2000}{90 - 2t}\,dt$$

$$\Rightarrow \quad \ln\left|\frac{90 - 2t}{90}\right| = -\tfrac{1}{4}$$

$$\Rightarrow \quad 90 - 2t = 90\,e^{-\frac{1}{4}}$$

$$\Rightarrow \quad t = 45(1 - e^{-\frac{1}{4}}) = 9.95$$

The time taken before the spacecraft stops is 9.95 seconds.

3 (a) $M = 10\,000 - 50t$

(b) $\quad M\dfrac{dv}{dt} = -Mg + 100\,000$

$$\Rightarrow \quad \frac{dv}{dt} = -10 + \frac{100\,000}{10\,000 - 50t}$$

Integrating,

$$v = \left[-10t + \frac{100\,000}{-50}\ln|10\,000 - 50t|\right]_{0}^{180}$$

$$\approx 2805$$

After 3 minutes the rocket is travelling at $2805\ \mathrm{m\,s}^{-1}$ approximately.

4 (a) Assumptions are:

- gravity is constant at $9.8\ \mathrm{m\,s}^{-2}$;
- air resistance is modelled by $R = kv^2$ newtons;
- the rate and speed of the fuel ejection is constant;
- there are no other external forces, such as attraction from other bodies.

(b) Possible reasons are:

- as the rocket ascends into the upper atmosphere and beyond, the air resistance will decrease;
- gravity will decrease as the rocket moves away from the Earth;
- the rocket may not continue to travel vertically upwards;
- there may be discontinuities in the change of M due to 'stages' of the rocket being ejected;
- the fuel may be ejected at a different rate or speed as the rocket travels farther away from the Earth.

5 The lander takes off when

$$\mu C \geq Mg_M$$

i.e. $180 \times 150 \geq (1.8 \times 10^4 - 180t)g_M$

The lander takes off after 7.4 seconds.

4.4 Simple harmonic motion
4.4.1 Vibrations everywhere

4.4 Exercise 1

1 (a) The seagull moves up and down on the sea. It has a maximum displacement of 0.7 m and each oscillation takes about 4 seconds.

The amplitude a is 0.7 and $\omega = \dfrac{2\pi}{4}$, so a suitable function is

$$x = 0.7 \sin\left(\frac{\pi}{2}t\right)$$

(b) The centre of the spin-drier vibrates up and down with an increasing amplitude. The amplitude doubles in 0.5 second. The time for one oscillation is approximately 0.26 second and this appears to be constant.

The amplitude a increases from 0.01 after 0.05 second to 0.02 after 0.55 second.

The gradient $\dfrac{da}{dt}$ is $\dfrac{0.01}{0.5} = 0.02$ and the intercept is approximately 0.01.

Therefore the amplitude is growing linearly according to $a = 0.02t + 0.01$ and ω is $\dfrac{2\pi}{0.26} = 24.2$.

A suitable function is

$$x = (0.02t + 0.01) \sin(24.2t)$$

2 (a)

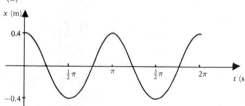

(b) A possible function is

$$x = 0.4 \cos 2t$$

(Note: The graph represents a simplification of the true motion.)

3 The rule vibrates quickly. The period is small and the amplitude decreases quickly to virtually zero after one second.

If the initial displacement of the ruler tip is 6 cm, a graph of the displacement against time might be as shown.

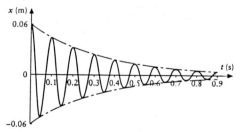

From this graph, the amplitude might be modelled as

$$a = 0.06\,e^{-3t}$$

The period of oscillation is approximately 0.1 second. So the displacement x is

$$0.06\,e^{-3t} \cos(20\pi t)$$

4.4.2 Simple harmonic motion

4.4 A

$$a \cos(\omega t + \varepsilon) = a(\cos \omega t \cos \varepsilon - \sin \omega t \sin \varepsilon)$$
$$= (a \cos \varepsilon) \cos \omega t - (a \sin \varepsilon) \sin \omega t$$

So $A = a \cos \varepsilon$ and $B = -a \sin \varepsilon$

4.4 **Exercise 2**

1 (a)

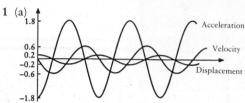

(b) **(i)** When the acceleration is zero, the displacement is zero.

(ii) When the acceleration is maximum, the displacement is minimum.

(iii) When the velocity is zero, the displacement is maximum or minimum.

(iv) When the velocity is a maximum, the displacement is zero.

2
$$x = 0.18 \cos(10.5t)$$
$$\Rightarrow \quad \dot{x} = -0.18 \times 10.5 \sin(10.5t)$$
$$\Rightarrow \quad \ddot{x} = -0.18 \times (10.5)^2 \cos(10.5t)$$
$$\Rightarrow \quad \ddot{x} = -x \times (10.5)^2$$
$$\Rightarrow \quad \ddot{x} + (10.5)^2 x = 0$$

This is the SHM equation, $\ddot{x} + \omega^2 x = 0$, where $\omega = 10.5$.

3 (a) Initial angle $\varepsilon = \dfrac{\pi}{2} + 0.8$

$$\Rightarrow \quad x = 0.2 \cos\left(3t + \frac{\pi}{2} + 0.8\right)$$

(b) Initial angle $\varepsilon = \pi + 0.8$

$$\Rightarrow \quad x = 0.2 \cos(3t + \pi + 0.8)$$

4
$$x = A \cos \omega t + B \sin \omega t$$
$$\Rightarrow \quad \dot{x} = -A\omega \sin \omega t + B\omega \cos \omega t$$
$$\Rightarrow \quad \ddot{x} = -A\omega^2 \cos \omega t - B\omega^2 \sin \omega t$$
$$\Rightarrow \quad \ddot{x} = -\omega^2 (A \cos \omega t + B \sin \omega t)$$
$$\Rightarrow \quad \ddot{x} = -\omega^2 x$$
$$\Rightarrow \quad \ddot{x} + \omega^2 x = 0$$

Hence $x = A \cos \omega t + B \sin \omega t$ is a solution to the SHM equation. It is a general solution since it has two arbitrary constants, A and B, corresponding to the two integrations which are required to solve a second order differential equation.

4.4.3 Modelling an oscillating body

4.4 **B**

1 The equation of motion is $\ddot{x} = -\omega^2 x$, which has a general solution of the form

$$x = A \cos(\omega t + \varepsilon)$$

Using the initial condition $x = a$ when $t = 0$ gives $a = A \cos \varepsilon$.

Differentiating the expression for displacement gives $\dot{x} = -A\omega \sin(\omega t + \varepsilon)$.

Initially, $t = 0$, $\dot{x} = 0$
$$\Rightarrow \quad 0 = -A\omega \sin \varepsilon \Rightarrow \varepsilon = 0 \text{ or } \pi$$

Hence *either* $a = A \cos 0 = A$,

or $a = A \cos \pi = -A$

But $-a \cos(\omega t + \pi) = a \cos(\omega t)$

So in either case, the solution is $x = a \cos(\omega t)$ where

$$\omega = \sqrt{\left(\frac{k}{m}\right)}$$

$$\Rightarrow \quad x = a \cos\left(\sqrt{\left(\frac{k}{m}\right)}t\right)$$

2

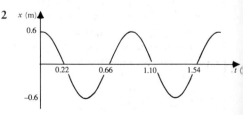

3 From the graph, the period of one oscillation is 0.88 second. So a baby of mass 10 kg on a spring with a spring constant of 500 N m^{-1} will oscillate with a period of just under 1 second.

4.4 C

1 $v \dfrac{dv}{dx} + \omega^2 x = 0$

Separating variables,

$$\int v \, dv = \int -\omega^2 x \, dx$$

$$\Rightarrow \quad \frac{1}{2}v^2 = -\omega^2 \frac{x^2}{2} + A$$

$$\Rightarrow \quad v^2 = -\omega^2 x^2 + \text{constant}$$

2 With the initial condition $x = a$, $v = 0$,

$$0 = -\omega^2 a^2 + \text{constant}$$

$$\Rightarrow \quad \text{constant} = \omega^2 a^2$$

Substituting this in the solution,

$$v^2 = -\omega^2 x^2 + \omega^2 a^2 = \omega^2(a^2 - x^2)$$

$$\Rightarrow \quad v = \pm\omega\sqrt{(a^2 - x^2)}$$

3 The graph of v against x from $x = -a$ to $x = a$ is as shown.

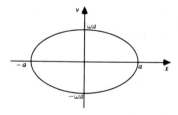

The motion is such that when the displacement is at its maximum (or minimum) the velocity is zero, and when the displacement is zero the velocity is a maximum (or minimum).

4 Writing $v = \dfrac{dx}{dt}$,

$$\frac{dx}{dt} = \pm\omega\sqrt{(a^2 - x^2)}$$

Separating variables,

$$\int_0^t dt = \int_a^x \frac{1}{\pm\omega\sqrt{(a^2 - x^2)}} \, dx$$

$$\Rightarrow \quad t = \left[\pm\frac{1}{\omega}\cos^{-1}\left(\frac{x}{a}\right) \right]_a^x$$

$$= \pm\frac{1}{\omega}\left[\cos^{-1}\left(\frac{x}{a}\right) - \cos^{-1}1 \right]$$

$$\Rightarrow \quad t = \pm\frac{1}{\omega}\cos^{-1}\left(\frac{x}{a}\right)$$

$$\Rightarrow \quad \frac{x}{a} = \cos(\pm\omega t) = \cos\omega t$$

$$\Rightarrow \quad x = a\cos\omega t$$

5 For the mass on the spring,

$$\ddot{x} = -\frac{k}{m}x \quad \Rightarrow \quad v\frac{dv}{dx} = -\frac{k}{m}x$$

Separating variables and integrating gives

$$v = \pm\sqrt{\left(81 - \frac{k}{m}x^2\right)}$$

Separating variables and integrating again,

$$\int_0^t dt = \int_0^x \frac{\pm 1}{\sqrt{(81 - kx^2/m)}} \, dx$$

$$\Rightarrow \quad t = \pm\left[\sqrt{\left(\frac{m}{k}\right)}\cos^{-1}\left(\sqrt{\left(\frac{k}{m}\right)}\frac{x}{9}\right) \right]_0^x$$

$$\Rightarrow \quad t = \pm\sqrt{\left(\frac{m}{k}\right)}$$

$$\times \left(\cos^{-1}\left(\frac{x}{9}\sqrt{\left(\frac{k}{m}\right)}\right) - \cos^{-1}0 \right)$$

$$\Rightarrow \quad \cos^{-1}\left(\frac{x}{9}\sqrt{\left(\frac{k}{m}\right)}\right) = \pm\sqrt{\left(\frac{k}{m}\right)}t \pm \frac{\pi}{2}$$

$$\Rightarrow \quad x = 9\sqrt{\left(\frac{m}{k}\right)}\cos\left(\frac{\pi}{2} \pm \sqrt{\left(\frac{k}{m}\right)}t\right)$$

Then

$$x = +9\sqrt{\left(\frac{m}{k}\right)}\sin\left(\sqrt{\left(\frac{k}{m}\right)}t\right)$$

to satisfy the initial conditions.

These initial conditions may occur if the mass is struck from its equilibrium position with an initial speed of $9\,\text{m s}^{-1}$.

4.4 Exercise 3

1 (a) Displacement $x = a \cos \omega t$

The initial conditions are $t = 0$, $x = 0.01$

$\Rightarrow \quad 0.01 = a \cos 0 \quad \Rightarrow \quad a = 0.01$

The time period

$$T = \frac{2\pi}{\omega} \quad \Rightarrow \quad \frac{8}{10} = \frac{2\pi}{\omega}$$

$$\Rightarrow \quad \omega = \frac{5\pi}{2}$$

(b) The displacement of the bob is

$$x = 0.01 \cos \left(\frac{5\pi}{2} t \right)$$

$$\Rightarrow \quad \dot{x} = -0.01 \times \frac{5\pi}{2} \sin \left(\frac{5\pi}{2} t \right)$$

So the maximum speed of the bob is

$$\dot{x} = \frac{5\pi}{200}$$

Differentiating again,

$$\ddot{x} = -0.01 \times \left(\frac{5\pi}{2} \right)^2 \cos \left(\frac{5\pi t}{2} \right)$$

This has a maximum of

$$\ddot{x} = 0.01 \times \frac{25\pi^2}{4}.$$

The maximum speed is $\frac{5\pi}{200} = 0.08 \, \mathrm{m \, s^{-1}}$

and the maximum acceleration is

$$\frac{25\pi^2}{400} = 0.6 \, \mathrm{m \, s^{-2}}.$$

(c) When the speed is a maximum, the displacement is zero. When the acceleration is a maximum, the displacement is -0.01 m.

2 (a) In equilibrium, $1 = 0.3k$

$$\Rightarrow \quad k = \frac{10}{3}$$

Thus the tension is given by
$T = \frac{10}{3}(x + 0.3)$ newtons.

(b) Using Newton's second law downwards,

$$1 - T = 0.1\ddot{x}$$

$$\Rightarrow \quad 1 - \frac{10}{3}(0.3 + x) = 0.1\ddot{x}$$

$$\Rightarrow \quad -\frac{100}{3}x = \ddot{x}$$

So the initial acceleration (when $x = 0.02$) is $\ddot{x} = -\frac{2}{3}$.

The initial acceleration is $\frac{2}{3} \mathrm{m \, s^{-2}}$ upwards.

(c) The equation of motion for the mass is $\ddot{x} + \frac{100}{3}x = 0$ which is the equation for SHM where $\omega^2 = \frac{100}{3}$.

Hence $\omega = \frac{10}{\sqrt{3}}$ and the time period is given by

$$T = \frac{2\pi}{\omega} = \frac{2\pi\sqrt{3}}{10} = 1.09$$

The time period of the oscillations is 1.09 seconds.

3 (a) Using Newton's second law downwards,

$$30 - T = 3\ddot{x}$$

From Hooke's law, $T = 15x$

$$\Rightarrow \quad 30 - 15x = 3\ddot{x}$$

$$\Rightarrow \quad \ddot{x} = 10 - 5x$$

(b) Try the solution $x = 2 + \cos \sqrt{5}t$

$$\Rightarrow \quad \ddot{x} = -5 \cos \sqrt{5}t$$

$$\Rightarrow \quad 10 - 5x = 10 - 10 - 5 \cos \sqrt{5}t$$

$$= -5 \cos \sqrt{5}t$$

$$= \ddot{x}$$

Therefore $x = 2 + \cos \sqrt{5}t$ is a solution.

Also, $x = 3$ and $\dot{x} = 0$ when $t = 0$, so this solution satisfies the initial conditions.

(c) The minimum extension of the spring occurs when $x = 2 - 1 = 1$, which is positive.

The string never compresses since the extension is always greater than 1 metre.

4 (a) N is the normal reaction.

T_1 and T_2 are the tensions in the springs.

12 N is the weight of the particle.

(b) From Hooke's law, $T_1 = 24x$

$\qquad$ and $\quad T_2 = -24x$

Using Newton's second law in the direction of increasing x,

$$T_2 - T_1 = 1.2\ddot{x}$$

$$\Rightarrow \quad -24x - 24x = 1.2\ddot{x}$$

$$\Rightarrow \qquad\qquad -40x = \ddot{x}$$

$$\Rightarrow \qquad\qquad \ddot{x} + 40x = 0$$

This is the SHM equation where $\omega^2 = 40 \;\Rightarrow\; \omega = 6.32$.

The particle performs SHM with angular velocity of $6.32\,\mathrm{rad\,s^{-1}}$.

4.5 Other oscillations
4.5.1 The pendulum

4.5 A

1 Using a program you should find that θ becomes zero at time 0.50 second. The time period is therefore 2.0 seconds, as is predicted by the solution of the SHM equation.

2 In this case, a quarter of the time period is 0.58 second. Hence the time period is approximately 2.3 seconds. This is significantly greater than the value of 2 seconds predicted by the SHM equation which is only valid for small amplitudes less than about 0.2 radians.

3 The time period is $\tau = 2\pi\sqrt{\left(\dfrac{l}{g}\right)}$ and so $\tau \propto \sqrt{l}$. To increase the time period you should therefore increase the length of the pendulum. If a clock is running fast then the time period is too short, so l must be increased. If the clock is running slow, then the time period is too long and l needs shortening. Your results from tasksheet 1 (page 369) should validate these conclusions.

4.5 Exercise 1

1 (a) This is SHM with $\omega = \frac{5}{3}$. The general solution is

$$\theta = a \cos\left(\tfrac{5}{3}t + \varepsilon\right)$$

The initial conditions give the particular solution

$$\theta = 0.12 \sin\left(\tfrac{5}{3}t\right)$$

(b) $\tau = 2\pi \div \frac{5}{3} \approx 3.77$

The time period is 3.8 seconds.

(c) The main assumptions are:

- the amplitude is small and constant;
- the mass is a particle;
- there is no air resistance or damping;
- the string is light and inextensible.

2 (a) $0.9 = 2\pi\sqrt{\left(\dfrac{l}{g}\right)}$ $\Rightarrow$ $l \approx 0.205$

The pendulum is approximately 0.2 m long.

(b) The general solution is

$$\theta = a \cos (7t + \varepsilon) \quad \text{since} \quad \frac{2\pi}{0.9} \approx 7$$

When $t = 0$, $\theta = 0.17$ and $\dot{\theta} = 0$. Therefore

$$\theta = 0.17 \cos 7t$$

$$\Rightarrow \quad \dot{\theta} = -1.2 \sin 7t$$

The maximum angular speed of the bob is 1.2 rad s^{-1}.

3 (a) Assume that:

• friction and air resistance are negligible;
• the oscillations have small amplitude.

0.15 $0.2\ddot{\theta}$

(b) Using Newton's second law tangentially

$$0.015 \times 0.2 \times \ddot{\theta} = -0.15\theta$$

$$\Rightarrow \qquad \ddot{\theta} + 50\theta = 0$$

(c) The time period is $\dfrac{2\pi}{\sqrt{50}} \approx 0.9$ second.

4 (a) $\qquad 2\dot{\theta}\ddot{\theta} = \dfrac{2g}{l}\dot{\theta}(-\sin\theta)$

$$\Rightarrow \qquad \ddot{\theta} = -\frac{g}{l}\sin\theta$$

$$\Rightarrow \quad \ddot{\theta} + \frac{g}{l}\sin\theta = 0$$

(b) $\dot{\theta} = \pm\sqrt{\left(\dfrac{2g}{l}\cos\theta + C\right)}$

with $g = 10$ and $l = 1$

$\dot{\theta} = 0$ when $\theta = \dfrac{\pi}{2}$ $\Rightarrow$ $C = 0$

So $\dot{\theta} = \pm\sqrt{(20\cos\theta)}$

(c) $\dot{\theta} = \sqrt{(20\cos\theta)}$ $\Rightarrow$ $\displaystyle\int \frac{d\theta}{\sqrt{(20\cos\theta)}} = \int d$

The pendulum oscillates from

$\theta = \dfrac{\pi}{2}$ to $\theta = -\dfrac{\pi}{2}$ and back again, so a quarter of the time period is given by

$$\int_0^{\pi/2} \frac{d\theta}{\sqrt{(20\cos\theta)}}$$

Using the mid-ordinate rule

$$\left(\text{to avoid problems at } \theta = \frac{\pi}{2}\right)$$

with 100 strips gives an approximate value of 2.28.

The time period for small oscillations is

$$2\pi\sqrt{\left(\frac{l}{g}\right)} \approx 2$$

so it appears that the time period increases as the amplitude increases. It should be possible to validate this result experimentally.

4.5.2 Damping

4.5 B

1 $\qquad\qquad mg - T - R = m\ddot{x}$

$$\Rightarrow \quad mg - k(e + x) - C\dot{x} = m\ddot{x}$$

$$\Rightarrow \qquad m\ddot{x} + C\dot{x} + kx = 0$$

2 $\dot{x} = Ap\,e^{pt}$ and $\ddot{x} = Ap^2\,e^{pt}$

$$\Rightarrow \quad mAp^2\,e^{pt} + CAp\,e^{pt} + kA\,e^{pt} = 0$$

$$\Rightarrow \qquad mp^2 + Cp + k = 0$$

3 $mp^2 + 20p + 10 = 0$

$$\Rightarrow \quad p = \frac{-20 \pm \sqrt{(400 - 40m)}}{2m}$$

The auxiliary equation has real, equal or complex roots depending on the value of $\sqrt{(400 - 40m)}$. If

$400 - 40m > 0$ (i.e. $m < 10$)

the roots are real;

$400 - 40m = 0$ (i.e. $m = 10$)

the roots are equal;

$400 - 40m < 0$ (i.e. $m > 10$)

the roots are complex.

4 $7.5\ddot{x} + 20\dot{x} + 10x = 0$

$\Rightarrow \quad 7.5p^2 + 20p + 10 = 0$

$\Rightarrow \quad p = -\frac{2}{3}$ or -2

$\Rightarrow \quad x = Ae^{-\frac{2}{3}t} + Be^{-2t}$

When $t = 0$, $x = 2$ and $\dot{x} = 0$

So $2 = A + B$ and $0 = -\frac{2}{3}A - 2B$

Then $A = 3$ and $B = -1$, so

$x = 3e^{-\frac{2}{3}t} - e^{-2t}$

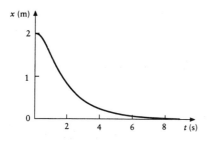

The mass has an initial displacement of 2 metres. When released it slowly returns to its equilibrium position. It does not oscillate and takes approximately 9 seconds for the mass to be within 0.5 cm of equilibrium.

5 $10\ddot{x} + 20\dot{x} + 10x = 0$

$\Rightarrow \quad 10p^2 + 20p + 10 = 0$

$\Rightarrow \quad p = -1$ (repeated)

$\Rightarrow \quad x = (A + Bt)e^{-t}$

When $t = 0$, $x = 2$ and $\dot{x} = 0$

So $2 = A$ and $-A + B = 0$

Then $x = (2 + 2t)e^{-t}$

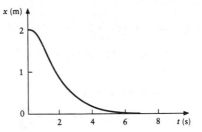

As with the overdamped case, the mass does not oscillate but returns to equilibrium. In this case, the displacement initially decreases more slowly than in question 4 but, after 2.8 seconds, the displacement is less than in question 4 and equilibrium is reached faster. After 7 seconds, x is less than 0.5 cm.

6 $100\ddot{x} + 20\dot{x} + 10x = 0$

$\Rightarrow \quad 100p^2 + 20p + 10 = 0$

$\Rightarrow \quad p = -0.1 \pm 0.3j$

$\Rightarrow \quad x = Ae^{-0.1t}\cos(0.3t + \varepsilon)$

When $t = 0$, $x = 2$ and $\dot{x} = 0$

So $2 = A\cos\varepsilon$ and

$0 = -0.1A\cos\varepsilon - 0.3A\sin\varepsilon$

Then $x = 2.11e^{-0.1t}\cos(0.3t - 0.322)$

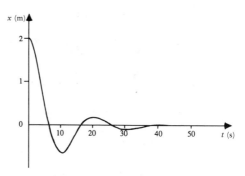

The mass oscillates about the equilibrium position, performing approximately two complete oscillations. The time period is about 20 seconds. The amplitude decreases less quickly than in questions 4 and 5. Amplitude ≈ 3.5 cm when $t \approx 37$ s.

7 As $C \to 0$, $\quad n \to \sqrt{\left(\dfrac{k}{m}\right)}$ and

$$x \to A\cos\left(\sqrt{\left(\dfrac{k}{m}\right)}t + \varepsilon\right)$$

This is the solution for SHM of a mass–spring oscillator.

4.5 Exercise 2

1

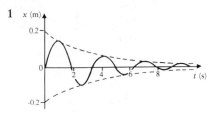

- The mass is initially struck from rest at its equilibrium position.
- The period of oscillation is π seconds.
- The amplitude is decaying exponentially and has maximum displacement of 0.14 metre after 0.67 second.
- After 8 seconds the oscillations have almost disappeared. There are about $2\frac{1}{2}$ oscillations.

2 (a)

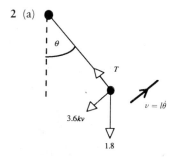

(b) Using Newton's second law tangentially, in the direction of increasing θ,

$$0.18 \times 0.2 \times \ddot{\theta} = -1.8\sin\theta - 3.6k \times 0.2\dot{\theta}$$

$$\Rightarrow \qquad \ddot{\theta} = -50\sin\theta - 20k\dot{\theta}$$

For small angles, $\theta \approx \sin\theta$

$$\Rightarrow \quad \ddot{\theta} + 20k\dot{\theta} + 50\theta = 0$$

(c) $p^2 + 20kp + 50 = 0$

$$\Rightarrow \qquad p = \dfrac{-20k \pm \sqrt{(400k^2 - 200)}}{2}$$

It is underdamped if

$$400k^2 < 200 \quad \Rightarrow \quad k < 0.71$$

3 (a) In equilibrium, $T_1 = 50$

$$\Rightarrow \qquad 45e = 50$$

$$e = 1.11$$

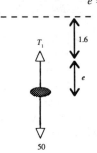

The equilibrium position is 2.71 metres below the support.

(b) Using Newton's second law vertically downwards,

$$50 - T_2 - R = 5\ddot{x}$$

$$\Rightarrow \quad 50 - 45(e + x) - 30\dot{x} = 5\ddot{x}$$

$$\Rightarrow \qquad \ddot{x} + 6\dot{x} + 9x = 0$$

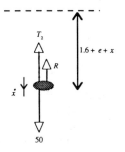

(c) $p^2 + 6p + 9 = 0$

$$\Rightarrow \qquad p = -3$$

The auxiliary equation has equal roots, hence the motion is critically damped.

$$x = (A + Bt)\,e^{-3t}$$

To satisfy the initial conditions,

$$x = 2t\,e^{-3t}$$

4E (a) Using Hooke's law,

$$5 = 0.02k \implies k = 250$$

The spring constant is $250\,\mathrm{N\,m^{-1}}$.

(b) $(M + 0.5)p^2 + 10p + 250 = 0$

$$\implies p = \frac{-10 \pm j\sqrt{(1000M + 400)}}{2M + 1}$$

$$\implies x = A_0\, e^{-10t/(2M+1)} \cos(nt + \varepsilon)$$

where $n = \dfrac{\sqrt{(1000M + 400)}}{2M + 1}$

(c) $e^{10t/(2M+1)} = 0.25$

$$\implies t = \frac{2M + 1}{10} \ln 4$$

(d) Removing the damping would mean that the scales would continue to oscillate and would not settle down to allow a reading to be taken.

4.5.3 Forced oscillations

4.5 **C**

1 (a) To increase the amplitude of the swing, the push should be applied at the end of each swing, in the direction in which the swing is about to move.

(b) If the swing were pushed at other times, the effect would not be so great. If it were pushed in the opposite direction to which it was moving, the amplitude would decrease.

2 This is quite straightforward to test practically. To increase the amplitude, the upward force should be applied when the mass is at its lowest point (i.e. at maximum displacement).

Note that the effect on the amplitude depends on the frequency with which the force is applied. If this is very much less or very much greater than the frequency of the oscillations then the force will have little effect on the amplitude. The closer the frequencies are, the more the force affects the amplitude, as in 1(a) above when the frequencies are equal.

4.5 **D**

1 Length of spring $= l + e + x - y$

Extension of spring $= e + x - y$

$$\implies T = k(e + x - y)$$

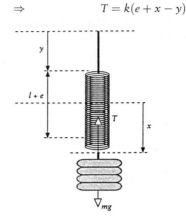

2 $mg - T = m\ddot{x}$

$$\implies mg - k(e + x - y) = m\ddot{x}$$

When in equilibrium, $mg = ke$ and so

$$-kx + ky = m\ddot{x}$$

Substituting $y = b \cos pt$,

$$\implies m\ddot{x} + kx = kb \cos pt$$

$$\implies \ddot{x} + \omega^2 x = b\omega^2 \cos pt$$

3 Try $x = A \cos pt$

$$\implies \ddot{x} = -p^2 A \cos pt$$

Substituting in the equation of motion,

$$-p^2 A \cos pt + \omega^2 A \cos pt \equiv b\omega^2 \cos pt$$

$$\implies A = \frac{b\omega^2}{\omega^2 - p^2}$$

$$\implies x = \left(\frac{b\omega^2}{\omega^2 - p^2}\right) \cos pt$$

4.5 **Exercise 3**

1 (a) $\ddot{x} = -2\omega \sin \omega t - \omega^2 t \cos \omega t$

$$\implies -2\omega \sin \omega t - \omega^2 t \cos \omega t + \omega^2 t \cos \omega t = F(t)$$

$$\implies F(t) = -2\omega \sin \omega t$$

(b)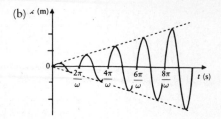

The mass is at rest and is then given an initial velocity. Resonance occurs, the mass oscillating with amplitude growing linearly. The time period is $\dfrac{2\pi}{\omega}$.

2 (a) $\omega = \sqrt{100} = 10$

For resonance, $p = \omega = 10$

(b) $\qquad x = 0.05 \cos 10t + t \sin 10t$

$\Rightarrow \quad \ddot{x} = 15 \cos 10t - 100t \sin 10t$

Then $\ddot{x} + 100x = 20 \cos 10t$ as required.

When $t = 0$, $x = 0.05$ and $\dot{x} = 0$, satisfying the initial conditions.

(c)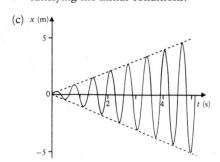

(d) The amplitude of the oscillations is growing linearly. The time period is approximately 0.63 second. The flag-pole would soon break.

In practice there would be a damping force and the wind is unlikely to blow with consistent strength and frequency.

3 (a) Some possible assumptions are:

- the upward force is periodic, with angular frequency 3 rad s^{-1};
- the spring is Hookean, where $k = 108$;
- there are no damping forces;
- the baby is a particle.

(b) $\ddot{x} + 9x = 0.05 \sin 3t$

The angular frequency of the unforced oscillation is 3 rad s^{-1}.

(c) The frequencies of the driving force and unforced oscillation are equal. Hence the baby is resonating and the amplitude of the bouncing will grow.

The model is unrealistic because it assumes that the body can apply a force downwards as well as upwards.

Miscellaneous exercise 4

1 (a) $v = 80 \text{ m s}^{-1}$ (b) $v \approx 40 \text{ m s}^{-1}$

2 -12.5 m s^{-2}; 0 m s^{-2}; 10 m s^{-1}

3 (a) 0.8 second (b) 0.74 second

4 (a) $\dfrac{dv}{dt} = -\lambda v^2$; $\dfrac{1}{v} = \lambda t + \dfrac{1}{30}$

(b) $\lambda = \frac{1}{225}$; 37.5 seconds

5 36 seconds

6 (a) $v = 10(1 - e^{-3t}) \text{ cm s}^{-1}$; $x = 10t - \frac{10}{3}(1 - e^{-3t}) \text{ cm}$

(b) 10 cm s^{-1}; no

7 $\dfrac{u^2}{6k}(3 + 2u)$ metres

8 $\sqrt{\left(\dfrac{2}{kg}\right)} \tan^{-1}\left(u\sqrt{\dfrac{k}{2g}}\right)$ seconds

9 (b) $v = \dfrac{\lambda e^{-kt}}{k^2} + \dfrac{\lambda t}{k} - \dfrac{\lambda}{k^2}$

10 $\frac{1}{450} \text{ m}^{-1}$

11 —

12 10 cm; $\dfrac{\pi}{5}$;

8.4 cm below the centre of oscillation;
54 cm s^{-1} upwards; 840 cm s^{-2} upwards

13 $\dfrac{2}{\pi}$ m s^{-1}

14 With initial conditions $x = -\frac{1}{4}$ and
$\dot{x} = \sqrt{(2g)}$ at $t = 0$, the equation of motion
is

$$\ddot{x} + 4gx = 0$$

The maximum extension in the subsequent
motion is 1 m.

15 (a) 2.36 seconds, 1.875 m

    (b) 32 J

16 (a) $\frac{1}{24}$ m

    (b) (i) $\frac{5}{24}$ m

        (ii) $5\sqrt{\left(\dfrac{g}{24}\right)}$ m s^{-1}, $5g$ m s^{-2}

17 $\dfrac{3\sqrt{2}}{4} a$

18 (a) 3 m   (b) 184 N towards A

    (c) 0.294 second

19 Period $= 9$ seconds,   amplitude $= 10$ cm

20 $x = \dfrac{\lambda}{8}(4\sin\omega t + \cos\omega t - \cos 3\omega t)$

21 $\ddot{x} + 6\omega\dot{x} + 13\omega^2 x = 0$

22 (b) $x = A\sin\omega t + B\cos\omega t$

    (c) $x = \dfrac{pt}{2\omega}\sin\omega t$

Experiments Commentary

You may not understand any of the theory behind the experiments at this point. You must, however, learn how to record and interpret your results. The actual mechanics behind the answers will be explained at the appropriate point in the chapter. You will then refer back to the results you obtained here and see how they fit into the theory.

It is important that data for the experiments are collected and kept for later use.

1 *The bricklayer's lament*

Some practical details are:

- The pulley should be fixed securely in a vertical plane with the string moving freely without knots or snagging on the pulley.

- The system should be released from rest each time. This is easy to do if the string is held at the pulley and then released on the word 'Go'.

- Several runs will be needed to assess consistency and accuracy; obviously poor runs should be excluded.

Other practical problems may be encountered and you should learn how to solve them yourself.

The results should give a clear graph of time increasing with distance.

If the distances measured are great, the masses may reach a steady 'terminal' velocity due to the friction in the pulley.

If the distances are too small, then inaccuracies in timing may hide any clear relationship between distance and time. If friction is ignored, a relationship of the form $d = kt^2$ is expected.

Possible extensions include changing the masses, for example to $50\,\mathrm{g}$ and $60\,\mathrm{g}$, and repeating the investigation.

You should make use of the modelling diagram in writing up your results.

2 Find a model for the motion of a rolling ball

Check for accuracy and consistency as before. Release from the same point each time, choosing a point from which the ball takes at least 3 seconds to roll 1 metre.

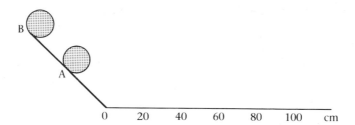

In the initial experiment the results depend on whether the times are measured from the release point A, or from when the ball reaches the start of the track at 0. These are shown by the thinner and thicker lines in the graph. The release point also affects the gradient of the graph.

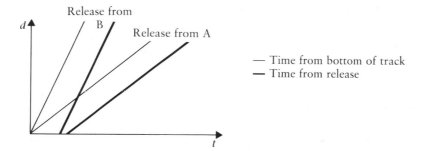

The second set of data collected for the ball rolling along the felt or ribbon can be used later to find the friction force involved. In this case, the (t, d) graph will not be linear as the ball will soon come to rest on the track.

3 Find a model for the motion of a ball rolling across a sloping plane.

The horizontal line at the base of the plane should pass through the base of the ramp as shown overleaf. Release points 1 and 2 are too low to give a curve that fits most of the paper. Once again, to be consistent you must always release the ball from exactly the same height.

Care must be taken to avoid soaking the sugar paper with water or the ball will not roll properly.

The path traced out should be a parabola in all cases. The axis of symmetry may be found by folding the cut-out shape.

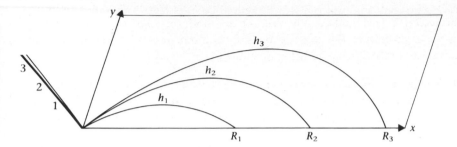

Discrepancies are caused by energy loss through friction or malformation of the ball. A snooker ball is probably best. The graph should have an equation of the form $y = kr(R - x)$, where R is the range.

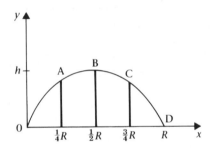

The release height is proportional to both h and R. It is also proportional to the square of the velocity at the bottom of the ramp.

If a ruler is laid across the path, then the times for the ball to travel through equal horizontal distances across the table can be found. This should show that the horizontal component of speed is constant.

Jumping buses

This practical should give you a feel for the factors which affect the flight of a projectile. You should quickly discover that both the angle of projection and the speed of projection will affect its path. Ensure that you only alter one variable at a time and record your results systematically.

1   You should be able to hit the target consistently. Obviously, pinpoint accuracy is not achievable, but with practice it should be possible to hit a target the size of a plate at a distance of between one and two metres.

2   The vertical height may be easier to measure accurately if you determine from what height you must fire the band in order to reach the ceiling.

3   The angle of elevation, i.e. the angle with the horizontal, can be measured with a protractor. To obtain the speed of projection, the theory from Chapter 1 can be used. A body of mass 1 kilogram, falling under gravity, changes its momentum by $9.8 \, \text{kg m s}^{-1}$ in each second.

   If an object is fired vertically upwards and reaches a height of 1 metre, for example, then the gradient of the graph of velocity against time is -9.8.

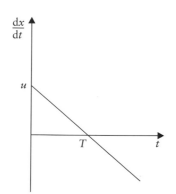

Let the initial velocity be $u \, \text{m s}^{-1}$ vertically upwards and the highest point be reached at time T seconds. Then

$$\frac{dx}{dt} = u - 9.8t \quad \text{and} \quad 0 = u - 9.8T$$

The area under the graph represents the displacement, so that if the band reaches a height of 1 metre, for example,

$$1 = \tfrac{1}{2}uT = \tfrac{1}{2}u \times \frac{u}{9.8}$$

and hence $u^2 = 19.6$.

4   (a)   The range (the horizontal distance between the point of projection and the point where the band lands) should be a maximum when the angle of projection is $45°$. (This may not be true in practice.)

   (b)   The maximum height (and minimum range) will occur when the angle of projection is $90°$.

   (c)   The time in the air is difficult to measure as the times are small. However, it is fairly easy to see that as the angle of projection decreases so does the time in the air.

Investigating forces

Commentary

1 Validation of statement 1 can be achieved using the apparatus shown for either the first or the second experiment.

(a) Using the rubber band

The rubber band can be extended to a fixed length by a single newton meter and the force recorded by the newton meter noted. (Remember to zero the newton meter carefully.) The band must then be extended an identical amount using two newton meters and the directions and magnitudes of the two forces can be recorded. The resultant of these two forces can be obtained by drawing and then compared with the single force needed. It should be noted that an infinite number of pairs of readings can be obtained for the two newton meters. This can be seen clearly from the vector triangle

$$\overrightarrow{AB} = \overrightarrow{AP} + \overrightarrow{PB}$$
$$= \overrightarrow{AQ} + \overrightarrow{QB}$$
$$= \overrightarrow{AS} + \overrightarrow{SB}$$

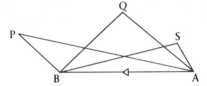

(b) Using the pulleys and masses

The force needed to support a mass can be measured by a newton meter. An identical force must therefore be produced by the combination of the two strings passing over pulleys. The tension in each string is equal to the force exerted by the mass suspended by it. Once again the directions and magnitudes of these forces can be noted and a triangle of forces drawn. The pulleys will need to be as frictionless as possible if this experiment is to achieve convincing results.

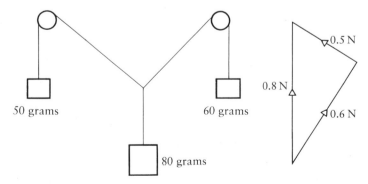

2 Statement **2** can be validated in a similar way to statement **1**. In both (a) and (b) the systems of forces are in equilibrium. Scale drawing of the vectors concerned will show that they combine to give zero. Note that in validating statement **1** with apparatus (a) the forces needed to produce a given extension in an elastic band are equated. In validating statement **2** the same apparatus is used to show that as the force in the elastic band is equal in magnitude and opposite in direction to the force given on the single newton meter, the three forces (those produced by the elastic band and the two newton meters) will add up to zero.

3 The apparatus in the third experiment can be used to validate statement **3**. The magnitudes and directions of the forces exerted by the four newton meters when the strings are in equilibrium can be noted. The hypothesis that they can be added by drawing a vector polygon can be validated by showing that there is a quadrilateral whose sides represent the four forces in both magnitude and direction. Note that the order of the sides of the quadrilateral will not affect this hypothesis. Care must be taken with the initialisation of the newton meters when used horizontally.

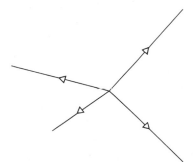

Any order can be used.

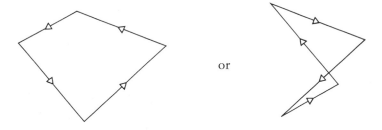

or

2.2 TASKSHEET 2

Modelling with force

Commentary

The aim of the practicals is twofold. Firstly, to enable you to experience the use of standard models in an unfamiliar situation. This should enable you to include practical experimentation in your own investigations. Secondly, to help you to discover that the models are there as aids. They do not provide a perfect fit for the data collected but can be used to give a reasonable approximation for analysis. You are strongly discouraged from attempting to 'improve' your data to fit the model. Any discrepancies (it is suspicious if they do not occur!) should be noted, discussed and their effects evaluated. For example, 'Does this mean that the standard model cannot be used for all values of the variables?', or 'Can a better approximation be found?'.

A reporting session at the end of the tasksheet is very useful. The class as a whole can learn from the experiences of others and will appreciate the importance of a clear presentation. By pooling the experiences of the class it is possible to show that a worthwhile model can be found in most cases. Even the fact that a good analytical model cannot be found is significant. It need not indicate a lack of success.

A The experiments here can be set up to test one of the standard models for tension (see page 355). As the strings and springs are stretchy, the model chosen should be either 4 or 5.

Standard model 4

$$T = kx$$

This model states that the graph of tension against extension for a spring or string is linear. A table of results can be found from any of the three practicals. It is unlikely that any of the three experiments will give a perfectly straight line through the origin. However, parts of the graph will indeed be linear and can be used to predict tension for a given extension. Possible graphs for each of the three sets of apparatus are:

Tension in a rubber band   Tension in a spring   Tension in elastic

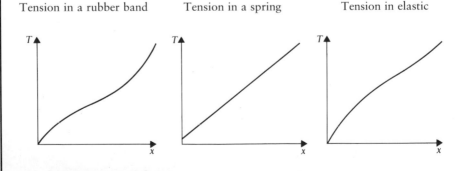

Care must be taken with the spring to avoid reaching the point where the spring fails. The elastic and rubber band can be regarded as expendable and can therefore be tested to destruction and a complete graph obtained.

B After dropping the balloons a few times it should become apparent that the larger the surface area of the balloon, the longer it takes to reach the ground. An appropriate standard model is one which deals with balloons of different areas.

$$R = kA$$

However, the resistance can only be measured by looking at the effect it has on the time taken for the balloon to fall.

Newton's second law gives $ma = mg - R$ or $a = g - \dfrac{R}{m}$

But $v = 0$ when $t = 0$ and $x = 0 \Rightarrow v = gt - \dfrac{Rt}{m}$

$$x = \frac{gt^2}{2} - \frac{Rt^2}{2m}$$

$$R = m\left(9.8 - \frac{2x}{t^2}\right)$$

R can be calculated from the measured values of m, x and t, and a graph plotted of A against R. It should be linear and pass through the origin if the theory is correct. Once again you should look for occasions when the standard model might not be valid. What if all the balloons were dropped from the top of a tall tower? Would they all reach the same limiting speed? This would suggest the need to use $R = kv$ as a model.

2.3 TASKSHEET 1

Satellites

Commentary

1

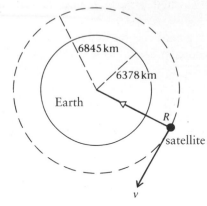

Possible assumptions are:

- The Earth is a perfect sphere of mass 5.973×10^{24} kg and radius 6378 km.

- The gravitational constant is 6.673×10^{-11} N m^2 kg^{-2}.

- The astronaut travels in a perfectly circular orbit $(467 + 6378)$ km above the centre of the Earth.

- The astronaut is a particle of mass m kg and his speed is constant, v m s^{-1}.

- The force of attraction of the Earth on George Nelson is R newtons towards the centre of the Earth.

- The satellite travels from west to east above the equator. (You might choose east to west.)

2 Using Newton's law of gravitation,

$$R = \frac{5.973 \times 6.673 \times 10^{13} \times m}{10^{12} \times 6.845^2} = 8.507m \text{ newtons}$$

But by Newton's second law of motion, as the astronaut is travelling in a circle at constant speed v,

$$8.507m = \frac{mv^2}{6.845 \times 10^6}$$

$$v^2 = 58\,230\,000$$

$$v = 7631 \text{ m s}^{-1}$$

The angular speed of the astronaut is $\dfrac{v}{r}$ or $\dfrac{7631}{6\,845\,000} \text{rad s}^{-1}$

so one complete revolution takes 5636 seconds or 1.566 hours.

So in 24 hours the astronaut rotates 15.3 times around the centre of the Earth. If he travels in the same direction as the Earth, i.e. west to east, then he will travel over Singapore 14 more times in the next 24 hours. If, however, the satellite travels in the opposite direction, east to west, then he will pass over Singapore 16 more times.

Modelling the Fosbury flop

You should find that the centre of gravity of the high jumper is approximately in the position shown below.

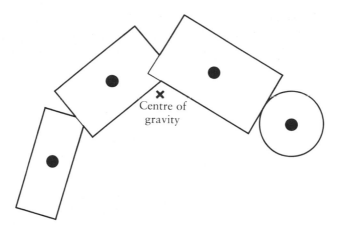

Centre of gravity

It is interesting to note that with this style of high jump, the athlete can clear the bar while her centre of gravity passes below the bar! Once the athlete has taken off she becomes a projectile. Her centre of gravity will follow a simple parabolic path. However, just as the tennis racket at the start of section 2.4 (pages 141–2) was seen to rotate about its centre of gravity, so the high jumper can rotate about her centre of gravity. A successful high jump style is one which enables athletes to 'raise' themselves above the centre of gravity at the crucial point of clearing the bar.

Which slides first?

Commentary

Problem

Which finger slides first?

Set up a model

Assume that the track is uniform and of mass M and is held horizontally in equilibrium on two fingers at A and B.
Let each finger exert a normal force N_a and N_b.
Assume that the finger at A is farther away from the centre of the track and that the coefficient of friction is the same for each finger.
Let the friction due to the push of each finger on the track be P inwards.

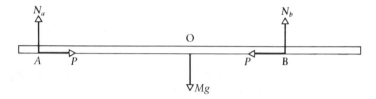

Analyse the problem

The weight of the track acts downwards through its centre at O. Taking moments about the centre of the track,

$$\text{AO} \times N_a = N_b \times \text{OB}.$$

Since AO > OB then $N_a < N_b$ and so $\mu N_a < \mu N_b$
As P increases, it reaches the value of the limiting friction at A before it reaches the value at B.

Interpret

The finger at A starts to slide. As the finger gets closer to O, the normal contact force at A increases and so the friction increases until it becomes greater than that at B. When this happens the finger at B starts to move and that at A stops slipping. The finger that is farther away from the centre will slide.

Validate

You should have found that your results agree with this interpretation.

A full analysis of the motion can be found in *Mechanics in Action* by Savage and Williams, Cambridge University Press, 1991 (ISBN 0 521 38941 0).

Sporting collisions

Commentary

1 A good approximation to the speed of the head of the club can be obtained using the distance between successive positions of the head of the club just before the ball is struck. A similar method can be used for the ball.

3 cm represents the length of the metric rule.

1.3 cm represents the distance between the positions of the head of the club.

This distance is therefore $\frac{1.3}{3}$ m.

The speed of the head of the club is $\frac{1.3}{3} \times 100 = 43.3 \, \text{m s}^{-1}$.

1.9 cm represents the distance between successive positions of the ball in flight.

The speed of the golf ball after being struck is $\frac{1.9}{3} \times 100 = 63.3 \, \text{m s}^{-1}$.

2 The golf ball is a very 'bouncy' object and it is not unreasonable to consider the collision between the club and the golf ball as being perfectly elastic.

The most significant difference between the mathematical model and reality is that the model relates to motion in a horizontal straight line, whereas the ball is driven into the air, because the club head is angled so that the impact is at an angle to the club head's velocity.

3 (a) Assuming the collision is perfectly elastic, the speed of the approach $= u =$ the speed of separation. As m separates from M, v must be greater than the speed of M and, as all velocities are in the same direction, the difference of the speeds after separation must be u. Therefore the speed of M is $v - u$.

   (b) As all the velocities are taken in the same direction, this may be taken as the positive direction for momentum. The total momentum before collision is Mu and after the collision it is $M(v - u) + mv$.

   Since momentum is conserved, these two expressions are equal.

   (c) Since $m > 0$, $\quad M + m > M$, and therefore

   $$\frac{2M}{M + m} < \frac{2M}{M} = 2$$

4 The following neat method avoids the use of calculus.

$$\frac{4x}{(1+x)^2} = \frac{(1+x)^2 - (1-x)^2}{(1+x)^2} = 1 - \frac{(1-x)^2}{(1+x)^2} = 1 - \left(\frac{1-x}{1+x}\right)^2$$

Now, being a perfect square, $\left(\dfrac{1-x}{1+x}\right)^2 \geq 0$. The least value, 0, only occurs when $x = 1$. Therefore, the greatest value of $\dfrac{4x}{(1+x)^2}$ is 1, occurring when $x = 1$.

Alternatively, the graph may be plotted on a graphic calculator, or you may use calculus.

If $y = \dfrac{4x}{(1+x)^2}$

$$\frac{dy}{dx} = \frac{(1+x)^2 \times 4 - 4x \times 2(1+x)}{(1+x)^4}$$

$$= \frac{(1+x)(4+4x-8x)}{(1+x)^4} = \frac{4-4x}{(1+x)^3}$$

$$\frac{dy}{dx} = 0 \quad \text{when } x = 1$$

x	$\rightarrow$	1	$\rightarrow$
$\dfrac{dy}{dx}$	$+$	0	$-$
	/	—	\

$\Rightarrow$ $x = 1$ gives a maximum value of $\dfrac{4}{2^2} = 1$

So for all KE to be transferred, $M = m$.

5 A 'bouncy' collision in sport, where the masses are equal, occurs in snooker.

Tension

1 Various springs will give different graphs.
   As you saw in Chapter 2, *Force and motion*, the likely graphs are as shown.

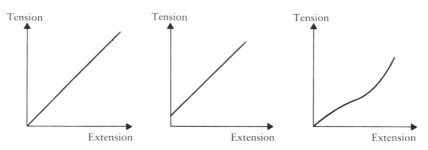

   However, most springs will obey Hooke's law for at least part of their extension.

2 The gradient of the line of best fit, passing through the origin, will give an estimation of k, the spring constant.

4.1 TASKSHEET 1

Sky-diving

1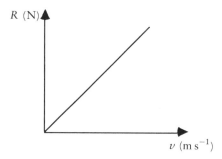

2 The sky-diver jumps and accelerates due to her weight. As her speed increases, the resistance force increases and so the resultant force acting on her decreases. At some point, the upward resistance force will balance her weight and though she continues to fall, her acceleration is zero. At this speed the forces are balanced; this is her maximum speed, called the terminal speed.

3 Her maximum speed occurs when the resistance force equals her weight. To increase her maximum speed she must reduce the resistance force. She can do this by changing her posture, so that a smaller area is facing the oncoming air. To reduce her speed she must increase her area, for example by opening the parachute.

4 As speed increases, the air resistance force increases.

5 Two possibilities are:

(a) $R = Kv$, for some constant K (b) $R = kv^2$, for some constant k

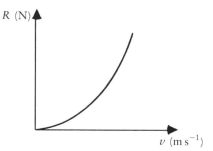

In this case the relationship is linear.

In this case the relationship is quadratic.

Resistance experiments

1, 2 Your experiment

3 You should find that the object reaches its terminal speed very quickly.
The graph of distance against time is therefore linear for most of the distance fallen.

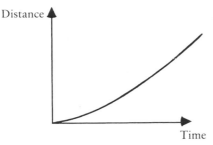

The terminal speed is the gradient of the straight-line section (where the object's speed is constant).

4 As the mass increases, other things being equal, the terminal speed will increase. It may be necessary to drop the object from a considerable height for it to reach terminal speed, w.

5 A linear graph for w against m suggests the $R = Kv$ model for resistance.

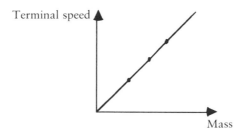

A graph such as the one below suggests that $w \propto \sqrt{m}$ and therefore indicates that the $R = kv^2$ model for resistance is appropriate.

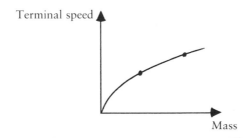

6 You can use your own data to find an appropriate value for K or k.

Validating the formula $T \propto \sqrt{m}$ Commentary

1 Attach the spring to a support and measure the extension for different masses suspended in equilibrium. In equilibrium, the tension equals the weight suspended.

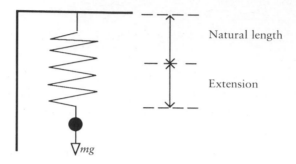

Assuming Hooke's law is valid, then the spring constant is simply

$$k = \frac{\text{weight}}{\text{extension}}.$$

Drawing a graph of weight against extension, an approximate value for k is the gradient of the line of best fit.

You will find that some springs are pre-tensioned and do not extend until a certain weight is applied. A better model for the tension in these springs would be $T = T_0 + kx$, where T_0 is the pre-tensioning force.

2 Timing a number of oscillations, for example 5, 10 or 20, and calculating the average should give an accurate and reliable value for the time period of oscillation. Springs oscillate fairly consistently if the mass on the end is not too small or too great and you can assume that the oscillations are all equal. Decide on the initial amplitude of release to ensure consistency and repeatability.

3 Collecting data for the time period for a range of masses will enable you to plot a graph of time period against mass. By fitting a curve to the data points you can compare the theoretical result that $T \propto \sqrt{m}$ $\left(\text{i.e. } T = A\sqrt{m}, \text{ where } A = \frac{2\pi}{\sqrt{k}}\right)$ with your experimental result.

It should be possible to compare the value of k in the model for tension derived from the graph with the value obtained in the earlier experiment.

(An alternative approach is to time the period when the mass is, for example, 60 grams and then to check that the period is doubled when the mass is 240 grams.)

Pendulum clocks

For the best experimental results:

- the string of the pendulum should be fixed at one end so that it swings freely;

- the string should be long enough for the size of the bob to be insignificant (i.e. it can be considered to be a particle);

- use a fairly light string or thread so that its weight is negligible compared with the bob;

- time a number of oscillations, for example 5 or 10, and calculate an average time period (for small amplitude oscillations the amplitude is reasonably constant for a few oscillations, though for larger initial angles of displacement the amplitude decreases quickly);

- take care that when investigating the effects of one variable the others are kept constant.

Possible observations are:

Mass: Provided the mass is sufficiently large so that the string can be assumed to be light, you should find that increasing the mass has little or no effect on the amplitude. This can be tested by comparing the time period for a light bob with that for a heavy bob. The time period appears to be independent of mass.

Length: The time period increases as the length of the pendulum increases. The graph shows time period against length for possible data.

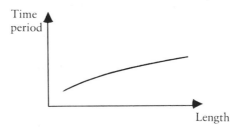

From the graph, a possible relationship is that $\tau \propto \sqrt{\text{length}}$. You should be able to use your data to find the constant of proportionality. Note that for small lengths it is difficult to collect reliable data as the size of the mass or bob is no longer insignificant.

4.5 TASKSHEET 1

Amplitude: For small initial angles of displacement the oscillations are similar and the amplitude does not decrease noticeably. Provided the initial angle is small (it does not exceed, for example, $\frac{1}{12}\pi$ radians or 15°) then the time period appears to be unaffected. For larger initial angles, the time period appears to increase as the initial angle increases. This is more noticeable for angles greater than $\frac{1}{4}\pi$ radians. However, as was stated earlier, it is more difficult to obtain reliable results for large amplitude oscillations as the amplitude decreases quite quickly.

Appendix 1

Physical data

Densities of some fluids (at 0 °C, and 1 atmosphere pressure, unless otherwise noted)

Density of dry air at 0 °C	$1.29\,\text{kg m}^{-3}$
Density of dry air at 20 °C	$1.20\,\text{kg m}^{-3}$
Density of water at 4 °C	$1000\,\text{kg m}^{-3}$
Density of sea water at 15 °C	$1025\,\text{kg m}^{-3}$
Density of helium	$0.178\,\text{kg m}^{-3}$
Density of hydrogen	$0.0899\,\text{kg m}^{-3}$
Density of olive oil at 15 °C	$920\,\text{kg m}^{-3}$
Density of crude oil at 15 °C	$875\,\text{kg m}^{-3}$

Some masses

The *Queen Elizabeth II*	$7.6 \times 10^7\,\text{kg}$
Oil tanker – empty	$2.2 \times 10^8\,\text{kg}$
– full	$6.6 \times 10^8\,\text{kg}$
Boeing 747 (empty)	$1.6 \times 10^5\,\text{kg}$
Skylab	$8.2 \times 10^4\,\text{kg}$
Automobile	$1.5 \times 10^3\,\text{kg}$

Gravitational constant $G = 6.67 \times 10^{-11}\,\text{N m}^2\,\text{kg}^{-2}$

Earth		
	Mass	$5.98 \times 10^{24}\,\text{kg}$
	Radius	$6.378 \times 10^6\,\text{m}$
	Mean density	$5520\,\text{kg m}^{-3}$
	Acceleration due to gravity at surface	$9.81\,\text{m s}^{-2}$
	Period of rotation	23 hrs 56 min 4 s $(8.616 \times 10^4\,\text{s})$
	Mean distance from Sun	$1.50 \times 10^{11}\,\text{m}$
	Period of orbit around Sun	1 year = 365 days 6 hours

Moon		
	Mass	$7.35 \times 10^{22}\,\text{kg}$
	Radius	$1.74 \times 10^6\,\text{m}$
	Mean density	$3340\,\text{kg m}^{-3}$
	Acceleration due to gravity at surface	$1.62\,\text{m s}^{-2}$
	Period of rotation	27.3 days
	Mean distance from Earth	$3.84 \times 10^8\,\text{m}$
	Period of orbit around Earth	27.3 days

Sun	Mass	1.99×10^{30} kg
	Radius	6.96×10^{8} m
	Mean density	$1410 \, \text{kg m}^{-3}$
	Acceleration due to gravity at surface	$274 \, \text{m s}^{-2}$
	Period of rotation	26 days (approximately)

The planets in the solar system

Planet	Mean distance from Sun (10^6 km)	Period of revolution (years)	Mass (kg)	Equatorial radius (km)	Surface gravity (g_E)	Period of rotation (days)
Mercury	57.9	0.241	3.30×10^{23}	2439	0.38	58.6
Venus	108	0.615	4.87×10^{24}	6052	0.91	243
Earth	150	1.00	5.98×10^{24}	6378	1.00	0.997
Mars	228	1.88	6.42×10^{23}	3397	0.38	1.026
Jupiter	778	11.9	1.90×10^{27}	71 398	2.53	0.41
Saturn	1430	29.5	5.67×10^{26}	60 000	1.07	0.43
Uranus	2870	84.0	8.70×10^{25}	25 400	0.92	0.65
Neptune	4500	165	1.03×10^{26}	24 300	1.19	0.77
Pluto	5910	248	6.60×10^{23}	2500	0.72	6.39

Some artificial satellites of the Earth

Satellite	Mass (kg)	Mean distance from centre of Earth (km)	Period (minutes)
Sputnik I	83	6970	96.2
Sputnik II	3000	7330	104
Explorer I	14	7830	115
Vanguard I	1.5	8680	134
Explorer III	14	7910	116
Sputnik III	1320	7420	106
Skylab	82 000	6820	93

Appendix 2

Programs for modelling free-fall

A straightforward program can be used to analyse the motion of an object in free-fall. An acceleration of $10 - 0.004\,V^2$ has been assumed in the Euler step programs given below. To adapt the programs to other situations, change the formula for A and check that the expressions for V and H have the correct sign.

Casio graphical calculators

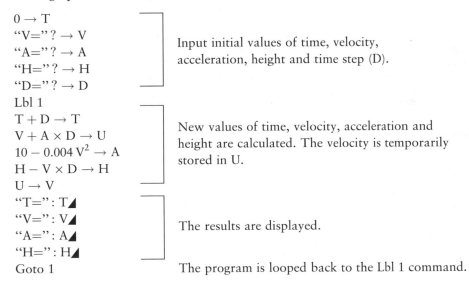

$0 \rightarrow T$
"V="? $\rightarrow$ V
"A="? $\rightarrow$ A   Input initial values of time, velocity,
"H="? $\rightarrow$ H   acceleration, height and time step (D).
"D="? $\rightarrow$ D

Lbl 1
$T + D \rightarrow T$
$V + A \times D \rightarrow U$ New values of time, velocity, acceleration and
$10 - 0.004\,V^2 \rightarrow A$ height are calculated. The velocity is temporarily
$H - V \times D \rightarrow H$ stored in U.
$U \rightarrow V$
"T=": T◢
"V=": V◢
"A=": A◢   The results are displayed.
"H=": H◢
Goto 1   The program is looped back to the Lbl 1 command.

- If you do not require all the results to be displayed, then instead of the command of Goto 1, the command

  $$H > 0 \quad \Rightarrow \quad \text{Goto 1}$$

  can be put *before* the display instructions. The program will then only display the values of T, V and A when the ground is reached.

- You might also wish to modify the program to display the results at chosen intervals of time, for example every 5 seconds. One suggestion is to input an end time, E.

Lbl 2
"E="? → E   Insert before Lbl 1.

$T \neq E \Rightarrow$ Goto 1   Insert before the results are displayed.

Goto 2   Replaces Goto 1.

Texas graphical calculators

$0 \to T$
Disp "V?"
Input V
Disp "A?"
Input A   Input initial values of time, velocity
Disp "H?"   acceleration, height and time step (D).
Input H
Disp "D?"
Input D
Lbl 1
$T + D \to T$
$V + A * D \to U$ New values of time, velocity, acceleration
$10 - 0.004\,V^2 \to A$ and height are calculated. The velocity is
$H - V * D \to H$ temporarily stored in U.
$U \to V$
Disp T
Disp V
Disp A   The results are displayed.
Disp H
Pause
Goto 1   The program is looped back to the Lbl 1 command.

- If you do not require all the results to be displayed, then instead of the command of Goto 1, the commands

  If $H > 0$
  Goto 1

can be put *before* the display instructions. The program will then only display the values of T, V and A when the ground is reached.

- You might also wish to modify the program to display the results at chosen intervals of time, for example every 5 seconds. One suggestion is to input an end time, E.

Lbl 2
Disp "E?"   Insert before Lbl 1.
Input E

If $T \neq E$ Insert before the results are displayed.
Goto 1

Goto 2   Replaces Goto 1.

Index